THE DAY OF THE HOLIDAY EXPRESS

Richard Woodley

Publishing

First published 1996

ISBN 0 7110 2394 8

Published by Ian Allan Publishing

an imprint of Ian Allan Ltd, Terminal House, Station Approach, Shepperton, Surrey TW17 8AS.
Printed by Ian Allan Printing Ltd, Coombelands House, Coombelands Lane, Addlestone, Surrey KT15 1HY.

DEDICATED TO

Alison, Andrew, Lucie, Owain & Sïan

Front cover: Holidaymakers wait for their train at Torquay in August 1958. *Torquay Herald Express*

Front cover, inset: On Saturday 9 July 1960, No 6875 *Hindford Grange* and No 8702 seen near Quintrell Downs with the 12.42pm Newquay-Cardiff. *Peter W. Gray*

Title page: No 4080 *Powderham Castle* climbs effortlessly up the 1 in 80 towards Nantyderry with the 9.30am Manchester-Swansea on Saturday 4 August 1962 when much of No 4080's work was still concentrated on this line. The engine has now acquired a straight-sided tender in place of the original flared design with which it was running in 1960. *R. O. Tuck*

Back cover, top: The last set of roofboarded Great Western stock is prominent in this picture of No 5923 *Colston Hall* attacking the 1 in 98 of Brewham Bank, after negotiating the junction slowing at Castle Cary, with the 10.20am Weymouth-Wolverhampton on Saturday 30 July 1960. The 14W designation on the smokebox door is the Weymouth shed turn number. *Richardson Bros/Ian Allan Library*

Back cover, bottom: The scene outside Torquay station on a Saturday morning in August 1958. *Torquay Herald Express*

This page: On Saturday 9 July 1960, No 6000 *King George V* returned to London after working the Down 'Cambrian Coast Express' with the 2.35pm Shrewsbury-Paddington. Here on its up journey the 'King' is accelerating hard out of Leamington with a full head of steam ready for the climb towards Fenny Compton. It is running 10min late but all except about four of those minutes were made up before No 6000 reached Paddington. *R. J. Blenkinsop*

CONTENTS

Foreword   4

Bibliography   4

Acknowledgements   5

1. Dawn Chorus   7
2. Too Good to Last?   21
3. Finding the Power for the Job   31
4. Punctuality — Good and Bad   87
5. Valleys Interlude and Suburban Summary   107
6. Personal View — Swindon Junction   115
7. Return Trip   129
8. Oxford — Operating Success on a Shoestring   135
9. The Big West of England Rush   141
10. Carmarthen Snapshot   159
11. Evening Round-up   163

Appendix   167

FOREWORD

This book recounts events which occurred 35 years ago on the Western Region of British Railways during a single day.

That date was 9 July 1960, a busy summer Saturday in the period of transition from steam to diesel power. So that readers can place the events in context, information and photographs from other dates between 1956-63 are included for amplification.

'Why choose 9 July 1960?' was the question I was continually asked about this book. The answer is straightforward: simply that it is the only day I know of when reasonable coverage of the whole Region can be achieved. Information has surfaced about most summer Saturdays on the Western between 1954-64, but never to quite the extent required to compete with coverage obtained for 9 July 1960. Even that day there are inevitably gaps, veritable black holes west of Truro and on much of the Cambrian. Less is known than I would like about activities west of Newton Abbot, beyond Whitland, around Worcester and Hereford or northwest of Shrewsbury. Night trains, of which there were plenty on the Western Region in 1960, were always going to be a problem, together with the identity of the engines which worked them.

But in the end, locomotives on a very high proportion of daytime trains have been traced, sufficient to lead to an assessment of how well the Western Region used its power resources, both steam and diesel, in handling the holiday traffic at this time.

Although the speed of change on British Railways was quickening, much that was described as Western in 1960 still meant pure Great Western. It was easy to visualise what the old company had stood for, and to respect the legacy it handed down. The time of the wholesale scramble for change was still 18 months away. Meanwhile, the Western Region had pledged all its resources to maintain the old GWR's fine reputation for dealing with huge holiday crowds. Many enthusiasts appreciated its sterling efforts enough to take a complete record of everything they saw, and this book relies heavily on those observations which were made during 9 July 1960. Many who were at the lineside responded not just to my requests for information, but sent expressions of encouragement too.

The lists I received varied enormously in style and content. Most ignored diesel units, some left diesel locomotives unidentified and not all included loco numbers more than once, regardless of how may times an engine reappeared later in the day. Nevertheless every contribution was invaluable and provided fresh information, so in June 1990 it was time to ask *Railway World* to publish a request for more. This the Editor kindly did. Gaps in coverage were gradually whittled down and incorrect identifications ironed out, until in August 1990 a crucial set of Shrewsbury notes appeared. Then a whole bundle of Carmarthen sightings came through the letterbox a week later, closely followed by an envelope full of Oxford photographs, all taken on The Day. That was the green light to proceed. This book is the result and I hope it captures some of the steamy atmosphere of those days.

Any comments, corrections or additional information will be welcomed and should be forwarded to the author via Ian Allan, the publishers.

BIBLIOGRAPHY

The Churchward 2-6-0s by David Andrews, Line One, 1985

Britannia — Birth of a Locomotive by Phillip Atkins, Irwell Press, 1991

Organised Chaos by Brian Macdermott, S. & D. J. R. Trust, 1989

Diesel Hydraulic Locomotives of the Western Region by Brian Reed, David & Charles, 1975

Main Lines to the West by Simon Rocksborough-Smith, Ian Allan, 1981

Summer Saturdays in the West by Simon Rocksborough-Smith and David St John Thomas, David and Charles, 1971, is required reading

Trains Illustrated Summer Annual, Trains Annual, Trains Illustrated, Railway Magazine, Railway Observer BR Timetables & Working Documents

Regrettably no WR Weekly or Daily Passenger Notices for 1960 have been located at any official sources. The assumption is that many have been destroyed or a few may have been sold off singly.

ACKNOWLEDGEMENTS

I spent 9 July 1960 at Swindon Junction, amongst many summer Saturdays all around the Western Region between 1958–1965. However, there were some locations I failed to visit and when this project began 20 years ago I still had much to learn. So I was very fortunate that three experts agreed to help, and, if this book has merit, it is largely thanks to their guidance. Any errors are my responsibility. Derek Frost generously supplied many years' West Country expertise. His help has been immeasurable, but above all he exerted a vital element of discipline. Tony Icke entrusted me with his priceless original records and answered many queries. John Hodge shared long experiences of summer Saturdays together with vital inside information on a whole range of topics. His photos were a revelation. All three provided accurate records I could always rely on.

I am equally indebted to Peter Gray, not only for his superb photographs but for his hospitality and his grasp of summer operating requirements, and also to Maurice Dart, Chris Foren, David Maidment and Christopher Napper for material I could not readily have obtained from any other source. Many other people gave me extensive assistance and I thank Gerald Adams, Clive Carter, Larry Crosier, Barry Heywood, Mike Lake, Gordon Moorhead, Terry Nicolls, Derek Phillips, Chris Potts, John Sparkes and James Tawse.

Below: The Friday prelude. Paddington coped efficiently with the busy demands of a summer Friday evening's business, though Fridays before a Bank Holiday could be hectic. Here on Friday 19 August 1960 No 6010 *King Charles I* sets off punctually for Bristol with the 5.6pm semi-fast to Weston-super-Mare, while No 6006 *King George I* is standing right out under Bishops Bridge Road with 14 coaches waiting to go on the 5.10pm to Wolverhampton. 'Kings' Nos 6016 and 6015 will be arriving shortly from Plymouth and Wolverhampton, while Nos 6000, 6007, 6022 and 6028 will also be in the station within the next hour or so. All departures are leaving on time.
John Hodge

Many eminent photographers did much more than just photograph; they also knew exactly what was happening all across the Western Region. Richard Riley helped with a sheaf of hard facts as well as a fine choice of photographs and so did Hugh Ballantyne, Dick Blenkinsop, Michael Mensing and Bob Tuck. Many other photographers willingly contributed, and I hope my selection finds favour.

Others who helped are no longer with us but they are certainly not forgotten, especially Huw Daniel, Reginald Jennings, Kenneth Leech, Tom Hayworth, Ray Miller, John Thane and Peter Tunks. My thanks go particularly to Huw's son Ieuan.

I consulted many organisations. They are run by people who deserve just as much gratitude as the individuals mentioned above. Pre-eminent is the Steam Railway Research Association (SRRA), guided by Richard Strange. Many SRRA members helped too, including Mike Thompson, Ben Brooksbank, Brian Green, Michael Hedges, Geoff Hobbs, Frank Hornby, Mike Lynch, George Pearce, Bill Rear and Don Steggles. Generous assistance also came from the Great Western Society archives, Great Western Study Group, PRO at Kew, NRM York, the RCTS, Plymouth Railway Circle and the Monmouthshire Railway Society, which is still going strong. My thanks go to Dave Mathew, MRS President, for permission to make use of the valuable WR Restaurant Car Survey carried out by the Society on 9 July 1960, and also to Ray Caston of the Signalling Record Society.

This book could not have been written without the contribution of those who took notes on 9 July. With their locations they are:

Birmingham area	Tony Icke, Colin Stevens*
Bristol	R. A. Cooper*,
	Mike Cornick*,
	F. J. Cullis*, Mike Pollard
Burton-on-Trent	Mike Thompson
Cardiff	David Griffith,
	David Burton
Cardiff Valleys	Robert Thomas
Carmarthen	John Lewis
Exeter	John Hodge,
	Eric S. Youldon,
	R. N. Giles*, Bob Stone,
	Richard Browne,
	David Hardy
Frome	Barrie Williamson
Newport	B. J. J. Jelf*
Newton Abbot	Derek Frost, Tony Goss
Oxford	Tony Icke, Mike Lake
Paddington/Ealing	John Faulkner,
	John R. Jones*,
	G. R. Lloyd*
Par/Truro	Peter Gray
Salisbury	D. J. Mant
Savernake	Bernard Cooke
Shrewsbury	Peter Ogden
Swindon	Richard Woodley
Taunton	John Cornelius
Tondu	Roland Pittard
Twyford	Christopher Napper,
	U. W. R. Casebourne
Westerleigh	Richard Adams
Weymouth/Dorchester	Peter Foster
Whitchurch (Salop)	Philip Nash
Wolverhampton Stafford Rd	Collection of John James
Worcester Abbots Wood Jc	Wilf Carey
Yate	Colin Roberts
Journey Notes	Maurice Dart,
	Griffyd Evans,
	Reginald Jennings,
	H. Poole, David Wallis
Shed Notes	Roger Bond, Chris Bush,
	James Graham,
	Richard Strange and others

*Monmouthshire Railway Society Survey Team.

Jean Pearce made a marvellous job of the typing, willingly assisted by her husband Ron who helped to interpret the more incomprehensible bits.

Last but not least, thanks go to John Tiley, Mike Hedderly and Hugh James with whom I have shared many open carriage windows and enjoyed the music.

Left: The very early morning. No 6013 *King Henry VIII* stands in No 8 platform at Paddington waiting to leave with the 12.45am down newspapers to Carmarthen on Thursday 15 December 1960. No 6013 will run over the down empty carriage line as far as Subway Jc before crossing on to the main line there. The 12.45 was the first regular 'King' turn to Cardiff, and from 25 November 1959 until 12 September 1960 it was the only one. No 6013 was a regular engine for the 12.45 and also worked it on 16 and 17 December. *R. O. Tuck*

I. DAWN CHORUS

9 July 1960. The early morning. Just north of Wolverhampton, the usual dark pall of coal smoke was rising above the blackened brick buildings of Oxley Locomotive Depot. But today was different — here the shed staff were busy preparing no less than six of Oxley's 'Halls' and 'Granges', plus a couple of foreign engines, for summer Saturday express work. Instead of their usual daily diet of freight haulage, Oxley engines were to work passengers to all corners of the Western. There was no time to wipe off the week's layer of goods train grime.

Nos 4963 *Rignall Hall* and 6907 *Davenham Hall* would go out travel-stained on the long haul to Taunton and Newton Abbot. Over other routes Nos 6857 *Tudor Grange* and 6925 *Hackness Hall* would be off to Basingstoke and South Wales. Later No 4984 *Albrighton Hall* would work to Swindon. Tyseley engines also had an extensive express programme to cover, on which they ranged far and wide across the Region. On these holiday trains Oxley and Tyseley engines could hold their own amongst more illustrious express 4-6-0 counterparts from along the Stafford Road.

This certainly did not mean that exact time was always kept. Far from it in fact, as summer Saturday trains between Birmingham and the West Country were often late runners week by week for much of the summer. But what it did mean was that the availability of engines like those Oxley workhorses was just one sign of success in matching the resources available to meet summer Saturday requirements. There were to be plenty more signs of success in unlikely quarters before the day was out.

Below: No 5965 *Woollas Hall* pauses at Pokesdown with the 8.35am Newcastle–Bournemouth on Tuesday 30 June 1959. No 5965 has recently been overhauled and is working from Oxford shed. A year later No 5965 looked rather less smart when it was used at Oxley to power the 6.40am Wolverhampton–Paignton on 9 July 1960. *D. K. Jones*

The crew of Exeter-bound 'Hall' No 5965 *Woollas Hall* took it off Oxley shed punctually at around 5.45am to collect empty coaches from Cannock Road sidings. These then formed 1C63, the 6.40am holiday express from Wolverhampton to Paignton. The coaches came straight back from Paignton at 3.10pm that afternoon, but the Oxley Night Foreman had no idea when his engine would return from Exeter. He already had his 'Halls' and 'Granges' scattered around as far afield as Laira, Didcot and Chester. Some of these would be going in any direction but towards home. One of them, No 6925 *Hackness Hall*, would make the earliest arrival of the day 12min before time at Newport, *en route* to Swansea with the 9.55am express from Paddington. By contrast, No 5965 was hard-pressed long before it reached Exeter. Fourteen minutes late at Taunton, not even a prolonged stop there was sufficient for the engine crew to rally matters before they set off to climb Wellington bank. They made it to the top at Whiteball all right but by the time *Woollas Hall* pulled into Exeter at 12.18pm, 23min had been lost on a typically easy Saturday schedule. As it happened, No 5965 was still at Exeter shed the following Tuesday, but that was Exeter's problem. It was up to the Exeter running foreman to send No 5965 back towards home when he could. The Oxley Foreman had done his job as No 5965 moved out. The day was under way.

Down at Bristol, finding enough footplatemen to cover all the varied demands of summer weekend operations was always a headache. Friday evening freights, extra overnight expresses and Saturday reliefs all had to be planned out and catered for. The sectional Freight Marshalling Instructions called for a dozen Western region 'DX' power category six-coupled engines to satisfy Friday night freight requirements from Bristol. But these DX 'Halls' and 'Granges' were also just what was needed for the weekend's extra passenger trains. So whatever the Marshalling Instructions might say, there would be a scramble to substitute as many '9Fs', 2-8-0s and 2-6-0s as possible on the freights. Even after fully utilising the 25% of engine capacity which was spare during wintertime, the supply of 4-6-0s to deal with Saturday's passenger programme would be tight.

Nearby, at Bristol Bath Road loco depot, change was in the air. The fully-equipped passenger steam shed complex was only 26 years old, but now it faced closure and demolition in two months' time, ready for a diesel depot to be built on the site. Until then it still had a busy daily role to play, but clean engines no longer figured among the main priorities. Only a handful of the most recently overhauled locomotives were in presentable condition. Others which had been well groomed only six months earlier, like 'Castles' Nos 4079 *Pendennis Castle*, 5085 *Evesham Abbey* and 5092 *Tresco Abbey*, now faced an uncertain future running around beneath thick layers of dirt and grease, but during 9 July that did not stop these three performing well on the road.

Below: This picture of Bath Road shed has been published before, but it was taken at 4pm on 9 July 1960 and so is strictly relevant to this book. It shows the depot virtually cleared out of main line engines at this time of day and largely frequented by Standard Class 3 2-6-3Ts between suburban workings. From the left the 'County' at the coaling stage is probably No 1011 *County of Chester* off the 1pm Salisbury–Bristol. No 5090 *Neath Abbey* has been to Paignton and back. Now it is already returning from a visit to the coaling stage. The engine with a flat-sided tender disappearing towards the turntable is perhaps No 5001 *Llandovery Castle* off the 8.35am Liverpool–Penzance. The tender-first '43xx' in front of the shed is likely to be No 7302 of Westbury which is expected to go out in place of a DMU on the 5.50pm Bristol–Taunton. Finally No 5078 *Beaufort* carrying reporting number M96 is just about to come off shed ready to takeover the 10.5am Penzance–Crewe, reported 14min late through Taunton with 'Hall' No 4916. Bath Road steam depot closed on 11 September 1960 and 'Castle' No 5075 was the last engine off shed at 11.55pm ready to work the 12.10am Bristol–Shrewsbury job early on 12 September. *Hugh Ballantyne*

Above: Grimy and unkempt, running 44min behind time at Exeter while hauling a notoriously late-running service, No 5085 *Evesham Abbey* has worked right through from Shrewsbury with the 7.42am Manchester–Penzance. Even after leaving five coaches for Kingswear at Newton Abbot, No 5085 still has to take nine coaches unaided through to Plymouth, where another Castle, No 5069, will be entrusted with the final stage to Penzance. Now nearly at a stand No 5085 struggles gamely to the top of Dainton on 30 July 1960, while many of the passengers lean out to gain a breath of fresh Devon air. *Hugh Ballantyne*

Bristol being so centrally placed on the Western, Bath Road engines were all too often apt to be borrowed by other sheds because they could be returned relatively easily. Around breakfast time No 5085 was at Landore and later worked 12 coaches to Paddington. No 5092 was at Laira and headed north for Wolverhampton. Two more were at Old Oak Common where Nos 7018 *Drysllwyn Castle* and 7034 *Ince Castle* were being readied to work direct to the West of England via Westbury. Yet another, No 5048 *Earl of Devon*, was at Newport Ebbw Jc preparing for a Newport–Paddington–Cardiff round trip. With so many engines away, was it any surprise that improvised power would have to be chalked up on the Bath Road roster board to cover the day's top-link 'Castle' turns?

Now at 5.45am Train Running Control was

anxiously watching the progress of the last of a busy night's programme of westbound trains through Temple Meads from other Regions. They had already been responsible for integrating a steady stream of overnight reliefs off the London Midland Region into the Western Region traffic flow to Devon and Cornwall.

All these trains from the northeast needed fresh engines at Bristol, and the responsibility for supplying them fell mainly on the local fleet of mixed traffic steam 4-6-0s allocated to St Philip's Marsh shed. So much so, that on 9 July not many hours of the night or day passed when there wasn't at least one hard worked 'Grange' displaying an 82B shedplate to denote its SPM origin, as it slogged up to Whiteball Summit from one direction or the other with a fully loaded train of holidaymakers. No less than eight 82B 'Granges' were involved, plus perhaps No 6833 *Calcot Grange*, which had already reached Newton Abbot and from there penetrated even further west across Cornwall during Saturday morning.

All regions were represented in the overnight traffic at Bristol from the Scottish Region southwards, and amongst this succession of trains were nine expresses coming down the North & West main line from Shrewsbury. There were through engine workings from Shrewsbury to Exeter, and Pontypool Road to Newton Abbot and Plymouth amongst these, but the last three

Left: Typical of the Bristol SPM 'Granges' which worked so many holiday expresses over Whiteball on 9 July 1960, and almost every other summer Saturday weekend as well, is No 6852 *Headbourne Grange* as it tops Whiteball with the 12.5pm Paignton–Cardiff on Saturday 1 July 1961. *Peter W. Gray*

Left: On the last lap from Bristol, No 6811 *Cranbourne Grange* starts the descent of Hemerdon bank with the 8.35am Liverpool–Penzance on Saturday 9 July 1960. No 6811 took over a 12-coach train from No 5001 at Bristol, and five of these vehicles were detached at Newton Abbot to go forward to the Torquay line with 2-6-2T No 4174. This left No 6811 with seven coaches, which was just right to be taken on to Plymouth unassisted. *John Spencer Gilks*

Below: On 9 July 1960 the 1.50pm Paddington–Carmarthen passes West Ealing and makes for Reading behind No 5099 *Compton Castle*. The four Canton express turns to London on this date were evenly split between two 'Castles' and two 'Britannias'. 'Concertina' restaurant car No W9526W is prominent marshalled midway down the train. *John Faulkner*

all changed locos at Temple Meads. Between them, on their long journeys south from Liverpool, Glasgow and Manchester, these trains had accumulated endless scope for delays over the years. If they were late enough to get into the daytime flow of westbound traffic they would have to occupy non-existent peak-time paths west of Taunton, and they would disrupt the intricate pattern of stock and engine workings right through to Penzance.

But today the 11.30pm Liverpool-Penzance had already arrived at Temple Meads about 5.20am. It was booked in with a Pontypool Road 'Grange', which then went off to turn on Bath Road shed ready to return north at 8.15am. In its place 'Castle' No 5075 *Wellington* was waiting to hook up, while the 6.54pm Glasgow-Plymouth changed engines and went on ahead as booked with Tyseley 'Hall' No 7912 *Little Linford Hall*. Nearby 'Warship' diesel No D817 *Foxhound* was ready to couple on the front of the 12.45am Manchester to Plymouth sleeper. Both trains left on time and No D817 followed No 5075 west in quick succession. At Control the night staff could heave a sigh of relief and begin to contemplate a well-earned breakfast.

At Swansea High St it wasn't just breakfast that was on the mind of the restaurant car Conductor of the 6.15am relief to Paddington as he checked in stocks of food and drink for the day. He had already come on duty over an hour earlier than usual. Because his Saturday restaurant car circuit ran an hour or so earlier than during the rest of the week, he had to think not just in terms of breakfast and tea but of supplies to serve lunch as well on the return trip from Paddington at 1.50pm. Food for hungry travellers was big business and British Transport Hotels and Catering who ran the train refreshment service had a reputation for good food and excellent value when a three course lunch cost 9s 6d (47½p). This ensured that the restaurant cars generally ran well filled. The Swansea Conductor had 42 seats at his disposal in gas-fired car No W9526W weighing 46 tons. This superb maroon vehicle towered over the BR Standard coaches forming the rest of the train, and carried its age well. It dated right back to 1906 and though modernised since then in three distinct phases, it still bore characteristic hallmarks of its Churchward 'Concertina' design origins. The first of these was its 70ft length, which together with its 9ft 0in width involved the panelled side doors being set back into the bodywork. Though the sides themselves were now steel sheeted with large vented windows, its mouldings along the waist, panelled ends and a sweeping canvas-covered arc roof set off an unmistakable vehicle. Originally first class, it rode well on its modern six-wheel bogies, boasted a spacious 19ft 11½in long kitchen-cum-pantry, and its three saloons of generous 2 x 1 seating across the car avoided the need to run a separate second open saloon coach to satisfy the demand for meals.

In mid-1960 No W9526W, on a 2,280 mile weekly circuit, was the oldest of 161 restaurant cars in Western Region stock; 115 of them, all built prewar, were handed down by the GWR. Even with 117 WR cars in regular use at the busiest time, many extra trains would inevitably have to go without refreshment facilities. As 6–10hr journeys were not uncommon within the Western Region alone, these could develop into something of an endurance test for passengers on hot summer days.

For No W9526W and its crew, Saturday's 380-mile stretch began behind local 'Hall' No 5913 *Rushton Hall* which should have a clear run at least as far as the junction with the Swansea District Line outside Neath. After that it would have to pick its way to Cardiff amongst the early morning paths of the up Fishguard boat expresses.

Surprisingly enough, even at 5.45am, the summer Saturday morning rush had already come and gone at Fishguard Harbour. Action there had started in the dead of night at about 1.15am with the arrival of the Friday night boat trains from Paddington, bringing sleepy travellers ready to patronise the 2.15am sailing to Rosslare. The incoming Rosslare steamer then berthed at 2.30am and the *Innisfallen* was due to tie up from Cork an hour later. So after what could often be a rough Irish Sea crossing, the weary passengers had to turn out in the middle of the night and go through Immigration before boarding the trains. Small wonder that a Customs posting to Fishguard in those days was not the most popular way to earn a living. The trains themselves were basic, taking over 6⅔hr for the 260-mile trip to Paddington inclusive of some shuttling about between the fast and slow lines at Reading, with no sleeping cars and the smell of fish from fully-loaded Siphons or General Utility Vans coupled at the front wafting along pungently in the wake of the train.

On 9 July three up boat expresses were due to run, leaving Fishguard at 3.30, 3.55 and 4.55am. Though the first was nominally nonstop to Cardiff, the 3.30 went no further than ½ mile to Goodwick where it ground to a halt alongside the locomotive shed to take assistance for the two-mile climb at 1 in 50 to Manorowen. Safety valves roaring, what was often small cab pannier tank No 7747 came on behind to bank the train to mp 285 8ch. It then scuttled back down to Goodwick in time for the nine-coach 3.55 to sally out unaided up the single line to Letterston Jc, first stop to change engines at Llanelly. Then, in view of the 13-coach load exceeding the 400-ton limit for a banked train, the fireman would put up express headcode on the pannier lamp irons and couple it on in front of 'Castle' No 4090 *Dorchester Castle* which was hauling the 4.55 as far as Cardiff. This assorted pair would then have their work cut out climbing to the top of the 1 in 50 before the pilot came off at Letterston Jc. It would by no means be the only pannier tank to sport express headlamps that day, for

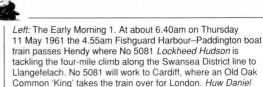

Left: The Early Morning 1. At about 6.40am on Thursday 11 May 1961 the 4.55am Fishguard Harbour–Paddington boat train passes Hendy where No 5081 *Lockheed Hudson* is tackling the four-mile climb along the Swansea District line to Llangefelach. No 5081 will work to Cardiff, where an Old Oak Common 'King' takes the train over for London. *Huw Daniel*

until 8.50am. By then the up rush had already been under way for two hours and station staff were getting ready with their 'queue' boards to deal with the crowds ejected from their lodgings immediately after breakfast. The throng would descend on the station even though their trains might not be leaving for some time. They could not be allowed on the platform, where they would impede passengers joining earlier departures, so they were held in two or three separate queues outside the station buildings.

With platform facilities at both Paignton and Torquay so severely restricted to just a pair of through platforms, the utmost efficiency was required to keep traffic moving on schedule every summer Saturday. The steeply-graded single line from Paignton to Kingswear could only accommodate 10 through expresses in each direction (not counting Kingswear–Newton Abbot local trains or through portions). Often loads had to be reduced at Paignton before trains could proceed to Kingswear. Activity at Paignton was further constrained by level crossings at each end of the station layout, yet departures every 10-15min together with similarly phased arrivals were common at peak periods on summer Saturdays. During 9 July up trains from the Torbay line came into Newton Abbot very close to booked time throughout the day. Some were early and only No 6830 *Buckenhill Grange* on the 2.25pm Paignton-Sheffield was noted as much as 7min late

Gloucester, Newport, Swansea and Newquay would see their share of them too.

If the steamers were held up by rough seas, connecting boat trains were subject to delay and indeed on 16 July they were 30-60min late. But on 9 July all was well, and 8min booked against the 4.55 was the sum total of lost time as the boat trains left Newport and prepared to cross into England, all re-engined now as they raced down into the Severn Tunnel behind Nos 5018 *St Mawes Castle,* 5054 *Earl of Ducie* and 6015 *King Richard III,* in that order.

At Paignton the scene already bore little resemblance to a normal early morning, as the first returning holidaymakers formed a steady stream staggering into the station with their heavy suitcases. Passengers off overnight arrivals were still hanging around in the chilly morning air, waiting until a more civilised time when they could claim their holiday accommodation. Down trains had been coming in since 5.14am and on 9 July the last of about 10 overnight arrivals, the 9.5pm from Newcastle, was not due to reach Paignton

Below: The Early Morning 2. On Saturday 15 June 1957 two 'Halls', Nos 6909 *Frewin Hall* and 6999 *Capel Dewi Hall,* pass Graigola Coal Yard on the Swansea District line with the 4.55am Fishguard–Paddington. *Huw Daniel*

until express workings off the branch ceased at 6.45pm.

Travelling ticket collectors pocketed pads of excess fare tickets in preparation for the task of covering a much wider range of trains than usual. Even so, they would be unable to inspect tickets on more than a fraction of the cross-country reliefs where four trains might be running in place of the daily one. Collectors at crowded station barriers would have to collect tickets from many of these extra trains. This made the Ticket Regulation system currently in force a doubly effective instrument for controlling the holiday flow of passengers, despite the additional administration it involved. To guarantee themselves access to 75 of the day's main return services from the West Country, passengers had to be in possession of a free seat regulation ticket obtained in advance as well as the ordinary rail ticket. This requirement served both to keep the number of passengers within predetermined limits, thus maintaining manageable train loads, and also ensured that sales of tickets in advance reached budgeted levels. At the same time, holders were guaranteed a seat, although the four-a-side seating arrangement found in ex-GW corridor coaches, and even the WR's allotment of modern BR standard stock, did tend to penalise those who had tucked

Below: The scene outside Torquay station on a Saturday morning, with passengers denied access to the up platform until their train is announced. Lines of passengers are standing under the canopy waiting in a queue which extends out of sight to the right of the picture. A separate queue has formed up around the perimeter fence behind a queue board beneath the far end of the station canopy. This board shows the train's reporting number, also shown on passenger's seat regulation tickets, and the train's destination. Thank goodness for a dry day. *Torquay Herald Express*

into plenty of Devon cream teas during their holidays.

All sheds across the system were busy marshalling their engines ready for the weekend onslaught. On summer Friday evenings the Running Foreman at Cardiff Canton had advised the Cardiff District Locomotive Controller, based at Cardiff Queen St, about the engine arrangements which had been made to cover Saturday's traffic requirements at Canton. The Cardiff Controller had then contacted Headquarters Control at Paddington to report all engine movements which were likely to be of interest. Headquarters' staff were receiving similar information from other Districts on the Region. Cards for each relevant engine were kept in a large rack on the control room wall and filled in as necessary. Engine movements were therefore closely supervised, but normally Control would only intervene to hasten the return of engines to their home sheds if a shortage of power had developed in a particular area.

At Canton the large blackboard on the shed wall would be full of chalked locomotive numbers covering all the shed's duties during the day. But despite the rush that preparation of so many engines entailed, Canton still took its reputation for having clean locomotives seriously, even on a summer Saturday. It was the time-honoured routine to send its London engines up to the General station and parade them along the centre road in front of an admiring crowd of passengers. Only spotless engines would create the right impression, so Canton cleaners were busy putting the finishing touches to two 'Castles' for the early turns to Paddington. This was unusual, because generally at least one was a 'Britannia' Pacific, but double-chimney 'Castles' had recently been making something of a comeback there. Both engines were in

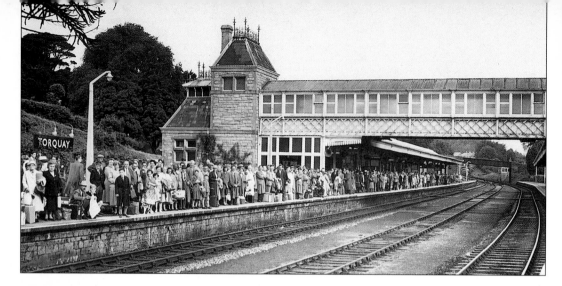

Above: Torquay station on a Saturday morning in August 1958 with the homeward rush of holidaymakers in full swing. *Torquay Herald Express*

Left: A Canton line-up with 'Britannias' Nos 70022 *Tornado* and 70020 *Mercury* on Tuesday 9 May 1961. No 70020 is numbered to work the 8am Neyland–Paddington at midday, and another 'Britannia', No 70026 *Polar Star*, is being prepared for the 1pm Cardiff–Brighton as far as Salisbury. *John Hodge*

Left: A classic example of glossy Canton polish on a lovely engine. No 7006 *Lydford Castle* is on the climb to Badminton near Chipping Sodbury with the up 'Red Dragon' on Wednesday 15 June 1960. The previous day No 7006 worked the up 'Capitals United Express' from Cardiff but was badly delayed by No 7920 on a Bristol–York troop train after Swindon. Although newly fitted with a double-chimney, No 7006 still has its mechanical lubricator fitted in the original position behind the off-side steampipe. *Rev A. C. Cawston Collection, National Railway Museum*

good condition, but when it came to the awkward and dirty task of oiling up between the frames on the four-cylinder GW 4-6-0s their drivers might well have preferred to settle for a Standard Pacific instead.

No 5099 *Compton Castle* had spent the previous day at Canton being prepared and it was first out ready to relieve No 5913 on the 6.15am from Swansea, while nearby 'Capitals United Express' headboard and reporting numbers were cleaned and then hoisted up on the front of double-chimney engine No 7023 *Penrice Castle*. Both 'Castles' had 380 miles to cover, 290 of them with one crew. For No 7023 it was at least the second day running on this working. Their tenders were well stacked up with Welsh coal of a quality which was becoming rare by 1960. As the sun rose, it glinted on shining brass. Scattered showers were forecast too and stormy showers did affect Cornwall, Devon and Somerset during the day, but for engine crews, and especially firemen, the weather would be quite acceptable: mainly dry but not too hot.

If the spit and polish applied to Canton's top-link engines was a reassuring reminder that a summer Saturday could still look like business as usual in some quarters, even here it was an illusion that was no more than skin deep. It masked a hive of activity in and around Canton's main six-road straightshed while a wide variety of eight different steam classes were being prepared for holiday express work. They ranged from a 'King', through other GW 4-6-0 classes (though not a 'Modified Hall' or 'County' until much later in the day), to 'Britannias', '9Fs' and also a trusty '43xx' Mogul. The significance of this variety was that by 11am Canton was cleared out of spare passenger engines, and until incoming locomotives could be turned round again, its extra Saturday commitments could be met only by using freight power or borrowing engines from other sheds. A similar shortage of 4-6-0s on 9 July also developed at Westbury, Weymouth and, as usual, Tyseley. By 1960 St Blazey, which in former years generally found itself the most strapped of all depots for suitable power, had begun to benefit from dieselisation. Now it even had a couple of 'Counties' to its name: Nos 1002 and 1006 displaced from the far west by the diesel hydraulic hordes. Even so, St Blazey still depended heavily on Laira to plug the gaps, a role Laira had never shirked, and in consequence Laira locomotives had been diagrammed to help out at all three Cornish main line sheds for many years.

Laira shed at Plymouth had all its long-standing responsibilities to fulfil, and now, with dieselisation, a lot more too. In fact by 1960 its importance in providing summer Saturday power over an area extending far beyond the West Country can scarcely be exaggerated and was constantly growing with the concentration of all new main line diesel-hydraulics there.

Though Laira shed staff had evolved their own answers to the challenges involved, running the place in summer must still have required men with a strong nerve. Most expresses needed to change engines on arrival at Plymouth. To minimise loco movements at Laira shed, and also along the ¾-mile of congested double track main line between North Road East and Lipson Jc, many workings were arranged so that the engines did not have to visit Laira between duties. Locos from as far away as Bristol, and those coming off piloting operations over the South Devon banks, would be turned instead at Cornwall Jc, together with engines from the Royal Duchy which were waiting to return across the Tamar. Despite these measures to ease overcrowding, routine servicing of steam power at Laira was still very time consuming during busy periods. Coaling facilities in particular were restrictive and an engine might easily occupy two hours on one of the coal roads.

Diesel locomotives could avoid any need to visit Laira by working through Plymouth without an engine change, or by stabling outside North Road before taking up their next turn of duty.

Extensive differences in passenger workings which had to be covered from week to week were dictated by the timetable and various passenger train notices throughout the summer. The locomotive diagramming office would be busy well in advance, so that Laira had continual access to enough power for its requirements. Incoming engines could then be made available to work incidental duties like empty stock services, of which there were a number most weekends. Even then any specials, such as Ocean Liner Expresses or trainloads of passenger-rated fruit traffic from Brittany, which might have to be rearranged at short notice to tie in with shipping arrivals at Plymouth, could still stretch motive power resources which were already fully committed. However, there were no such specials to be catered for on 9 July.

By 7am that morning 14 down arrivals had already reached Plymouth since midnight. Laira yard was full of engines, some of them well used, others freshly prepared waiting for work. The pivotal importance of Laira's position was clearly evident from the heavy calibre of engines on shed, their constant movement in and out, and the number of distant depots already represented there. Early on 9 July these included engines like Nos 6024 *King Edward I* from Old Oak Common, 5033 *Broughton Castle* from Oxford, 5045 *Earl of Dudley* of Wolverhampton Stafford Road, 73026 from Shrewsbury, 6932 *Burwarton Hall* from Cardiff and others from many points in between.

These steam locomotives would be serviced and then sent out again, though on many summer Saturdays this was not necessarily in the direction their home sheds would have chosen. Some were purloined for a trip into Cornwall, others for a run to Newton Abbot piloting over the banks. So it was not altogether surprising that sometimes foreign sheds didn't send their best engines to the West Country unless they were on a diagram with a reliable return working.

All WR main line diesels were based at Laira. By this stage only the four-road steam straightshed had been equipped with specialist diesel repair facilities, and in here the 58 diesel-hydraulics so far delivered, less those out of service for testing or overhaul, had to be maintained to comply with the Divisional Mechanical Engineer's weekly schedule. Twenty-four D800 Type 4 'Warships' in service at this stage needed to be intensively utilised to make the best use of their capabilities. On the other hand, two types of diesel built by the North British Locomotive Co for the Western Region had constant reliability problems and availability rates were poor. Nos D6300-5 of the initial Type 2 series could hardly be trusted to run properly at all and not one of these was in fact observed at work on 9 July. Of the other 24 D63xx Type 2s, those noted in service were exclusively engaged in the area west of Newton Abbot. They all ran either double-headed or in multiple, which provided a useful insurance against failure. Despite their deficiencies, however, these diesels managed to accomplish a surprisingly large amount of work. Similarly the five big NBL Type 4 D600 'Warships' had an indifferent reliability record, but they managed to attain at least 60% availability on 9 July even though one of their number, No D603 *Conquest*, was back at the North British factory for major repairs.

There were many other considerations to take into account which were special to Laira shed. Finding crews who were trained and passed to handle each particular type of diesel was no easy task. 'Granges' with small 3,500gal tenders, of which there were a large number in the Newton Abbot division, were kept off London jobs or long nonstop runs wherever possible. Their tenders had insufficient water reserves where troughs failed to fill between trains with tight margins.

When there were not enough diesels to cover diagramming requirements Laira was responsible for supplying steam substitutes. Now that turns like the 'Torbay Express' had been absorbed into Laira diesel rosters, it was up to Laira and not Newton Abbot to find a suitable steam engine if there was no diesel available for the train from Kingswear. On 30 July 1960 No 7916 *Mobberley Hall* was supplied by Laira for the up 'Torbay' and it is likely that a similar situation applied to No 6966 *Witchingham Hall* which also worked this train on 9 July.

During the morning Laira was in the fortunate position of having three 'Kings', Nos 6016, 6024 and 6028, available for up expresses, and all of them were used to work trains which were generally diesel-hauled. Laira's own No 6016 *King Edward V*, which ran strongly all that summer, was used to spearhead the midday rush of Cornish expresses. It came out for the up Perranporth on 9 July, and that was only the fourth time this train had been steam-hauled since July 1958.

However, looking at the amount of time lost on

important up expresses from Plymouth over a number of weeks through the summer of 1960, it is hard to resist the view that, with so much concentration on diesels, standards of fire cleaning and locomotive preparation at Laira were perhaps slightly past their best by then. This is not to imply criticism, because with so much daily express work now undertaken by diesels, the amount of manpower required for labour-intensive work on the ashpits by a massive influx of steam engines once a week was bound to cause problems. As it was, three of the 'Castles' turned round at Laira lost time heavily on their return journeys with weighty trains on 9 July.

Regular arrangements were adopted to work power down in advance ready for the weekend. On many summer Fridays in 1960 the 9.5am Liverpool–Plymouth came down from Bristol with two engines. Friday 8 July was no exception with No 6910 *Gossington Hall* from Didcot piloting 'Castle' No 4095 *Harlech Castle* ready to bring back loaded trains on Saturday. The spare engine in front was booked to be supplied from Cardiff to Exeter ready to return with the 10.10am ex-Paignton on Saturdays, but in fact it often went back on any train except that one. The only occasion it adhered to the diagram over seven 1960 weekends was when No 6980 *Llanrumney Hall* worked the 10.10 back on 30 July. No 6910 actually returned east on 9 July hauling the 1.30pm Paignton–Paddington, and on a couple of other occasions the engine involved went off to Wolverhampton. Canton very wisely kept its own engines well away from this working!

In some contrast, the staff at Hinksey Up Yard, Oxford, could contemplate a reasonably quiet day with time to catch up on paperwork and make sure that any crippled wagons on hand were ready for dispatch at the earliest opportunity after the weekend. The passenger service over all main lines converging at Oxford was so heavy that southbound freight traffic was due to be suspended all day, after arrival of the 6.45am Banbury Class 7, from 9.7am until the 2.30pm Washwood Heath-Eastleigh Class 5 passed at 5.35pm. Various trip freights ran to Morris Cowley and the 6.10am Wellingborough Class 8 arrived via Bletchley with Crosti '9F' rebuild No 92028 at 12.44pm, but otherwise the railway's lifeblood was at a standstill.

This was the normal summer Saturday freight situation throughout the Western Region. Main line mineral and goods traffic was largely suspended everywhere. Only on the South Wales valley lines did an appreciable amount of freight flow as the day's record at Tondu shows. Elsewhere just a couple of vacuum-brake-fitted freights like Friday's 5.5pm Marazion–Crewe and the Saturday 1.5pm Saltney–Cardiff were allowed to intrude amongst the holiday expresses, and they were expected to keep strict time. No 6872 *Crawley Grange* working through on the 1.5 was about 5-10min late passing Shrewsbury,

Right: The morning after. On Sunday morning 17 July 1960 a build-up of engines awaiting coal at Laira stretches right back over the connection on to Lipson down running loop. They mostly comprise two-cylinder engines, among them Nos 1004, 5385, 6804 and 6878, but also include 'Castle' No 4092 in foreground. *R. C. Riley*

Right: Empty stock operations were an important aspect of holiday traffic. Many empty trains were worked over long distances, but this view of 2-8-0 No 3862 bringing 12 vehicles tender-first towards Teignmouth on Tuesday 2 August 1960, the day after August Bank Holiday, is likely to be a fairly local run to a convenient coach stabling point like Exminster. Earlier that morning seven down ECS workings had been programmed through Exeter St Davids between 12.50pm–2.5am, starting from Paddington (three), Bristol (three) and Oxford (one) to Exminster, Penzance (two), Newquay, Paignton (two) and Falmouth. Four more came down later in the day, one of which was hauled by No 7034 (see picture on page 145). *Hugh Ballantyne*

Right: During its last weekend of booked 'King' haulage the up 'Cornish Riviera' leaves Plymouth on 12 September 1959 hauled by No 4955 *Plaspower Hall* and No 6025 *King Henry III*. The down train was hauled by No 6002 *King William IV*. The stretch of double track shown in the photo was highly congested, carrying not only WR main line trains, but also Launceston branch trains, light engine movements and the empty stock of trains off the former SR route into North Road. *Terry Nicholls*

but it recovered this lost time reaching Newport High St at 6.42pm, 5min early with a light load equalling 250 tons.

The busiest freight arteries from Cardiff to Swansea, through the Severn Tunnel and between Swindon and Didcot were on full stop for 8–10hr. Crucial loaded freight traffic from South Wales eastbound into Cardiff saw only four trains scheduled in 10hr, but in fact traffic was so pressing on 9 July that four extra down freights ran west out of Cardiff in the morning and one up, insinuated into the passenger flow whenever there was a glimpse of a spare path. Even where there was adequate capacity for freight on four-track sections, adjoining double-track bottlenecks prevented much goods being moved. Between the London yards and Reading, through freight movement ceased from around 6am until just after 3pm. Then at 3.5pm No 6956 *Mottram Hall*, already way off the beaten track for a Shrewsbury engine and which had found its way to Southall via Swindon and Didcot the day before, set off west from Acton with 5C51, the 3.5pm express freight for Hackney yard, Newton Abbot. No 6956 picked up speed on the down relief line through West Ealing 6min late as it got its train rolling on the long haul towards Devon, punctuated by frequent pathing stops along the way. This was the first WR freight from London to the West of England for more than 24hr.

Freight dislocation was even more severe in the West Country itself. In effect, no down main line goods moved from Taunton for 20hr after the Friday 6.30pm Bristol–Tavistock Jc Class 4, except a solitary

Bristol–Barnstaple train at 4.5am on Saturday. Friday night's 10.20pm Banbury–Hackney 8C61 freight was dumped at Frome for 15hr from 6am Saturday morning until 8.50pm that evening. There was a 13hr gap in the up direction too. Special arrangements had to be made to restart goods service on Saturday evenings with a series of local freights from Hackney to Tavistock Jc. This helped to clear traffic which had been standing waiting all day, but inevitably transit times suffered as a result of these unavoidable Saturday delays.

Even if main line freight paths had been available, which they certainly weren't, all mixed traffic locos and crews were far too busy to be spared from passenger work. Thus an Old Oak '9F' 2-10-0 No 92238, which worked the 2.30pm fast freight from Paddington to Tavistock Jc on Friday 8 July, was fully occupied hauling the 12.42pm Newquay–Cardiff express through from Plymouth next day, and arriving at its destination early. Extensive use of suitable engines off freight diagrams was made when possible on Saturdays, but again this required foresight and careful organisation. It was no good, for example, Westbury sending down one of its '28xx' 2-8-0s on

Below: No D600 waits to leave Paddington with the 5.50pm Plymouth departure on Wednesday 24 May 1961. Two porters are ready to load their consignment of parcels in the front luggage compartment when the platform trolley arrives. The restaurant car conductor will be busy in the second and third coaches answering passengers' meal enquiries and, if demand is heavy, handing out dinner tickets for one or more sittings. The Paddington Platform No 3 RA indicators are visible on the right suspended beneath the bridge girders. *John Hodge*

Right: The tender of No 6016 *King Edward V* is topped up with water before the engine leaves its home shed at Laira and runs light to North Road station on Friday 22 July 1960. From there it will work 12 coaches on the last daily 'King' turn from the West of England to London, the 9.30am Falmouth. I saw No 6016 come off the Berks & Hants line at Reading during this journey. No 6016 was running 2min early at 3.40pm and sounded very fit as it picked up speed after slowing to 40mph over the junction. On 23 July No 6016 returned to Plymouth on the 9.30am Paddington–Newquay. *Frank Tweddle*

Thursday night's 10.20pm Banbury–Hackney Class 8 arriving 1.24pm Friday, when it was a 4-6-0 which was required to work a weekend express back. Control needed to exert a firm hand here because Westbury shed had enough commitments of its own supplying engines for Salisbury to South Wales, and Weymouth traffic, on Saturdays without having too many of its engines tied up further west.

Good planning was the key to a successful summer Saturday, and on 9 July 1960, a high standard of operating was actually achieved. Through the season, each weekend had its own blueprint of extra trains evolved during previous years and put to the test in a special weekly 'Notice of Passenger Train Arrangements' published separately for every Western Region Division each Friday. Any deviations or additional movements were covered by a duplicated Daily Notice.

Regular annual features of the second weekend in July were up and down West of England specials for the middle weekend of Swindon Works Trip fortnight, and returning Wakes Week extra traffic to Wigan and Colne. These extras over the busy North & West main line, which was already well extended, were enough to tax motive power resources to the utmost.

Preparations for Saturday were in hand behind the scenes all week, and at Old Oak Common the carriage and wagon examiners had a leading part to play. Faulty coaches had to be removed from weekend sets and replaced with suitable substitutes, always assuming that coaches with Pullman-type gangway adaptors were available to couple GW design corridor connections to BR Standard stock when required.

There was little opportunity to match up coach liveries. All named trains in chocolate and cream colours required strengthening at weekends and maroon vehicles generally had to be used. The 'Cornishman' sets were so diluted on Saturdays that the name was abandoned. Spare chocolate or red and cream stock often infiltrated into maroon sets. Many ordinary GW coaches dated back to the 1920s with only a handful of earlier Toplight corridor coaches, all 70ft stock, now remaining. Considering their age, prewar vehicles were very creditably turned out, and modern coaches forming trains like the 'Torbay Express' received special attention to cleaning at Kingswear and Old Oak Common regularly.

Some of the coaches used on dated services commencing 9 July 1960 might not have been used since Christmas 1959 or even the previous August. They required checking, oiling, cleaning, labelling and a battery charge to prepare them for service. But the first tangible sign of the approaching weekend was the arrival on Friday morning at Paddington's No 4 platform of two empty trains. These were formed of restaurant cars from Old Oak being stocked up with supplies ready for Saturday departures. The second of these attached a passenger engine, which on Friday 22 July was No 6965 *Thirlestaine Hall,* and at 12.5pm it was due out for Truro, running nonstop to Exeter where the restaurant cars were booked to be topped up with gas. These cars would disperse to Penzance and Newquay later in the evening, where they would be marshalled into the stock of up expresses ready for use next day.

From then on the level of activity built up through a busy programme of sleeping car and relief services on Friday night to reach a midday peak on Saturday. By then even Old Oak Common's vast array of carriage sidings was looking deserted and it was time to think about positioning all the incoming trains which would arrive during the afternoon. All wheels that could move were already turning, and the railway's resources were stretched to the limit.

Above: One of the few freights to penetrate over Western metals on 9 July 1960 was the 6.10am Wellingborough–Hinksey Class 8. This is making its way gingerly through Oxford at 12.44pm behind rebuilt Crosti '9F' No 92028. *Mike Lake*

Below: No 5008 *Raglan Castle* leaves Newport on Friday 1 July 1960 with the 2.55pm Paddington–Swansea. Behind the tender is restaurant car No W9602W being worked down 'light' as usual on Friday for use in the 1.30pm Swansea–Paddington service next day. *John Hodge.*

2. TOO GOOD TO LAST?

To move the holiday crowds on a summer Saturday in July 1960, British Railways Western Region needed to run over twice the usual number of daily express trains. Normally about 190 long-distance expresses were scheduled each day. On an early July Saturday this total increased to around 450 trains, all now numbered under the new four-character identification system recently introduced on the Western in June 1960.

For many years the Great Western had carefully nurtured the growth of its holiday business, not just to the West Country but also promoting Weymouth for the Channel Islands, resorts like Tenby in West Wales and the two routes through Wales to Cardigan Bay. Weston-super-Mare enjoyed great popularity and the Cotswolds was a choice of many tourists who preferred to holiday away from the coast.

Serving resorts in so many areas involved operating extra trains over all the main lines from Paddington, as well as handling heavy inter-regional traffic and

catering for business generated at intermediate towns and cities along the way. Thus all important routes, except the Oxford-Worcester-Hereford line, saw an

Below: A succession of bridge repairs, a derailment and a landslip disrupted each of the last five summer Saturdays while steam still worked the majority of Western Region summer Saturday expresses in 1961, and one of these situations is the cause of this fascinating photograph. The date is Saturday 19 August 1961 and the tender of an engine, presumed to be the Wellington banker No 6999 *Capel Dewi Hall,* has been derailed on points leading into Whiteball loop. So here at Norton Fitzwarren four down trains are in sight, stopped at every signal until normal services can be resumed. From the rear of the queue they are: No D800 on the 12.21pm Cardiff–Newquay, No 5075 *Wellington* with the 12 Noon Paddington–Plymouth, then what is thought to be No 7029 *Clun Castle* on the 10.18 Wolverhampton–Kingswear, and No 6963 *Throwley Hall* stopped at Victory Siding signals in a most inconvenient location with 14 coaches in tow on the 11.40pm Paddington–Penzance. This incident meant all four trains were 61–74min late when they passed through the Newton Abbot area. *Mike Fox*

increase in express services and even here train loads were often substantially increased on Saturdays.

The Great Western had invested heavily in building up capacity to cope with heavy holiday traffic, and by the time Nationalisation took place, many of the most cost-effective measures which were justified by the limited length of the holiday season had already been carried out. Some schemes like a 1914 proposal for a flyover at Aller Jc, extension of the Swansea District Line to avoid Llanelly, and a 1935 project for a spacious five-platform station at Paignton had not progressed beyond the planning or initial building work stages. Even so, such was the foresight of the GWR that BR inherited sufficient capacity to be able to channel more trains over its Western Region routes than ever before.

British Railways in turn enthusiastically endorsed Great Western policy towards holiday traffic, to such an extent that by 1957 so many trains were running over the main line west of Bristol that it was saturated with traffic. On four or five peak Saturdays a year in the late 1950s more trains were programmed for much of the day than could realistically be handled over the double tracks between Newton Abbot and Taunton or through the Severn Tunnel.

Once the saturation point was reached, measures to increase line capacity were either prohibitively expensive, as in the case of structural work to relieve congestion at bottleneck locations, or else already

under active consideration, as in the case of diesel locomotives to handle longer and faster trains. Similarly, the cost of moves to improve loco utilisation or lift weight restrictions could not be justified in view of the restricted life expectancy of steam engines, despite the fact that they still handled most of the traffic. Trying to make use of what little room for manoeuvre which did remain, to help feed the press of trains through acute bottlenecks, was virtually self-defeating. Instead of being in the position of speeding trains up to achieve greatest line capacity, schedules had to be slowed down and special allowances provided to cover likely delays.

These allowances could take a number of forms, but the ones most applicable were in the shape of recovery margins, which by 1960 were mostly hidden among intermediate timings, pathing stops, and specific signal check allowances. Both the first two expedients had to be adopted in order to funnel traffic from the

Below: No 6827 *Llanfrechfa Grange* assists No 4963 *Rignall Hall* up past Whiteball Siding on Saturday 1 July 1961 with the 7.50am Newquay–Manchester. No 4963 could do with all the help it could find on this arduous turn from Plymouth to Pontypool Road. The 7.50 was therefore regularly double-headed as far as Bristol in 1961 when other 82B 'Granges' such as Nos 6830 and 6878 were also involved on this train, as well as 'Halls'. *Peter W. Gray*

Right: The Severn Tunnel was a major bottleneck, and the climb out of the English side was a severe test for the engines of heavy South Wales or North & West expresses. No 5084 *Reading Abbey* approaches the top of the steepest part of the incline near Patchway with the up 'Pembroke Coast Express' on Saturday 10 September 1960. Lots of extra coaches have been added to both portions to take up a full load of 13 vehicles. *Richard Picton*

southwest over conflicting junctions at Reading. The usual daily 17min nonstop schedule from Newbury was inflated by anything up to 13 extra minutes as the main Saturday afternoon rush developed around 3pm. A few minutes later, trains from the Basingstoke line were booked to stand on the branch at Southcote Jc until a main line path to Reading West was available. It didn't take many recovery margins like that to add half-an-hour to the schedules of a whole block of trains. Alternatively it meant that trains which did not have to make use of their recovery margins would be running disruptively early as they approached major junction points.

Further west 'Castle' No 5063 *Earl Baldwin* on the Saturday equivalent of the down 'Cornishman' was due to make a pathing stop on the relief line at Creech Jc. This was to enable the 10.35am Paddington–Penzance to clear before a slot was available for the Wolverhampton train to restart in the notorious queue to climb Wellington bank. However, that was a stop this train didn't often have to make because it was usually running late long before reaching Creech Jc.

In other situations build-up of traffic was such that even in ideal circumstances of exact timekeeping, signal checks were often inevitably interspersed among a press of trains. Virtually everything possible had already been done to maximise line usage by increasing the frequency of signalling block sections. Hardly a section exceeding two miles in length existed between Paddington and Oxford, Severn Tunnel Junction and Bridgend or Exeter and Dainton. With the 'open as required' Saturday signalboxes in operation few busy main line sections exceeded four miles and the 5 3/4-mile section between Hullavington and Badminton was of wholly exceptional length.

Trains were worked at speed through short sections of as little as 14 chains (308yd) using the old GWR block regulation 4A which permitted block working protected by the next signalbox in the rear. Even then signal delays could not be avoided and were so predictable along some sections of line that special allowances for signal checks were built into the working timetable. Train after train coasting down from Church Stretton to Shrewsbury on Saturday mornings had four, five or even seven minutes extra shown for signal delays. The driver on 'Hall' No 4928 *Gatacre Hall* hauling the 7.35am Cardiff-Blackpool was unlikely to work his engine hard up the climb from Ludlow knowing he had a 7min signal check allowance after Church Stretton Summit, but if he didn't go well enough to keep time past Craven Arms he would delay Fowler 2-6-4T No 42387 on the 6.15am from Swansea Victoria to Shrewsbury due to come off the Central Wales line only 3min behind. The 6.15 then had its own 4min signal check allowance so that if it needed to use an island bay platform at Shrewsbury, its booked 10.55am arrival didn't conflict with the 10.52am departure of the 8.35am Liverpool–Paignton and Penzance, storming out for the south fully laden behind 'Castle' No 5001 *Llandovery Castle*.

Headways past other bottlenecks were tight for long periods of the day. Therefore smooth passage was bound to depend as much upon the judgement of railwaymen on the spot as on the likelihood of exact observance of the timetable. This was particularly true of other places where signal slowing allowances applied. These included the descent south into Hereford, both sides of the Severn Tunnel, Wellington bank, over the whole Torbay line, and across the single-line Royal Albert Bridge. Was it any surprise that a heavy train like the 7.42am Manchester–Penzance and Kingswear which had to negotiate all these obstacles was last seen dividing at Newton Abbot over an hour late. Its engine, No 5029 *Nunney Castle*,

Above: No 5016 *Montgomery Castle* and 5953 *Dunley Hall* pick up speed away from Carmarthen with the 2.30pm Neyland–Paddington on Friday19 February 1960. *Huw Daniel.*

had already been steaming hard for 7½ hr from Shrewsbury and now had to take an unassisted eight-coach load over the South Devon banks to Plymouth, before reaching its home shed at Laira after 247 gruelling miles.

Lots of time was often lost by trains negotiating the Marsh loop at Bristol, where expresses avoiding Temple Meads queued up to stand on what was in effect a busy Saturday main line. Here during 8-10min they had to change crews or engines, pull coal forward, frequently take water too and then set off over a maze of conflicting junctions. During Birmingham holiday fortnight no realistic amount of recovery margin was likely to compensate for a procession of delays over the Snow Hill approaches, while Oxford afforded many passengers a much more prolonged view of the cemetery south of the station than of the church spires for which the city is famous.

A concentration of continuous tight margins for many hours through the Severn Tunnel probably had the most widespread effects of all, and these could be seen in the schedules of Saturday trains as far apart as Bath, Swindon and Abergavenny as they began jockeying for position to take their turn through the 'Big Hole'. Of course in reality the consequences of many missed paths could rapidly spread over a far larger area than that. Only the closest co-operation between all railwaymen involved served to limit resulting disruption. Staff were

well aware of really troublesome trains like the 11.10am Penzance–Wolverhampton, 9.25am Weymouth–Wolverhampton and 7.42am Manchester–Penzance which ran well behind time week after week, and they moved quickly to fill these vacant paths so that no time was wasted. Occasionally there were spectacular problems regarding timekeeping, but this was generally on predictable peak July and August weekends. Otherwise a sprinkling of very late running trains could usually be accommodated without upsetting the rest of the service. In fact the heavy timetabled Saturday traffic was generally handled creditably right up to the full capacity of the track mileage available.

What money could be spared by BR for improvements to trackwork was used to complete carriage sidings and a loco turntable at Goodrington in 1958 thus bringing at least part of the GW's prewar Paignton improvement scheme to fruition. However, remodelling of the four-track layout through Newport High St in 1962/63 came too late to help ease the peak summer Saturday load there. In any case this was more a solution to the long-standing problem of conflicting slow freights delaying down passenger trains all week at Newport than a specific response to summer Saturday operating difficulties.

One of the proclaimed advantages of Nationalisation was the prospect it held out of closer Regional co-operation. But as far as handling summer traffic was concerned, any actual evidence of this was still thin on the ground, and limited largely to shifts in traffic on competing routes from London to Weymouth and Wolverhampton. There were obstacles to all the other more obvious avenues. Though the Western Region had now taken over the Bristol–Barnt Green section of the Midland main line to Birmingham, the locomotive demarcation point for services to and from the LMR at Bristol, or in a couple of instances, Weston-super-Mare, was still absolute. There were already enough problems arranging steam power for the busy Birmingham–Bristol service without contemplating through engine workings any further west.

Similarly, unfavourable configuration of junctions prevented the Western making any use of the SR Exeter–Plymouth route, or its stock of capable light Pacific locos, to relieve congestion. This was because inevitable reversals at both Exeter St Davids and Plymouth would have been largely impractical at peak periods. When the SR West of England route had to be used in emergency the only realistic point of access without excessive mileage penalties was as far east as Basingstoke. For its part, the Southern Region had already gone its own way, losing money on the 'Devon Belle' Pullman service because it was not in a competitive position to tap Plymouth or Cornish traffic.

Passengers ought to have been spared the more inconvenient features of inter-regional rivalry, but this was not always the case. Only one Saturday service from the West of England originated on the SR before joining the WR traffic flow up from Exeter. This was the 9.18am Exmouth–Manchester, a nice through service which ran year after year. But as far as the Western Region was concerned, this train was known as the 10.4am from Exeter St Davids, with no mention of its true origin in the timetable. No hint of the useful service it could provide was shown on any poster advertising. Compared with this facility there was nothing available for Exmouth passengers off the WR in the southbound direction. They either had to change at both St Davids and Central; or at St Davids and Starcross, followed by a 15min ferry trip across the estuary. For the northbound journey No 4942 *Maindy Hall* went up light engine to Exeter Central on 9 July and it took over the train from Exmouth there. No 4942 then ran well on its working right through to Shrewsbury. Here No 4942 arrived about four minutes late at around 3.50pm ready for Stanier Class 5 No 44911 to continue haulage on to the LMR.

By 1960 the degree of saturation on summer Saturdays had begun to diminish slightly, and so the pressure to look for alternative traffic solutions, as distinct from finding financial solutions to the problem of congestion, was becoming less acute.

If the traditional railway summer Saturday was just past its peak in 1960, this fact was hardly evident on the day. An odd Wakes Week extra to Lancashire ceased running, and one or two coaches were trimmed off the load of a few less popular reliefs, but that was about all the adjustments made which arose from changes in passenger demand. Much more significant in 1960 were alterations arising from policy initiatives at the British Transport Commission, BR's ruling body. Transfer of London–Weymouth and Channel Islands traffic to the Southern Region took out three Saturday departures from Paddington; though of course Weymouth still received other boat train and holiday traffic from Bristol, Birmingham and Cardiff routed via Castle Cary and Dorchester. The loss of Weymouth business at Paddington was more than compensated for by concentration of Birmingham services there, while the LMR route from Euston underwent electrification work between November 1959 and March 1967.

A start, tentative at first, was also made in summer 1960 towards tidying up the long-established Saturday timetable on the West of England main line. It was a first move to begin ironing out the enormous peaks of demand that had built up, by spreading departures from Paddington at more regular intervals, and also to ease intermediate timings still more during the busiest periods of the day. This move also employed a measure of realism because while the pre-war GWR had found it possible to have Saturday 10.25, 10.30 and 10.35am departures from Paddington, and then run them at virtually weekday 'Riviera' schedules right through to destination regardless of load, the operating situation in BR days had changed out of all proportion. So much more cross-country traffic now intruded that there was much less opportunity for time lost to be recovered *en route*. Intermediate stations required additional calls. Empty stock and special workings had to be insinuated into an already crowded programme. Crews could not be expected to work such long hours; nor were they all familiar with the latest forms of traction. All these features contributed to the difficulty of handling summer services, and it was now a well-accepted principle that Saturday schedules were drastically slower than those which applied during the week, though even then not as slow as the awful service run on Sundays.

Everywhere the gradients faced were the limiting factor, a constant aggravation as train weights and frequency increased. Almost all Western Region main lines involved gradients of 1 in 80 or steeper at some stage *en route* to the holiday resorts. Only Weston-super-Mare escaped this handicap, but on the other hand, climbs steeper than 1 in 60 along the Weymouth line, over Cockett near Swansea and of course the South Devon banks meant either restricting train loads

or facing up to the complexities of arranging pilot assistance. Even where westbound gradients might be easier, as in the case of the Torbay and Cambrian routes, or where the Cockett climb could be avoided by using the Swansea District Line, loads were still restricted to a weight which could be worked back up 1 in 52 to Talerddig, 1 in 55 out of Torquay, or 1 in 50 to Manorowen box by the Fishguard boat trains, in the reverse direction.

That 1 in 55 climb out of Torquay was particularly damaging in terms of the operating problems it generated. It highlighted the difficulties of having to keep assisting engines ready whenever they were needed, and then of finding light engine paths back down to Torquay for them when the line was already fully occupied. To avoid this, train loads had been restricted to 10 coaches on all services starting or finishing at Paignton since 1959 and this was one ruling that was pretty much universally observed.

The supply of summer Saturday bankers and pilots on a grand scale was by no means restricted to the West Country, however. During the afternoon when traffic between Cardiff and Swansea was at its height a line of five or six tank engines would form at Neath General station. These would shove every train from the platform end up two miles of 1 in 99/88 to Skewen East Jc in order to keep Neath station clear for business, especially when the longest trains had to draw up twice there.

An express like the 11.55am Paddington–Pembroke Dock coming down with 'Castle' No 5091 *Cleeve Abbey* had time allowed to stop for assistance at Pilning through to Severn Tunnel Jc. It would also get a banker at Neath and then, when the 11.55 reversed at Swansea only eight miles further on where No 4076 *Carmarthen Castle* took over, there was provision in the working timetable for another pannier tank here to pilot the 'Castle' up to Cockett. In fact on 9 July the load did not warrant either the Severn Tunnel or

Cockett stops, but the 11.35am Paddington relief did have No 5067 *St Fagans Castle* coupled inside 0-6-0PT No 9484 bunker-first out of Swansea amidst a welter of busy traffic to West Wales.

On the Salisbury to Cardiff route gradients were so steep and speed restrictions so numerous that the whole busy main line service was restricted to overall speeds averaging not much more than 30mph. Along here the best schedule of 171min for 91½ miles was actually only accomplished on summer Saturdays. Many cross-country services over the North & West main line struggled to better a similar average, whatever the timetable might suggest.

Even in 1960 locomotive weight restrictions were still rife. For example 86ton '9Fs', despite weight distributed over a long wheelbase, could not cross the Tamar Bridge into Cornwall. Quite why this prohibition should apply when heavier 'Britannias' were permitted, or a 'Castle' and a 'County' were allowed to double-head a train over Brunel's viaduct together, is difficult to understand. The east–west routes across central Wales were so handicapped that they could take locos no heavier than power Class 4 and there were not even enough of these to go round when two were required to haul many trains. Whilst most regions still had their own examples of rare power combinations on summer Saturdays there could be few pairs so bizarre as a 'Dukedog' 4-4-0 and '2251' class 0-6-0 taking a 10-coach restaurant car express to London up five miles of 1 in 50-65 on the Dolgellau–Ruabon line. No wonder there was sometimes a pair of well-cooked smokebox doors by the time they breasted the summit beyond Drws-y-Nant.

Attempts to find worthwhile alternative spheres of operation for displaced Laira 'Kings' were to be thwarted to the bitter end by weight restrictions on the class west of Cardiff, so when a Canton allocation did eventually materialise in September 1960, all

'King'-hauled trains into South Wales had to change locos at Cardiff. This made two engines necessary on what were previously through workings for just one. Could that be called progress over 30 years after the GW's bridge-building programme first began to permit engines with 22.5ton axle loads to run on main lines?

All these limitations posed a summer challenge of daunting proportions for the considerable number of railway staff involved at all levels. With so many trains running, it called for resourcefulness and ingenuity at every point where services conflicted and converged to achieve the best results. In practical terms this meant achieving the most punctual running possible, while the financial aspects of mounting such a labour-intensive and resource-sapping peak service were inevitably of secondary consideration.

Despite the best intentions, so many extra trains were running that not all of them could be scheduled at times which were actually convenient for travellers. Due to increased prosperity in the area, holiday traffic from South Wales had increased enormously during the 1950s. To help cater for this, three unbalanced services were introduced in 1958 which ran from the western valleys of Monmouthshire to Paddington on Saturday mornings, sweeping up traffic omitted by a succession of Cardiff-Paddington services passing nonstop through Newport.

These three trains each required a lot of early morning empty stock activity to get them ready for departure from Blaina, Abertillery and Ebbw Vale. But for some reason they were then not shown in the local section of the public timetable at all, so publicity was less than dazzling. They also required two engines each. A branch tank worked as far as Bassaleg Jc where the train was then made up for Paddington by a main line locomotive. At that time the cramped layout at the east end of Newport High St station did not readily allow engines to be changed there. Light engine mileage from Canton was also necessary for one tender loco every week, while the return working of the express engine on the Blaina train was at best erratic and often very time consuming.

Passengers had to hold seat regulation tickets in advance to avoid overcrowding, but on the 5.55am Blaina service there was no fear of that. When I appeared at Newport on Friday 29 July 1960 to obtain my regulation ticket the day before I was due to travel I was given ticket No 11. Once aboard next morning behind Southall 'Modified Hall' No 6967, I had the first two coaches entirely to myself. *Willesley Hall* was in nice condition and made light of the schedule. It could have cut over 20min off the 160min timing, and eventually reached Paddington 5min early. But it was no surprise when this lightly-patronised Blaina service disappeared from the timetable for good at the end of the summer.

British Railways' 265,000 traffic staff were fully committed to keeping all the holiday wheels turning as sweetly as possible, making the best use of the equipment at their disposal. Much of it was prewar and ageing. At the same time modern equipment coming into use was often unfamiliar and many of these staff had the job of bedding in a variety of new diesel locomotives and signalling of types which were totally different from anything to which they were previously accustomed.

The fruits of the 1955 Modernisation Plan were now beginning to make themselves felt in no uncertain way on a day-to-day basis five years later, but so concentrated were motive power demands on a summer Saturday that the impact of dieselisation was severely neutralised at weekends. It was hoped that diesels would help to handle the traffic more efficiently and indeed they did, but the sheer intensity of movement meant that the limiting factor was still the slowest train in a procession of 7–12min headways, and any contribution to improved efficiency by 58 new diesels was never going to be enough to satisfy the requirements of the day.

These requirements arose from universal paid holidays which enabled many families to afford weekly accommodation at resorts. Ideally in this pre-package tour era most holidaymakers wanted to arrive at their destinations between 2–6pm on Saturday afternoon. However hard the railways tried, it was an impossible goal to fulfil, and by 1960 the practicality of concentrating so much of the Western Region's weekly resources into a single day's operation was beginning to be seriously questioned. Perversely, over the last two or three years the weekend peak had become even more acute as Saturday to Saturday accommodation bookings became a well-established pattern in the popular market, but those who could afford hotels which were less particular in this respect often chose to use their cars when they travelled on holiday midweek. So trains like the 10.30am down 'Riviera' hardly ever warranted a 10.35am relief from Paddington on a weekday in 1960. Similarly, the usual midweek South Wales reliefs to the 11.55am and 1.55pm trains did not penetrate beyond Swansea.

However slight, not only did this trend increase Western Region reliance on summer Saturday traffic, but it also cut back the scope for utilising expensive sets of reserve coaching stock outside weekends. At the beginning of 1960 only half the WR's stock of corridor coaches was in regular rostered working throughout the year. Some coaches in the reserve fleet might make only 5–10 journeys a year, and the loss of loaded midweek work meant that their already uneconomic sphere of action was further reduced. Greater concentration on the day of the week when BR's service could be at best mediocre was bad news all round. Hence the need to start levelling out the Saturday peak quickly gained top-level attention when Regional finances came under the microscope during the next 18 months.

Above: With its usual two engines on a 14-coach train the 2.55pm Paddington–Swansea and Bristol comes powering through Didcot on Friday 8 July 1960. A disreputable looking Swindon 'County', No 1004 *County of Somerset,* heads No 4076 *Carmarthen Castle* which will take the Swansea portion on from Swindon. No 4076 has left Swansea only at 7.30am that morning so this is a very demanding 390-mile diagram. The up main signals are off for No 4084 *Aberystwyth Castle* approaching with the 12.15pm Dr Day's Sidings–Old Oak Common parcels. Next day No 4076 would work only to Carmarthen while No 1004 penetrated to Salisbury. *Mike Lake*

The fact was that in 1960 individual BR Regions enjoyed considerable independence from their masters at the British Transport Commission. The Western Region made extensive use of this independence, but not always wisely, and on occasions paid only lip-service to the directives from its Marylebone Road masters. Thus when mileage reductions were imposed by the BTC in response to new economy measures ordered by the Government on 4 April 1960, Western Region observed the letter but not the spirit of some BTC instructions. Mileage economies were accomplished, for example, by amalgamating the midweek 2.55pm and 3.5pm departures from Paddington as far as Swindon. The mileage was certainly saved but what happened was that two engines and crews still worked the same two sets of coaches as one train. It was a great sight seeing two 4-6-0s powering through Didcot together, and some good running followed but no actual financial economy resulted at all. Instead passengers were 10min late arriving at their destinations right down the line to Swansea.

There is no doubt, however, that the Western Region did all it could to cater successfully for such large numbers of passengers. Many of the facilities on offer were efficiently organised, like the Passengers' Luggage in Advance arrangements which were an absolute boon to travellers. Instructions for maintaining connections at major stations like Bristol Temple Meads

were set out in detail and gave passengers a realistic chance of completing their journeys with a minimum of disruption. Meanwhile the Region's management was pursuing sensible policies with regard to new motive power, introduction of resignalling schemes and train identification. Even if regional finances were far from satisfactory, operations ran smoothly enough on a day-to-day basis.

On the other hand there were lapses, and not all of them were just of regional origin. The Western shared with the LMR a marked lack of confidence in the new 'Blue Pullmans'. Already two years late entering service, they were eventually introduced by the WR in September 1960 on very modest schedules five days a week, with one of three units spare and idle all the time. Five days' use of two units could not possibly cover the financial burden involved. Unfortunately, the

Western also misjudged levels of 'Blue Pullman' patronage, and, after a couple of months, embarrassing alterations to routeing and extra stops had to be introduced. A number of other ordinary services were inevitably affected, so that a train like the one to Plymouth which, except for a short spell after the last war, had left Paddington at 4.15pm for 50 years, was suddenly altered to start at 4.5pm. The old 4.15 departure was still shown in the public timetable for a further eight months, while some disgruntled passengers found themselves arriving at an empty platform.

The reputation of the Western Region with its customers also suffered from other self-inflicted pitfalls which contributed to the frequent late running of some services. Paddington was a well-organised and efficiently run station but recent changes to traffic patterns meant that it was subject to overcrowding at peak times. Dieselisation of suburban services should have helped. But, due to the use of some diesel units without ATC shoe clip-up gear which could not use the electrified suburban platforms, they actually made the difficulties at Paddington worse for a while early in 1960.

Another problem was a persistent tendency to overload important trains so that sometimes extra minutes were added to working schedules, and at other times the trains just ran late. It made very little difference to passengers which option was taken. As far as they were concerned the train was late anyway.

It should be pointed out at once that this strengthening of loads was not on a scale which would have presented problems either historically to 'Kings' and 'Castles' in GW days, or currently in 1960 by comparison with loads regularly worked over the LMR Western Division by similarly sized 4-6-0s. Both would have taken the extra tonnage involved in their stride. But the WR was not in a position to exert quite the discipline that its predecessor had enjoyed, so where the overloads exceeded timetabled limits they were enough to upset the delicate balance of punctuality and some very poor running could result.

For example, among others, both the 10.55am down 'Pembroke Coast Express' and the 11.5am 'Merchant Venturer' from Paddington were in different loading categories as between their up and down stock workings. In the case of the 'Merchant Venturer' this situation no doubt dated back to the days when the up train conveyed an extra slip coach for Reading, but this practice had ceased in 1958. The up trains could both be loaded to 100 tons more than

Below: No 5087 *Tintern Abbey* makes an exhilarating start from Paddington with 15 coaches on the down 'Merchant Venturer'. The date is Saturday 6 August 1960 as No 5087 comes under Westbourne Bridge and passes Ranelagh Bridge loco yard, where two Oxford-based 'Castles' await work. No 5012 *Berry Pomeroy Castle* in the foreground is probably marked down for a turn back to Didcot on the 2.3pm departure, while No 5025 *Chirk Castle* is on standby in the pilot spur beyond. *R. C. Riley*

the down workings, and both the 10.55 and 11.5 often ended up carrying two, three or more extra coaches daily on the down trip as well. The 11.5 was an Old Oak turn with the facility to use a 'King' so that the limits could be observed, but when exceptionally the Saturday train was loaded to 15 coaches on 6 August 1960, which, mostly with standard stock, must have grossed 535 tons, just one 'Castle', No 5087 *Tintern Abbey*, was supplied for haulage.

In the case of the 10.55am down, however, a Landore lodging turn through to Swansea, there was no alternative but to use a 'Castle' and it was never anything else except the odd 'Britannia' seen years before. The 10.55 should have been a 'Special Load' set of nine coaches on its fast weekday timing, but it exceeded this limit for at least half the year, not because down traffic demanded it but because the return working at 5pm formed the most popular evening service from Cardiff to London on much slower timing. Not only did it overshoot the down 'Special Load' limit but it also frequently exceeded the more liberal 350-ton maximum coming back on the up train too. In August 1960 the 'Pembroke Coast Express' was made up to 12 coaches both ways day after day, and day after day there were late arrivals in Cardiff coming down. Some were very late, not far in advance of the Saturday schedule which allowed an extra 30min to Cardiff with a weekend load of 13 coaches. The retiming of working schedules was no consolation to passengers in a situation like this.

Such policies eroded the goodwill of staff and customers alike, and unfortunately they did nothing to help arrest the Western Region's alarming financial deficit. The Western Region could never be said to have conducted its operations with much consideration for the feelings of its paymasters at the BTC, but when this lack of diplomacy was coupled to such poor results, the hatchet could not be far away. The size of its losses gathered pace through 1960 and 1961 so that when the time came to reshape British Railways in 1962 the Western Region was in the front line for a fundamental shake-up. At the cost of considerable expenditure of taxpayers' money the new Regional management then fell into the trap of sweeping away much that was worth keeping along with what wasn't, and by the end of 1962 changes resulting from a complete change of management philosophy were obvious all over the Western.

But in 1960 there was still a fascinating spectacle of variety and individual enterprise which helped to extract every passenger mile from the resources available. The inevitable problems arising within streams of densely packed traffic were often dealt with amazingly quickly, as we will see from two of the engine difficulties which were promptly overcome on 9 July 1960. This was just one part of a story which was repeated on many steam summer Saturdays.

It may have been TOO GOOD TO LAST, but it was also FAR TOO GOOD TO MISS.

Below: No 5077 *Fairey Battle* was well thought of at Landore. It is on the last stage of the journey from Paddington to Swansea passing Lon Las with the down 'Pembroke Coast Express' on Thursday 9 February 1961. It will probably have made up time on the easier schedule from Cardiff and at 2.35pm is now running only 5min late. *Huw Daniel*

3. FINDING THE POWER FOR THE JOB

To haul summer Saturday express traffic on 9 July 1960 the Western Region had at its disposal 187 four-cylinder steam 4-6-0s and 466 two-cylinder 4-6-0s of Great Western design. In addition to these were 12 BR Class 7 'Britannia' Pacifics, 29 BR Standard Class 5s and 12 BR Standard Class 4 4-6-0s allocated to ex-GW sheds, a total of 706 steam locomotives. There were also 29 Type 4 diesel-hydraulics in stock and, as it happened, 30 Type 2 diesel-hydraulics too. However, unsatisfactory trials had delayed one of these, No D6326, at the North British factory.

Diesel multiple-units played a very restricted part in the proceedings. Ideal for suburban services, their limitations in coping with peak period holiday expresses were ruthlessly exposed on summer Saturdays. Despite making up three-car units into sets of nine coaches they still could not offer enough accommodation to deal with all Cardiff–Birmingham traffic and a number of steam-hauled reliefs were necessary. In those days the object was to offer passengers the best service possible and when through trains were run from Birmingham to Pembroke Dock and Fishguard Harbour, that meant putting on a steam job as well. And, with the doubling up of individual multiple-units on most services, there were not enough diesel sets left to cover every normal weekday commitment on the Saturday Cardiff–Bristol service or even the Cardiff Valleys interval workings. That involved more steam substitute workings again. One other DMU managed to make it in stages from Newton Abbot to Porthcawl. Except for the 7.10am Paddington–Wolverhampton via Oxford, and a handful of Weymouth trains, most other DMUs were engaged on Class 2 semi-fast and local services.

Below: Both lines were bidirectional through the interesting junction station at Johnston (Pembs). On Wednesday 22 June 1960 No 6909 *Frewin Hall* shunts stock off the Neyland line while to the right a cross country diesel unit forms the 4.45pm Milford Haven-Bristol passenger. *Gerald Adams*

Even so one might have expected that the WR's passenger complement of 764 engines outlined above would have been sufficient to power all the day's 450 or so main line expresses. But in fact that was far from being the case. Just how far the day's locomotive resources fell short of expectations depended on how fully the loco stock was utilised. Many of the fleet were engaged on their regular overnight freight, parcels and daily local passenger workings. They were either otherwise committed, precluded by weight restrictions, undergoing servicing or wrongly located to play any part in hauling holiday express traffic. Others were under repair, awaiting parts or restricted by poor condition to light work.

To take the 30 'County' Class engines as examples, only one, No 1015 *County of Gloucester*, was at Swindon Plant, its repair in abeyance during the Works annual holidays. But No 1026 *County of Salop* had been stopped awaiting shopping at Shrewsbury since 6 July 1960, and troublesome 'County' No 1023 was inactive, thought to be under repair at Exeter. No 1005 *County of Devon*, due to be taken out of traffic at Bath Road for shopping on 22 July 1960, was too run-down to be used on express work, though it managed a local trip to Taunton and back. By complete contrast No 1010 *County of Caernarvon* could not be used on fast work either, because it was running in on Swindon–Didcot locals after overhaul.

Of the remaining 25 engines, 15 were observed on express work, three on parcels and one exclusively on local passenger trains. Three more were accounted for at sheds on Sunday. Half the 'Counties' being concentrated at the far west extremities of the Western Region meant a couple of Cornish 'County' workings and at least one of the Neyland engines were bound to have been missed because of the limited time for which observations are available at Par and Carmarthen. But it is fair to say that out of this class of 30 locos which were an ideal versatile type for summer Saturday work,

not more than 20 actually made it on to expresses during 9 July 1960.

Then of course many trains, the majority, in fact, required more than one engine in the course of a journey across the Western Region. Anything up to six locomotives per train were needed, as in the case of the 8.15am Perranporth–Paddington and also of various portions forming the 8am Neyland–Paddington. Exceptionally on 2 July 1960 the 8.55am Wolverhampton–Penzance also needed six in a glorious technicolour of double-headers and a triple-header, possibly even seven if No 5031 *Totnes Castle* had to stop at Wellington for the occasional banking assistance required on this train. Back on 9 July five engines were required for the 10am Newquay–Paddington with its triple-header to Plymouth, and five more on the 11.10am Penzance–Wolverhampton in which three different pairs of engines were involved *en route*. (I realise three x two doesn't make five, but 'Castle' No 5045 *Earl of Dudley* with its 14-coach load had to take two separate pilots during a through trip from Plymouth to Wolverhampton.) Further north almost all through trains to central and west Wales needed three or more locomotives and inevitably the consequence of this was that there were never quite enough suitable engines where they were most needed. Saturday rearrangements and the resulting impossibility of changing engines at Shrewsbury meant that the three locomotives usually required to work the daily 'Cambrian Coast Express' in both directions between Paddington and Aberystwyth were expanded to at least five plus one assistant. And it might need eight engines on peak Saturdays even before the coast line portions were taken into account.

One of the biggest surprises in looking at locomotive utilisation on the day was to find that some sheds like Swindon actually had 'Castles' on hand for which they did not have adequate Saturday work. Every one of these inevitably contributed to a shortage of passenger engines elsewhere. Stafford Road was another example of a surplus situation on 9 July and Nos 5022 *Wigmore Castle* and 5046 *Earl Cawdor* were not steamed there even though both were in action either the day before or the day after. A couple more, Nos 5026 *Criccieth Castle* & No 5047 *Earl of Dartmouth,* were only used on pilot, standby and local work. Any of them would have been most welcome at a wide number of other depots including a couple not at all far away. Worcester had no pressing commitments for three spare 'Castles' (excluding Nos 4085/7005 which were in works), once its six London jobs had been dealt with. To be

fair though, Worcester was always ready to lend a good 'Castle' or two at the height of the Birmingham holiday fortnight. In fact No 5081 *Lockheed Hudson* ran a return trip to Plymouth on 22/23 July 1960 and again on 29/30 July 1960, with No 7006 *Lydford Castle*, an old Laira engine, appropriately filling this role on 6 August 1960. No 7006 had also penetrated to Newton Abbot on 30 July 1960, returning via Paddington on that Saturday afternoon.

Further west the amount of 'Castle' working between Swansea and Carmarthen was extensive enough to rival 'Castle' activity on many other more heavily trafficked routes during the afternoon, while 'Granges' and 'Halls' were left to handle some of the more ambitious Saturday diagrams east of Swansea. One of these engines, No 6843 *Poulton Grange* of Llanelly, worked from Swansea to Salisbury and then Westbury to Birmingham during the day, 270 miles excluding light engine running. A Landore 'Hall' No 6941 *Fillongley Hall* made a return trip to Banbury on the Swansea–York trains and clocked up 342 miles in the process.

One sure way to improve loco utilisation on Saturdays was to devise quicker turn-round times between trips, but generally nothing very ambitious was attempted. Too many tight turn-rounds were likely to backfire in the event of late running, and with one notable exception taking in the engine off the 11.30am ex-Paddington at Taunton, nothing much quicker than ordinary weekday turn-rounds was

ventured. Outside Paddington, Ranelagh Bridge loco yard contained limited stabling space and this was fully utilised every day. The only way to speed up operations there on Saturday was for an engine simply to turn and take water before leaving again. This could certainly be useful at peak weekends, and on Saturday 6 August 1960 the 81A '9F' No 92238, already mentioned in connection with passenger work on 9 July, was out again. It arrived at Paddington on the 5.55am South Wales express from Blaina at 10.15am. After some delay it was not released into Ranelagh Bridge yard until 11am. The '9F' 2-10-0 was then turned and reversed out again at 11.23am ready to work the 11.35am down departure to Neyland, booked straight through to Swansea (on this occasion), and No 92238 duly left Paddington right on time on its way back west.

On 9 July similar incoming London engines sent back to Old Oak Common for servicing certainly did not feature in any repeat appearances at Paddington that day. Whereas the first 81A 'Castle' safely received back from Llanelly on a Saturday morning Fishguard train would often reappear for the 6.55pm down Fishguard later that evening, there was no pressure for Old Oak locos to be reused so intensively on this occasion. The 6.55 engine was actually No 5037

Monmouth Castle which had come in on Friday's 4.15pm from Bristol 24hr before. Old Oak was still turning out fresh 'Castles' of its own like No 5043 *Earl of Mount Edgcumbe* at midnight on Saturday and one wonders whether it was really necessary for Old Oak to have been busy plundering engines from other depots to fill its lists earlier in the day. At Old Oak they would undoubtedly see the matter differently, with a daunting programme of express workings to be powered from 6pm Friday right through the night until 1.30pm Saturday, and very few easy jobs among them. No passenger engines would be wasted; borrowing was a way of life and anyway other sheds had locos they could spare.

Old Oak was well-known for this habit and whilst Southall, Reading and Didcot sheds had their own regular summer Saturday turns from Paddington, their engines and those from Swindon and any other shed as far west as Carmarthen were fair game too. The 87E 'Castle' No 5080 *Defiant*, for which no workings were recorded on 9 July, was not available to help with any of Landore's own duties for two Saturdays running at the turn of the month. On 23 July it was borrowed by Old Oak, probably at short notice, to take the place of a diesel on the 3.15pm Paddington–Kingswear. No 5080 then took until Monday afternoon 25 July to make its way back as far as Cardiff on the Penzance–Swansea. It would probably be Wednesday before No 5080 was ready to resume its regular Landore workings. On 30 July *Defiant* was again well off its normal patch when Stafford Road used it for a relief turn to Paddington, and finally on 6 August No 5080 found itself on Landore Turn 3 handling the 7.55am Paddington as far as Swansea. By then it was absolutely filthy after spending so much time wandering all over the system.

One other aspect of current policy which could affect engine utilisation at that time was the Western Region's habit of shuttling its fleet of express engines around between sheds to equalise mileages. This had meant the loss of some well-established favourites at most sheds over the last few years. Two other considerations further increased this movement of four-cylinder engines around the Region in 1960. The first was replacement of 'Kings' and 'Castles' by dieselisation, and the second was the concentration of 70XX series 'Castles' newly fitted with Alfloc water treatment apparatus at Worcester Division sheds. It might have seemed wise to arrange these movements well in advance of the summer timetable both to reduce dislocation and leave time for sheds to acclimatise to their new engines. But all through late June and early July reallocations were in full swing. Among them on 9 July was the exchange of two ex-works double-chimney 'Castles', Nos 5094 and Alfloc-equipped 7003, between Bristol Bath Road and Gloucester. Such engines as these in course of reallocation were ripe for plunder. No 5094

Tretower Castle bound for Bath Road found its way from Gloucester on to a Swindon diagram which it worked through from Paddington to Swansea, returning as booked with the 3.50pm Whitland milk. No 7003 *Elmley Castle* moving from Bath Road had overshot its new home at Gloucester and on Friday 8 July was purloined by Stafford Road for a return trip to Paddington. It then set off in the right direction from Stafford Road at 3.33am on Saturday morning but did not reach Gloucester until 6pm that evening, passing Abbots Wood Junction on what must have been the 4.45pm Worcester–Gloucester Eastgate local. More wasteful summer Saturday use of a crack ex-works 'Castle' would be hard to find. By the following Saturday No 5094 was safely established on the 8.20am Weston-Paddington and No 7003 had begun what was to be a notable association with the up 'Cheltenham Spa Express'. But by being deprived of either of these engines on 9 July, Gloucester had nothing larger than No 7926 *Willey Hall* available for its up 'Cheltenham Spa Express' turn. Such a shortage could feed right down through the links, and when the supply of 4-6-0s on shed did run out, it was no easy job for running foremen casting around the yard to find suitable substitutes to fill in.

First in line to plug the gaps should undoubtedly have been the Western Region's stock of over 50 '9F' 2-10-0s, but on 9 July the participation of these was limited to only about eight engines standing in for 4-6-0s. They were handicapped by their physical distribution around the system, and a blatant prejudice against the use of '9Fs' on express work by the regional operating authorities.

Nine '47xx' 2-8-0s were few in number but giants in every other way. Though their overall impact on the summer Saturday scene was inevitably limited, they commanded instant attention whenever they appeared on passenger traffic over the Paddington–Bristol–Plymouth triangle within which most, but not quite all, their express work during BR years was carried out.

And then there was the main line of reserve, the same as it had been for well over 25 years in the shape of the '43xx' mixed traffic Moguls. With at least 21 of these 2-6-0s out on main line express work in addition to their regular operations on secondary routes all round the Region, the contribution of these sturdy but ageing machines forms a fascinating insight into how the problems of finding enough motive power to cover holiday demands were solved, sometimes satisfactorily, sometimes less so.

By 1960 the days of '28xx' 2-8-0s on passenger traffic were over, always barring the completely unexpected, which occurred about once a year in the early 1960s. The first time was on 13 August 1960 when a Pontypool Road 2-8-0 No 3826 arrived relatively punctually at Cardiff on the 8.50am Birmingham–Swansea dated relief. The second was on 5 August 1961 when No 3854, also strangely enough

Right: After wandering all over the Western Region for the last two weekends No 5080 *Defiant* is in dire need of a good clean as it curves past Landore with the 7.55am Paddington–Carmarthen on Saturday 6 August 1960. 'Britannia' No 70018 *Flying Dutchman* is waiting in the loop with the 9.25am Cardiff–Neyland parcels. This is composed of the usual selection of empty coaches and parcels vans, plus the regular Cordon gas tank wagon which used to be sent down by this train from Cardiff to West Wales four times a week. *Huw Daniel*

Right: '9Fs' had one or two fairly regular turns between South Wales and the West of England in summer 1960, notably the 9.5am Swansea–Kingswear and the Newquay–Cardiff. '9F' No 92248 is passing Undy Halt on Saturday 30 July 1960 with the 9.5am Swansea train which the 2-10-0 worked throughout to Kingswear. It usually received assistance between Taunton and Exeter from the engine off the 9.40am Paddington–Minehead, which on this occasion was No 5943. *R. O. Tuck*

Right:: '47xx' No 4706 runs in to stop at Reading on Saturday 1 August 1959 with the 1.25pm Paddington–Kingswear. The next two Saturdays '9Fs' worked this train and it might be thought that the days of '47xxs' on expresses from Paddington were numbered, but on 29 August No 4706 was back on the 1.25 again. There were three other '47xx' 2-8-0s out on passenger work on 1 August as well as No 4706. Traffic was heavy and No 4706 arrived at Newton Abbot 30min late among a press of trains. No 4706 was an SPM-based 2-8-0 which would probably have been appropriated for the 1.25 off Friday night's 9.15pm Temple Meads–Acton Class D freight. *R. C. Riley*

Left: Tyseley engines were seen on a regular basis working over the Cambrian on summer Saturdays. They spent the following week on the coast before returning at the weekend. Here 2-6-0 No 5369 waits at Aberystwyth with the 9.55am Shrewsbury train on Tuesday 15 July 1958. *Frank Hornby*

Left: At Newton Abbot the last recorded appearance of a '28xx' 2-8-0 on a holiday express was this occasion on Saturday 5 August 1961 when No 3854 unexpectedly worked the 8.50am Swansea–Paignton relief on from Bristol. '9F' 92210 had brought the train in from Swansea and was 8min late leaving Cardiff. As No 3854 was only 10min late reaching Newton Abbot, including a dead stand for signals outside Newton Abbot station, it had certainly run well. No 3854 averaged 49mph between Exminster and Dawlish Warren on the way from Exeter in 32min, or 29min net. Neither of the '47xx' 2-8-0s on down express services that day could compete with this standard of timekeeping. The 'Castle' on the right is No 4096 *Highclere Castle* and the down through line signal behind the engine is clear for No 5072 and its assistant to depart for Plymouth with the 8.55am Wolverhampton
–Penzance. The small inspector's cabin on the down platform, where locomotive movements in the Newton Abbot area were arranged at peak periods, is visible on the left. *Frank Tweddle*

Left: '28XX' 2-8-0s helped on milk and parcels traffic at weekends while 4-6-0s were busy on holiday traffic. On Saturday 16 July 1960 the 12.20pm Penzance–Kensington milk has a relatively light load as No 3840 clears Hackney, on a loco working which will not be completed until No 3840 reaches Old Oak Common at 7.5am next morning. *Derek J. Frost*

from Pontypool Road, appeared at Exeter on 1C73, the 8.50am Swansea–Paignton relief. Furthermore, it was running early and making such good progress that No 3854 had been allowed out of Taunton ahead of the down 'Riviera' instead of following it as usual when 1C73 ran. Their passenger forays had never been frequent, but the '28s' still had a limited summer Saturday part to play on empty stock, parcels and occasional milk trains, so releasing 4-6-0s for other work. The last gas turbine — Brown Boveri No 18000 — was now parked withdrawn outside Swindon Works, almost within sight of the station. Here I had seen it come whistling through, on what must have been one of its final workings, with the 1.15pm down on 15 October 1959.

That leaves only one further Western express engine which was available for consideration — a certain double-framed 4-4-0 which in 1960 was still enjoying its first revival. No 3440 *City of Truro* was not required for railtour use on summer Saturdays. Its regular daily job was a return Swindon–Bristol local via Badminton most evenings, but it should technically have been quite capable of helping out on some of the main line express work for which 2-6-0s were marked down. Unfortunately, No 3440 was based at Swindon shed where there were already ample numbers of very grubby 4-6-0s on hand to cover all likely Saturday requirements. Thus on 9 July there was neither the scope nor the temptation to use the famous 4-4-0 on anything more venturesome than its usual Bristol local, though Tyseley would perhaps have been more than happy to have it for a trip to Oxford and back in place of No 6364 on the 9.5am from Snow Hill to Portsmouth.

A closer look at the major classes involved reveals some interesting trends at what was a crucial point in the transition from steam to diesel power during 1960.

8P 'King' class 4-6-0s

9 July was a good day for 'Kings'. Six worked in the West of England, thought to be the last time so many of them were seen in the west on one day. Fourteen more were also active elsewhere, 12 of these on the Birmingham line. As usual all worked expresses, though there was a milk train involved on the way back after the modest sortie by No 6003 *King George IV* to Swindon in the evening.

The availability figure of 66% for the class which these 20 active engines represented was above the usual 55-61% level of many years' standing, even if it was nothing special for a summer Saturday. Those 'Kings' performed well, and their punctuality record without heavy time losses was the best on the day of any class with a significant number of engines involved in express haulage, steam or diesel.

Ten 'King'-hauled up Birmingham line expresses averaged under 2min late per train at Paddington. Down traffic was only prevented from achieving a similar record by congestion during the afternoon, when the 11.10am, 1.10pm and 2.10pm expresses lost between 11-19min into Snow Hill. All three were 12–14 coach trains with 'Kings' Nos 6010, 6011 and

Below: No 3440 *City of Truro* stands at the up platform in Swindon Junction station waiting to leave with an eastbound excursion on Friday 18 July 1957. At this stage No 3440 was shedded at Didcot, moving to Swindon in 1958. *Hugh Davies*

6027 which ran well on their up journeys.

At least six 'Kings' worked the same equivalent rosters to and from Wolverhampton on both Friday and Saturday, though the 'Special Load' 8.30am down Birmingham 2hr was not one of these. On Friday it was hauled punctually by No 6028 *King George VI* just a month out from works, but by 8.30am Saturday No 6028 was already down at Plymouth, and so a much higher mileage engine, No 6029 *King Edward VIII*, was put on in its place. Despite perhaps 56,000 miles to its credit since overhaul in May 1959, No 6029 also did well and ran into Snow Hill at 10.31am.

No 6029 was not actually timed anywhere on its way back from Wolverhampton to Paddington with the 7.20am from Pwllheli. However, after changing from 0-6-0s Nos 2287 and 3200 to No 5970 *Hengrave Hall* at Ruabon the train was running well up from Shrewsbury. No 6029 then left Stafford Road shed at 12.20pm in plenty of time to make a punctual departure for London. With a light load on an easy 135min nonstop schedule from Snow Hill, No 6029 could be expected to improve the day's punctuality ratings rather than the reverse.

Meanwhile, just as No 6029 was due to run into Paddington at 3.25pm its brother engine, No 6028, was facing up to a vastly different proposition way down west at Newton Abbot. No 6028 had to tackle a hefty load of 13 vehicles on the 12.30pm Newquay–Paddington and, after dropping the 'Manor' pilot at Newton East up through line home signal, No 6028 was off on its way at 3.28pm.

As usual this was a run of three phases — delays to Taunton, healthy time recovery on to Reading and beyond, followed by more delays into Paddington. Two minutes' arrears at Newton had expanded to

Above: On Thursday 16 June 1960 'King' No 6015 *King Richard III* comes flying over Aynho Troughs with the 11.40am Birkenhead–Paddington. *Rev A. C. Cawston Collection, National Railway Museum*

15min by Taunton, due to two cross-country services from Penzance in front which were running 24 and 18min late. These squeezed the 12.30pm Newquay into the path of the following train at Exeter, and it was not until the Penzance trains diverged towards Bristol that No 6028 could expect to show its paces. This it certainly achieved. No 6028 covered 112 miles from Taunton to Twyford in 124min including a lengthy booked call at Reading. So every minute of the time lost earlier on was now regained.

No 6028 would have been going good and hard up hill and down dale right across Somerset and Wiltshire to reach Reading in about 110min from Taunton. While 120 or so diners were contentedly munching toasted tea cakes, followed by a liberal helping of sandwiches and fruit cake in the triple restaurant car unit, they were being whisked along at speeds not far short of those needed on the much lighter up weekday 'Riviera'. No doubt No 6028 was on full song as it swept through Lavington and vigorously tackled the eastbound ascent to Savernake with a continuous roar of crackling exhaust.

Soon after Twyford, however, No 6028's crew would have sighted adverse signals ahead from a procession of four preceding trains making for Paddington. No remedy was readily available for the checks which followed. No 6028 was 9min late when it slotted into one of the long platforms at Paddington, booked to be No 9. Nevertheless it had been a good day's work on two heavy trains to and from Plymouth, not to mention Friday's Wolverhampton turn as well.

Only one 'King' came seriously unstuck for punctuality. It was a pity this had to be No 6024 *King Edward I* which was currently in very good shape. It was the first steam loco of 1960 to appear on what had always been a long-standing Saturday 'King' turn, the 11.15am from Plymouth, and could have been expected to stay well out of trouble on its way up to Paddington. Unfortunately, No 6024 lost its path when a defective coach with a hot box had to be detached from its train at Newton Abbot and it then suffered the consequences.

After Canton 'Castle' No 7023 with 764 miles, No 6028 managed the next best mileage of any WR steam locomotive over 8/9 July, running up 697½ revenue-earning miles in the process. No 6029 covered 492 miles in only a fraction over 24hr, but this was more a quirk of rostering a late turn on Friday followed by a morning turn on Saturday, than giving any real idea as to what could be achieved regularly. Some ER Pacifics were sustaining over 500 miles a day on diesel workings around this time, but the loss of high mileage Plymouth steam duties on the Western, and a reluctance to turn round any WR steam engines in order to maintain diesel diagrams even if it might have been desirable, meant that for 'Kings' little regular improvement was possible on the usual daily 246-mile scope of a Paddington–Wolverhampton return trip. Unfortunately, increasing the number of through Shrewsbury jobs would have caused stock marshalling difficulties at Wolverhampton. The single daily through engine working which did operate between Paddington and Shrewsbury, on the weekday (SX) 'Cambrian Coast Express', was currently the preserve of No 6000 *King George V* which was seen on it at least twice earlier in the week.

If the 'Kings' were handicapped by what work remained for them, there were other clear indications that now after 30 years' service they were no longer indispensable. 1960 was the first year that the 'Cornish Riviera' was not steam-hauled on summer Saturdays. Most of the other traditional Saturday West of England 'King' workings had been dieselised, as well as all but

Right: Both Laira 'Kings' were frequently used to cover non-availability of diesels throughout the summer of 1960. Here No 6002 *King William IV* is seen west of Twyford on the last stage of its journey with the 11.15am Plymouth–Paddington on Saturday 16 July 1960. No 6002 is running 19min late but it has now overtaken the failed 'Warship' diesel on the Perranporth–Paddington which had delayed No 6002 earlier. *Ben Brooksbank*

Right: By 1960 the arrival of a 'King' from Plymouth was one of the main events to watch out for at Paddington, with the 9.30am from Falmouth providing the best chance. On Friday 19 August 1960 No 6016 *King Edward V* has not experienced such a successful trip on this train as the one four weeks earlier, and because of a diesel failure on the up 'Torbay Express' it is arriving 45min late. No 6016 made up the resulting deficiency in diesel numbers by returning to Plymouth that night, and next day, 20 August, it was back at Paddington again with the 8.20am Penzance–Paddington. *John Hodge*

Left: On 9 July 1960 No 6000 *King George V* had been regular engine of the down 'Cambrian Coast Express' at least three times during that week. Here it is coming through Hatton with a clear exhaust ready to arrive punctually at Snow Hill on the dot at 12.31pm. *D. K. Jones*

Right: The engines on the 11am and 12 Noon trains from Snow Hill to Paddington were the same on both 8 and 9 July 1960. The first of these trains pictured here on Friday 8 July is the 7.35am Birkenhead–Paddington and it is climbing up past Fosse Road Loop behind No 6022 *King Edward III.* Next day, after No 5088 had worked VO3 from Chester–Wolverhampton, No 6022 brought it into Paddington at 1.16pm, a minute late, hauling 14 bogies. *R. J. Blenkinsop*

one of the midweek trains, but so far no attempt had been made to arrange alternative summer duties for them. Surplus 'Kings' just fitted in on 'Castle' work when available. Only three good 'King' workings to the West of England remained on Saturdays, leaving Paddington at 9.30, 11 and 11.30am. As the summer progressed employment of 'Kings' even on these fell off badly. By the beginning of September there were hardly any Old Oak 'Kings' circulating in the West Country at all, until finally on Saturday 10 September not one 'King' appeared at Exeter during the day. Slow schedules on the Birmingham route, an ignominious start on the South Wales main line which involved the single 'King' working being downgraded on to a secondary train for 10 months, and the need to double head the 10-coach 7am Weston-super-Mare–Paddington express up the Bristol line every Monday morning, all pointed to one conclusion which no one was yet willing to face — surplus 'Kings' were now verging on borrowed time.

The main loss of mileage following dieselisation of West of England trains had already taken effect in 1959, annual usage of 'Kings' falling from a peak average of 55,291 miles per loco in 1958 to 48,426 miles in 1959 and 47,620 miles in 1960. As the 1956 figures were around 50,000 miles per annum, the damage could have been worse.

Only the two remaining Laira 'Kings' were still competing with diesels for West of England express work. When Old Oak had to supply steam for a dieselised Plymouth express, a 'Castle' was very often used, even to the extent of turning out an immaculate but heavily overloaded No 7017 *G. J. Churchward* for the down 'Riviera' on Friday 22 July 1960. This was a job No 7017 completed in some style by returning the same night from Plymouth on the up Penzance Postal. Luckily the two remaining Laira 'Kings', Nos 6002 and 6016, were a really good pair, well able to hold their place in the line. No 6002 *King William IV* was on a

diesel job working the 1.20pm ex-Penzance on 8 July, and so was No 6016 with the up Perranporth on 9 July. To see No 6016, two months beforehand, come roaring through the Pewsey dip at 65–70mph from a standing start at Westbury on the up 'Royal Duchy' was to gain a real insight into how 'Kings' had reigned supreme on this line for over three decades.

In previous years every effort would have been made to ensure as many 'Kings' as possible were in service for the summer traffic. But when the Swindon Works holidays began on 1 July 1960, no less than six engines were marooned there under repair. No 6005 spent virtually the whole summer in works from 30 May to 25 August. No 6019 was still at Swindon on 4 September. Another two were at Stafford Road works where No 6006 had arrived for a week's adjustments on 6 July, joining No 6020 which came out after casual repairs on 15 July. No 6014 had just returned from Stafford Road works on 7 July after a light casual repair. As it required running-in, No 6014 was not steamed on 9 July. In any case, by 4 September No 6014 was back at Swindon again for a more extensive classified overhaul.

That leaves just one 'King' unaccounted for on 9 July, No 6009 *King Charles II* of 81A. In fact it remains unaccounted for except on Old Oak shed lists between working the 8.30am Paddington-Wolverhampton on 25 June 1960 and reappearing again with the 3.10pm down on 26 September. I do not have enough definite evidence to claim that 6009

Right: On Friday 8 July No 6017 *King Edward IV* shows off its immaculate paintwork to good effect as it steams up towards Fosse Road box with the 8.55am Birkenhead–Paddington. Next day it replaced No 7026 *Tenby Castle* on the same train at Wolverhampton and kept good time all the way to Paddington where No 6017 arrived a minute behind time. Later it returned with the 6.10pm down and passed Tyseley 5min in arrears. *R. J. Blenkinsop*

Above: No 70018 *Flying Dutchman* is still waiting in the loop at Landore as No 5043 *Earl of Mount Edgcumbe* comes blasting up towards Landore with the 11.5am Milford Haven–Paddington, 1.30pm off Swansea on Saturday 6 August 1960. *Huw Daniel*

did not work at all between these dates; in fact it could conceivably have worked an occasional 'King' turn like the 6pm to Westbury or 6.35pm to Swindon on 8 July, but this is not thought to be likely. Certainly, No 6009 did not work on successive summer Saturdays when it would be expected to appear. It was eventually recorded under repair at Old Oak on 25 August and 10 September, so in any event it must have covered very little work all summer. With so many engines being repaired the surprising thing is that 'King' mileage for the year held up as well as it did.

7P 'Castle' class 4-6-0s

'Castle' withdrawals now spanned 10 years after the first disappeared in March 1950 and had since claimed 13 engines. Despite this, only five more were to go during the next 18 months and in July 1960 there were still plenty of 'Castles' around looking their best, many sporting new double-chimneys and taking a big share of the heaviest and fastest trains.

Out of 157 'Castles' still in stock, 112 were observed in traffic on 9 July, two were seen in steam on standby duties and four more were to be found working on Friday 8 July or Sunday 10 July. These are assumed to have been available if required on Saturday. One more 'Castle' was not steamed after Thursday and probably needed attention. Two locos were reckoned to be under repair at foreign sheds, being No 4096 *Highclere Castle* at Southall and No 5025 *Chirk Castle* at

Tyseley, while No 5072 *Hurricane* had been out of traffic since 24 June awaiting entry to Swindon on 14 July. Similarly No 7032 *Denbigh Castle* had been stopped at Old Oak to await shopping since 1 July. Compared to eight 'Kings' in Works, the total of 15 'Castles' in and around Swindon Plant was fairly modest, although no less than one might expect from the 20-month average overhaul cycle to which 'Castles' worked. This accounts for the whereabouts of 138 engines on 9 July plus two more, Nos 5056 and 5097, noted on 10 July, but whose availability on Saturday cannot be vouched for.

It is possible to speculate endlessly and not very profitably about where the missing 17 'Castles' which were not traced over the weekend might have been. Usually my speculations of this sort have not turned out to be very helpful. The unexpected happened too often on summer Saturdays to justify making specific assumptions, however realistic they might seem at first. Laira would have an engine on standby, but it might just as easily be '47xx' No 4705 as one of the two untraced 'Castles' shedded there, Nos 5053 *Earl Cairns* or 7022 *Hereford Castle*. Equally the Reading down end pilot, though usually a 'Hall' by 1960, might be expected to employ a 'Castle' with No 5076 *Gladiator* unaccounted for.

Not so; it was No 6923 *Croxteth Hall* on standby which was called upon to take over the 1.20pm ex-Paddington from Reading at short notice and successfully worked 13 coaches on this Kingswear train.

Old Oak would often use its very competent fleet of 12 'Modified Halls' to cover a Saturday shortage of 'Castles' and at least five were used in this way on 9 July, penetrating far and wide in the process. But out of five untraced 81A 'Castles' there were a few unobserved Old Oak workings which would probably have featured a couple of them: the 9.15am down to Hereford being the most likely. The 9.15am down has so far defied all efforts to identify its engine. It was just missed by two separate observers arriving at Oxford and was out of sight, by perhaps ½ mile, of the observer at Abbots Wood Jc near Worcester. As this engine was on a 299½-mile round trip to Hereford, a 'Castle' was booked and would be expected if the loading limits were to be observed, but a 'Hall' was still by no means unknown.

Those 'Castles' working, or noted and considered fit for traffic on 9 July, totalled 119 engines, which represents an excellent minimum availability figure of 75% out of 157 in the class. 'Castle' availability was generally about 10% better than 'Kings' because operationally 'Castles' enjoyed a couple of advantages over the bigger engines.

Firstly, 'Castles' could economically work a much wider range of duties than 'Kings'. While the best ex-works 'Castles' would be expected to reach a standard approaching average 'King' performance, there were a fair number of 'soft' duties to occupy the weaker engines and those on high mileages. This was not of course true of summer Saturdays when 'Castles' were first choice for so many express services, but even then, on 9 July, much of the Swindon-Didcot local service was 'Castle'-worked with three engines of a more or less run-down nature.

By contrast, 'Kings' were expected to work expresses all the time and did virtually nothing else. It was one thing to declare availability figures including engines hauling 150-ton stopping trains, but quite another to compare them with a class which had to be in tip-top form all the time. Two of the highest mileage Stafford Road 'Kings', Nos 6007 *King William III* and 6022 *King Edward III*, were among those which successfully worked the same cycle of London expresses both days on 8/9 July. By contrast, of the 84A 'Castles' shopped at around the same time as these two 'Kings' in February and June 1959, No 5022 *Wigmore Castle* for example was steamed only on 8 July and No 5026 *Criccieth Castle* was used just for a single trip to double-head from Wolverhampton to Birmingham on 9 July. All could be expected to appear

as equally available in the running and maintenance records, however.

Secondly, 'Castles' were still top-link power at almost all the depots where they were represented. Even where they had been displaced, the Laira boat engines were still well maintained for Ocean Express duty, and at Old Oak good 'Castles' were always in strong demand to work over routes where 'Warships' and 'Kings' did not operate, as well as standing in as required where they did. Numerically there were enough 'Castles' allocated to major sheds for there always to be low mileage engines available in good condition to cover the best express turns. Crews could therefore be confident of getting an engine in good condition when the job required it, and they might well prefer one of these to a high mileage 'King'.

Twenty-five early '40xx' 'Castles' now approaching 40 years old were well represented on 9 July. Eighteen were at work, with only three engines, Nos 4077, 4092 and 7013, unaccounted for. They were active all over the system, penetrating to Newquay and Fishguard on the one hand while no less than eight others were to be found on expresses at Paddington. Although these earlier engines were reckoned to become run-down more quickly than the later ones, and a few like Nos 4075, 4077, 4084 and 4092 were in poor shape, there was little actual evidence to show that their overall work was to any degree inferior in terms of availability, mileage or punctuality. The high standards of overhaul at Swindon Works had a lot to do with the evergreen aspect that 'Castles' were still able to present to the world, but the pampering that engines received at sheds like Landore, where there were five '40xx' series 'Castles' allocated, was also a contributory factor. Here any four-cylinder engines which had run about 30-35,000 miles since shopping would regularly be revitalised by an intermediate valve and piston overhaul which gave them a renewed lease of life on the Landore turns to London. 'Castle' No 5051 *Earl Bathurst* working the down 'Pembroke Coast Express' was in this category on 9 July. Under the keen eye of Chargehand Cleaner Cliff Rowlands, it was rare to see a Landore engine turned out for London in anything but resplendent condition, complete with freshly painted silver buffers. This standard also applied to turns west of Swansea like the up 'Red Dragon'.

Landore was in the fortunate position of being able to shuffle its less favoured engines off down the line to Carmarthen shed, but it was notably the sluggishly inclined BR-built 'Castles' like Nos 7012 and 7016, still running with mechanical lubricators set at the original feed rate, which were disposed of in this way, as distinct from any of the double-chimney engines old or new. Early '40xx' series double-chimney rebuilds with new inside cylinders like Nos 4090 and 4093 had a definite edge over some BR-built locos still carrying single chimneys, and it is a matter of regret that none

Left: On Saturday 9 July 1960 'Castle' No 5088 *Llanthony Abbey* was recently ex-works and looking very spruce. It was the only engine to cover the whole of the Chester–Paddington main line during the day, with a return journey back as far as Wolverhampton added in as well. No 5088 is seen here on the 9.45am Pwllheli–Paddington, which had been running about 15min late with 2-6-0 No 6312 at Severn Bridge Jc before No 5088 replaced it at Wolverhampton. No 5088 left Snow Hill 20min late and is now climbing out of Leamington 24min late. Twelve of these lost minutes were recovered to Paddington where No 5088 arrived at 6.17pm. The first three coaches are from the regular 'Cambrian Coast Express' Pwllheli portion and behind them comes one of the original GW quick lunch cars No W9631W.
R. J. Blenkinsop

Left: This is a photograph which captures all the atmosphere of Landore. Its cavalcade of 'Castles' is lined up at 1.30pm on Monday 2 January 1961. From the left background the engines are:
No 4076 *Carmarthen Castle* off the 10.5am Cardiff–Neyland parcels, coming in for coal;
No 5082 *Swordfish* leaving to take the 2.30pm departure from Swansea–Paddington;
No 5006 *Tregenna Castle* for the up 'Pembroke Coast Express';
No 7021 *Haverfordwest Castle* hauled the up 'South Wales Pullman' next day on Landore Turn 2, with an early morning trip to Carmarthen beforehand working the 12.45am ex-Paddington Newspaper Train from Swansea;
No 5035 *Coity Castle,* a Swindon engine, brewing up ready to go over to Felin Fran and collect the 3.50pm Whitland–Kensington milk;
No 5004 *Llanstephan Castle* for the 5.30pm departure from Swansea–Paddington. It returned on the 10.55am down next day, but was 22min late at Cardiff;
No 5041 *Tiverton Castle*, no known working until the 11.50am Swansea-Manchester next day.
   The engine beyond the coaling stage may be No 5013 *Abergavenny Castle*, backing in after arriving at Swansea with the down 'Pullman' at 1.10pm. *Huw Daniel*

Left: On 29 July 1961 the crew of No 5072 *Hurricane* working the 9.45am Pwllheli–Paddington through Tyseley lean out to watch No 5018 *St Mawes Castle* come tearing past with lots of time to recover on the 8.47am Ramsgate–Wolverhampton. The Ramsgate must have been handed over late by the Southern at Reading and passed Didcot 23min in arrears, but No 5018 has lost another 20min since then, so this trip has deteriorated beyond recall. *Gerald Adams*

of that modified '40xx' series with high superheat boilers survived into preservation.

Annual mileage of 'Castles' was bound to suffer at once with the onset of modernisation because at first steam withdrawals did not keep pace with the rate of new diesel deliveries. Only nine 'Castles' and three 'Halls' had been scrapped since 1958 to balance the arrival of 28 Type 4 diesels, each of which should in theory accomplish well over double the work rate of their steam predecessors. The 'Castle' average therefore fell by 12% from 48,879 miles in 1958 to 42,981 miles in 1960.

The daily mileage covered by all 'Castles' was around 150 miles, while those actually in service averaged about 200 miles. These were not unreasonable figures for engines with a narrow firebox and nothing in the way of labour-saving devices to help with fire cleaning. It would be interesting to know how mileages varied from shed to shed but no official figures are available. It is only possible to make an assessment based on total mileages of later engines allocated to one shed for most of their lives. Therefore, as one would expect, No 7008 *Swansea Castle* on Oxford's very limited 130/150-mile daily roster of 'Castle' duties to London and Chester was averaging about 32,250 miles a year, while a crack Laira unit like No 7031 *Cromwell's Castle* managed 56,370 miles. So class averages could mask a significant variation between individual engines.

On 9 July 'Castles' certainly had their ups and downs, with some variable timekeeping and performance on heavy trains, but this was only to be expected in a situation where the Western Region relied confidently on this large class of engine to bear the brunt of powering its express services.

There was a casualty requiring replacement on the road, and another 'Castle' needed unscheduled assistance. However, the total failure rate seems to have involved only two locos on the Region thought to have needed removal from their trains during the day. That was an enviable situation.

Depots like Old Oak Common, borrowing relatively unfamiliar 'Castles' and pressing all their own fleet into express service regardless of condition, inevitably meant some 'Castles' were going to be pushed to keep time with substantial loads. 'Castles' worked nearly a third of the 54 loco-hauled services from Paddington between 6.50am and 1.30pm on 9 July, all on express turns exceeding 190 miles duration during the day.

Except No 5036 *Lyonshall Castle*, light engine up from Reading at 5.35am for the 7.40am to Paignton, and No 7004 *Eastnor Castle*, turned at Ranelagh Bridge for the 12.45pm down Hereford, all had been prepared at Old Oak. Not one of these engines was more than five minutes late arriving at Oxford, Bristol, Newport or Exeter, except the three West of England services leaving Paddington at 12.5, 1.20 and 1.30pm which experienced varying fortunes threading their way through the afternoon rush.

'Castles' were most plentiful out of Paddington on the South Wales and Worcester services. Here they enjoyed a virtual monopoly over both routes, except on a couple of morning departures when 'Halls' were substituted. Later on, two 'Britannias' also appeared for the 3.55 and 5.55pm South Wales trains, but these amounted to much less than half the usual number of Pacifics seen at Paddington compared to previous years. Bristol traffic would normally have been even more heavily dominated by 'Castles' on Saturday, and indeed it was until lunchtime. But the plunder of Bath Road 'Castles' by other sheds earlier in the morning took its toll as the day wore on, and then gradually more and more 'Counties' began to appear.

Forty per cent dieselisation on the West of England main line meant there were 9 or 10 regular 'Warship' departures from Paddington on Saturdays between 6.30am and 6.30pm. Those took out five old 'King' turns, two for 'Halls' and two 'Castles'. Though nine of these diesel rosters operated normally on 9 July, disruption to the usual level of 'Castle' activity at Paddington so far was still minimal. Only the down 'Torbay Express' was a serious casualty. In the opposite direction diesel appearances at Paddington were rather more fluid depending on Type 4 availability. Again it was inevitably the old 'King' workings which tended to suffer most severely, but even so 'Kings' were able to find their way on to a few regular diesel arrivals during the afternoon. The opportunity also arose to restore 'Castle' haulage of the up 'Torbay Express' and though a 'Modified Hall' happened to be used instead, at least it was steam.

Good availability of 'Kings' meant that only three 'Castles' were called up to cover shortages. The trio involved were all Old Oak Common engines, and of these the 8.20am Penzance–Paddington with No 5065 *Newport Castle*, whilst heavy, had been worked by 'Castles' more often than anything else in the past. The very moderate size of the 3.10pm Paddington–Wolverhampton headed by No 4082 *Windsor Castle* meant it was nicely weighted for a 'Castle' going down.

The 11.30am down Ilfracombe and Minehead express to Taunton coming back at 3.31pm was, however, a turn which usually saw a 'King' well extended, both on account of a 13 or 14-coach load each way and the smart 81min turn-around scheduled between trains. It was not unknown for the 11.30 to be so late reaching Taunton that the stock of the engine's return working was already standing in the up relief line platform amalgamating its Minehead and Ilfracombe portions. This was of course exceptional and even then not quite as disruptive as it might have seemed. Only one subsequent train needed to use that platform at Taunton during the following 40min while the locomotive had time to go off and turn, but a serious delay to the up Minehead was still a certainty when this happened.

Frequently by mid-morning on Saturdays Old Oak

had only one or two 'Kings' left to cover three heavy departures from Paddington at 11.0, 11.10 and 11.30am. In this situation the 11.30 had been first choice for a 'King' so far during 1960. But just to show that nothing was sacrosanct, on 9 July the other two trains had the 'Kings', leaving the crew on the 11.30 to make do with No 5034 *Corfe Castle*. Whilst a good engine, it was still in original single-chimney form and over a year out of Works. No 5034 was certainly not a picked unit.

The 11.30 to Minehead used to enjoy an unusually clear path on Saturdays to start with, and by running nonstop to Taunton it was able to keep up with the Mondays–Fridays 11.30 to Penzance schedule right out as far as Fairwood Jc Westbury. However, at Clink Road Jc a notable laggard was due to emerge on to the main line only 14min ahead of the 11.30 and trouble could develop from there. The 9.25am Wolverhampton–Paignton ran via Oxford and Swindon to Westbury, and on 9 July with No 5926 *Grotrian Hall* in charge the 9.25 lost so much time from Oxford, where it left only ½min late, that No 5034 was able to stay ahead after Westbury. Instead it was following trains which felt the 9.25's chilly draught, while No 5034 carried on to reach Taunton only 4min late at 2.14pm.

After uncoupling, *Corfe Castle* made straight for the shed turntable. While the shed staff were on hand pulling coal forward in the tender, it might also have been prudent, had No 5034 been a double-chimney 'Castle', to open the smokebox door and see if the accumulated pile of char inside was large enough to need removal before it impaired steaming on the way back. However, with a properly prepared single-chimney engine like No 5034 this was unlikely to be necessary.

No 5034 could then make its way back round to Taunton East without obstructing any passenger lines in the station by utilising Taunton West Goods loop. With V88 and V89 expresses off the North & West running late as usual, only two trains (Nos 4963 *Rignall Hall*, early on the 10.50am Wolverhampton–Minehead, and 4916 *Crumlin Hall* with the 10.5am Penzance–Manchester) then impeded No 5034's freedom to cross on to the up side at any convenient time between 3.6 and 3.29pm. So No 5034 was ready and waiting when the first portion of its train came into No 8 bay platform from Ilfracombe with 2-6-0 No 7319, and then 2-6-2T No 6155 arrived early from Minehead to complete the 14-coach formation.

Due out at 3.31pm in the working timetable, No 5034 must have been delayed at the start for a couple of minutes because 'County' No 1017 on the 1.55pm Torquay–Paddington was not cleared through on the up main until 3.29pm. Unfortunately the engine on the 1.30pm from Paignton, No 6910 *Gossington Hall*, which was in front of No 1017, must have been badly held up between Athelney and Castle Cary by the 2.30pm all stations local passenger from Taunton. This meant that Nos 6910, 1017 and 5034 were closely bunched together after Westbury. By Savernake both Nos 1017 and 5034 were 14min late. After that a hefty slice of recovery time made the schedule very much easier to Twyford and here No 5034 was only 4min late. Even then the remaining tight allowance of 31min in from Twyford virtually ruled out a punctual arrival by that stage and in addition six other expresses had to be accommodated at Paddington first, all of them arriving between 6.16 and 6.31pm. No 5034 would have turned up outside the terminus to find a full house, and so it was around 6.38pm, 13min late, before a clear platform was available for the Minehead.

Despite this, No 5034 had run the whole round trip of 286 miles, including time spent at Taunton, in only 428min or so. With 450-ton trains its crew had achieved all that could be expected of them and it is unlikely a 'King' would have done any better.

Even the softest Old Oak 'Castle' job on Saturday involved a 228½ mile journey working the 2.40pm Wood Lane–Plymouth milk empties. Two well-worn engines were used for West of England milk traffic, No 7024 *Powis Castle* down on Saturday and No 5056 *Earl of Powis* up with the 12.35pm from Penzance on Sunday. Both were 'Castles' which, in their prime a year earlier, had participated in the last down steam worked 'Bristolian' runs. No 5056 was involved during the first two weeks of February 1959 and again in May, making its last run of a long 'Bristolian' association which dated back to prewar days, on 20 May 1959. No 7024 made 26 appearances after 24 March 1959, culminating in the last regular down steam-hauled 'Bristolian' on Friday 12 June 1959. It reached 95mph on this trip and covered the distance in 99min 20sec.

Back on 9 July 1960 the only Old Oak 'Castle' which appeared to have a relatively easy time of it was No 7036 *Taunton Castle*. This was borrowed by Gloucester shed to help cover its own shortage of 'Castles' by working a regular Gloucester–Cardiff–Swindon–Gloucester circuit of stopping trains, parcels and London portions in place of a local engine. Otherwise Old Oak 'Castles' were busy everywhere that through workings from London penetrated. At least 10 81A 'Castles' made their way back into Paddington from every direction after 4.15pm. In order of appearance they were Nos 5040, 7020, 7030, 5065, 5034, 5057, 4075, 5042, 5084 and finally No 4082 *Windsor Castle* which arrived at about

10.15pm on the 4.30pm from Birkenhead. These Old Oak Common engines outnumbered all other 'Castles' which came in during this period by two to one, whilst also exceeding all arrivals by either 'Kings' or diesel locomotives. This aspect emphasises the essential role still being performed by 'Castles' on top-link expresses at Paddington in 1960.

'Castles' were thoroughly popular engines. The high regard in which they were held had more to do with good overall performance than their ability in terms of maximum power output. By the standards of the 1960s this was not unlimited, yet 'Castles' could still undertake all but one or two of the express jobs offered on the Western, and work them with a realistic prospect of success.

6MT 'County' class 4-6-0s

The 30 'County' class two-cylinder 4-6-0s have already been mentioned in connection with the number seen on express work. Overall availability was at least 66%, but as the location of four engines is unknown, an estimate of those ready for work points towards a respectable figure around 73% for the whole class. I am not aware of annual mileages for these WR two-cylinder 4-6-0s but as the basic shopping period for 'Counties' was about 22 months or slightly longer than for 'Castles' it seems likely that their mileage rate was also about 10% lower than that of the four-cylinder engines.

During the 1959/60 winter, plentiful deliveries of NB Loco Type 2 diesel-hydraulics prompted a redistribution of five 'Counties' around the West Country, with a clear tendency for them to gravitate eastwards in the process. This severely curtailed 'County' activity on better class work in Cornwall during 1960. Fortunately, however, No 1008 *County of*

Cardigan kept a single 'County' foothold in place at Penzance through the year and events proved that the initial intention to replace them altogether in the far West was premature. It was clear before the end of 1960 that the NB diesels were never going to make the grade, and by November 'County' strength at Penzance was back to the same representation of four engines as in previous years. Three of these engines survived through until the shed's closure to steam in September 1962. On 9 July 1960 only one 'County' was specifically identified in Cornwall, but the actual working total might have rivalled the previous weekend's tally of three seen there: Nos 1002/6/18. Only the sole Penzance engine was not noted on either occasion.

Just one of Shrewsbury's six active 'Counties' found itself on a really long distance working, and here was a classic example of a shed holding on to its best engines while it packed off No 1017, which was definitely its most run-down 'County' in terms of time elapsed since last overhaul, on the longest job of the day. No criticism is implied here, because this was probably a lesson learnt from bitter experience in previous years. On 9 July Shrewsbury was equally wary what work was put to its seven 'Castles', and all but one of these were safely back on shed by Sunday ready to start a proper week's work next day.

Meanwhile, No 1017 *County of Hereford* left Salop overnight on Friday, probably hauling the 10.30pm Manchester–Paignton. It hauled this over the North & West main line, through the Severn Tunnel and on via Bristol Temple Meads as far as Exeter. Here it was serviced, before relieving 'Hall' No 6928 on the 8.10am Newport–Paignton at 11.20am. On arrival, No 1017 turned at Goodrington and then worked a regular turn to London for the engine off the Newport train, taking the 1.55pm Torquay–Paddington. This train ran nonstop to Newbury, and in the early stages was delayed for 13min between Exeter and Taunton. But by Savernake No 1017 had closed right up on the

1.30pm from Paignton with No 6910 *Gossington Hall*, which had left Taunton 24min in front of the 'County', and so none of the lost time could be regained at this stage. At about 5.35pm No 1017 was still just too late approaching Reading for it to be able to overtake the 4.20pm from Swindon there before that train, pulled by No 6957 *Norcliffe Hall*, emerged back on to the up main line. The space created by No 1017's call at Newbury enabled No 6957 to follow No 6910 up to Paddington, leaving No 1017 kicking its heels behind. But No 1017 had regained 4min lost time by Twyford and it was only some more concluding delays which prevented it recovering all but about 7min lateness. By this means No 1017 had successfully accomplished 433½ miles. It provides perhaps a first inkling that, far from being the liability that some observers would have us believe, the 'Counties', all now standardised with redraughted double-chimneys, and whether run-down or not, were very handy machines. They were not only able to cope with high steam rates required for climbing steep gradients, but also the sustained hard steaming needed to master fast nonstop runs.

Further evidence of this comes to light at Bristol Bath Road where three 'Counties' managed to appear on a trio of the best London turns. One of them kept ahead of time going back to Bristol on a schedule which demanded a mile-a-minute run from Paddington to the stop at Bath during the height of the Saturday rush.

The better one of Exeter's pair, No 1007 *County of Brecknock*, also added its distinctive exhaust note to the length of the West of England main line, booked nonstop over 202 miles from Paignton with the 9.45am Churston–Paddington. To reach Churston

Below: Displaced from the West Country and now allocated to Shrewsbury, No 1008 *County of Cardigan* heads the 2.35pm Birkenhead–Paddington express out of Chester on a hot summer day in 1963. *E. N. Kneale*

ready for this working, No 1007 took over the 10.22pm Manchester–Paignton at Exeter, probably from Shrewsbury 'Hall' No 5971 *Merevale Hall*. It then turned at Goodrington before proceeding light to Churston. No path for this light manoeuvre was shown in the working timetable, thus leaving the option open for No 1007 to double-head a down train tender-first, if this was more expedient, to save a separate path along the branch.

One hundred miles to the north, but over double that distance by rail, two of the Neyland engines were busy on regular parcels traffic, and at least two more 'Counties' penetrated to Chester with London through portions from Wolverhampton.

Another engine contributed what was probably the most interesting Western loco working of the day, when No 1018 *County of Leicester* infiltrated right through over the Great Central to Leicester. This was surprising because, although No 1018 was now nominally a Laira engine, it was still recorded around this time carrying a Penzance shedplate. For such an engine to be seen at Leicester Central was certainly a very rare event in the course of normal service.

The previous Saturday No 1018 had been busy as usual with haulage of the 8.15am Perranporth-Paddington between Truro and Plymouth. This was a substantial 12-coach train over the Cornish main line on which a 'County' could show to good advantage. When on 9 July No 1018 was 250 miles away and no 'County' was available the Perranporth had to be double-headed.

No 1018 must by then have found its way to Basingstoke via Reading, which was unusual because, although Laira 'Counties' still made occasional trips to London on milk traffic, they did not generally stop off on the way. No 1018 would have picked up the 11.4am Bournemouth Central–Sheffield express in place of the usual Banbury 'Hall' at Basingstoke, before weaving its way across all the conflicting

streams of Western traffic at Reading and Didcot. In quick succession the Bournemouth–Sheffield was tight behind the 9.45am Churston–Paddington at Southcote Jc, then the dated 12.55pm Paddington–Swansea at Reading West and the 10.20am Weymouth–Wolverhampton at Didcot North. Though nominally nonstop from Basingstoke to Banbury, so heavy was the throng of other services also trying to get from Didcot to Banbury that the Sheffield train had a first pathing halt at Didcot North, and then another one booked on the through line in Oxford station. In fact No 1018 would not have had to make either of these stops because it came round the avoiding line at Didcot North Jc ahead of the 10.20am Weymouth. This curved in from Foxhall Jc behind No 7911 some 11min late, after No 1018 had already managed to squeeze through. No 1018 therefore had a relatively clear road, passing Oxford 8min early, just 5min behind No 6813 *Eastbury Grange* working throughout on the 9.10am Kingswear–Birmingham Moor St. Only a handful of trains ran nonstop northbound through Oxford even on Saturdays, and this successfully disposed of two of them.

The Bournemouth–Sheffield was due to reach Leicester at 4.10pm, on a not untypical schedule of 180min for 110¼ miles from Basingstoke, and then there was the problem of what to do with No 1018. 'Counties' like No 1019 from Swindon were occasional visitors to Leicester, but finding a way of pointing *County of Leicester* back in the right direction, when it was quite so far off its home patch, was a different matter altogether.

No 1018 probably started off on the 5.20pm Leicester–Woodford local, percolating back into Banbury at 7.8pm. One might then reasonably have expected No 1018 to be dispatched south towards Bristol or London, so it was a big surprise to find No 1018 tucked up on Shrewsbury shed around lunch-time next day. The 'County' may well have managed

Left: No 1018 *County of Leicester* gets to grips with Rattery bank on the evening of Tuesday 2 August 1960 with the 6.10pm Goodrington Sands Halt–Plymouth. No 1018 had come up earlier on the 10.18 Saltash–Goodrington. Regardless of whether it was still carrying an 83G Penzance shed plate or not during July, No 1018 is certainly displaying an 83D Laira plate in this photograph. *Peter W. Gray*

Below left: No 4986 *Aston Hall* descends Fosse Road bank running early with the 1.11pm Portsmouth Harbour–Birmingham Moor St on Saturday 9 July 1960. No 4986 passed Oxford 6min early and was still about a minute before time at Tyseley. The front coach is one of the WR's only remaining type of second class brake Saloon. There were 10 of these bow-ended vehicles in WR stock, and they were often marshalled into summer Saturday service as an end brake. *R. J. Blenkinsop*

this overnight move from Banbury on the 8.10pm Marylebone-Shrewsbury train of empty milk tanks. So it was Tuesday 11 July before No 1018 started to make meaningful progress back towards the West Country. Then its route lay through Severn Tunnel Jc on the 9.5am Liverpool–Plymouth, which No 1018 would normally haul as far as Bristol.

Certainly by Saturday 16 July it was Cornish business as usual again between Penzance to Plymouth when No 1018 was out single-handed on the 12 Noon Penzance–Crewe, which often loaded very heavily. None the worse for that, No 1018 then returned west on the 8.35am Liverpool–Penzance on which, between them, No 6841 *Marlas Grange* to Plymouth and then No 1018 appear to have made a good fist at some worthwhile time recovery. From 40min late at Newton Abbot the deficit seems to have been cut by more than half before Liskeard.

One final twist which raises a further doubt about where No 1018 was actually shedded, whatever the official allocation records might suggest, was that when on 21 July No 1018 required repairs, these were actually being carried out at Penzance.

Like many BR engines which fell into the Class 6 category, much 'County' work was in fact of Class 7 standard. They enjoyed the same passenger load limits as 'Castles' right round the Region, and some of those loads could be very taxing — 420 tons over 1 in 60 gradients in Cornwall was heavy going for any locomotive, and made the 371-ton limit on similar gradients from Kemble to Sapperton look like something of a picnic. 'Counties' were noted for fast surefooted starts out of difficult locations like St Erth, Lostwithiel, Totnes and Stapleton Road, where the rumpus they made, like the shot of a gun from those squat double-chimneys, could certainly be heard a good way off.

5MT 'Hall' class 4-6-0s
Altogether 182 'Hall' 4-6-0s and 53 'Modified Hall' varieties were identified over the weekend. Nevertheless coverage tended to be patchy. Whilst

most of the express jobs were duly observed, 'Halls' handled a much wider variety of duties than that, not all of which were likely to be pinpointed by observers on Saturday. 'Halls' were so valuable on overnight freight and early morning stock positioning work that locomotives thus occupied were often held over for the next leg of their booked diagrams and did not reappear again later the same day. Therefore, lack of coverage prevents a detailed picture of 'Hall' operations being offered on secondary and local services in some areas. This is particularly true in the zone including a central band right across the Region. A large number of 'Halls' shedded at Didcot and Reading were busy but unseen on early morning commuter, inter-regional and empty stock operations to Paddington, Basingstoke, Newbury, Oxford and beyond, while there were others working Worcester and Hereford turns which were not observed either. Nearly 50% of the 'Halls' allocated to these four sheds were unaccounted for, amounting to 27 engines. Except at Worcester a lot of them were from the 30-year-old '49xx' batch which were slightly less likely to be first choice selections for express duty.

It is not therefore possible to estimate any availability figures covering the whole class, but as an example, something over 47 out of 71 'Modified Halls' were working on Saturday, of which 28 took expresses. Looking at individual sheds a clearer picture begins to emerge, because seven depots were observed to achieve 80–100% availability of the 'Halls' on their strength. Sheds in holiday areas like Newton Abbot (87%) and Exeter (85%) were prominent among these, with Swindon (83%) and Bristol Bath Road (82%) heavily involved in providing power for Saturday expresses too. Perhaps more surprisingly, Landore and Carmarthen sheds both reached an 80% level while Neath, where the fledgling 'Hall' representation was only a month old, actually managed to have all five of its engines in service, even if they were hardly under the shed's direct control; No 4927 *Farnborough Hall* being away at Chester and No 4988 *Bulwell Hall* at Reading. No 6905 *Claughton Hall* was the best of this bunch and the engine paired with the experimental GW standard pattern eight-wheel tender. It was at Old Oak after working in earlier with Friday night's 8.55pm Birkenhead Sleeper from Wolverhampton to Paddington via Oxford.

Two more sheds would probably have achieved a service level of 80% if Canton and Oxley hadn't had so many locomotives in works. More undoubtedly achieved 80% unobserved, with Oxford closest at 77%.

Of the 326 engines which currently formed the complete 'Hall' strength, enough is certainly known to provide a good overall pattern of activity on 9 July and in the '69xx' series alone this ranged right across the board. Old Oak 'Hall' No 6974 *Bryngwyn Hall* worked the mundane 7.35am Severn Tunnel Jc–Hanwell

Bridge 8A63 coal train on Friday. Saturday's contrast could scarcely have been greater when No 6974 then had to cover the front line 8.45am Paddington–Paignton breakfast car express. With that, No 6974 did well to reach Exeter 13min early. However, the credit for this may well be due to a determined crew, who probably had rather a rough ride on an engine like No 6974 which was due for overhaul only two months later. Then there was No 6970 Whaddon Hall, just ex-works and as such a most curious choice to haul two coaches on the 1.20pm Oxford–Moreton-in-Marsh local. No 6903 Belmont Hall of Pontypool Road kept to its usual midweek type of work from this shed on the 6.30am Bassaleg–Margam 8F17 goods, and No 6954 Lotherton Hall was so run-down that it spent the day banking at Bristol Stapleton Road.

'Halls' worked everything in between too, including two named trains, milk, parcels and fish, as well as a very considerable share of the holiday expresses and whatever special traffic was on offer. A train like the 11.40am Paddington–Penzance was a fully fledged 'Castle' job on which No 7903 Foremarke Hall took the entire 13-coach load through to Plymouth, assisted by No D6320 from Newton Abbot.

The 7.10pm Paddington–Wolverhampton, loading to 13 or 14, definitely warranted a 'King'. However, due to a quirk of Saturday rostering no 'King' was booked, and out of six June and July Saturdays a 'King' was available only on one occasion. At other times a wide variety of 'Halls' or 'Castles' from a bewildering variety of sheds was provided; in fact on 2 July the 7.10am had two engines with Worcester's No 6992 Arborfield Hall coupled ahead of No 5063 Earl Baldwin. No 5063 was on a quick turn-around at Ranelagh Bridge off the 9.45am Pwllheli–Paddington. But on 9 July no similar move was made to use No 5088

Llanthony Abbey off the Pwllheli train, and instead Tyseley stalwart No 7918 Rhose Wood Hall, which had come up to Kensington Olympia earlier with the 10.10am Birmingham Moor St–Margate, had to work a hard passage home on the 7.10. This time with 14 coaches, mostly standard stock including a heavy triple dining car unit on Saturdays, and weighing perhaps 515 tons gross, it was a classic example of the sort of unsung filling-in work that common-user 'Halls' had been covering competently for years. The excuse for slow Saturday schedules having worn rather thin by this time in the evening, No 7918 was on the usual daily booking of 101min to Leamington.

9 July was a good day on the Paddington–Birmingham service, but even by those standards this must have been a really rousing run on the 7.10 over the Chilterns, then thunder and turf up to Ardley. However, a 500-ton load like this was too heavy to be taken through to Wolverhampton by a 'Hall' without assistance. The Banbury standby engine was in no position to help even if the men on No 7918 had been inclined to stop there, because the down end pilot, No 6979 Helperly Hall, had already been pressed into service for a trip to Wolverhampton earlier. It only set off back to Banbury from Stafford Road at 6.41pm. Obviously No 6979 would not yet be ready to go out a second time when No 7918 came hustling its long train headlong through Banbury and set about the climb towards Fenny Compton just after 8.30pm. On arrival at Leamington No 7918 was well over the 420 ton single-handed weight limit for a 'Hall' up Hatton Bank, so it had to uncouple and cut Prairie No 4112 inside for the next stage on to Birmingham Snow Hill. Despite the delay this entailed, the pair came racing triumphantly through Solihull only 4min late at 9.19pm with 8min left for a punctual arrival at Snow Hill, and

an ample margin behind 1H44, the 3.10pm from Paignton, for a clear run in.

The engine on the Paignton train was No 6928 *Underley Hall* which had also had a busy day. Displaced from Cardiff Canton soon after the first influx of inter-city diesel multiple-units in 1957, No 6928 now hailed from Pontypool Road. Besides covering Saturday extras on the North & West line 86G shed also had to top-up power for some of the trains starting from Newport now that Ebbw Jc shed had parted with all its 'Halls', so No 6928 had first started out on the 8.10am Newport–Paignton that morning. It worked this to Exeter and then went on shed there for service, before picking up the usual (as opposed to regular) return working on the 3.10pm Paignton–Wolverhampton back from Exeter. Unexpectedly though, No 6928 was then apparently coupled in front of No 6829 *Burmington Grange* which had brought the 10-coach train in from Newton Abbot, where No 6829 had itself arrived double-heading No 6919 *Tylney Hall* from Paignton. It is not clear how far No 6829 worked with No 6928, either to Taunton or Bristol (though it was not on any of those sheds next day) or (more unlikely) beyond. Certainly No 6928 was running solo by the time it came off the North Warwickshire line at Tyseley 2min behind schedule at 8.52pm. By then it had recovered 7min of a late start from Exeter. This was the last of 10 Saturday expresses from the West Country to Birmingham, half of them pulled by 'Halls', and when it reached Wolverhampton No 6928 parked the stock in Cannock Road sidings and arrived on Stafford Road shed for disposal at 11.25pm. Its coaches were the same ones which No 5965 had collected first thing in the dawn chorus earlier that morning for 1C63. Now they had completed their Saturday circuit they would not be needed for another

week until No 7915 *Mere Hall* arrived from Oxley early on 16 July to start that day's Paignton working over again.

No 6928 meanwhile spent Sunday at Stafford Road and would then be ready to resume its regular daily freight workings when it left shed at 10.16pm that evening. It might continue in a homeward direction on one of the three Monday Class '8' goods trains which were due to run from Stourbridge Jc to Pontypool Road, possibly along with fellow 86G engine No 6819 *Highnam Grange* which was at Oxley running-in after being released from Stafford Road Works only 10 days before. It might even take over the place which had been vacated by another Pontypool Road 'Grange' in the middle of its working on Saturday. This was No 6867 *Peterston Grange*, borrowed for the usual Stourbridge Jc 'Hall' turn on the 8.30am Birmingham–Weston-super-Mare which No 6867 worked through in the southbound direction only. Nor was this all, because three more 86G Pontypool Road engines were in the area: No 5970 *Hengrave Hall* was also at Stafford Road on Sunday after being purloined off another freight diagram for the 7.20am Pwllheli–Paddington between Ruabon and Wolverhampton, while No 6958 *Oxburgh Hall* had been in the Wolverhampton District since Thursday at least. On Saturday it was commandeered for the 8.10am Birmingham–Birkenhead as far as Chester. No 6958 later returned to Shrewsbury, probably on the 4.30pm or 5.37pm from Birkenhead and was still awaiting a passage home from there on Sunday. Finally No 6812 *Chesford Grange* was at Tyseley after working the 7.15am Cardiff–Birmingham via Hereford, so that of 13 'Halls' and eight 'Granges' at Pontypool Road a lot ended Saturday many miles from home.

These were rather makeshift workings, but not only

were Pontypool Road engines scattered about far and wide in the Northern Division, they were highly active all the way down west too, and some of these regular turns were both hard and heavy. Between Shrewsbury and Pontypool Road on summer Friday nights three southbound freights were cancelled because their paths were needed for overnight holiday expresses. So a couple of 86G 'Granges' off the freights found themselves working well-laden express runners instead. Rather than hauling the 1.15am (MSX) Coleham–Pontypool Road 7T52 goods the 'Grange' shown in the Freight Marshalling Instructions came back from Shrewsbury on the 9.15pm (FO) Manchester–Newquay. Another 'Grange' which had come north on Friday afternoon's 4.10pm Pontypool Road–Coton Hill 6J48 fast freight, then worked Shrewsbury to Bristol with the 11.30pm (FO) Liverpool–Penzance in place of the usual 9.5pm (FSX) 4V62 vacuum goods from Copley Hill. We have already noted this engine arriving at Temple Meads on the express in Chapter 1.

From Pontypool Road westwards 86G handled the 9.15pm Manchester–Newquay and 11.10pm Manchester–Penzance trains through to Plymouth, this time using 'Halls' with a crew change at Bristol, both well loaded to between 12 and 13 LMR coaches. Nos 4916 Crumlin Hall and 4937 Lanelay Hall appear to have been used for this purpose on the night of 8/9 July.

So around 1.30am alongside the dark windswept island platform at Pontypool Road all should have been ready for a snappy 6min engine change. As the incoming 'Grange' came steaming up from Little Mill Jc on the Newquay, its stablemate, No 4916, would be waiting at Pontypool Road station south end ready to take the strain of 420 tons on the hard slog to Plymouth. Upon arrival there the complete train went forward to Newquay with Nos 1002 County of Berks and 4095 Harlech Castle double-heading, while No 4916 went off for service.

No 4916 then reappeared from Laira later on Saturday at about 12.30pm, and worked the 13-coach 10.5am Penzance–Manchester back as far as Bristol. It handed over to No 5078 Beaufort at St Philip's Marsh, while No 4937 Lanelay Hall followed its shedmate closely up the West of England main line on the 10.45am Penzance–Sheffield. This had been double-headed from Penzance by an NB Type 2 diesel piloting a 'Hall', thought to be No 6931 Aldersey Hall, and No 4937 then had assistance for the 12-coach train from D6316 out of Plymouth over the banks.

This would position Nos 4916 and 4937 at Bristol where one of them might be required to pilot yet another Pontypool Road engine on the 12 Noon Penzance–Manchester North & West mail back towards home. This train regularly loaded above the 385-ton limit allowed for any power Class 5 engine up Filton bank, so it often needed two locomotives.

Sure enough on 9 July the mail was still loaded to 13 coaches after No D601 coming in from Plymouth had detached the Sheffield van at Bristol. This would form a full load for Canton 'Castle' No 5061 Earl of Birkenhead which was due to take over haulage of the mail from Pontypool Road to Shrewsbury. This 'Castle' reached Pontypool Road on the 7.20pm connecting service from Cardiff, bringing with it a large influx of South Wales passengers who would then try to find vacant seats on the mail at Pontypool Road. Often the mail was already full leaving Bristol, and then the train had to be run in two sections from Pontypool Road to Crewe or Manchester. There was a conditional 'Q' path already shown in the working timetable for that purpose. In this situation No 5061 would have worked the first portion and then one or both of the pair of 86G engines coming in from Bristol would be called on to haul the second Penzance section of the mail through to Shrewsbury. No 4937 was at Shrewsbury shed on Sunday, and it is therefore possible that it worked the whole of this tough Pontypool Road–Plymouth–Shrewsbury assignment on Saturday.

It need only be added that No 4937 had not been overhauled since November 1957 and it duly went for works repair shortly afterwards on 5 September 1960. Its overall condition cannot have been good and this indicates that there was little element of selection when it came to choosing 'Halls' for the hardest jobs. No 4916's condition was little better, and no doubt the engines didn't look very trim either. A clean 86G loco was a rarity. The busiest passenger sheds had their best 'Halls' reserved for regular express turns, but otherwise there is little evidence to show that weekday loco diagrams could be manipulated in such a way as to make the best mixed traffic engines available where they would be most useful on Saturdays. It was largely due to the dedication of loco crews in making the best of the engines they were given that such a lottery could be made to work successfully in practice. Their reward at Pontypool Road, where fortunes had ebbed and flowed for years with the profitability of the coal trade, and where they had fought hard through the days of their high performance 'Saints' to keep a good share of the lucrative North & West express runners, was to have the whole place razed to the ground,

Right: Standing in for the usual 'King' on the up 'Cambrian Coast Express', No 6934 *Beachamwell Hall* has quite enough to cope with working from Wolverhampton to Paddington without having to wait at Birmingham Snow Hill while brake trouble is rectified on the 12.25pm Wellington–Lapworth three-car suburban DMU in front. The date is Saturday 10 September 1960 and this 'Hall' has found its way on to the 'Cambrian Coast Express' because the balancing Saturday 9am Paddington–Pwllheli down working for its normal 'King' ceased to run after 3 September. No 6934 managed this working all right and returned next day on the 4.10pm Paddington–Birkenhead, running via Thame because of engineering work on the main line. *M. Mensing*

Right: The 12 Noon Penzance–Manchester north mail has just restarted from Bristol Stapleton Road and its two engines, Nos 6904 *Charfield Hall* and 5099 *Compton Castle*, are struggling to get this heavy train moving up the 1 in 75 of Filton Bank. No 5099's Cardiff–Shrewsbury–Bristol–Pontypool Road–Cardiff circuit did not operate on summer Saturdays and then two smaller 4-6-0s had to be used between Bristol and Pontypool Road instead. The exact date of this photo is unknown, but it was taken between 27 June and 14 July 1960. *Richard Picton*

Right: The 12.46pm Ramsgate–Birmingham was a relief train which ran once a year at the end of the Birmingham Holiday Fortnight. It was also one of a select band of expresses to the WR which ran via the West London line changing engines at Kensington Olympia. Unfortunately, on this occasion, Saturday 6 August 1960, the passengers have had to contemplate Olympia station for far too long because of vacuum trouble experienced by the incoming loco from the SR, Type 2 No D5007, when it was being uncoupled from the train. No D5007's removal took from 3.5 to 3.40pm, and so No 5923 *Colston Hall* is seen here departing at 3.51pm. It was a long, slow journey and by the time No 5923 reached Tyseley at 6.48pm it was 56min behind time. *R.C. Riley*

along with the five busy Pontypool marshalling yards. Main line work had all been wiped out, together with No 4916 and the other last 'Halls' by June 1964. The rest of the Pontypool Road infrastructure followed within a year.

In 1960 there were other major sheds where 'Halls' were top-line power, notably Banbury, Taunton and Westbury with 47 members of the class between them, of which four were in works and 27 observed in traffic. These were depots with a lot of regular passenger work. By contrast with 'Halls' from some of the other sheds already mentioned, all but a couple of those noted were to be found on workings which, while not necessarily all regular, took them to, through or from their home stations.

The Banbury turns involved plenty of interesting inter-regional work, which was another 'Hall' strength, because they could operate over most SR main lines west of Basingstoke, the Great Central to Sheffield, as well as to Crewe via Shrewsbury or Market Drayton. No 6976 Graythwaite Hall from Banbury ran the regular down Newcastle–Bournemouth (West) express through to its destination on Friday, and would have returned to Oxford as usual that night starting out on the 9.20pm Bournemouth–Reading. Next day it reappeared to take over the 11.16am Bournemouth–Newcastle from 'King Arthur' No 30781 Sir Aglovale at Oxford and worked this to Leicester Central. It should have regained Banbury promptly on the 5.20pm Leicester–Woodford local but it seems likely that 'County' No 1018 worked that train leaving No 6976 to come back on the 3.5pm Hull fish.

One or two Westbury engines were waylaid when they reached their outward destinations, notably No 4957 Postlip Hall which is thought to have hauled the 8.15am Frome–Paddington, and was then borrowed for a trip to Cardiff on the 3.58pm West Ealing–Whitland milk empties. Interestingly, No 4957 is shown on its record card as being on loan to Weymouth from 25 May to 16 August 1960. However, there is no evidence that No 4957 carried a 71G shedplate, or that it was actually based at Weymouth except as part of the regular Westbury arrangement to supply Weymouth shed with engines as required, when for example No 4957 worked the 11.12am Weymouth–Paddington on 23 July. Otherwise No 4957 was frequently on normal Westbury turns like the 4.35pm Newbury–Westbury passenger and other locals over the Berks & Hants line. Weymouth was of course SR territory now, and, regional co-operation being what it was, plus recent loss of the Channel Islands boat trains being a bit of a sore point on the WR, the fact that Weymouth shed was desperately strapped for suitable engines to work on to the WR met with a less than sympathetic response. Basically Weymouth was left to cope as best it could on a shoestring.

Despite a lot of light engine running to Salisbury as well as Weymouth, Westbury's own requirements were rather easier to organise now that dieselisation meant fewer 'Halls' were likely to be borrowed to cover West of England holiday trains. But old habits died hard. And at 12.20pm on 9 July No 4917 Crosswood Hall duly took over the 7.43am Nottingham–Plymouth on time from 'Jubilee' No 45612 Jamaica at Bristol. Unfortunately, No 4917's westbound path was hindered by a crush of trains and it lost 11min on a very easy schedule by running to Exeter in 151min including calls at Bridgwater and Taunton. However, No 4917 then regained five of these before reaching Newton Abbot. There it collected NB Type 2 No D6328, which had only been newly delivered the previous month, and this pair worked the 7.43 through to its destination.

No summary of 'Hall' activity would be complete without an assessment of their contribution towards moving holiday expresses from the west. About 22 'Halls' were involved on up trains between 7am and 4pm at Exeter and Newton Abbot, and no other classes were involved to a greater extent than 13 'Castles' and 12 'Warships'. Many 'Halls' worked as far as Bristol on trains for the LMR but there were two going through to Shrewsbury, others to Pontypool Road or Cardiff and four to the Birmingham area. Two took Paddington trains, pride of place going to No 6966 Witchingham Hall ex-works on the up 'Torbay Express', though it didn't experience an easy trip.

Only three 'Halls' remained stationed in Cornwall and seven at Laira. Inevitably dieselisation had largely edged them out of the Duchy, but there was around a handful still to be seen at work on both 2 July and 9 July, mostly double-heading on Newquay trains. The small number of 'Halls' was largely offset by the interesting combinations of engine power involved. In fact, except for two solo locomotives engaged on the main line to Penzance, no two motive power combinations were the same.

A final comment appropriately involves the last locomotive of the Class, No 7929 Wyke Hall which worked from Penzance to Plymouth on what appears to be the 2.15pm Penzance–Swindon Works Trip special. If so, it was the only express of the day from Penzance to the east which was seen to be steam-hauled all the way through Devon and Cornwall. On this No 7929 handed over to No 6837 Forthampton Grange assisting Shrewsbury's No 6904 Charfield Hall from Plymouth to Newton Abbot.

No 6904 had originally left Stafford Road shed at 10.47pm Friday night, apparently to haul empty stock from Wolverhampton down to Plymouth. It then worked the Trip passengers back to Swindon, running via Westbury where footplate crews were changed. Finally No 6904 took the empty coaches from Swindon on to Cannock Road sidings, and eventually arrived back outside Stafford Road shed at 5.35am Sunday morning after covering some 510 miles. It wasn't a

Above: Looking highly disreputable on 9 July 1960 without its safety valve cover, and still carrying VO4 reporting numbers off its up working on the 9.20am Chester–Paddington earlier, No 5990 *Dorford Hall* is not a credit to its home shed at Banbury. However, it is coming through Hatton station in fine style on the 4.34pm Paddington–Wolverhampton semi-fast and will pass Tyseley with time in hand to reach Snow Hill punctually at 7.57pm. *D. K. Jones*

bad day's work for a Shrewsbury engine which hadn't been seen anywhere near its home shed in the process.

5MT 'Grange' Class 4-6-0s

Every summer Saturday was a good day for 'Grange' 4-6-0s and on most of them the Western could have done with another 20 of these engines. 9 July was no exception and not even the presence of a large number of diesels firmly camped right in the middle of traditional 'Grange' territory could damp down their level of activity. Briefly, out of 80 engines, 66 were located and 55 were seen in service. Of these, over half were still involved down in the West Country beyond Bristol, but the remainder were so well distributed right across the rest of the system that almost every main line east of Chester and Carmarthen saw at least two 'Granges' appear during the day, except routes through High Wycombe, Stroud and Yeovil.

Alone among main line steam classes, 'Granges'

retained an allocation at all three WR sheds in Cornwall and they had the largest hand in what steam work remained. Despite the fact that much of the daily work left for Penzance's eight 'Granges' was meant only to involve standby duty, milk trains or local traffic to Truro, at least half of them managed to cross the Tamar on 9 July. If you were spending that day in Cornwall the all-steam Saturday equivalents of the 'Cornishman' were definitely among the trains to see. Three of the four engines involved on these were 'Granges'.

Interestingly, one of the Penzance summer Saturday steam workings to Newton Abbot seemed to be at least partially still in place when No 6826 *Nannerth Grange* arrived there piloting No 5065 *Newport Castle* on the 8.20am Penzance–Paddington. But whereas in 1959 No 6826 would have been one of the pair of two-cylinder 4-6-0s to relieve a 'King' on the down 'Riviera' and work it through to Truro where the train divided, on 9 July 1960 No 6826 was held over to pilot No 6021 *King Richard II* with the 11am Paddington–Penzance and only went as far as Plymouth. It then returned to Newton Abbot, again later piloting No D808 *Centaur* on the 4.50pm Penzance–Manchester.

In all, five 'Granges' were still to be found assisting over the South Devon banks on 9 July but most of these engines were on filling-in or positioning turns rather than competing with the 'D63xx' Type 2s on

exclusive assistant duties. No 6854 *Roundhill Grange* came up coupled to No 5092 *Tresco Abbey* from Plymouth on the 11.15am Newquay–Wolverhampton, and then was itself piloted by No 4992 *Crosby Hall* when it took over the 12.21pm Cardiff–Newquay from No 5945 *Leckhampton Hall* at Newton Abbot. No 6854 may well have worked through to Newquay on this train, though it would need further assistance up the 1 in 35 of Luxulyan bank. The balancing 12.42pm Newquay–Cardiff service had set off up the branch earlier with No 6875 *Hindford Grange* attached to Pannier No 8702, both from St Blazey shed, over 1 in 71 gradients to Roche where No 8702 came off. The Pannier then returned light to Newquay and tackled the 1.45pm local to Par while No 6875 continued on to Plymouth. A little earlier No 6873 *Caradoc Grange* of Laira, an engine with good Celtic associations well suited to doing battle with the ups and downs of the Cornish gradients, had undertaken a fairly typical 'Grange' assignment for the weekend. It was coupled inside No 4095 *Harlech Castle* on the 11am Newquay–York as far as Plymouth where No 6804 *Brockington Grange*, one of the plentiful SPM '68xx' which had worked down overnight on Friday, took over on its return leg to Bristol assisted by No D6328. No 6873 went on to haul the 4.45pm Plymouth–Exeter later in the afternoon and came back on Sunday with the 4.15pm all stations to Plymouth.

Taunton also had a handful of 'Granges' to complement its large 'Hall' allocation and these were active on all sorts of work. Curiously the one which should have been in best condition, No 6874 *Haughton Grange*, was only seen the day before when it took Friday's 4.30pm Taunton–Exeter slow passenger. First 'Grange' out on Saturday was No 6814 *Enborne Grange*, surplus at St Blazey and now working from Taunton. This engine took what had been a Penzance 'Grange' turn until 1959 on the 6.35am Taunton–Neyland as far as Cardiff. Here it arrived 12min late before handing

Above: The 12.5pm Paddington–Plymouth has collected its Dainton pilot at Exeter as usual and on Saturday 30 July 1960 it climbs to Dainton Tunnel hauled by Nos 6813 *Eastbury Grange* and 4995 *Dalton Hall*. They were reported just 2min late at Exeter. Stoneycombe box is switched out, so the up line distant signal will be off all day, not just for No 6025 which is due shortly, unassisted and running early on the 1.45pm Newquay–Paddington. *Hugh Ballantyne*

over to No 5913 *Rushton Hall*. No 6814 then went to Canton to turn and 65min later returned to the station. It was now ready to take over the 8.17am Carmarthen–Penzance from No 6818 *Hardwick Grange* of Llanelly which arrived from Swansea 2min early. This was a full load job through the Severn Tunnel when No 6814 worked the 13-coach train of mixed stock on to Bristol, where No 5055 *Earl of Eldon* relieved it for the run to Plymouth. No 6814 should then have reappeared for the 5.15pm Bristol-Taunton local but Canton 'Hall' No 6932 *Burwarton Hall* covered that instead. However, No 6814 may have eventually reached home last thing that day on the 10.40pm Bristol to Taunton semi-fast.

Next off Taunton shed in the morning was No 6868 *Penrhos Grange* which hauled a 9.35am Taunton–Paignton seaside excursion formed of a GW open vestibule set branded 'Bristol 12', returning from Goodrington Sands at 6.20pm. No 6815 was at Taunton shed on Sunday but not otherwise observed, so that left what was probably the hardest Taunton turn of the day on the 10.40am Minehead–Paddington to be worked by a very run-of-the-mill high mileage engine, No 6871 *Bourton Grange*. This may well have happened because there was no obvious way for the engine to return home from London within a reasonable time, and that factor no doubt contributed to a wide variety of engines provided for the 10.40 in 1960, resulting in some fairly indifferent running. They were mostly 'Halls', but No 1009 *County of Carmarthen* and '9F' No 92241 both appeared on successive weekends and even the 'County' certainly had no success with timekeeping. Finally on 27 August No 4994 *Downton Hall* ran abysmally and reached Paddington 50min late.

In this context No 6871 on 9 July didn't do at all badly, but it also didn't appear to do well enough to avoid holding up other trains either. After a buffet car section had been added to the Minehead portion making up 11 coaches, No 6871 got away from Taunton 8min late at 11.55am into a procession of trains which had left Exeter 5–10min late. In a similar situation the previous Saturday when No 4955 *Plaspower Hall* was on the job, the 10.40 was also held for 10min to take its proper place in the up line traffic, crossing from the up relief platform to the up main line at Taunton East after the 9.45am Churston had passed. No 6871 was then unable to maintain its proper headway to Westbury. Here it was around 13min late, and probably took about 135min to run 107 miles from Taunton to Reading, delays no doubt included, against a booking of 125min. In a series of tight margins this affected following trains and must have cost No 4083 *Abbotsbury Castle*, right behind on the 10.35am Torquay–Paddington, its path at Castle Cary ahead of the 11.12am Weymouth–Paddington. The Weymouth train with Standard 5 No 73042 then had three stops to make before No 4083 could get past at Frome. So No 4083 was 31min late at Savernake, but only 19min late, following right behind No 6871 again, into Paddington.

At Reading No 6871 on the Minehead had to jockey for a path across to the up main platform. The 11.5am from Weston which should have overtaken the Minehead train at Reading was long gone behind No 5087 *Tintern Abbey*, and instead No 5041 *Tiverton Castle* running early on the 7.30am from Pembroke Dock was allowed to pass on the through line. It was an excellent piece of traffic regulation to allow No 5041 ahead at Reading even though it was running early, because No 6871 continued to lose more time, passing Twyford 18½min late and West Ealing 20min late. The real irony is that No 6871 had now built up a large enough leeway in advance to be able to sail into Paddington quite undelayed and it actually recovered 4min in the process. So the measure of lost time from Taunton was only about 8min but it was enough to be quite disruptive to neighbouring trains.

The only other 'Grange' to work into Paddington that day did rather better, even though it was something of a freight train habitué from Newport

Below: SPM 'Granges' took whatever work came along in their stride, and that includes No 6809 *Burghclere Grange* coming out past Old Oak Common in fine style on the down 'Royal Duchy' 1.30pm Paddington–Penzance on Saturday 13 August 1960, which No 6809 will work to Plymouth. No 6809 is in good condition, less than a month out of works, but its moment of glory on the 'Royal Duchy' is marred by massive engine failure problems suffered by the 11am Paddington–Penzance which was 190min late at Newton Abbot. No 6809 got off more lightly than most following trains and was 49min late at that point. *R. C. Riley*

Above: With steam off and the prospect of a good breather down Hatton bank to come, No 6857 *Tudor Grange* approaches Hatton station with the 9.20am Birkenhead– Bournemouth on 9 July 1960, which No 6857 will take as far as Basingstoke. No 6857 had relieved 'Crab' No 42856 at Wolverhampton. It then left Snow Hill 14min late and recovered 7min before Oxford. *D. K. Jones*

Ebbw Jc. This was No 6838 *Goodmoor Grange* on the 5.55am Blaina-Paddington which it took over from a Valleys tank engine at Bassaleg Jc. No 6838 then worked nonstop up from Newport leaving on time at 7.15am, carrying one of the Paddington observers to reach his vantage point in the process. With nine coaches No 6838 must have approached Wootten Bassett about 10min late and the 7am from Weston, which was diesel on Saturdays only, was allowed to go ahead, but after passing Swindon 12min late No 6838 ran well from there to Paddington in about 78min, only just outside even time, and arrived 7min late.

Few 'Grange' runs were made in the wide open spaces like this. As surplus engines were gradually being released from West Country sheds they became more closely associated with work of all sorts in and around Birmingham, which kept no less than 14 'Granges' busy on 9 July, or over slack infested stretches of the South Wales–Salisbury line on which Welsh based engines Nos 6822 *Manton Grange* and 6843 *Poulton Grange* performed successfully with trains to Portsmouth and Brockenhurst.

The biggest batch of 'Granges' was quartered at St Philip's Marsh and this centrally-located base offered opportunities for these engines to operate over a wide area of the Western Region's Red category route mileage. No 6827 *Llanfrechfa Grange* was a case in point, ex-Swindon Works after overhaul eight months before and still in good condition. No 6827 was at Paignton ready to take on the 9.30am to Swansea, usually worked either by 82B or 83A locomotives depending on how well the overnight 10.5pm from Hull was running, bringing down an incoming engine for the 9.30. In view of what followed it is likely that No 6827 had started its day at Newton Abbot, after working a freight like the 3.45am Stoke Gifford–Hackney Yard 8C58 or a series of local passenger trains down the day before. No 6827 hauled the 9.30am from Paignton throughout to Swansea, running

nominally nonstop from Torquay to Newport except the usual break for a crew change on the Marsh avoiding line at Bristol. It arrived in the Welsh capital 3min late at 1.45pm, and then left for Swansea only 13min ahead of No 5051 *Earl Bathurst* on the down 'Pembroke Coast Express'. To avoid delaying No 5051, the 'Grange' would have to pick up its heels along here, because, whereas No 6827 had to make the usual stops at Bridgend, Port Talbot and Neath, No 5051 was due through nonstop to Swansea. Even if No 6827 ran punctually its margin in front of the 'Pembroke Coast' was only 3min on arrival at Swansea. There was no scope for any slackening of effort climbing to Llanharan, Stormy Down and Skewen summits along the way. At Swansea the stock of the Paignton train was drawn out into the carriage sidings while the 'Pembroke Coast' reversed and No 6918 *Sandon Hall* took it on to Carmarthen, departing at 3.30pm in the timetable.

By the time No 6827 reached Landore it was probably in need of a good fire clean and ashpan rake-out but the day wasn't over yet. When No 7011 *Banbury Castle* ran into Swansea High St terminus on the 3.55pm down 'Capitals United Express' No 6827 was waiting to back on to an exceptional 11-coach set forming the West Wales portions for Carmarthen and beyond. On that, it would need assistance up to Cockett, probably from '57xx' Pannier No 8789 which had piloted No 4099 *Kilgerran Castle* out on the 3.45pm down Fishguard boat express 30min before. With such a load, some hard steaming at the end of an arduous day would be required to keep an extremely tight 24min booking for 20.1 miles from Llanelli to Carmarthen. This would mean some fast running that summer evening, charging along the shores of Carmarthen Bay with the crew on their well-loaded 'Grange' trying hard to keep time, before they had to ease for the slow curving run in from Carmarthen Jc to the Town station. No 6827 was finally seen arriving there pretty punctually complete with headboard soon after 9.20pm.

It might have arrived at Carmarthen on a named train but No 6827 was unlikely to go back on one. There was a 9pm 5B15 express freight from Carmarthen to Bristol on weekday nights and, even if No 6827 was borrowed for a filling-in turn or two in the meantime, it would still be ideally placed to work this freight back from Carmarthen late on Monday.

Such were the 'Granges', versatile and willing. Their qualities are among the first to spring to mind whenever summer Saturdays are mentioned.

4MT 'Manor' class 4-6-0s

With over two thirds of the 30 'Manor' 4-6-0s positioned primarily for work on to the Cambrian section (otherwise officially known as 'Section "L" Shrewsbury District (Oswestry Area)'!) and the remainder very thinly spread among six other sheds, it was inevitable that the contribution of this class to handling much long distance express traffic was going to be strictly limited. But as much of their work was well off the beaten track it is worth a closer look.

In the event, of the 16 'Manors' observed on Saturday, nine got on to express work of some description, but two of these were only in the capacity of assistant engines. Four more were located at sheds over the weekend, mainly Oswestry.

The most substantial chunk of engines covered Cambrian routes and associated lines to Carmarthen and Ruabon on which eight were seen. There would certainly have been much more 'Manor' activity than was actually observed, both on Oswestry–Aberystwyth and Machynlleth–Pwllheli traffic because information has only surfaced covering workings on the Cambrian fringes at Shrewsbury, Whitchurch and Carmarthen. However, most expresses over the Cambrian main line were covered at some stage. These were vastly increased on a summer Saturday to seven down and six up passengers carrying express headcode, with a similar number over the Coast line, though 'Manors' had nothing like a monopoly of these trains.

Even when there were 'Manors' available they required piloting at least part of the way when loads exceeded nine or 10 coaches, while further pressure on resources was exerted by the need to change engines at Welshpool every Saturday on trains like the 'Cambrian Coast Express' in both directions and the 10.15am Aberystwyth–Shrewsbury. The Saturday 'Cambrian Coast Express' skirted Shrewsbury on the Abbey Foregate loop, so an extra set of engine workings had to be added to the weekday arrangement because the usual engine change at Shrewsbury was obviously not possible. The same Machynlleth 'Manor' or occasionally '43xx' Mogul with assistance as required worked the 'Cambrian Coast Express' in both directions between Aberystwyth and Welshpool, and then the trains were worked by a similar selection of Shrewsbury-based

locomotives between Welshpool and Wolverhampton, the up and down trains passing near Hollinswood Summit if they were running on time with their hard-pressed engines.

The 'Cambrian Coast Express' was usually a daily 'Special Load' set of seven coaches west of Shrewsbury with some very smart timings. On Saturdays it would load to 10, 12 or however many coaches up to 14 that the traffic would bear, and to cover this extra tonnage just 2min was added to the eastbound timing as far as Welshpool. It was small wonder that the train often needed double-heading throughout, but on 9 July the load was within single engine capacity both ways except for the climb to Talerddig from Machynlleth. Lost time on the Cambrian was not readily tolerated as all crews were only too well aware of the crossing difficulties this created on the single line. Keeping schedule therefore meant heavy work for engines and firemen both ways for most of the distance between Aberystwyth and Wolverhampton. On the down run No 7821 *Ditcheat Manor* was supplied at Wolverhampton, taking over punctually from 'King' No 6000 after the 'Manor' had worked up earlier on the 8.47am parcels from Shrewsbury. No 7821 was only on loan to Salop shed at this stage, after it had been released from Newton Abbot a week or two before, now that there were so many diesels available at Laira to cover South Devon bank work. No 7821 worked to Welshpool where it was due at 2.22pm and here the incoming Aberystwyth engine would be waiting on the Pit Road ready to take over. This engine was not identified, although No 7818 *Granville Manor* was a regular 'Cambrian Coast' locomotive around this time. No 7821 regained Shrewsbury later on the 3.55pm Welshpool–Shrewsbury passenger after covering just over 100 miles in the day. This modest figure proved to be not much out of the ordinary for 'Manor' mileages on 9 July, and only No 7802 *Bradley Manor* was seen to approach 200 miles.

No 7802 of Machynlleth arrived in the area on Thursday and then made for Wolverhampton that night on the 11.40pm Welshpool–Victoria Basin 4H70 vacuum freight conveying empty vans and cattle traffic. Later on Friday No 7802 was called out for the Stafford Road breakdown vans from 9.20am until 1.16pm — fortunately nothing serious, as there were no delays to scheduled services. It then departed Stafford Road at 1.51am Saturday morning, probably to take over the 2pm Penzance–Crewe perishables from another 4-6-0 which had brought the perishables from Bristol. No 7802 would have proceeded on from Crewe to Whitchurch for the 9.45am passenger as far as Welshpool. Here it picked up the 10.15am from Aberystwyth, calling at the stations on the joint line to Shrewsbury which were to be closed only two months later. No 7802 was finally due to make tracks in the direction of home on the 4.22pm Shrewsbury–

Aberystwyth, leaving Shrewsbury to find an engine for the last through Cambrian train of the day at 6.30pm. Surprisingly it wasn't worked by one of Salop's own engines, as all the local 'Manors' and '43xx' were safely tucked up on shed next day. And nor was it No 7827 *Lydham Manor* of 89C. This was at Shrewsbury all day on Saturday and Sunday after taking the weekly RAF train from Cardington in Bedfordshire on from Coleham to its destination at Bridgnorth over the Severn Valley line on Friday evening 8 July, though 'Grange' No 6838 was an even more unusual 4-6-0 visitor to this line a week later on the same train.

Many locomotive diagrams over the Cambrian included successive duties over quite short stages, but longer workings were involved on the Manchester to Aberystwyth service. The 10.45am down train from Manchester Exchange was powered by No 7810 *Draycott Manor*, which reached Whitchurch to pick up the westbound train there on the 8.53am freight of two wagons and one van from Oswestry. The 10.45 duly arrived from Manchester headed by No 44780 of Longsight and No 7810 left punctually at 12.35pm with its 12-coach train stretching out well beyond the end of Whitchurch platform. This Manchester–Aberystwyth train was dated to run for part of the summer service only, but in July and August it was subject to massive peak loadings and sometimes had to be divided. On 23 July 1960 two nine-coach trains were taken by Nos 7807 and 7827 and on 13 August it was divided again with 'Manors' Nos 7801 and 7827.

One straightforward out and back duty was fulfilled by No 7814 *Fringford Manor* on the 7.35am Aberystwyth–Shrewsbury and 3.15pm back after connecting with No 5019 *Treago Castle* on the 11.10am from Paddington. Any aspiring passengers for Cambrian stations hoping to make a tight connection off the 9.5am from Paignton, with No 1013 *County of Dorset* due at 3.7pm, were totally out of luck. Their train didn't reach Salop until about 3.45pm and they had to await the next down Cambrian departure at 4.22pm.

No 7814 had been another of the West Country engines displaced on South Devon bank work after 1958. In fact there was now only one 'Manor' remaining in position at either Newton Abbot or Laira for such duties. That was No 7808 *Cookham Manor*, though on 9 July it didn't make its first noted appearance until well into the afternoon. There at Plymouth No 7808 was appropriately attached ahead of 'King' No 6028 on the 12.30pm Newquay–Paddington, so there was still a glimpse of the classic 'Manor'/ 'King' combination which had successfully ruled the South Devon banks in recent years. Moreover, this 13-coach train came into Plymouth behind a Cornish combination of Nos 7816 *Frilsham Manor* and 6913 *Levens Hall* so a full steam changeover of double-headed pairs was still possible there. No 7808 later returned to Plymouth on the 10.20pm Hackney–Tavistock Jc freight, collecting traffic which had been unable to

proceed from Newton Abbot earlier in the day.

No 7816 was one of five 'Manors' stabled in Cornwall for duties of this latter sort of fairly mundane nature, taking in weekday trains like the three-coach 6pm Newquay–Plymouth and numerous freights not always running in obvious working timetable paths, but including ones like the 8.18pm Tavistock Jc–Truro class 'K'. On Saturdays however they could still thrive, as when Nos 7813 *Freshford Manor* and 6805 *Broughton Grange* made a striking pair bringing the 8.15am Perranporth up from Truro. With 'King' No 6016 waiting to take over at Laira Jc it was only the addition of a wretched Type 2 diesel No D6311 as pilot which robbed this exchange of another quality line-up.

No 7820 *Dinmore Manor* of St Blazey did not look particularly smart in those days. It had not had a classified repair since November 1955 and had got through some hard graft over the South Devon banks in the intervening years. This was usually characterised by a vertical column of exhaust as No 7820 came hammering up Rattery, relieving the train engine behind of a good share of work. All that exertion had taken its toll and by 9 July No 7820 was pretty run-down. It left St Blazey light engine for Newquay at 10.15am, in the usual path of the assistant engine for the 12.42pm Newquay–Cardiff, but in fact returned on the 11.53am Newquay–Par local, leaving the assistant job to be handled by Pannier No 8702. No 7820 left the West Country shortly after, going to join No 7805 *Broome Manor* at Canton.

Before No 7805 arrived in August 1958 'Manors' were always rare visitors to Cardiff. There were none shedded closer than the pair at Gloucester and those two were usually outstationed at Cheltenham for work over the Midland & South Western Junction line to Andover before its services were mutilated in 1958. Canton received No 7805 to supplement its reduced '43xx' Mogul allocation for use on banana traffic from Barry, though for some reason it very rarely worked there. Instead, except for all but the 'Cambrian Coast Express', No 7805 had charge of the most important 'Manor' duty of the day, working the 8.30am

Above right: On Saturday 9 July 1960 Nos 7816 *Frilsham Manor* and 6913 *Levens Hall* climb up past mp 299 between Quintrell Downs and St Columb Road with the 12.30pm Newquay–Paddington. At Plymouth these two engines will be relieved by Nos 7808 and 6028, which later reached Newton Abbot 2min late. *Peter W. Gray*

Right: Pictures of solo 'Manors' on main line expresses are not very plentiful. Here is No 7825 *Lechlade Manor* putting its improved draughting to the test as it picks up speed beyond Whiteball summit with the 8.45am Liverpool–Penzance on Saturday 8 July 1956. The use of this Carmarthen 'Manor' on what was usually a very substantial train of at least 12 coaches has all the signs of a rush job. Chester 'Hall' No 5962 was recorded on 284 earlier in the journey and the following Saturday 284 had 'Castle' No 5057. *Kenneth Leech*

Cardiff–Newcastle as far as Gloucester and the 8.15am balancing express from Newcastle back again.

The 8.30 was usually a Gloucester turn during the week but on Saturdays that engine worked the 8.10am Cardiff–Filey Holiday Camp instead, leaving Canton to find a loco for the easy undulating run along the banks of the Severn with the Newcastle train. On 9 July No 5914 *Ripon Hall* took the 8.10am and as Canton was already short of larger engines No 7805 got the 8.30 job. Rather a comical situation developed at Gloucester in both directions where the relatively diminutive 'Manor' handed over to a pair of Millhouses engines Nos 73065 and 45570 *New Zealand* going north, and on the way back No 7805 relieved both 'B1' No 61223 and Holbeck's No 45566 *Queensland*, all on 11-coach trains. In front, coming south from New Street, was another 'B1', No 61195. This was losing time and ended up running over an hour late on the 7.36am Sunderland–Bristol. It held up the Newcastle–Cardiff badly. Despite an easier Saturday schedule, No 7805 was unable to make much impression on such lateness and it pulled into Cardiff 55min behind time at 5.32pm. Even so, it cannot have done too badly because 2hr later No 7805 was back off to Gloucester again on the 7.35pm from Cardiff, this time stopping at all stations.

Finally to bring 'Manor' activity round full circle back towards the Cambrian No 7815 *Fritwell Manor* came into Carmarthen during the afternoon on the 10.18am Penychain–Carmarthen. This curious conveyance was a holiday train originating from the Butlin's Holiday Camp station near Pwllheli which enjoyed a busy and interesting Saturday train service. Campers trains to Stoke, Manchester, Liverpool and Warrington were worked from Penychain to Bangor by LMR 2-6-4Ts, often in pairs, but the Carmarthen service around this time was generally hauled by a BR Standard Class 3 2-6-2T to Aberystwyth. This was able to effect the necessary reversal at Dovey Jc simply by running round. When the train reversed again shortly

afterwards at Aberystwyth No 7815 took over there. Running under express headcode as 1F80 the 108½-mile journey from Penychain to Carmarthen took 333min. All the way between Aberystwyth and Carmarthen speed was limited to 40mph over gradients as steep as 1 in 41. Curvature was so severe that the final 14½ miles were further restricted to 35mph. A weight limit of 200 tons for the largest engines allowed meant that six coaches was certainly the maximum on this train.

The Carmarthen–Aberystwyth line was quite an outpost of 'Manor' and Mogul workings although the 'Manor' on the corresponding northbound 10.10am Swansea-Pwllheli was unfortunately misidentified. Like many Saturday extras, the 10.10 was simply a weekday local from Swansea to Carmarthen extended, with the same set of stock strengthened as necessary. But the need to reserve the most powerful permitted locomotives on through Saturday services like this let in other engines on the regular locals. Smaller tender classes down to the '22xx' 0-6-0s therefore got a look in on these trains, as well as a wide variety of other Cambrian passenger duties.

7MT 'Britannia' class Pacifics
By 1960 the Western Region's 12 remaining 'Britannia' Pacifics had been allowed to wither on the vine. In their earlier years the first five Canton 'Britannias' had carried out good but not outstanding work — the slow schedules of the South Wales expresses did not permit that — but the antipathy of Western Region management to what had immediately

Below: On the last day of booked Canton top-link 'Britannia' workings to Paddington, No 70019 *Lightning* passes Subway Jc at 1pm with the up 'Red Dragon' on Saturday 10 September 1960. The following Monday 'Kings' were due to start taking over the three main diagrams, though No 6023 has already arrived at Canton and been used on the morning of the 10th for the up 'Capitals United Express'. The third Canton working on 10 September was worked by 'Castle' No 4080. *R. C. Riley*

been seen as interlopers was well known. Mileages run up by Pacifics on the Western did not even begin to approach those achieved on the Great Eastern section or even the London Midland. The potential for economies of operation by rostering the Pacifics intensively, in a way with which 'Castles' and 'Kings' would have found it difficult to compete, was never put to the test even when all 15 WR 'Britannias' were concentrated at Cardiff in 1957. Without suggesting that 'Britannias' would ever have been preferred to 'Kings' and 'Castles' for the fastest and heaviest work on other Western Region routes, in South Wales they could have been programmed to take over all the London services on their modest schedules with a useful saving in operating costs. Instead the extra 'Britannias' just inherited 'Castle' duties and achieved 'Castle' mileages.

Much was made of complaints about various design features on the Pacifics. Some, like defective smokebox spark arrester plates, were relatively easily sorted out. Others, like smokebox saddle bolts working loose, were not. Otherwise it seemed that these could be largely attributed to matters of comfort and convenience on the footplate, coupled to the unaccustomed demands of a left-hand driving position. Draughty and harsh riding, together with the need to adopt a different firing technique, were often causes of irritation. But in fact many crews were gladly prepared to put up with these features in return for an engine with 'Britannia' boiler capacity and access to its gutsy performance, particularly on the taxing 20½-mile climb from the Severn Tunnel up to Badminton.

There was nothing wrong with the engines themselves as No 70024 *Vulcan* was to prove during the eleventh hour for Pacifics on the Western Region in May and June 1961. It proved to be the last Pacific overhauled at Swindon and ran 9,782 miles in 35 possible working days between examinations, at a time when the location where major repairs to these engines were to be carried out was under intensive review.

But the heart had gone out of their work before that. All too often the 8.30am from Bristol was getting ahead of what should have been the crack morning 8am up 'Capitals United Express' from Cardiff at Wootton Bassett as early as April 1959. By 1960 the 'Britannias' could actually be claimed to be the hardest hit casualties of dieselisation anywhere on the Western Region. Mileage fell from an average of 49,296 miles per engine in 1959 to only 38,597 miles in 1960; 'Britannia' availability was disastrous, and their best work was all under threat from double-chimney 'Castles' and then 'Kings'.

Official indifference could manifest itself in all sorts of ways, but the interminably slow progress of these Pacifics through Swindon Works was one aspect of their maintenance which puts the whole matter into clear perspective. No 70028 *Royal Star* was taken out of traffic for overhaul on 6 May 1960 and didn't get

back to Canton fit for work again until November. No 70026 *Polar Star* took from 9 May to 16 June out of traffic before it was even admitted to Swindon and then didn't complete its overhaul until 11 October. Meanwhile Nos 70019 *Lightning* and 70022 *Tornado* were also in Swindon Works for long periods over 9 July, so 33% of the engines were out of commission in the medium term for a start. This was at a time when nine weeks was quite normal to undertake and complete the repair of a postwar 'Castle'. No 70016 *Ariel* had only just escaped a similar fate by being released from a light casual repair at Caerphilly Works on 30 June. It was the only Pacific ever to receive attention there. No 70016 was at Canton on Friday 8 July and may have been used for the 5.20pm up Milford fish from Canton to Swindon late that evening.

Only seven of Canton's 'Britannias' were therefore to be seen at Cardiff during the day so it was hardly surprising that there was a shortage of passenger engines there. This was countered by some quick turn-rounds, doubling up of a couple of turns and perceptive use of '9Fs'.

A tight situation may well have played its part in the selection of No 70023 *Venus* for the up 'Red Dragon' to Paddington because it was already sitting on a high mileage accumulated over the previous 15 months. No 70023 was not up to the usual standard of engine chosen for this job. Nevertheless it was clean, ran on time or early both ways and was only removed from the 3.55pm down 'Capitals United Express' at Cardiff to suit Saturday operating requirements. No 70029 *Shooting Star* showed what might be achieved on intensive cyclic diagrams by taking up workings which usually required two separate Class '7' engines. It handled the Friday 7.20pm Cardiff TPO to Shrewsbury, returning with the same mail van on the 1.25am Crewe–Cardiff due at 5.32am. At 12 Noon No 70029 was off to Paddington on the heavy 8am Neyland and it came back with the 5.55pm down 'Red Dragon'. At the end of this 500-mile stretch No 70029 showed no ill effects and pulled into Newport 5min early.

The other four active Pacifics were nicely divided up among the other areas where they saw frequent use: west of Cardiff as far as Carmarthen and on the North & West line, but with a Saturday twist. This involved one of the North & West turns which on Saturday took No 70018 *Flying Dutchman* from Cardiff through to Chester on the 12.38pm 1M12 to Manchester (Exchange) via Warrington, while No 70025 *Western Star* followed straight after at 12.45pm for Shrewsbury on the 11.15am Swansea–Manchester Central which ran via Crewe. No 70018 had only made it back to Shrewsbury by midday on Sunday but No 70025 came straight home on the 2.55pm Liverpool–Cardiff. The 'Britannias' could also justify their 7MT mixed traffic rating when they were used for fast freight work on

occasions. No 70024 *Vulcan* was seen at Carmarthen on one of the evening Milford fish trains. This was probably the passenger-rated 5.20pm Milford Haven–Paddington which ran under express headcode all the way and mainly comprised Insul-6-X refrigerated six-wheel fish vans. This train changed engines in the up loop alongside Canton shed where No 6935 *Browsholme Hall* took five vehicles over from No 70024, which it was due to work on to Swindon.

With the appearance of 'Kings' at Canton two months later it was not difficult to see which way the wind was blowing for the 'Britannias'. By mid-1961 overhauls of Nos 70018/23/27 were being carried out much more promptly in 7/8 weeks at Doncaster, and during September 1961 came departure for good from the Western Region and wholesale transfer northwards, some to Carlisle Canal depot. Despite a complete failure on the part of locos like No 70018 to satisfy the rigourous demands of the Waverley route, the ex-Canton 'Britannias' lasted much longer on the LMR than they ever would have on the WR.

In June 1965 the familiar galloping beat of No 70017 *Arrow* could still be heard, building up speed through the Lune Gorge in the middle of the night ready to attack Shap single-handed on the Summer Friday 7.2pm Euston–Inverness Sleeper. Listening to the musical sound of its chime whistle passing Tebay served as a reminder that there was unrealised potential in these engines which the Western Region had totally failed to recognise.

5MT BR Class 5 4-6-0s

If there was something of a case for the Canton 'Britannias' there was absolutely no following at all on the Western Region for the '73xxx' Standard Class 5s. Disregarding the Barrow Road and Bath Standard 5 allocations, where they were viewed with greater esteem but worked only over former LMS routes, these numbered just 20 WR-based engines. They had been progressively shuffled out to sheds where there were inter-regional services to be worked. They were hardly expected to appear on internal WR traffic at all, though in fact they did. Fifteen Shrewsbury engines largely worked over ex-LMS routes, including the Central Wales line along with two '73xxx' at Llanelly. The Swindon trio were diagrammed for GC line workings like the 7.30pm Swindon-Sheffield worked by

No 73012, with No 1021 *County of Montgomery* coupled inside.

On the Western much the same sort of problems afflicted Standard Class 5s as 'Britannias' — only more so. For instance Barrow Road's supply of ex-works engines was quite badly disrupted by delays as their BR Standard 5s passed through Swindon Works. No 73031 was stopped awaiting overhaul at the shed on 9 December 1959 but work did not commence at Swindon until 24 March 1960. It was 1 July before repairs were completed and No 73031 was only just back in time to work the 2.15pm Bristol–York on 9 July. To complicate matters still further, an engine like No 73003 which had spent four months at Swindon then took a further month after completing its overhaul before being returned to Barrow Road.

In October 1959 No 73027 went for overhaul at Swindon about the same time as No 73042 from the Southern's fleet at Weymouth was sent for repair to Eastleigh Works. Both received general repairs. No 73042 was back in service after only three weeks on 14 November 1959. No 73027's overhaul took eight months and it wasn't back in traffic until June 1960. Even taking into account any differences in the degree of general repair, this was clearly an absurd situation.

Both these '73xxx' were busy on 9 July: No 73042 was on the 11.12am Weymouth–Paddington semi-fast which finished up about 6min late after recovering 11min from Savernake. No 73042 then returned as usual with the 6pm down Weymouth service coupled inside 'Castle' No 7010 *Avondale Castle* to Newbury. There the train divided and No 73042 took on the rear coaches which left at 7.18pm for Trowbridge, calling at all stations. Finally, it returned the empty stock to Westbury for stabling.

No 73027 was at Bristol in the morning and the bush telegraph had obviously broadcast the news about it being in good condition — as well it might be after such a protracted overhaul. Instead of going back towards its home base at Swindon No 73027 was therefore appropriated for a trip to Paignton on the extended 8.50am Swansea–Bristol. There was a regular path for this train to run beyond Bristol when required at about 11.57am, but it was a fairly inauspicious time of day to be setting out for the West Country. As a result No 73027 had to thread its way down after the 'Riviera' and all its reliefs, landing up at Newton Abbot 12min late at 2.49pm.

With Standard 5s so thin on the ground it was something of a coincidence that the following 9.5am Swansea–Kingswear service also saw haulage with another one. This was No 73023 of Llanelly which worked to Cardiff and handed over there a minute or so late to '9F' No 92237. There were very few other concentrations of Standard engines to be found elsewhere on the Western Region that day and it was certainly no coincidence that this one occurred at Cardiff. The other Llanelly engine, No 73021, was on the work for which it had been assigned to this shed — one of those fascinating Saturday trains which offered infinite possibilities for unusual motive power over interesting routes. This was the 9.30am Pembroke Dock–Shrewsbury worked by Neyland '22xx' No 2283 as far as Llandovery. Here No 73021, which had come up from Llanelly earlier, was waiting to replace it for the heavy climb over Sugar Loaf Summit. The 9.30 was booked to cross the return train from Shrewsbury beyond there at Llangunllo in the middle of another long 1 in 60 climb. This passed behind Stainier 5 No 45283 but it could just as easily have been one of Shrewbury's Standard 5s.

The Caprotti Standard 5s, which had always seemed so unsuitable for the hard flog required out of Shrewsbury in every direction, had now left the Western Region for more level prospects on the North Wales Coast line workings from Patricroft; though not before a couple of them, Nos 73130 and 73133, had penetrated right through to Devon on Friday night reliefs in July and August 1958.

But the Shrewsbury Summer turn for a Standard 5 to Plymouth still continued and No 73026 went the whole way on 8 and 9 July 1960. It is possible that the engine travelled south on the 10.15am Friday Glasgow–Plymouth which, despite the addition of a buffet car at Shrewsbury when engines were changed, only loaded to about nine coaches. But on Saturday No 73026 was turned out by Laira for the 7.50am Newquay–Manchester which No 73026 was due to work to Pontypool Road, usually taking a pilot through the Severn Tunnel. With 13 coaches it would have been a real handful for a 'Castle'. Not a lot can be said about the running. At Newton Abbot No D6320 was detached and No 73026 was on its own. At Exeter it was 20min late increasing to 38min behind time past Taunton. From Bristol No 73026 left at about 2.18pm, behind No 6859 *Yiewsley Grange* on the 9.22am Ilfracombe–Cardiff which should have departed 17min after the Newquay train. Unfortunately the Shrewsbury observer had to leave for Crewe at 5.35pm and the 7.50, due at 5.25pm, had not arrived by then. One can only say it would have done well to be in by 5.45pm, though to judge from the two preceding North & West trains coming in about 60 and 15min late, one suspects it would be well after 6pm when the 7.50 actually made its appearance behind returning 'Jubilee' No 45680.

The other Salop Standard 5 turns were fairly ordinary by comparison, and those noted were divided between a couple working south on the WR, two on trains over the Central Wales and one heavy LMR North & West service to Liverpool. Nevertheless with Weymouth's contingent active in the direction of Bristol and Wolverhampton as well as Paddington, and examples stationed on the Great Central line very likely to have been running through High Wycombe on trains like the 11.35pm Sheffield–Hastings, there were few WR centres which failed to see a '73xxx' on 9 July.

4MT BR Class 4 4-6-0s

There were only twelve BR Standard Class 4 4-6-0s in Western Region stock and they kept a disconcertingly low profile for much of the time. The six engines located on 9/10 July were mainly conspicuous by their absence from any meaningful work at all, though Nos 75020/6/7 at Machynlleth would certainly be busier on the Cambrian.

Four Tyseley examples were not even preferred to '43xx' Moguls, but then neither was the sole 'Manor' there, No 7824. The three Oxford '75xxx' Standard 4s, which were used to run car trains from Morris Cowley during the week, totally failed to graduate to anything more interesting over the weekend. No 75001 had made it to Bristol St Philip's Marsh on Sunday but this was only likely to be another freight working. The sole double-chimney example was No 75029 which hauled a semi-fast service from Swindon to Bristol during the morning. It returned from Weston-super-Mare to decant a full trainload of seaside day trippers back at Swindon around 8.20pm.

In fact the only significant WR working for a Standard Class 4 wasn't run by a WR engine at all. Now that the old GW shed at Chester West was closed, there were a couple of turns which bought LMR locomotives up from Chester and Birkenhead. On one of these No 75039 appeared from Chester Midland on the 9.20am Chester–Paddington as far as Wolverhampton, where it gave way to No 5990 *Dorford Hall* for the rest of the journey. After service at Stafford Road from 11.30am to 1.30pm No 75039 took over the 9.45am Paddington–Wrexham which had travelled down sedately via Oxford with Old Oak 'Hall' No 4919 *Donnington Hall*. Altogether it was a very modest contribution from a modern class with such wide route availability. It was also a drastically reduced range of Standard 4 sightings compared to earlier years like 1957.

BR Class 9F 2-10-0s

The Western Region had the lion's share of BR double-chimney '9F' 2-10-0s. With some 50 of these superbly versatile machines came a responsibility to make the best possible use of them, but unfortunately this was a hurdle which the WR failed to clear. Instead of making sure that they were concentrated to ensure punctual operation of fast freights, and to improve the running of an increasing number of partially vacuum-fitted services, the '9Fs' were frequently drafted on to loose coupled goods work formerly handled quite adequately by engines like WD 2-8-0s.

The South Wales area was the main generator of freight traffic and, therefore, freight revenue on the Western Region. The final Freight Marshalling Instructions covering the Wales Division before

dieselisation started there were issued in January 1962. They showed just 17 freight trains booked for '9F' haulage. Of these only five were fully fitted and seven of the rest could have been handled by WDs.

Low utilisation should have meant that lots of 2-10-0s could be spared from slow freight work to help out on summer Saturday passenger trains. And in 1959 they were. On the peak day, 15 August 1959, no less than seven '9Fs' worked Paddington departures to Plymouth, Kingswear, Cardiff, Swansea and even Wolverhampton. Others brought arrivals into Paddington, at least four more hauled cross-country services and just for good measure another eight '9Fs' were busy on LMR holiday relief traffic at Derby, so their use was extremely widespread.

1960 looked as if it might shape up the same way when a contingent of 2-10-0s was drafted into Laira ready for the summer service. Until, that is, Canton successfully put No 92220 *Evening Star* on the up 'Red Dragon' job for three days around the end of June. This proved it wasn't just 'Britannias' which could run the South Wales service; '9Fs' might also, given half a chance. Well, they weren't. I saw No 92220 come romping through Swindon on Tuesday 28 June with the 3.55pm down 'Capitals United Express'. It had a load of 12 and was making a comfortable 60mph or so, having caught up to within 5min of No 6962 *Soughton Hall* working the lighter 3.45pm down Fishguard in front. Authority really took fright and banned '9Fs' from further long runs of this sort because it so clearly showed up the slow standard of service they were offering if a '9F' could time the heaviest expresses competently.

As well as route restrictions already mentioned, other impediments were allowed to remain in the path of '9Fs' which effectively prevented their full potential being exploited. The clearest example of this related to the maximum loads '9Fs' could haul over various routes on passenger trains. Up the 1 in 52 of Cockett bank '9Fs' were limited to 280 tons which was actually 25 tons less than the maximum for 'Castles' and 'Counties'. Not a hundred miles away on the S&D '9Fs' were taking 410 tons up a similar curving 1 in 50 gradient five times longer.

Other sections of the WR Working Timetable ignored '9Fs' altogether from their maximum engine load tables. As late as 1961 the Gloucester District passenger book showed no '9F' load entries at all, and that included important main lines between Birmingham and Bristol; also Severn Tunnel Jc to Swindon where '9Fs' were very likely to be found.

The practical consequences of omitting '9F' load limits over the Bristol-Birmingham line from any of the relevant WR passenger working timetables could be awkward. On 6 August 1960 the driver of No 92137, faced with 14 coaches at Bristol on the 8.5am Newquay-Newcastle, claimed the engine was overloaded and called for assistance at short notice.

Above: On Saturday 9 July 1960 BR Class 4 No 75025 sorts out its stock at Birmingham Snow Hill before drawing it into the platform to form the 5.45pm from Birmingham to Stratford-upon-Avon and Worcester.
M. Mensing

Right: Driver Eddie Broome was Chairman of the Canton LDC and he insisted on being allowed his trip to London driving *Evening Star.*
No 92220 was therefore turned out on the 'Red Dragon' for the third and last time and it looks a real picture coming light up from Canton to Cardiff General at 9.34am on Friday 1 July 1960.
R. O. Tuck

Right: Hauling rather less than its own weight, '9F' No 92207 passes Solihull with the 3.30pm Oxford–Birmingham Snow Hill passenger train on Saturday 27 August 1960. Many WR '9Fs' were either idle or similarly under utilised on summer Saturdays in 1960.
M. Mensing

Above: On Saturday 16 July 1960 No 92223 is accelerating out of Newton Abbot beyond Hackney with the 12.42pm Newquay–Cardiff, one of the few holiday expresses which did not normally take assistance over the South Devon banks. In place of the Old Oak '9F' found on this train the previous week, No 92223 is one of the Laira '9Fs' imported for the summer. *Derek J. Frost*

Barrow Road had no reason to be prepared for this extra demand on what was already a busy August Bank Holiday. But equally there were no grounds on which to dispute the driver's claim. A considerable delay elapsed before '4F' No 44296 could be found to couple inside No 92137 and this unusual pair then managed to get started. Nevertheless there was still no rush to rectify the omission in the timetables.

Some mechanical problems could still arise with '9Fs'. Whilst initial trouble with sticking regulators had soon been overcome out of sheer necessity, effective cylinder lubrication had not. This had been a difficulty with 'Britannias', and deficiencies in this department also caused valve and piston wear to '9Fs' once they got on to fast work. No 92208 of Laira was stopped for attention to valves and pistons at Newton Abbot between 5-16 December 1959 within six months of its delivery new from Swindon. '9Fs' were therefore officially limited to the same 60mph maximum speed as the '47xx' 2-8-0s, though for very different reasons.

No 92208 was in trouble again during early February 1960 with a defective brick arch, and another Laira engine, No 92221, experienced the same complaint later during the same month. As late as August 1960 Southall shed staff reported a series of brick arch failures on the seven '9Fs' stationed there. This had nothing to do with any very occasional use on express duties, but similar complaints were quickly reported at Bath Green Park when '9Fs' started work on the S&D in June 1960. This brick arch weakness may have been more pronounced on '9Fs' equipped with double-chimneys. This could be the reason why remedies were still being sought as late as 1960.

However well developed they became, '9Fs' would never have been able to stem the diesel tide. But they should still have had a valuable role to play. Bath

Green Park used all four of its 2-10-0s for S&D express work on both 16 July and 23 July. No doubt they were also out in force on 9 July. By contrast, only around 10 WR '9Fs' were seen to be mobilised during daytime on 9 July which was a low proportion out of 50 engines, when comparatively few of them were required for freight traffic over the weekend. Just half of those 10 were on passenger duties, and by no means all of those were beyond the capability of a '43xx' 2-6-0.

No 92220 itself was not to be seen at work on 9 July although it was at Canton on 8 July and again on 10 July along with seven other '9Fs'. No 92220's most regular 1960 working on the 10.30am Cardiff–Portsmouth as far as Salisbury was taken by No 4973 *Sweeney Hall*. However, the Bristol turn on the 8.5am from Cardiff, which No 92220 had hauled the previous Saturday was again worked by a '9F'. Unusually this was a Laira engine, No 92249, which later regained Cardiff as booked on the 7.40am from Newton Abbot. No 92249 then returned overnight to Plymouth after 10.30pm in time to be seen at Laira again next day, presumably starting off for home on the 11pm Cardiff–Bristol mail.

The most obvious exception to the concentration of what '9F' activity there was on traffic to and from Cardiff, came with No 92218. This 2-10-0 was seen at Bristol in the evening, probably before taking on the 7.30pm Temple Meads–Oxley 7H34 which was quickly promoted to a Class 'D' 5H04 freight from Stoke Gifford onwards. The most extraordinary sight, however, was of another Laira '9F' No 92222 standing in for a 4-6-0 or 2-6-0 on the 10am Weymouth–Birmingham as far as Swindon where No 5981 *Frensham Hall* took over. I arrived too late to see this engine change take place there myself, and was inclined to disbelieve it when I was told — until I saw No 92222 arrive again on exactly the same train a week later. After that I could hardly argue.

No 92233 was the only '9F' seen which managed to maintain any semblance of its normal activity on a daytime freight working. It came gingerly off the Greenford loop at West Ealing with the 11.5am Banbury-Old Oak Common 8A52 Class 'H'. On Saturdays in 1959 '9F' duties had ranged right up among the best 'King' workings, as on 8 August when No 92206 hauled the up 'Mayflower'. But fairly typically in 1960 only one 2-10-0 was seen with what was usually reckoned to be a Class '7' express engine turn on 9 July. Even that was concerned more with haulage of heavy parcels traffic from Swindon to Paddington and back to Cardiff than any demands of outright speed. Nevertheless in conjunction with an up overnight milk train to Swindon this did provide No 92216 with a 290-mile round trip in little more than 24hr. It followed 'Castle' No 4084 *Aberystwyth Castle* which hauled the same series of trains on Friday, but No 4084 then carried out a return express trip to Salisbury on Saturday.

One or two long distance fast freight duties like the Llandilo Jc-Paddington services could also provide a fair mileage for their booked '9Fs', especially if there were any Saturday fill-in turns for which they could be utilised. One possibility in this direction was No 92219 on the 3.25pm Carmarthen–Cardiff slow passenger as far as Swansea. By next day it was back at Canton ready to resume regular freight workings. But by and large it has to be admitted that the '9Fs' offered power and performance which was not seen to its best advantage on 9 July.

7F 47xx 2-8-0s

The main drawback in selecting 9 July 1960 to survey summer Saturday traffic was that no 5ft 8in-wheeled '47xx' 2-8-0s worked passenger trains. These attractive engines had proved themselves amazingly resilient and adaptable in BR days, such that their passenger appearances at one time or another had ranged across much of the cream of weekend services to the West Country, always excepting the actual 'Riviera' and 'Mayflower' trains themselves. In recent years Old Oak was not averse to turning out No 4701 for the 10.15am Paddington–Kingswear as on 15 August 1959 to head the procession of down pre-'Riviera' portions that morning. Similarly in the corresponding crush of up Cornish expresses Laira was willing to use No 4705 for nothing less than the 10am Newquay–Paddington

on 14 June 1958, though not with a full 15-coach load on that particular occasion. Far from being shunted aside by the initial influx of 'Warship' diesels and '9F' 2-10-0s, in 1959 '47xx' 2-8-0s were out on express work every weekend except 27 June, and by the end of August 1959 they had regained the initiative on their common working of the 1.25pm down Paddington–Kingswear. They even broke new ground with two successive weekend appearances on the 8.20am Penzance–Paddington, which was usually very much a preserve of four-cylinder engines up from Plymouth. For this, Nos 4705 and 4708 left Laira with their tenders stacked right up with coal, as well they might, ready to pull out all the stops on what was always a heavy train. Finally on 19 September 1959, when Laira probably had any number of engines to choose from, No 4703 was on shed there, just after being outshopped from Swindon on 2 September after a heavy repair. It was mustered for the first of two reliefs to the up 'Riviera', probably the 9.55am Newquay-Paddington, and on this occasion No 4703 would have to work its 11-coach train nonstop up from Newton Abbot to a weekday schedule of about 205min. This was tight for a 2-8-0 over 193.7 miles. Fine though it looked as No 4703 breasted Savernake Summit in full cry at 3.20pm, $9\frac{1}{2}$min late, the 60min margin which remained was not quite going to be enough to secure a punctual arrival at Paddington.

That seems to have been the last eastbound Plymouth–Paddington express run for a '47xx'. Most summers they were slow starters, until peak weekend power demands thrust them into the limelight as July progressed. 1960 was no slower than 1959, chiefly on account of a couple of early season express appearances as part of a Bristol SPM freight diagram by No 4703. This engine turned up twice from Plymouth on the 7.30am Penzance-Bristol, a train on which I can trace only one '47xx' appearance before, so even as late as this they were still finding fresh employment. On 2 July 1960 No 4703 was into Taunton by 12.48pm on its way to Bristol and again it was maintaining virtually a weekday schedule at that point.

The train which everyone looked out for hoping to see a '47xx' in action was the 1.20pm Paddington–Kingswear and after a couple of barren weekends for 2-8-0s on 9 and 16 July, No 4705 hauled the 1.20 on 23 July, and No 4703 a week later. 2-8-0 timekeeping on this train was rather suspect. The 1.20 was always heavy, exceeding 420 tons tare, and over considerable distances scheduled passing times called for progress somewhat in excess of the official 60mph limit laid down for the class. They could certainly run well, but nosed about disconcertingly at speed if they had been out of shops for any length of time. Over the years SPM's Nos 4703 and 4706 were often used for this train, regardless of condition, as part of another freight diagram. This strategy did not often seem to work successfully. Better results were achieved when

Above: '47xx' 2-8-0 No 4705 passes Newbury at speed on the down through line with the 1.20pm Paddington–Kingswear on Saturday 23 July 1960. The front four coaches of BR standard stock were in chocolate and cream livery and formed the regular down 'Royal Duchy' Kingswear portion. Behind these came an assorted set of ex-GW coaches making up the train of 13 carriages. The 1.20 down was hauled by a 2-8-0 only twice during the 1960 season, the second time being a week later on 30 July.
D.E. Canning

Below: The sight of an NB Type 2 diesel piloting a Churchward 2-8-0 on an express happened very infrequently. On this occasion Nos D6321 and 4705 climb to Dainton Tunnel with the 7.43am Nottingham–Plymouth on Saturday 5 August 1961. The train is running 36min late but the two engines are successfully maintaining the 18min schedule from Newton Abbot to Totnes where they arrived at 4.16pm.
Hugh Ballantyne

Old Oak was able to select the best from its own stud of five '47xxs'. Finally the 1.20's path was likely to become seriously impeded by four late-running North & West services converging in front of it at Taunton, so good work done to this point could easily be wasted by a whole series of delays from there on down.

No 4705 had little chance on 23 July because the North & West trains ahead were 51–60min late. It reached Exeter 33min in arrears. No 4703 looked very scruffy on 30 July — not a bit like the well groomed ex-works thoroughbred on 19 September 1959 — and it was subject to a similar situation when it actually got in among the late Liverpool and Manchester trains at Taunton. However, No 4703 had to contend with an additional 11.5am Leicester-Paignton relief right ahead as well, so it landed up at Newton Abbot 40min late.

Despite dieselisation nearly half the class could still be seen in the West Country over a 1960 weekend. On Sunday 24 July Nos 4703/5/6 were at Laira, and No 4702 came in with a down goods which was frequently '47xx'-hauled on Sunday mornings.

However, this was not the case on 9 July when most '47xx' activity was concentrated on the Birmingham main line. No 4700 had worked the 6.12am Old Oak-Bordesley freight on Friday and probably returned early Saturday morning on one of three London-bound fitted freights due up from Banbury. No 4701 was in Swindon Works. No 4703 appeared from SPM, probably for the 8.45pm Bristol TM goods–Acton 5A15 fast freight on Saturday evening. No 4705 was seen on the afternoon Bristol–Plymouth parcels the previous Saturday and No 4707 had been in Oxley Yard two days later on 4 July. Finally on 9 July No 4708 may have worked the 6.20pm Paddington–Salop 4J86 Class 'C' freight in the evening, and it was at Oxley shed on Sunday.

So it was left to the Somerset & Dorset's 2-8-0s to provide what must have been the only eight-coupled passenger power over a very wide area of southern England on 9 July. No 53807 had been nicely cleaned up the previous day to feature in the BBC television *Railway Roundabout* series, and it was used to haul the 10.40am Exmouth–Cleethorpes from Templecombe back to Bath on Saturday. No 53809 had a longer assignment, working south on the 5.40am Derby–Bournemouth relief earlier.

Eight-coupled express operations may have been few and far between, but the sight of these pre-Grouping 2-8-0 designs working passenger traffic for BR was an effective response to the peak weekend situation, when power output was a more important consideration than anything in the realms of speed.

4MT '43xx' Class 2-6-0s

By 1960 the '43xx' Moguls had had a long and honourable career stretching back over all but half a century. Whilst none of the earliest engines were still active, some survivors were over 40 years old. A few were veterans of overseas service with the Railway Operating Division in World War 1. But now in many ways time had caught up with them.

Withdrawals had already been in progress for 23 years. Recent introduction of diesel multiple-units had drastically reduced both the number remaining to 140 engines, and also their daily participation in main line passenger services. Just as important, a series of one-way journeys to the scrapyard had interfered with the normal cycle of repairs for this class. Few 2-6-0s had received recent attention. So the ones that survived were all too often in poor condition, rough riding, with tenders full of freight train slack. Not a happy proposition for footplate crews hoping to find themselves with a 'Hall' to cover their summer Saturday shifts.

Being such lively little engines '43xxs' had always been subject to overloading. Now some of the passenger load limits laid down were due more to what they used to achieve way back in their pre-1939 prime than to any realistic expectations of what was practical on BR summer Saturdays 20 years later. A 370-ton maximum meant they could still be expected to haul 11 coaches plus a van from Plymouth to Penzance for example, taking in ruling gradients of 1 in 55 on the way. This was an unlikely event by 1960 but down in the west No 7311 was still involved with express work from Paignton to Bristol on 2 July and during 9 July No 7335 covered the whole length of the Cornish main line on the 7.58am Plymouth–Penzance parcels. Two more, Nos 5318 and 5358, were hobnobbing alongside NB Type 2 diesels at Laira next day. With another smart pair of Moguls at Exeter, together with No 6313 of Didcot visiting, and Taunton's 2-6-0s busy belting up and down the secondary lines across Somerset on Barnstaple and Minehead expresses, they were well placed to seize on any serious deficiency in main line diesel numbers even as late in time as this.

Almost everywhere else Moguls were permitted to take loads within one coach of the maximum for 'Halls' on the same timings. 420 tons or more was allowed over most level routes. On the North & West a maximum of 406 tons represented 13 coaches of older stock and this would mean hard going through the Severn Tunnel, on up over Llanvihangel and all the way to Shrewsbury.

In practice an 11-coach train was usually the heaviest task for a 2-6-0 by 1960. That was just as well because eight coaches was a much more realistic load if time was to be kept, and one or two of the schedules on regular Mogul turns were quite tight. Between Banbury and Birmingham the 9.2am from Margate had a similar 60min schedule applying to daily Birkenhead expresses like the 9.10am and 1.10pm down from Paddington, all of which made the same intermediate stop at Leamington. On the 9.32am from Bournemouth Central with a 62min timing No 6364

ran pretty well. However, the other northbound Mogul runners along here on 9 July were subject to Reading shed's problems in covering its specialised jobs like these. Reading possessed only three '43xx' of its own, one of which was always kept as up end pilot at Reading General station. Another, No 6324, still carrying GWR livery on its tender, spent the day on station pilot work at Oxford. Yet Reading had to find at least two more Moguls suitable for the through Redhill-Birmingham duties off the SR, so borrowing was the only answer. That generally involved lifting one or two of Didcot's seven 2-6-0s, but whatever happened it was Hobson's Choice, using whatever was available regardless of fitness for a 140-mile through run.

In the event, No 6366 on the 9.2am Margate–Wolverhampton was a Swindon engine in quite acceptable condition, but it was preceded by No 7332 with 11 SR coaches on the 8.50am from Margate. Now No 7332 was a rough old dog, far from home at Canton, and by the time it reached Oxford 44min late at 1.20pm, No 7332 seems to have been in dire trouble. The fact that there was another Mogul, No 6350, right behind in even more serious difficulty meant that the whole main line service from the Banbury direction into Snow Hill was badly dislocated for 2hr as No 7332 lost an extra 30min before reaching Tyseley. No 6350 never made it that far at all

Above: Except for one appearance by 'Manor' No 7808, the 9.2am Margate–Birmingham via Reading was a rock solid '43xx' 2-6-0 working on at least 10 Saturdays in summer 1961. A Reading 2-6-0 was generally used, but No 7324 of Didcot managed to appear twice. On the first of these trips from Redhill, dated Saturday 29 July, No 7324 had passed Didcot at 1.25pm, 10min late. Unfortunately by the time it appears at Tyseley in the photograph No 7324's arrears have grown to 38min. Such a deficit made this the least successful trip noted on this train all that summer, though it was never seen less than 7½min late at Tyseley. *Gerald Adams*

and No 6366 behind that inevitably got caught in the backlash.

The story of No 6350 clearly illustrates a whole range of difficulties in obtaining optimum use of second string engines like this one. No 6350 was allocated to an ex-LMS shed, working from the SR at Weymouth right up the spine of the WR on the 9.25am to Wolverhampton. With 10 coaches to handle throughout over 193 miles it was a daunting prospect. To cap it all, the 9.25 had an unrealistically fast schedule even when there was a 4-6-0 on hand to spare for it.

On 9 July Weymouth shed faced its usual Saturday shortage of engines to work six morning expresses for WR destinations, and especially one to handle the 9.25 turn No 2W. Standard Class 5s used for it on at least five 1960 Saturdays were fully committed elsewhere,

'Halls' were in short supply and there was already a '9F' 2-10-0 booked for the 10am turn No 12W. That left the three 71G-based '43xx' 2-6-0s in the front line, but Weymouth was well aware of the limitations of these, its own engines, of which No 7303 was generally retained for banking work up to Bincombe box, and No 6344 worked the 4.30pm stopping passenger from Maiden Newton to Weymouth. Instead foreign Moguls were dug out from Bristol Barrow Road, SPM and Severn Tunnel Jc sheds when necessary to plug the gaps. Unfortunately No 6350 could hardly have been a more unsuitable choice.

Allocated to Barrow Road and generally used for local trip goods work from Westerleigh and Avonmouth to the other Bristol yards, No 6350 had only received sufficient mechanical attention to maintain it for this menial task. Lots of unpopular tender-first running meant maintaining a properly fitting cab storm sheet was just about the most important aspect of its mechanical condition in the normal way. In fact, under a repair regime where a four-year interval was usually the limit even for a 2-6-0, No 6350 had received no classified overhaul since 26 May 1954 when it was outshopped from Caerphilly. No 6350 was taking ages to accumulate its mileage, and all the time its condition was deteriorating. No 6346 of Barrow Road was in a similar state, both with ageing black livery well hidden under layers of dirt.

No 6350 had only got out into general circulation by being loaned from Barrow Road to Swindon the week before, probably to help with the rush of outward bound Swindon Works trip specials on 1/2 July. However, it would be one thing to work one of these over the Tiddly Dyke from Swindon Town to Portsmouth or Poole, quite another to run from Weymouth to Wolverhampton without causing mayhem on the way.

Out of Weymouth assistance would be necessary up the initial 1 in 50 through Bincombe Tunnel, but after that No 6350 was on its own with 10 coaches over Evershot summit, up Brewham and Dauntsey banks. All took their toll. By the time No 6350 pulled into Swindon to change crews they had already been hard at it for three hours. No 6350 came to a stand about 37min late and only just avoided delaying the 11.45am up Bristol two-hour which came roaring through at 12.30pm on the fast line with 'Castle' No 5049 *Earl of Plymouth* well extended, while No 6350 drew what fresh breath it could at the platform.

At Didcot North Jc the paths of Nos 7332 and 6350 converged, with both trains running so late it was a moot point which should go first. No 6350 had to take second place here too, and occupied some 54min to cover the tightly scheduled 34 miles from Swindon to Oxford, by which time it was 55min late. Moguls were tricky engines to fire and, as No 6350 laboured towards Banbury, after $5\frac{1}{2}$hr steaming conditions on

the footplate can only be imagined. The 2-6-0 was unfit to go any further, and appears to have been exchanged there for No 6979 *Helperly Hall* which was probably the Banbury down end station pilot. The 9.25 eventually passed Tyseley at 3.32pm, 89min late. No 6979 reached Stafford Road at 5pm for a quick visit to turn and then got off back to Banbury at 6.41pm.

No 6350 was not seen again until Friday 15 July when it came back light from SPM to Barrow Road. It was then laid up at once, unfit for further use. Officially out of traffic from 19 July onwards, No 6350 did not actually leave for another full repair at Caerphilly until 5 September. On this showing it was lucky to survive that visit at all, but it did and went on working for another $2\frac{1}{2}$ years.

As for the 9.25 it continued its wayward habits regardless of motive power until it ceased to run in September 1961. Four Weymouth Standard 5s and two 'Halls' could do no better than record passing times at Tyseley between 27-80min late Saturday after Saturday in 1960. The Tyseley signalman must have been tempted to do a double take when he was offered the last 9.25 of the year on 10 September and Shrewsbury Standard 5 No 73093 appeared from Weymouth with 12 coaches running only 18min late.

These events south of Birmingham certainly marked the low point of Mogul fortunes during the day on 9 July. Other areas provided rather more fruitful theatres of operation. North of Birmingham they were spearheaded by 22 2-6-0 engines still kept at Tyseley, Shrewsbury and Croes Newydd sheds.

Tyeseley '43xxs' were often involved on Birmingham–Aberystwyth through runs of 124 miles duration in place of booked Standard Class 4 4-6-0s. Sunday excursions on to the Cambrian almost invariably saw '43xxs' rostered, as on 28 August 1960 when No 6363 worked a public excursion from Snow Hill as far as Shrewsbury, where No 7309 took it over for the day's 215-mile round trip to Minffordd and back.

On 9 July the Shrewsbury area provided a happy hunting ground. Apart from No 7330 on Welshpool stopping trains, No 6312 of SPM was well off the beaten track working the Welshpool to Wolverhampton section of the 9.45am Pwllheli-Paddington journey. No 6312 was running this Oxley turn No 9 in place of the sole surviving 84B 2-6-0 No 7339 for which it was booked. There was even a '43xx' on the up 'Cambrian Coast Express', though this one was unidentified as it negotiated the far side of the Abbey Foregate triangle, well on its way ready to hand over the train pretty punctually at Wolverhampton to 'King' No 6012.

But the most evocative sight at Shrewsbury was No 5339, the third highest mileage Mogul of all, knocking on 1,450,000 miles, and whose first home shed had been at Salop way back in January 1918. This engine was gamely fighting its way up from the south on the 7am Paignton-Colne relief.

That train had first been seen earlier in the day at Newton Abbot behind Worcester 'Hall' No 6947 *Helmingham Hall*, and when it ran the 7am usually changed locos at Bristol Temple Meads. With so many engines already earmarked for work elsewhere, it is likely that the Bristol sheds had nothing larger than a 2-6-0 to spare for the stage on to Shrewsbury. Being a train running only on an 'as required' basis, the 7am inevitably came close to the back of the queue for power. Although SPM had a substantial allocation of 14 '43xx' which was currently the largest anywhere, like the 'Granges' there, they got around far and wide. So even releasing one of these 2-6-0s was no easy matter. Six were on express work during the day working as far afield as Paddington, Wolverhampton, Minehead, Barnstaple, Salisbury and Cardiff. Others were on freight duty, and No 5385 had found its way to Croes Newydd by Sunday. At the same time only two other old '43xxs', Nos 5311 and 5337, were left at SPM, both of them on their last legs and shortly due for withdrawal. They were presumably even less desirable mounts for the 7am Paignton than No 5339, which itself had under five months left in traffic before the final call.

So No 5339 it had to be, probably on its last express run, and the unfortunate crew were likely to be only too well aware that they were in for a hard time before

they had even taken the engine off shed. Although the 7am Paignton had a relatively clear path following No 4975 *Umberslade Hall*, which was working right time through to Shrewsbury on the 6.35am Paignton–Wigan, a lot of time was lost. By the time No 5339 reached Salop at around 2.5pm, where 5A Class 5 No 44761 took over, the 7am had fallen about 80min behind the 6.35. However, it is likely that some of the arrears may have been debitable to No 6947 earlier in the journey, as No 6947 was anything between 15-30min late passing Taunton.

Another SPM engine with a different story to tell was green-liveried 2-6-0 No 6374 which on Friday worked the 4.35pm Millbay–Paddington parcels,

Below: This magnificent picture is full of summer Saturday atmosphere. It is a classic example of how '43xx' Moguls could be saddled with work which would stretch far larger engines than this one. No 5313 is roaring over the top of Nantyderry bank with 12 coaches on the 9.5am Birkenhead–Plymouth and Cardiff express on Saturday 14 September 1957. Despite working through from Chester, No 5313 still has plenty of steam, though no reports of its timekeeping have yet emerged. The train is made up with three Chester–Plymouth coaches on the front, then four from Birkenhead to Plymouth and five from Birkenhead to Cardiff. Chester or Oxley engines were generally used on the 9.5 that year, but No 5313 of Oxley was the only 2-6-0 recorded. *R. O. Tuck*

known in some quarters as the 'first perishables'. This was one of three weekday services bringing perishable produce up from the west and No 6374 hauled what was often a heavy train, clearing as many vans as possible from Plymouth before the weekend, as far as Bristol. After servicing at SPM overnight No 6374 coupled on to next morning's 5.30am from Paddington. On Saturdays the 5.30 ran to Minehead instead of Penzance, and No 6374 took it through from Bristol over the branch. Although it was too long for the tiny 4-4-0 sized turntable at Minehead and the awkward business of attaching turntable extensions had to be adopted, No 6374 then ran a couple of vital trips to Taunton. Along with No 5376, also of SPM, this helped release Taunton's own 2-6-0s for working through services to the SR serving Barnstaple Jc and Ilfracombe. They had complete domination of these trains by virtue of automatic token exchangers to facilitate running through the crossing loops at 40mph, and cut back cab steps to provide adequate clearance at Barnstaple. Dogged hard work by the 2-6-0s was needed to handle packed 280-ton through portions from London and Birmingham over a succession of 1 in 58/60 gradients, making full use of their marked ability to accelerate quickly from frequent slowings on the way.

Yet another SPM '43xx', No 7301, was at Cardiff Canton. Here they had suffered effects of run-down and grossly overloaded Moguls for years, and as late as 23 August 1958 had experienced eight down express arrivals at Cardiff behind 2-6-0s from all points of the compass. These recorded an average lateness between them of 30min each, which was nearly double the average of lost time for all down arrivals that day. Mogul movements had dropped by about half in summer 1959 and now for 1960 Canton was hardly expecting to need any at all on expresses. However,

there was the big advantage that if a '43xx' was required here, the best could now be selected from those available. On 8 July 1960 these included Nos 6326, 6338, 6352 and 7338 seen at Canton, with No 7301 working in later. Of these No 7301 with a 1960 overhaul date was clearly the best, so it was promptly marked down to fill a shortage next day on the 9am Cardiff–Portsmouth.

The stock was late reaching platform one at the General from Canton sheds, and so No 7301 pulled away 11min late before regaining a minute by Newport. The load was observed here as 13 coaches, but it is most unlikely that Canton would have risked even its best Mogul on a load of such magnitude by this stage. The booked and usual load on the 9am was 10 coaches which seems more probable. This would avoid any need to provide assistance through the Severn Tunnel, though it would still be tight against a 312-ton limit up Dilton Marsh bank where one of Westbury's 0-6-2Ts Nos 5689 or 6625 was usually on hand to assist. Anyway No 7301 must have held its own to Salisbury, arriving before midday. The Canton crew then had a couple of hours to turn the engine and rest before relieving an SR locomotive on the 11.37am Portsmouth–Cardiff. This was late coming in, so instead of leaving at 1.22pm No 7301 had to contend with a departure 24min behind time. It passed the Salisbury observer a mile west of the station, getting under way at 1.55pm, with No 5936 *Oakley Hall* also late on the 11am Brighton-Cardiff 11min behind.

Schedules on this route were certainly easy. They had probably been arranged as much with the extensive participation of 2-6-0s in mind as any other motive power. Even so, No 7301 did well with 10 coaches. It called at Westbury, filling a handy lull at the station while nearby the afternoon rush of

Left: On Saturday 9 July 1960 2-6-0 No 6365 runs into Oxford virtually on time with the 10.45am Birmingham–Brighton. Hauling 11 coaches through from Redhill on this train was a hard assignment for one of these engines. *Mike Lake*

Left: 2-6-0 No 7320 has dropped the Pembroke Dock portion of its train at Whitland and only three coaches now remain of the 8.55am from Paddington, 'Capitals United Express', to be worked to Neyland. 2-6-0s were economical power for these light West Wales services and No 7320 is seen near Clynderwen in June 1962. *Mike Esau*

Left: Even as late as June 1962, the 6.50pm up Mail from Neyland to Paddington might be worked by any variation of a 'County', 'Hall' or '43XX' 2-6-0 as far as Camarthen. With its Royal Mail van for Bristol attached behind the engine 2-6-0 No 7318 leaves Neyland and prepares for the climb to Johnston in a most attractive picture which, while it may look superficially familiar, has never been published before. *Alison M. Esau.*

Cornish expresses to Paddington was in full swing on the cut-off line. At Bathampton No 7301 was nicely placed to join the Bristol line procession right behind No 1009 *County of Carmarthen* on the 1.15pm from Paddington. No 7301 then called at Stapleton Road and despite having to climb Filton bank from a standing start No 7301 had regained enough time to stay ahead of No 6946 *Heatherden Hall* coming up the parallel relief line to Filton on the 12.5pm Paignton–Cardiff right behind it.

By that stage no less than nine minutes had already been recovered from Salisbury, but No 7301 was still one path adrift approaching the Severn Tunnel bottleneck. Luckily it was in a position to take the 12.5pm Paignton's path at Patchway and from there apparently enjoyed a remarkably clear road all the way to Cardiff. Here the train pulled up at 4.31pm, a mere 8min late. Even taking into account No 7301's charmed life on this run, 16min time regained was good going. After seeing 2-6-0s in such serious difficulty elsewhere it is a particular pleasure to be able to show this other side of the coin in what appears to be among the best examples of actual time recovery anywhere on the Western that day. No 5936 did nearly as well, recovering 12min on the Brighton. Having sorted out its '43xx' selection policy successfully, Canton was still regularly using 2-6-0s on Cardiff–Newcastle expresses in 1962 even though the place was already crawling with Hymek diesels by then.

Nine '43xxs' formed the backbone of secondary power at Gloucester and when required these were also to be found on Newcastle-Cardiff expresses. Whilst fulfilling this function was not necessary on 9 July, No 6381 was out early on the 6.43am Cheltenham–Cardiff stopping train and it then came straight back on the 500-ton 10.35am Pengam–Barnwood 7T91 freight. Through beautiful countryside other Gloucester engines would be storming the 1 in 60 climb up May Hill on Hereford line locals. They often put up performances along here which were every bit as exciting as anything to be found on the main line. A picked Gloucester '43xx' was well known as a good runner and during 1960 Tyseley managed to get its hands on three for one summer Saturday turn alone.

Of these No 6365 was ex-works in April, painted lined green, and on 9 July it appeared at the head of the 10.45am Birmingham–Brighton, Eastbourne and Hastings. With 11 coaches on, No 6365 had to make times like 27min to Leamington which would not have disgraced a 'Castle'; No 6365 did it too, and left Oxford nicely set for the through run to Redhill running 30sec early. Oxford was humming with 2-6-0 activity. Within two hours up to 1.50pm eight '43xxs' were to be seen at work, and without them the motive power situation would have been untenable.

Therefore it can be clearly understood that, despite their limitations, '43xx' 2-6-0s were still making a sterling contribution to the WR's summer Saturday effort. That day No 6364 was logged in detail with nine coaches on the 9.5am Birmingham–Portsmouth, and it must have run at speeds comparable to those attained by No 6365 on the 10.45 less than 2hr later.

No 6364 left Snow Hill on time and passed Olton in 8min making 55mph on the gradual uphill gradient. It then suffered a signal check to 36mph at Solihull, possibly after catching up with 'King' No 6011 on the 9am Snow Hill departure in front. No 6364 managed a good recovery back to 55mph on the level through Knowle and by Lapworth speed had increased to 61mph on more favourable gradients. Nevertheless the signal check had cost 1½min and No 6364 was still a minute late passing Hatton. The driver then let No 6364 go down Hatton bank, reaching close on 80mph, and they came to a stand at Leamington in 29min, a minute early. The net time was only 27½min from Birmingham and the concluding 6.1 miles from Hatton were covered in only 6½min.

Leaving Leamington on time at 9.38am No 6364 climbed the 1 in 187 past Fosse Road box at 43mph before falling off to 41mph at Harbury. With the train running comfortably on time there was no need to rush downhill after passing Cropredy at 58mph and No 6365 arrived at Banbury ¼min early. 19.8 miles from Leamington had occupied 26¼min. Leaving Banbury at 10.7½am the final 23.7 miles to Oxford were easily scheduled in 31min and after passing Heyford at 60mph No 6364 had no difficulty in reducing this time to 28½min. It reached Oxford 3min early after an excellent performance. This demonstrated how well No 6365 must have run with 11 coaches on a schedule which was one minute faster overall from Birmingham to Oxford than that maintained by No 6364.

The Oxford observer had a real Mogul day out on 9 July, coming back with No 6349 on the 3.30pm Oxford–Birmingham. However, this was an express of only three coaches delayed by a wait at Oxford which made No 6349's departure 13¾min late, while the 1.11pm from Portsmouth Harbour was allowed to go on ahead. The 1.11 with No 4986 *Aston Hall* preceded the 3.30 until the 1.11 was turned on to the relief line ready to go into Birmingham Moor St. Until then No 6349 was snapping at the heels of No 4986 the whole way from Oxford. No 6349's top speed of 62mph at Fenny Compton was largely incidental, but with No 4986 running early in front, No 6349 was nevertheless able to recover all but 4min of its late departure by Snow Hill. Here No 6349 arrived at 5.11pm in a running time of 82min from Oxford.

Far away from Oxford, but making an equally important contribution, were another seven active 2-6-0s seen working north and west out of Carmarthen. Five and six-coach through portions off

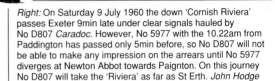

London trains were ideally weighted for '43xx' haulage, and on these Neyland and Carmarthen locos had plenty of brisk running every day under express headcodes. The services involved called at all stations beyond St Clears so the express bit was a little misleading, but these '43xxs' maintained a strong Churchward flavour down there on 9 July. At Carmarthen they took over the 10.55am, 11.35, 1.55pm and 3.55 trains from Paddington to West Wales as well as working to Aberystwyth. There was another diagrammed for the 8.55am down too on 87G turn No 200, but Carmarthen supplied one of its 'Halls', No 4962, for this, relieving No 5013 *Abergavenny Castle* when the train reversed there.

Even down in deepest west Wales not all the 2-6-0 turns were easy, however. There were only four big engines at Neyland and '43xxs' had to be ready to face up to any of the Neyland 'County' duties when required. So in the evening out came 2-6-0 No 7306 for the 6.50pm up mail, booked load seven for Paddington with TPO van to Bristol, though '43xxs' were allowed to take up to 11 bogies from Neyland when required. Having weathered the initial 1 in 75 climb away from the Cleddau estuary on to the moors before Johnston, the rest of this 40-mile journey was a series of sharp switchback gradients with six stops on the way. No 7306 reached Carmarthen on time at 8.20pm. Here No 5016 *Montgomery Castle* was waiting to add a sleeping car, before hauling the train on to Swansea. No 7306 then had an hour to turn at Camarthen before collecting the down 'Capitals United Express' loaded three coaches each for Fishguard and Neyland.

There were other 2-6-0 workings noted all over South Wales and no doubt plenty more too originating at Machynlleth and Croes Newydd. But No 7306 had probably the last '43xx' express turn of the day, so we leave it in the dusk, crossing the bascule bridge out of Carmarthen and then shooting stars as it tackled the 1 in 95 climb up to Sarnau. A well-maintained '43xx' was a great machine but if the thought of these frisky '43xxs' brings tears of nostalgia to your eyes, remember too that they brought tears to the eyes of their crews for very different reasons when allowed to fall into poor condition. Searching out all the soft spots in the track and with boiler pressure hard to maintain anywhere near the 200lb mark, these 2-6-0s were often an unnecessary trial when so many '9F' 2-10-0s were lying about unused on summer weekends. They must have made the prospect of dieselisation seem much more attractive, though of course in the case of places like Neyland that heralded an entirely false dawn. Other areas were more fortunate and already they were shaping the future.

D800 Type 4 Diesels

After two years of intensive evaluation the Swindon-built D800 'Warship' class diesels were now giving

Right: On Saturday 9 July 1960 the down 'Cornish Riviera' passes Exeter 9min late under clear signals hauled by No D807 *Caradoc*. However, No 5977 with the 10.22am from Paddington has passed only 5min before, so No D807 will not be able to make any impression on the arrears until No 5977 diverges at Newton Abbot towards Paignton. On this journey No D807 will take the 'Riviera' as far as St Erth. *John Hodge*

Below right: Taunton's No 5992 *Horton Hall* assists ailing 'Warship' No D839 *Relentless* out of Whiteball Tunnel with the 7.45am Paddington–Paignton which has come via Bristol. This train is now so late on Saturday 18 August 1962 that it is running some way behind the 10.5am Paddington departure. The leading Great Western Centenary coach is wide enough to emphasise the compact size of the 'Warship' diesel–hydraulic, as redesigned at Swindon from the more generously proportioned DB 'V200' class. *Mike Fox*

good results in service, even if not all their teething troubles had yet been overcome. To help offset an enormous building cost of £120,000 per unit they were proving capable of running 120,000 miles per year, whilst averaging 380 miles for every day's use in traffic. This was a big improvement on 45-55,000 miles a year being achieved by express steam 4-6-0s. Furthermore, the diesels were carrying out this work at a saving of some 40% in fuel costs. Official figures are hard to come by. This calculation of fuel saving is based on a price of 11d per gallon for diesel oil (DMU fuel cost 10.95d in 1962) at a consumption of 1.0mpg; and coal costing £4.5s per ton (an average 1960 price for all grades from NCB figures) at 40lb use per mile. No allowance is made for lighting up or idling. The end result is similar using figures quoted by Mr E. S. Cox during 1959 when he stated BR fuel oil costs were £16 per ton (1s 3d per gal) against £4 10s per ton for coal.

Of 24 'Warships' in stock, no less than 21 were seen at work on 9 July. So good was their availability that when a photo of an unidentified 'Warship' equipped with four-character indicator box on the front turned up, crossing Liskeard viaduct during the morning of 9 July, it could only be No D819 *Goliath*, because all the other 'Warships' of this series were already accounted for. No 'Warships' were in Swindon Works and there were no failures in traffic on 9 July either. Was it any surprise that Swindon was pursuing its diesel-hydraulic programme with enthusiasm? Even when tempered by an element of caution the potential savings were very great if these results could be maintained.

Unfortunately they couldn't. Quite apart from high initial outlay, the 'Warships' were still subject to expensive development costs to improve their riding, engine cooling capability and train heating reliability, not to mention heavy expenditure on routine renewals.

Three quarters of the 'Warships' in service were less than a year old, and could therefore be termed brand-new in summer 1960. They would be expected to perform at their best on the pick of intensive long distance diesel diagrams arranged specially and annual mileage figures tended to decline to a marked extent in future years, though they obviously still showed a significant improvement over what had ever been achieved with steam on the Western.

In the short term there was a price to pay in pushing utilisation of the diesel fleet beyond a certain point from week to week. Thus while availability of 'Warships' was good on 9 July they were much more intensively operated on the following weekend. What made 9 July such a good weekend for 'Kings' and for steam generally was that the 9.30am and 10.15am departures from Paddington were steam on 9 July but diesel on 16 July. Similarly, in the opposite direction the 8.15am Perranporth, up 'Torbay Express' and 12.30pm Newquay were diesel-worked to Paddington on 16 July. But that second Saturday there was a penalty for this extra activity with high profile failures of Nos D802 *Formidable*, D808 *Centaur*, and D823 *Hermes*.

Working the 10am Newquay–Paddington, one of No D802's motors cut out 14 times before Exeter, so this, the heaviest train of the day, had to stop at Exeter West box to obtain assistance. 'Castle' No 5020 *Trematon Castle* was fortunately on up standby duty and when No D802 came to a halt the 'Castle' was ready to couple on inside. Thirty minutes late at 2.6pm they set off again 'with No 5020 barking away and apparently pushing No D802 and hauling 15 coaches'. Meanwhile No D800 on the up 'Riviera' was kept waiting behind and eventually passed Exeter 17min late. Even so it came through long before the down 'Riviera' on which No D808 had had to attach the Reading pilot, which was again 'Hall' No 6923. This pair did not appear until 2.27pm running 44min late.

Still on 16 July a disastrous failure also overtook the 1.20pm Penzance-Paddington hauled by two 'D63xx' diesels when NB Type 2 No D6306 expired altogether on Hayle bank. As it was not permissible for the failed diesel to be dumped in a siding, the second 'D63xx' attached, No D6309, could not proceed with 13 coaches. The Drump Lane Shunter, Pannier No 3702, was therefore put on in front and this curious cavalcade took the train to Redruth. Here No 7806 *Cockington Manor* had been dispatched from Truro to replace No 3702, and eventually Plymouth was reached 93min late. By this time No 7022 *Hereford Castle* on the 1.45pm Newquay–Paddington had been held back to take up the path of the 1.20pm Penzance and No 7022 probably had to make all the 1.20's four calls on the way to London too, instead of running up nonstop. The 1.20 itself was also a regular Saturday steam turn beyond Plymouth, and, instead of the usual 'Castle', Laira had to use a Shrewsbury 'Modified Hall' No 7922

Salford Hall off an a morning arrival, probably the 6.58pm from Glasgow due at 10.22am. Nevertheless, with No D6312 as pilot, some modest time recovery had begun when No 7922 arrived at Newton Abbot 91min late. From there onwards, however, the 1.20 was far too fast to be timed successfully by a 'Hall' with 13 coaches. More lost time was unfortunately inevitable.

In terms of mileage covered, however, the Type 4 diesels were in a league of their own. During the mid-1950s only about four steam engines would be able to manage a return trip over the Paddington–West of England main line during daylight hours, even on the busiest summer Saturday. Although the service was not yet reorganised to increase the scope for round trips, seven diesels did so on 9 July, a marked improvement. But it was the ability of the 'Warships' to do yet another trip overnight which really gave them the edge.

No D806 *Cambrian* worked the 8.10am Paddington–Paignton on Saturday morning. It then came back with the 2.45pm Paignton–Paddington, clocking up over 400 miles in the process. No D806 then rounded this off by penetrating right through to Penzance on the 11.15pm Saturday night newspaper train.

All sorts of other permutations were now possible, even within the restricted Paddington–Bristol–Penzance area where crews were trained to drive 'Warships'. A Paddington–Bristol–Paddington–Kingswear–Paddington programme was handled by No D821 *Greyhound*. Penzance–Bristol–Plymouth–Paddington, taking in the 4.50pm Penzance–Manchester, 12.45am Manchester–Plymouth and the up 'Riviera', was part of No D817 *Foxhound's* routine when we encountered it at Bristol in the 'Dawn Chorus' earlier. No D817 must then have returned to Plymouth on Saturday night because it came up again next day with the 1.10pm Penzance–Paddington. By contrast 'Castle' No 5075, which had preceded No D817 west to Plymouth on Saturday morning, was only required to make a local trip to Newton Abbot. However, in the event of a diesel failure No 5075 might well have been needed for something more demanding.

In practice, 'Warship' timekeeping was good, and lost time was usually attributable to delays from conflicting traffic. Full power (notch 6 or 7 depending on the individual locomotive) provided something in hand for even the heaviest of 15-coach loads on summer Saturday schedules.

Right at the other end of the scale No D819 *Goliath* was being retained in the West of England on 9 July ready to take up the first 'Warship' workings on china clay traffic at St Blazey from the following Monday, 11 July. On services like the 10.10am St Blazey–Fowey a 'Warship' was allowed to take 22 loaded wagons compared to 20 for a '42xx' 2-8-0T. This move was immediately hailed as a great improvement, which it undoubtedly was when crews compared the comfort of a 'Warship' to threading the narrow steeply graded bore of Pinnock tunnel in the open cab of a hard-working steam tank engine. The reputation of 'Warships' for versatility was significantly enhanced by this success, especially at the end of the week when No D819 was released from china clay work in time to work the 12.30pm Newquay–Paddington on 16 July and down 'Riviera' back on Sunday. Not even a trusty '42xx' tank could achieve that in a week's work! The same Sunday afternoon, 17 July, No D816 *Eclipse* came down light from Plymouth to take the place of No D819 at St Blazey for the following week. By 2 August 2-8-OT No 5264, which had been on loan to St Blazey from Duffryn Yard, was making its way in stages back through Teignmouth to South Wales. However, doubts about diesel braking capability, and the effects of power surge caused when changing gear on these loose coupled freights, may already have been creeping in. It was to be 1962 before the last 2-8-OT in Cornwall could be finally dispensed with.

The newest 'Warships' on 9 July 1960 were No D823 *Hermes* from Swindon and D833 *Panther*, the first of the North British-built series, which were both commissioned three days earlier. Now No D823 celebrated its entry into traffic on 9 July with a Works Trip special from Swindon to Paignton and back. This run was successful, because No D823 was in regular service by the following Saturday, working the 8.15am Perranporth-Paddington in place of 'King' No 6016 which had appeared on 9 July.

Unfortunately its initiation on 16 July was not at all successful, and somewhere around Frome or Westbury No D823 also had to stop to pick up steam assistance. From being 2min early into Newton Abbot and just 3min late passing Exeter, things degenerated to such an extent that, by the time No D823 came through Twyford with No 5935 *Norton Hall* attached, it was 86min behind schedule. The Westbury and Frome avoiding lines were invaluable in this situation. Fortunately they enabled the press of up London trains which left Exeter behind the Perranporth to get ahead, and each of these was delayed only to the tune of 20min or so. However, it is a fact that with diesel problems on the 10am Newquay and 1.20pm Penzance already described, only two of the day's expresses from Cornwall to London on 16 July failed to feel the effects of delays resulting from diesel failures — and one of those was steam-worked by 'County' No 1014 on the up 'Royal Duchy' in place of the usual diesel.

Acceptance of No D833 from North British was a much more protracted business, no doubt because there were fundamental changes to engines and transmissions fitted on this series which required evaluation. Bitter experience of previous diesels from this source may also have encouraged a cautious approach.

D600 Type 4s

The five North British-built D600 diesels were still working alongside the Swindon 'Warships' on an equal footing, though they did have a couple of relatively regular passenger diagrams of their own. No D601 *Ark Royal* had charge of the most notable of these on both Friday and Saturday 8/9 July. During the week this involved taking the 12 Noon Penzance–Manchester from Plymouth as far as Bristol and then carrying straight on to Paddington with the 6.55pm from Weston. After a couple of hours turn-around the diesel then returned to Plymouth on the fast but light 12.30am down newspapers. No D600 *Active* also appeared on the 14-coach 10.37am Paddington–Penzance as far as Plymouth, a Saturday train with which it had been associated from its earliest days in 1958.

The last three North British D600 'Warships' with Glasgow-built engines were poor performers. They suffered from variable power output and uncertain reliability. Each of them in turn spent extended periods under repair during 1960, though not always as a result of mechanical shortcomings. No D602 *Bulldog* had suffered collision damage on 15 December 1959 which involved extensive repairs. It was still at Swindon in May 1960. No D603 *Conquest* received damage to both its cabs in another accident during 1960. This time repairs were undertaken by North British, when the opportunity was taken to carry out numerous minor modifications. In the event, virtually nothing was seen of these three on 9 July although one of the class was also noted at work in Cornwall on the 11.10pm Manchester-Penzance.

A very similar pattern of operations was evident the following Saturday when Nos D600 and D601 exchanged duties, though on this occasion No D600 must have worked right through from Paddington to Penzance on the 12.30am newspapers. It returned to Plymouth on the up 'Riviera' before making for Paddington again on the 12 Noon mail from Penzance. From 4pm Friday onwards it therefore amassed 874 miles in only 32hr. Again, however, nothing was seen of Nos D602–4 east of Plymouth.

No D603 was back in regular service shortly afterwards and spent much of its time around the turn of the month powering the 5.30pm down 'Mayflower'. On Saturday 30 July No D603 ran to Kingswear on the 'Torbay Express', and, with No D604 also back in traffic, the type's big day finally came round a week later on 6 August. No D602 was booked for the down 'Riviera', No D601 followed on the 10.37am from Paddington and No D604 was to haul the 'Torbay Express'.

Unfortunately the down 'Riviera' was remanned at Newton Abbot on the way, and Old Oak had overlooked the fact that the fresh crew were not trained to drive this type. No D602 therefore had to come off the train at Newton Abbot. It was sent

Left: Recent attention to North British 'Warship' No D602 *Bulldog* at Swindon has not extended to a repaint, but on Sunday 24 July 1960 No D602 is at least back in traffic. It waits at Didcot with a regular diesel trial turn on the 2.20pm Paddington–Swindon parcels, before resuming express work from Laira. *Frank Hornby*

Right: The 6.50am Paddington–Penzance crosses the Royal Albert Bridge into Saltash on 9 July 1960 powered by a pair of NB Type 2 diesels. On 2 July this express was hauled by No 6824 *Ashley Grange* beyond Plymouth, so there was considerable variation in motive power on some trains in Cornwall from one week to the next during 1960. *Hugh Davies*

straight off to Plymouth light diesel during the height of the afternoon rush, still in the charge of its London crew. A hasty search of Newton Abbot loco resulted in No 6800 *Arlington Grange* being called up to join No D6311 on the down 'Riviera', but all this manoeuvring severely delayed No D601 waiting behind on the 10.37.

No D604 made it solo no further than Newbury where one of its engines must have shut down. It was a Stafford Road 'Modified Hall', No 6987 *Shervington Hall*, probably whilst standing at Reading, where it would be facing down ready to leave for Basingstoke to collect a Portsmouth–Wolverhampton working, which received the summons to help the stricken diesel. Running on one engine No D604 might well be able to muddle through with a weekday load, but not when pulling 13 packed coaches on a Saturday. Even with No 6987 leading, they were 80min late passing Taunton and lost more time all the way to Exeter where the 'Torbay' was 88min late. No D604 was also detached at Newton Abbot and forwarded limping to Plymouth, leaving its train still standing at the platform.

Such serious set-backs left North British with little room for manoeuvre when the time came to fend off guarantee claims as more of its diesels entered service. Eventually this famous company collapsed altogether in 1962, though appropriately its surviving steam engines continued to uphold North British's great reputation as a locomotive builder for many more years on foreign railways throughout the world.

D6300 Type 2s

The D6300s were such a doubtful proposition that on 9 July not one was seen working any train on its own. They did have some solo midweek turns on Newquay locals by this time, but all their weekend work was carried out either in multiple or double-heading. The general attitude to the ability of a single 'D63xx' was

well illustrated by the reaction of the Southern Region to their daily use on exchange local passenger trains from Plymouth to Exeter via Okehampton. After a period which was characterised by call-outs to rescue some total breakdowns in remote locations, the Southern was understandably critical of the problems they caused. Poor availability of 'D63xxs' and the intention to dieselise as many trains as possible west of Plymouth resulted in the exchange services reverting to '43xx' steam haulage for a time after May 1960.

On 9 July there were probably about six 'D63xx' pairs operating in multiple between Plymouth and Penzance or Newquay, and another seven or so individually assisting over the South Devon banks. Next weekend there were at least seven pairs to be seen in Cornwall and another seven or eight handling assistant work during the day. On both occasions a disproportionate number of the earliest batch were tucked away out of view. These could only be coupled in multiple with one of the same early series which further affected their usefulness.

Economically there was not a lot of benefit in this mode of operation over the Cornish main line. In most instances a pair of diesels merely replaced one steam locomotive. On really heavy trains a Type 4 diesel or steam 4-6-0 was required as well as one or two Type 2s. Where a pair of Type 2s replaced one steam engine diesel fuel consumption was more costly than coal, and as mileages covered were similar to the old steam diagrams, there were few savings in this direction either.

The same Type 2 pairs did not apparently stay coupled for more than a day or two at a time, though Nos D6307 and D6317 did remain together on 14 and 16 July. Similarly Nos D6311 and D6322 worked in multiple on 16 July and were both noted at St Blazey on 19 July. There was no attempt to exploit operating flexibility at this stage by mixing work in pairs with solo duty over the South Devon banks in any one

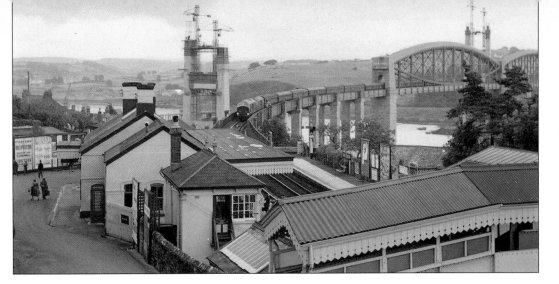

diagram. Once a pair were coupled they apparently stayed coupled until they returned to Laira or St Blazey. When one failed they still stayed coupled, relying on the other 'D63xx' to drag the casualty home. In this respect the work of the Type 2s was less adaptable than their steam predecessors. It also explains why, though there were a lot of diesels about in Devon and Cornwall, they still left plenty of summer Saturday work to be covered with steam power.

Having said that, the overall standard of Type 2 work cannot have been so bad, because assistant duty over the South Devon banks was not a job to be undertaken lightly. 'D63xxs' handled a large proportion of the daytime pilot turns, and it was only the unbalanced nature of Friday night assistant work, as the heavy westbound traffic built up, that prevented them taking a similar preponderance of the overnight activity. Clearly in a situation where a 'D63xx' diesel was assisting a heavily loaded 'Castle' or 'Hall' like No 5093 *Upton Castle* with 14 coaches on the 8.25am Paddington–Perranporth, a total engine failure on Dainton bank could cause massive disruption. But there is no evidence that anything of this nature occurred to cause serious delay on the South Devon banks during summer 1960.

All except the first eight of the Type 2s up to No D6333 were new in 1960 and they were going through what was probably the most productive period of their short lives. They had certainly been pitched in at the deep end when they had to tackle holiday loads over the South Devon banks and across Cornwall. It has to be said that, despite their deficiencies, the 'D63xxs' made a much better attempt at the job than the first cross-country type diesel multiple-units managed to achieve when they were drafted in down there, even though some steam locomotives had to be retained at Laira, Newton Abbot and Penzance to cover diesel shortcomings.

Despite such set-backs, the Western was steadily following its policy of extending total dieselisation area by area. The transition from steam was already well advanced in the West Country and, above all, it was orderly. The degeneration of this policy within a couple of years was to prove both wasteful and costly. Such a fundamental change of plan could only be justified by new management as part of a determined drive to reorganise all aspects of running the railway. This reorganisation was also to prove the downfall of diesel-hydraulics themselves before very long, despite the enormous expense of building them in the first place.

Right: Class '51xx' 2-6-2T No 4167 is assisting No D6322 in front of No D6312 which has failed with the 6.50am Plymouth–Penzance as they depart from St Austell on Monday 25 April 1960. No 4167 was attached at Par. Repeated attempts to dieselise this train during 1960 met with little success and it was December before any consistent degree of dieselisation was achieved. *Maurice Dart*

Left: The 2.10pm down to Birkenhead is ready to leave Platform No 4 at Paddington with No 6027 *King Richard I* on a 13-coach load for Wolverhampton. The 2.10pm was prone to delay in the mid-afternoon congestion beyond Banbury, as on 9 July 1960 when No 6027 was also in charge of this train, and on Saturday 20 August 1960, the date of the photograph, No 6027 was 27min late reaching Snow Hill. *John Hodge*

Above: At Paddington No 70024 *Vulcan* has already arrived on the 'Red Dragon' long enough beforehand for the A35 reporting numbers to be changed to F55 ready for the down journey on the 3.55pm 'Capitals United Express', yet there are still plenty of bystanders milling around on Platform No 8 beside the cab rank. It is Wednesday 24 May 1961 and No 70024 is in the middle of its month's high mileage running at Canton. *John Hodge*

Left: On 9 July 1960 Laira 'King' No 6002 *King William IV* comes through Taunton in a hurry running 6min early on the 9.30am Paddington–Newquay. The up main signals are clear for No 4083 *Abbotsbury Castle* to pass shortly with the 10.35am Torquay–Paddington. *John Cornelius*

4. PUNCTUALITY — GOOD AND BAD

On 9 July most trains ran well, according to undemanding schedules. Many expresses were sighted at a number of points during their travels across the Western Region, so a reasonable assessment of their progress — successful or otherwise — can often be made.

Beside the West of England main line at one stage during the afternoon there were observers on watch at Newton Abbot, Exeter, Taunton, Frome, Savernake, Twyford and West Ealing, as well as at Paddington itself. Even though there was endless scope for a succession of delays between these points, not much that was important seems to have escaped the eagle eye of one or more of these interested onlookers. At the same time, records of punctuality at Bristol, Swindon, Newport, Cardiff, Oxford and Birmingham Snow Hill give a good insight into operations on other Western main lines, as well as providing minute by minute information about flows of traffic through these major centres. First we are therefore able to examine movements at three different points for periods of ½ or 1hr during the morning.

Paddington

Few places could rival the sheer intensity of long distance departures which had to be dealt with at Paddington. From 6am onwards there was a constant procession of empty trains using the two up engine and carriage roads from Old Oak Common into the terminus. These fed six main line departure platforms and culminated in a series of 11 expresses starting out in one hour between 8.30 and 9.30am. All of them were steam-worked. Seeing 'Kings' and 'Castles' ranged right across the country end of the station, as each waited in turn for the RA platform indicators to light up, it was impossible to believe that this was a scene which would be decimated within three years.

The last coaches of the long 8.25am to Perranporth had barely disappeared with No 5093 *Upton Castle* before No 6029 *King Edward VIII* was on the move with the 8.30am 2hr Birmingham express, strictly limited to nine coaches on its 'Special Load' timing.

At 8.35am No 5039 *Rhuddlan Castle* was the first of the daily quintet of top-link Landore 'Castles' away off to Swansea. It was the previous evening's 'Pembroke Coast Express' engine and in good shape. At Reading, Swindon Works apprentice Gryffyd Evans, while returning home to Tregaron on holiday, joined this 10-coach train, and he clocked No 5039 leaving a minute

late at 9.20am. Despite the fact that No 5039 should have had a clear headway of 26min at Swindon, the 8.35 was heavily signal checked as it approached. Less surprising was another severe signal slowing after Pilning as No 5039 descended towards the Severn Tunnel. Possibly it was obstructed by the 10.44am Pilning-Severn Tunnel Jc car ferry train. This was due to arrive at the junction only 8min before the 8.35 was scheduled through. Even so, the 121min schedule for 97½ miles from Reading to Newport was easy. No 5039 was on time into Newport and a minute early at Cardiff. Later in the day after pausing for service at Landore No 5039 should have been out again on the 8.5pm Swansea–Fishguard, 3.45pm ex-Paddington, but Landore had no shortage of 'Castles' and an old 'forty', No 4099 *Kilgerran Castle*, was supplied for this train instead.

With only one down main track available through Reading there had to be a 10min interval for the 8.35am down to call there before the 8.45am Paignton departure could leave Paddington nonstop to Exeter. This involved 'Hall' No 6974 on its spectacularly successful run mentioned earlier when it arrived 13min before time. If the 214min schedule to Exeter was anything but a rush job, so too the 8.50am down Bristol and Weston-super-Mare train bore absolutely no resemblance to the weekday 8.45am 'Bristolian', even though it utilised the same stock. No 7030 *Cranbrook Castle* had nearly twice the weekday load, but was it really necessary for such an important train to be allowed 38min extra to Temple Meads on Saturdays? No wonder the 'Bristolian' destination boards were reversed at weekends. The 8.50 formed a surprisingly rare through engine working from Paddington to Weston, the enthusiasm for engine changing at Bristol amounting almost to an addiction, and sometimes a wasteful one at that.

The run of Old Oak-powered departures from 8.45 to 9.15am was broken only by the second Landore engine starting for home at 8.55am. A resplendent No 7021 *Haverfordwest Castle* was fresh off the up Friday 'Pullman' and although hauling a tonnage virtually up to the route limit of 455 tons, No 7021 had no trouble keeping time all the way down for another early arrival at Cardiff. The 8.55 reversed at Swansea High St where No 5013 *Abergavenny Castle* was the new engine, and again at Carmarthen where No 4962 *Ragley Hall* coupled on the nine West Wales coaches. At Whitland No 4962 had to uncouple while the main Pembroke Dock portion at the front left for the branch, probably with a small Prairie. No 4962 then collected the Neyland coaches again to cover the final stage of a 260-mile journey which it was due to complete at 4.5pm.

On the 9am down Pwllheli train, notes of the running by No 6012 *King Edward VI* were taken by distinguished schoolmaster and railway authority the late Mr R. A. U. Jennings, on his way to a speaking engagement at Birmingham later that day. I am not sure whether the notes were taken on 2 July or 9 July as the exact Saturday in July was not marked and No 6012 made successful runs on this train both days. It arrived at Snow Hill 6min and 5min early respectively, with 11 coaches in tow each time. Nevertheless, some details are well worth recounting as Tony Icke, who travelled with 2-6-0 No 6364 on the 9.5am Birmingham-Portsmouth, passed No 6012 on 9 July running 2min early at Aynho Jc. Reginald Jennings recorded No 6012 there at 10.15½am, 1½min early.

By contrast with Saturday schedules elsewhere, the 9am down was allowed only 2min extra to Snow Hill, as compared to the weekday allowance with a lighter load. In the event, No 6012 didn't need either of them. It left Paddington a fraction early and reaching 64mph at Denham had time in hand for a 40mph slack past Beaconsfield. No 6012 arrived at High Wycombe 30sec late and left again punctually at 9.37am, just before No 6001 *King Edward VII* would have come through fully laden with 14 coaches, but also running right time on the 7.25am from Wolverhampton. No 6012's crew took it fairly easy up the climb to Saunderton and dropped over a minute before Risborough, but then they reached 78mph at Haddenham and 76 at Blackthorn. By the time No 6012 was nicely stuck into the climb past Bicester, and encountered No 6011 *King James I* around here as it came haring down from Ardley full pelt on the fast and heavy 7.30am from Shrewsbury, No 6012 was back on time. Through Banbury 2min early, a top speed of 82mph was achieved near Fosse Road box and the job was in the bag. No 6012 pulled up in Snow Hill at 11.10am after taking 93min from High Wycombe, well within the weekday 'inter-city' schedule for this train.

No 6012 gave way to No 4954 *Plaish Hall* at Wolverhampton and then went off to turn at Stafford Road between 11.54am and 1.6pm. Its return working was on the up 'Cambrian Coast Express' and No 6012 regained Paddington 4min early at 4.16pm, after picking up all of a 6min late start from Birmingham.

Meanwhile No 4954 had 'Grange' No 6861 *Crynant Grange* in front on the 11.10am (SO) Birmingham-Pwllheli, but this kept well clear so that No 4954 could call at Shrewsbury punctually around 12.30pm. Unfortunately it is not known which engines relieved Nos 6861 and 4954 at Ruabon. The 11.10 load at eight

coaches was within the capacity of a single Croes Newydd '43xx', but the 11-coach Paddington train was a different matter. It could have been taken on by the pair of Oswestry 0-6-0s, Nos 2287 and 3200, which had stormed the mountain gradients up from the coast earlier on the 7.20am Pwllheli–Paddington. Then on the other hand it may equally have been a Croes Newydd pair, possibly including 'Dukedog' No 9014 which had been seen in steam at 84J the previous Wednesday 6 July. Moreover, further fresh engines were also required to work the nine-coach Pwllheli portion on from Barmouth. These could involve No 9017 which was performing station pilot duties at Pwllheli on 7 and 8 July. By now Nos 9014 and 9017 were the last two of a dwindling band of 'Dukedogs' remaining in service.

Back at Paddington in the morning, No 5040 *Stokesay Castle* was lined up on the 9.5am to Bristol and Cheltenham. Its best work was done on the return journey when No 5040 wound up at Paddington 7min early with the 1.50pm back from Bristol. Nearby No 6023 *King Edward II*, spick and span in two-week-old paint, was ready with the 9.10am to Birkenhead. It reached Snow Hill 4min late on this train, and unusually also handed over to a 'Hall', No 5900 *Hinderton Hall*, at Wolverhampton. Both Nos 6023 and 5900 are of course preserved and still together at Didcot. No 5900 would have some stiff pulling with 12 on up Hollinswood bank, but then the restaurant cars came off at Shrewsbury, leaving a more manageable eight coaches to be handled over the 1 in 83 ruling gradient before Ruabon on No 5900's way to Chester.

After the 9.15am left Paddington for Worcester and Hereford, attention concentrated on the morning's main flow of traffic to the West of England. The first couple of these departures came within our hour's timescale before 9.30am. In Platform 2 on the 9.22am to Paignton was borrowed Swindon 'Hall', No 5964 *Wolseley Hall*. Instead of the correct reporting number C70, No 5964 was still carrying an inaccurate chalked reporting number 1A10 off a previous duty on the 7.5am from Cheltenham. The stock for the 9.22 which consisted of 10 carriages was one of the sets which had been worked up from Didcot earlier that morning, usually marked Set No 3 and leaving at 6.35am from Old Oak Common. This empty stock was hauled by any engine available at Didcot ('Castle' No 5093 on 30 July 1960) which would then be available for use on a later departure like the 10.22am to Paignton or 11.15am to Cheltenham.

Across from No 5964, at Platform 4 the 9.30am down was also filling up with passengers. On Saturday it formed the main day service to Newquay, loading to 13 with a 70ft dining car. Of all these early departures, from the moment when Laira 'King' No 6002 *King William IV* came into view backing deceptively quietly past Royal Oak ready to couple up, this was one to savour. No 6002 had come up in place of a diesel on

Above: Among a series of double-headed trains across Cornwall Nos 6837 *Forthampton Grange* and 1006 *County of Cornwall* climb steadily over Clinnick Viaduct hauling the 9.20am St Ives–Paddington on Saturday 4 July 1959. With 14 carriages this is an arduous climb but the two engines are comfortably on time at 11.06am. Later in the journey No 6021 *King Richard II* will be in charge. Although right on the tail of the preceding train at Pewsey, and by then running 29min late, No 6021 was going strongly through there as it tackled the final stretch up to Savernake. *Peter W. Gray*

the 1.20pm Penzance–Paddington the previous day and now completed its Laira circuit with this return trip on the 9.30. As it had been 81A steam every Saturday up to now, but was diesel the following weekend, No 6002 on the 9.30 was a sight not to be missed. The fate of the 9.30 on the road was closely bound up with that of the 9.22 in front. Nos 5964 and 6002 did not disappoint.

No 6002 was booked out to Savernake in 83½min and it passed Westbury about 7min behind No 5964 at around 11.15am, 2min early. However, the 'King' could not afford to gain any more time than that before Castle Cary. Here the 10.20am Weymouth-Wolverhampton, with No 7911 *Lady Margaret Hall* coming from Yeovil, had to cross the main line at 11.36am between No 5964 at 11.31 and No 6002 due at 11.41. No 6002 must have negotiated this hurdle without undue hindrance, and it ran the 47½ miles

from Westbury to Taunton in under 50min. None of the 4min time allowance for signal checks after Castle Cary was needed, so No 6002 passed Taunton going great guns on the main line 6min early at 12.5pm. However, now No 4908 *Broome Hall* starting away with the 6.40am Leicester–Paignton was only 5min in front. This engine was running well with a light load, but being booked to precede the 9.30am down to Exeter in 1960, No 4908 would have been allowed out in front of No 6002 at Taunton West box. No 6002 probably ran into its signals as early as Norton Fitzwarren which would have killed any impetus for the climb to Whiteball. By Exeter all the 6min time gain had been lost.

Although No 4908 was safely tucked away in the platform line at Exeter as No 6002 came past, another obstacle now presented itself. The 7.30am from Paddington via Bristol was 14min late ahead and this had to call at all stations from Starcross to Newton Abbot. The 7.30 did not have the '9F' 2-10-0 or '47xx' 2-8-0 power encountered on some weekends, being worked this time by a Taunton 'Hall', No 4955 *Plaspower Hall*. Luckily at 1.12pm No 6002 was able to overtake this train as well while No 4955 called at Dawlish Warren, and that left the 9.30 with a clear run. At Newton Abbot No D6323 was attached to assist No 6002 over the banks to Plymouth and there both locomotives were replaced.

Above: Some very odd reporting numbers were utilised for up South Wales expresses on August Bank Holiday Monday 1960. The 11.5am Milford Haven–Paddington, usually A90, arrives at Cardiff behind No 5040 *Stokesay Castle* while the 11.55am down is already in from London, out of view on the left, with No 5039 *Rhuddlan Castle*. An hour later the 12.5pm Milford Haven appeared with No 5051 *Earl Bathurst* carrying reporting number A83 instead of its normal A11. Whilst A73 was a spare number, A83 usually appeared on the 1.50pm Hereford–Paddington. *Richard Picton*

The engines which hauled the 9.30 through Cornwall on 9 July are unknown. But when the 9.30 was seen west of Plymouth on other occasions during summer 1960 it was steam-worked. A week earlier on Saturday 2 July the locomotives taking over from 'King' No 6028 were an unidentified combination of 'Hall' and 'Grange'. On Friday 8 July No 1006 *County of Cornwall* took the 9.30 through to Newquay, and on Saturday 23 July the Cornish engines were Nos 7813 *Freshford Manor* and 4906 *Bradfield Hall*. They were banked from St Blazey to Luxulyan by 2-6-2T No 5198. On Saturday 27 August No 6854 *Roundhill Grange* piloted No 1006. So with power combinations like this to be found, the 9.30 was well up the list of any Saturday's most interesting trains.

Cardiff

Half an hour at Cardiff General from 9.30 to 10am is scarcely enough to do justice to the constant comings and goings of main line passenger, freight and valleys services. But it does illustrate some of the variety not to be found elsewhere on the Western. Across at the Valleys section's island platform 0-6-2T No 6626 of Radyr shed was just drawing away with empty stock of the 8.25am local passenger from Merthyr which had arrived on time at 9.26am. Earlier No 6626 had gone up the Taff Vale main line on the 5.20am newspaper train from Cardiff. This service also conveyed one

passenger coach and survived long enough to be easily the last steam passenger working on the Valleys section.

On the up centre road 2-8-2T No 7209 was waiting at the colour light signal gantry for the all clear from Cardiff East box. At 9.32am No 7209 got the road and crossed over on to the up relief line ready to diverge into Pengam sidings on 8T51, a Saturday version of the 6am goods from Margam.

The two main up Platforms, Nos 1 & 2, had been busy ever since 7am and now at 9.32am No 6941 *Fillongley Hall* arrived on the 8.10am Swansea-York routed via the Great Central line. The inter-regional flavour of this train was emphasised by its LNER stock and included an ex-Great Northern Railway coach, now a buffet car, No E43134E. No 6941 was on its way to Banbury, and reached Oxford 2min late solely due to a late running diesel unit occupying the main

Right: This is a scene which could have taken place on either 2 July or 9 July 1960 because No 70029 *Shooting Star* worked the 8am Neyland to Paddington on both days. Pictured here on 2 July, after a good clean during the morning, No 70029 is waiting on the centre road at Cardiff General for its train to come in. No 1028, bringing the 8am Neyland up from Swansea, is not steaming and will arrive 12min late. This is also holding up the 8.30am Pembroke Dock–Birmingham which will leave 12min late with the engine seen behind No 70029, No 6840 *Hazeley Grange* of Pontypool Road. *Gerald Adams*

platform there in front of it. On arrival at Banbury No 6941 had 3½hr turn-round before picking up the 10.8am Newcastle back to Swansea. This express was 18min late at Swindon but No 6941 managed to regain four of them before Cardiff, even though the train had lost its proper path from Patchway onwards.

Only one relief to the up 'Red Dragon' was booked, running into Cardiff at 9.37am with Landore 'Castle' No 5077 *Fairey Battle* just as No 6941 left. If there were two reliefs, as on the following Saturday when 'Hall' No 6973 *Bricklehampton Hall* was in charge of the 9.55am from Cardiff, that second extra would generally have to load inconveniently at Valleys Platform No 6. No 5077 set off at 9.44am nonstop to Paddington. On the way it would overtake No 6941 at Swindon. Fortunately the 8.15am from Abertillery which was next in front with No 7902 *Eaton Mascot Hall*, though losing more time up from Newport, just managed to keep far enough out of No 5077's path to allow the 'Castle' an early arrival at Paddington.

The engine for the 'Red Dragon' proper usually made its way up from Canton to the General in plenty of time for a leisurely engine change. So 'Britannia' No 70023 *Venus* — looking quite the part — was already on hand when No 7028 *Cadbury Castle* arrived with the West Wales portion, and while the train was made up to 13 coaches at Platform 2 the Pacific took over. No 70023 left on time at 10am and made a punctual run to Paddington, arriving at 12.59pm. No 7028 on Landore turn No 5 was due to make two Saturday return trips between Swansea and Cardiff. Its final assignment would be to pick up the down 'Red Dragon' again in the late evening from another 'Britannia', and return the same eight coaches to Swansea.

It was 11.15am before down traffic at Cardiff really livened up, but at 9.50am what should appear over the brow of the main line climb from Newtown West but 1Z90, a 10-coach excursion from Blaenavon to Barry

Island behind '56xx' No 6636. 1Z91 followed just over an hour later with No 5659, also from Pontypool Road shed. These services were well patronised and gave holidaymakers a full day at the seaside. They returned from Barry Island at similar intervals in the evening, starting with 1Z90 at 7.20pm, but only 1Z91 went all the way back to Blaenavon. There were some fearsome gradients to be faced climbing up the Eastern Valleys on the way home, and 10 wedged non-corridor coaches was well above the 180-ton weight limit for a singe-handed '56xx' tank engine beyond Pontypool Crane St. So at Newport taper boilered Pannier No 9468 was attached to pilot No 5659 up the valley at 9.5pm, and there would certainly be some sparks flying when this pair came to make a restart on the 1 in 42 climb out of Abersychan.

Bristol

Not 40 miles by rail separated Cardiff from Bristol, but the two cities were worlds apart in terms of their Saturday traffic flows. At Temple Meads long distance express traffic was heavily predominant all night and all day. On the down main line beyond Parson St there were only two gaps of 35min or more in passenger services between the time the down Postal passed just after 1am until 10pm that night.

During the mid-morning period from 10 to 11am Temple Meads had a wholly unexceptional total of 10 expresses to deal with, four of them changing engines at alternate ends of the station. You had to be really fit to see everything going on here, trekking up and down platforms of interminable length, but the amazing diversity of engines on view made it all worthwhile.

Right on 10am the 7.30am Blaina–Weston was due out, curving away under Bath Road bridge behind Mogul No 6348. This was the regular Ebbw Jc engine which reappeared again on this train a week later. Second up train of the day from the Torbay area was the 6.50am Paignton–Bradford which changed to

Left: On Saturday 9 July 1960 No 6025 *King Henry III* would normally seem to be unlikely power for a train like the 6.35am Walsall–Kingswear. However, No 6025 is working a Paddington–Bristol–Kingswear–Newton Abbot–Kingswear–Paddington circuit over the weekend, so its appearance arriving at Exeter on the Walsall train is only a convenient filling-in turn. *John Hodge*

Left: 2.5pm at Bristol Temple Meads on Saturday 15 July 1961 and 'Jubilee' No 45566 *Queensland* on the left awaits departure with the 2.15pm York express. Kentish Town 'Jubilee' No 45614 *Leeward Islands* should already have gone at 1.58pm, but its train, the 8.5am Newquay–Newcastle, is running late up from the West Country with 'Warship' No D817. So No 45614 is standing by until its train arrives, and it will be 2.25pm before No 45614 leaves with 11 coaches for the climb to Fishponds. *Richard Picton*

Below: On its epic trip to the Western, No 72005 *Clan MacGregor* makes its way cautiously out of Gloucester under adverse distant signals with the 7.45am Paignton–Newcastle. In the far background '2P' 4-4-0 No 40501 is on Gloucester station pilot duty, and to the right the 'Castle' on Horton Road shed is No 5002 *Ludlow Castle* awaiting a return working to Swindon in the evening. *T. D. Fry*

'Jubilee' No 45608 *Gibraltar*. The 6.50 was then routed to Yate up Fishponds bank and No 45608 emerged to pass Westerleigh 9min late.

'King' No 6025 *King Henry III* which went forward on the 6.35am Walsall–Kingswear from Bristol was something of a curiosity. This appeared to be the Old Oak engine off the 2.25am fast newspapers from Paddington. On weekdays it returned with the 7am Weston–Paddington express. But on Saturday mornings the 7am was diesel-hauled, and Bath Road shed then had difficulty deciding what to do with this spare 'King' — usually a good one too. The obvious answer would seem to have been to send it back on the 8.30am to Paddington, but it was sighted on this only once. The alternative procedure, adopted on four Saturdays up to the end of July but not afterwards, was to forward the 'King' to Kingswear or Paignton on the 6.35am from Walsall or 6.40am Leicester. The 6.40 was made up of SR stock on occasion, which provided the unique spectacle of a 'King' hauling green coaches.

On 9 July No 6025 was badly held up behind the 6.40am Wolverhampton-Paignton, which had bypassed Temple Meads on the Marsh avoiding line and then ran poorly. At Exeter No 6025 was 21min late. After reaching Kingswear No 6025 used the yard turntable, and then worked back with the 4.35pm Kingswear-Paddington as far as Newton Abbot, where it went on shed overnight. On Sunday No 6025 was back off to Kingswear again and finally departed for home hauling the 1.8pm Kingswear-Paddington passenger.

Within a minute or two of No 6025 leaving at the west end of Temple Meads, Barrow Road 'Jubilee' No 45577 *Bengal* started from No 12 platform in Brunel's original Great Western trainshed with the 10.20am to Newcastle. At 10.26am No 5087 *Tintern Abbey* was due to arrive, usually at Platform 4, on the 7.30am from Paddington while alongside No 4955 *Plaspower Hall* was waiting to relieve the 'Castle'. The 7.30 then travelled direct to Bridgwater on Saturdays without diverging off through Weston-super-Mare, but after reaching Taunton 5min late No 4955 soon caught up with the procession in front delayed by the 6.40am from Wolverhampton. At Exeter the nonstop 9.22am from Paddington overtook No 4955 on the centre road. However, any unscheduled delay at Dawlish Warren while No 6002 also went past on the 9.30am down Newquay can have caused only minimal inconvenience to passengers on the 7.30, while the Cornish traffic was kept moving sweetly along.

Next into Temple Meads, the 8.15am from Weymouth was due to arrive at 10.45am with one of that shed's Standard 5 4-6-0s, thought to be No 73022 or No 73041. Soon afterwards the 10.50am to Portsmouth Harbour set out along the same route as far as Westbury with No 5936 *Oakley Hall*. Once a Canton Standard 4 turn until these engines were drafted away with the spread of DMU services, the 10.50 was now more likely to have a Bristol or Westbury engine. However, although No 5936 now came officially from Reading shed, it had been at Canton the day before. This gave the 10.50 an unexpected link with the past. Arriving at Salisbury a minute or so early at 12.36pm after the usual leisurely trip on this route, No 5936 later returned to Cardiff on the 11am ex-Brighton. Its final task of the day was then to haul the 8.25pm Cardiff–Plymouth parcels, which was a light train mostly made up of loaded fish vans originating earlier in the day at Milford Haven.

Stanier Class 5 No 45264 and its successor from Bristol, 'Hall' No 4908, between them converted a 2min deficit at Westerleigh into a 3min early arrival at Taunton on the 6.40am Leicester–Paignton. Station work at Temple Meads was always carried out promptly and 13min booked for engine changing on this train left plenty of scope for time recovery if a departure slot could be found on the main line out to Yatton.

As 11am approached, the pace of incoming arrivals from the west was hotting up nicely, to an extent where about four expresses an hour had to start using the Marsh avoiding line. All that activity was of course invisible from the main station platforms, and at 10.55am it deprived watchers at Temple Meads of what was undoubtedly the sight of the summer. Laira double-chimney 'Castle' No 4087, with its distinctive Davies & Metcalfe lubricator reservoir high up on the side of the smokebox, was running right time north from Exeter at 9am on the 7.45am Paignton-Newcastle. *Cardigan Castle* drew up opposite SPM loco around 10.45am and there it was relieved by Carlisle Kingmoor-based Pacific No 72005 *Clan Macgregor*, a most unusual visitor to the Western.

'Clans' had been getting about to a remarkable extent that summer when working the twice-weekly 8.35pm Stirling–Sutton Coldfield 'Car Sleeper'. No 72009 went all the way through on Tuesday 5/6 July, but generally, as with No 72006 on 19 and 21 July, the Pacific came down from Stirling and was replaced at Derby. From there No 72006 piloted the 7.40am Bristol–Bradford on the first stage back to Carlisle. No 72005 apparently worked Stirling–Derby–Bradford on 7/8 July but then, instead of making for Carlisle, it was turned round and sent off south again on the 8.45pm Bradford–Paignton that Friday night. It duly arrived at Bristol around 3.30am where No 5090 *Neath Abbey* may have been the relief engine. No 72005 then retired to Barrow Road for a well-earned breather. It had so far amassed some 610 miles in only 31hr.

For a class with such an unfancied reputation No 72005 had a few more points to score, as the miles sped by beneath its wheels on the way back north. Carrying reporting number M314 the 'Clan' was away up Filton bank in good shape pulling a nice uniform rake of 10 LMS 'swingers' and it passed Westerleigh

6min early. This train called at Worcester and No 72005 had a rapturous reception all along the line. In territory where chime whistles were virtually unknown, No 72005 was finally seen by Mike Thompson as it passed Burton on time at 2.41pm with the crew waving from the cab and whistling furiously. No doubt the passengers wondered what on earth all the noise was about.

Another interesting train, though for very different reasons, followed the 7.45am Paignton into Bristol. This was the 8am Paignton–Manchester Victoria which every week during July varied its ultimate destination in the northwest according to which towns like Huncoat or Clitheroe were ending their Wakes holidays that weekend. So on 9 July the 8am from Paignton ran to Colne, with No 5003 *Lulworth Castle* in charge throughout from Paignton to Coleham. Here it stopped alongside Shrewsbury loco shed to change power and 'Jubilee' No 45704 *Leviathan* took over. However, somewhere along the way, possibly at Pontypool Road, the 8am Paignton seems to have spawned a relief to Colne, and, before No 45704 came nonstop through Shrewsbury station on the main train, it was preceded by 'Crab' 2-6-0 No 42868 of Agecroft on the Colne extra.

One further train should have rounded off our 10–11am timeframe at Bristol Temple Meads, but because No 6867 *Peterston Grange* was 28min late at Westerleigh on the 8.30am Snow Hill–Weston-super-Mare, it didn't manage to make it in time, and would not arrive before 11.25am. By then three more 'Castles' would have come and gone. Later there was an Oswestry 'Manor' running in after overhaul at Swindon, and a '9F' which departed on the 7.40am from Newton Abbot as far as Cardiff. The variety was amazing. There were 'B1s', '4Fs', 'Counties' and *City of Truro* still to come, and it was well into the evening before more than one main line diesel showed its face here.

The Choice — Paddington or Waterloo for Exeter and Ilfracombe

During the next hour, from 11am until midday, almost every major station could contend for attention. All were crowded with passengers and carrying on a roaring trade. No sooner had one fully-laden train left the platform than it was replaced by another, and slick operating was essential to keep things moving. Otherwise business would be lost, not just to other forms of transport, sometimes to competing railway routes.

Between London and Exeter these commercial considerations meant that Southern and Western Region express services were very finely balanced indeed.

The Western had for many years enjoyed the fastest (and the slowest) times to Exeter, the fastest by virtue of being able to run trains with fewer stops on the way. However, by 1960 that advantage had been severely eroded on summer Saturdays. Generally the quicker morning trains from Paddington did not even stop at Exeter. Those which did call were often more crowded. The various portions of the 'Atlantic Coast Express' with their capable Bulleid Pacific motive power now stopped only once or twice before Exeter anyway, so the fastest schedules on the Southern were more than competitive. Add to this equation the likelihood of better timekeeping on the more lightly used line from Waterloo, at least beyond Basingstoke, and it is obvious that on Saturdays from 9am to 1pm the Southern was in a position to carry the lion's share of Exeter passengers.

Both Paddington and Waterloo had departures for Devon or Cornwall around 10.35am and again at 11am. The Southern's 10.35am 'Atlantic Coast Express' to Padstow left Waterloo with 'MN' No 35019 *French Line CGT*, and the 11am 'ACE' to Ilfracombe behind No 35028 *Clan Line*. Both were late at Salisbury to the tune of one and 12min but they then ran so successfully that when the 10.35 reached Exeter St Davids with light Pacific No 34096 *Trevone*, it was back on time. No 35019 would therefore have reached Exeter Central about 1.55pm before No D600 on the 10.37am from Paddington came through St Davids at 2pm.

Approaching 11am Paddington was full of heavy 12, 13 and 14-coach trains leaving, in Platform order across the station, at 10.55, 11.10, 11 and 11.5am. Seven express arrivals also came in between 11–11.30am. All were steam-hauled both in and out, and prominent among them was No 6021 *King Richard II*, ready to go on the 11am down. The 'King' would be parked well out under Bishops Road bridge on a 14-coach load like this for Penzance and Kingsbridge. Steam from its safety valves eddied amongst the girders causing the first drips and smudges on its shining paint and polished brass as No 6021 waited to leave. Once on the move, No 6021 had the best of the running in the early stages. It came racing over the avoiding line at Westbury around 12.50pm, only just after No 35028 on the 'Atlantic Coast' had cleared

Below: A most atmospheric shot of Seaton Junction on a damp Saturday 23 July 1960, which shows how traffic over the SR West of England main line could rival that on the Western. 'BB' class 4-6-2 No 34049 Anti-Aircraft Command on the combined 1.45pm Exmouth and 2.35pm Seaton–Waterloo waits in the platform, as the last coach of the 11am from Padstow, the 'Atlantic Coast Express' disappears from sight on the up through line. Another 'BB' No 34051 Winston Churchill approaches under full steam with the 12.5pm Waterloo–Ilfracombe and Torrington ready for the climb up Honiton bank. Steve Derek

Salisbury. But from there No 35028 really got going, hardly unexpectedly for a 'Merchant Navy' but especially noteworthy because 10min in front of the Pacific was 'N15' 4-6-0 No 30453 *King Arthur* on the 10.45am Waterloo–Seaton. To keep out of *Clan Line*'s way the 'King Arthur' also had to run like a stag. It needed to be safely looped at Seaton Jc by about 1.50pm, before No 35028 came charging through on the middle road going hard ready to climb Honiton bank. No 30453 must have managed it too, because No 35028 was able to hand over to 'BB' No 34065 *Hurricane* at Exeter Central and the light Pacific reached St Davids only 4min late at 2.42pm.

Meanwhile No 6021 had run Westbury–Taunton in a gross time of about 52–55min, which, though not spectacular, did take account of a tight margin behind the 11.25am Chippenham–Weymouth diesel unit between Witham and Castle Cary. Any delay to the diesel would inevitably rebound on the express behind.

Cogload was flush with trains as No 6021 emerged under the flyover with the Bristol line, so it is difficult to know if the 11am had a clear run through Taunton. The 12.6pm Bristol–Taunton local was not far ahead on the down relief line, while the 7.43am Nottingham–Plymouth would have been almost alongside the 11am near Cogload. It arrived at Taunton a minute after No 6021 had gone through 2min late. On the up main No 6021 would have passed its final 'King' compatriot left from pre-diesel days at Laira as No 6016, freed at last from delays behind Bristol line traffic, came hammering past, getting well stuck into a sustained spell of fast running on the up Perranporth.

Beyond Taunton what looked like a safe 19min headway in front of No 6021 turned out in reality to

be nothing of the sort. No 73027 on the 8.50am relief from Swansea, which had been looped for the two portions of the 'Riviera' to overtake, now came out on to the main line again and No 6021 had to follow it over Whiteball. So No 6021 took 43min from Taunton to Exeter. By then the 11am from Waterloo had closed up to within a few minutes margin, and when No 6021 ran through St Davids 8min late at 2.27pm No 35028 with the 'ACE' was probably only about 3min out of Central behind it.

At Exeter No 6021 overtook No 6996 *Blackwell Hall* which was just uncoupling from Canton '9F' No 92237 at the down platform. No 6996 was the engine which had worked the 9.40am Paddington–Minehead as far as Taunton earlier, and then followed the usual procedure for the 9.40 engine by double-heading No 92237 to Exeter on the 9.5am Swansea–Kingswear. This was yet another 14-coach train as far as Newton Abbot where the load was reduced. However, back with the 11am, No 6021 still had to follow right on the tail of No 73027 around the seafront at Dawlish, and matters did not begin to improve for the 'King' until after it reached Newton Abbot 10min late at 2.54pm. Here, instead of one of the 'D63xx' Type 2s diesels which had so far monopolised all the down pilot jobs since early morning, Penzance 'Grange' No 6826 *Nannerth Grange* was already facing towards home and waiting to come on ahead of No 6021 for the stiff pull over the banks to Brent. There the three Kingsbridge coaches would be detached to go forward on the 3.40pm from Brent with a small Prairie, leaving the load on the 11am nicely weighted for a single 'County' to handle between Plymouth and Penzance. If the same procedure was followed at Plymouth as the previous Saturday, when No 1006 *County of Cornwall* was used on the 11am returning off the 11.15am Newquay–Wolverhampton, No 1002 *County of Berks* was the loco taking over the 11am to work it through Cornwall. With 11 stops, this stretch would take over 3hr, and

was due to end in Penzance at 7pm.

Meanwhile the 11am 'Atlantic Coast Express' had completed its journey across North Devon to Ilfracombe at 4.38pm, if *Hurricane* was back on time, but not before it ran into yet more competition from the Western. This came in the shape of a six-coach Ilfracombe portion off the 11.30am from Paddington. Despite traversing a single line and steep gradients most of the way from Taunton, the Western enjoyed a 23-mile distance advantage over the Southern route. So the scheduled times taken by the two trains from London tied exactly where their routes converged on arrival at Barnstaple Jc. The 11.30 had come down to Taunton in 164min with 'Castle' No 5034 *Corfe Castle* on 13 or 14 coaches, and 2-6-0 No 6337 was due to take over the Ilfracombe section from there. On this Taunton turn 70, No 6337 covered two punishing return trips from Taunton to Ilfracombe and back in the day. No less than 243 miles were involved and not many of them were easy ones.

Six coaches to Ilfracombe over the Western was only a gesture, however, and a dry one at that, because the 11.30 carried no refreshment facilities anywhere on the way. Only the fleet of foot could work in a visit to the station buffet while the train divided at Taunton.

Snow Hill for Penzance

For travellers from Birmingham to the West of England it was the LMR which was in no position to compete on Saturdays, as its trains from the north turned up at New Street already well filled. This left the Western to cope as best it could with enormous flows of westbound traffic over roundabout routes to Taunton via Stratford-upon-Avon and Filton or Oxford and Swindon.

For holidaymakers on 9 July the omens looked good. To be sure, the main day Penzance service at 8.55am from Wolverhampton was made up to 14

coaches but on the head end was No 5063 *Earl Baldwin*, one of the best medium superheat single-chimney 'Castles' around. The previous day it had worked the 'Cornishman' to Bristol and back. Now it was tackling the 237 miles through to Plymouth via Stratford and despite a very large increase in load, only 15min more than the weekday schedule was allowed. This train stopped four times before Snow Hill and the uphill start from West Bromwich was inclined to be tricky with a tare load of 480 tons, so No 5026 *Criccieth Castle* was supplied to pilot No 5063 over the first 12¼ miles to Snow Hill. Here the train left a minute late at 9.41am.

As things turned out it was a pity No 5026 didn't go the whole way to Plymouth because, quite uncharacteristically, No 5063's performance was well below par. Despite enjoying the falling tendency of the route via Hatton to Stratford, Cheltenham and Gloucester, time was lost, and once lost those minutes were unrecoverable. Passing Westerleigh well clear of any conflicting traffic, No 5063 was 15min late. It was therefore in no position to overtake the 7.43am Nottingham–Plymouth in the Bristol area as it should have done. The 7.43 ran to a much slower schedule so arrears on the Wolverhampton train had grown to 30min before No 5063 eventually managed to get ahead at Taunton. This represented such a loss of time that, if the 9.25am Wolverhampton–Paignton had been running punctually over its even more circuitous route through Oxford and Westbury, it could actually have converged at Taunton right behind No 5063 on the 8.55am from Wolverhampton. Unfortunately, however, the 9.25, with another Stafford Road engine, No 5926 *Grotrian Hall,* had fared no better. Having left Oxford only 30sec behind time, it eventually appeared at Taunton to change crews 34min late, with a queue of trains including the 'Torbay Express' held up behind it.

Back with the 8.55 matters on the 'Castle' footplate, with a fresh crew from Bristol, may by then have

started to rally a bit. Though another 6min were lost on to Exeter, No 5063 was almost able to hold its headway behind No 6021 on the 11am from Paddington, so it may have managed to climb Wellington bank unaided despite a 25-ton overload. But the effect of 36min lateness was bound to tell on No 5063's progress as trains piled up all around it, and after Exeter there were three expresses in front which No 5063 should have preceded.

Luckily the train directly ahead made a passenger stop at Newton Abbot, which left the through line there free for use by No 5063. Even so, a couple more minutes were lost attaching No 4920 *Dumbleton Hall* before the whole cavalcade set off 39min late to climb Dainton.

This 14-coach formation turning up at Plymouth so late in the day posed headaches at Laira. Finding sufficient power to work it on to the point where five Newquay coaches were detached at Par meant at least two engines. On 2 July a couple of Type 2 diesels plus 'Manor' No 7816 were supplied. But on 9 July 'Castle' No 5058 *Earl of Clancarty* was coupled on ahead of Penzance 'Grange' No 6825 *Llanvair Grange* and this pair worked the Wolverhampton through beyond Truro regaining what time they could on the way. No 5058 was a Laira engine in tip-top condition. On Monday after returning from Penzance it was off to London, and came back the following day in place of a diesel on the 5.30am from Paddington as far as Plymouth.

As for *Earl Baldwin*, they took no chances with it on the return trip to Wolverhampton next day. Though slow, the Sunday 10.30am through train from Penzance was also heavy, so No 5063 received assistance from No 6837 *Forthampton Grange* over the banks, and then again later from No 6863 *Dolhywel Grange* all the way to Wolverhampton. As No 6863 had been out piloting between Plymouth and Newton Abbot on Saturday, and was finally seen on the

Above: Saturday 9 July 1960 at Truro as 0-6-0PT No 3709 with spark arrester chimney departs with the 6.10pm to Falmouth. On the left No 5058 *Earl of Clancarty* which is coupled to No 6825 *Llanvair Grange* working the 8.55am Wolverhampton–Penzance will be following No 3709 up to Penwithers Jc shortly. Some 10min have been recovered since Newton Abbot, but the Wolverhampton is still around 30min late. *Peter W. Gray*

7.10pm Hackney to Tavistock Jc freight that evening, its probable place of attachment to No 5063 on Sunday was at Exeter.

When Nos 6863 and 5063 eventually made their way on to Stafford Road shed at 9.54pm the 'Castle' was in no fit state to be considered for the 'Cornishman' again next day. In fact it was still taking things easy the following Saturday when No 5089 took on the Plymouth job, though with little more success than No 5063 had enjoyed. This time *Earl Baldwin* was only the pilot engine double-heading No 5089 between Wolverhampton and Birmingham. Fortunately No 5063 lived to fight another day. It was still on these West of England trains as far as Bristol until summer 1964 by which time loads were lighter but their punctuality had improved considerably. No 5063 was by then the best remaining 'Castle' out of all those in LMR stock, both in terms of appearance and condition, and some excellent performances were achieved.

Progress on the Up Line

Right through until midday, incidence of serious late running was rare on all WR routes, but up trains were even less prone to lose time on 9 July than their down counterparts. The only three arrivals known to have reached Paddington before noon running over 10min late had originated from three different directions. Of these, one train each from Hereford, Fishguard and

Weston-super-Mare was 21-26min in arrears, though the last two seem to have suffered mainly through losing their booked pathing slots at Reading and Didcot. No problems with up line timekeeping were evident in the Birmingham area or through South Wales, while at Oxford most arrivals were coming in early between 10.30 and 12 Noon.

The 30¾-mile stretch over Whiteball between Exeter and Taunton was the main bottleneck. It was generally scheduled in about 37min early on, easing to 41–43min as traffic built up around 10.30am. Once the line became packed from 11.30 onwards, in order to funnel the maximum capacity through, 37 and even 36min schedules started to reappear. But in fact nothing was making it to Taunton in less than 41min by then, and for trains clearing Exeter between 12 Noon-1pm times of 54–59min became common. The upshot of this was that, while Exeter movements were back on time after 1pm, nothing approached Taunton punctually on the main line from the west after the up 'Devonian' had passed at 10.55am until after observations there ceased around 5pm.

There was often scope for time recovery after Taunton, however, and the first up train to lose its path from the west was able to recover it further north, thanks to some smart operating which contained any timekeeping problems within manageable proportions. The first Saturday morning express up from Cornwall was involved, leaving Penzance bright and early at 6am for Crewe and the north. By the time this train came to leave Newton Abbot it was late behind the 9.30am Paignton–Swansea which it should have preceded.

The 6am was the Saturday version of the service known in some quarters as 'The Lodger', being the return working for engine and crew of the celebrated Shrewsbury lodging turn to Newton Abbot. Here the 6am called to set down only and collect its through North & West engine.

Shrewsbury's star performer, No 4080 *Powderham Castle*, had been nicely fettled up and, despite its age, an engine with better credentials for this job would be hard to find. No 4080 was of course one of the earliest 'Castles', but it had now been fully modernised with all the most recent front end improvements. It was eventually, along with the original No 4082 *Windsor Castle*, longest-lived of the class in normal service, besides being the engine credited in perpetuity with the highest mileage of any 'Castle'. It went well too. Contrary to some expectations No 4080 was a more than adequate replacement for No 7023, which had been at Canton from new, when No 4080 was transferred to Cardiff 12 days later on 24 July. Within a week No 4080 had graduated up from relief work, through Canton turn 5 up the North & West, on to the 'Red Dragon', and there 'Forty-Eighty' stayed on Londons all summer until Canton received its first 'Kings'. No 4080 ultimately survived long enough to work the very last Welsh-based 'Castle' passenger assignment on 4 April 1964 and that again took it up the North & West for one final time with the 5.10pm Cardiff–Crewe.

On its way through Exeter 12min late at 10.33am on 9 July 1960, No 4080 was nicely into its stride. It passed only 4min behind No 6827 heading the 9.30am from Paignton. No opportunity to overtake was available however because No 4080 had to call additionally at Weston-super-Mare and Bristol Stapleton Road. But despite these extra stops and a load of 13 coaches, No 4080 apparently managed to hold its place behind No 6827 all the way to Maindee Jc East near Newport. Still running out of course the 'Castle' was fortunate to negotiate the Severn Tunnel without undue delay, as down traffic was solid on a succession of 7min headways around 1pm. Here No 4080 was allowed to encroach into the path of the 8.48am New Milton–Swansea. This must

have delayed the 8.48 with No 6972 *Beningbrough Hall*, but in the end it did not matter a lot because the 8.48 had a long stop at Cardiff, and was able to leave there for Swansea behind No 73023 facing a recoverable deficit of only 6min.

Even so, when No 4080 was able to diverge at Newport for the north it was at least 15min late. So heavy was the press of traffic here too, that the 6am from Penzance was fifth in a succession of seven up steam expresses passing Maindee Jc North and making for Hereford between 12.45–1.45pm. No 4080 also passed seven more down steam North & West expresses between Severn Tunnel Jc and Llanvihangel, with some of these engines like 'Hall' No 4928 *Gatacre Hall* on the 9.15am Blackpool–Cardiff probably showing clear signs of hard use. Their crews would be glad of a breather on this easier stretch for southbound trains just across the Welsh border.

At the same time margins over the down line water troughs at Undy near Severn Tunnel Jc could hardly be tighter. So it had to be assumed, following half an hour's constant use every 6½-7min, that eventually the level of the troughs here would not refill sufficiently to provide all the water supplies required. As a precaution, therefore, No 5050 *Earl of St Germans* following No 4080 on the 8.30am Ilfracombe–Manchester was booked to stop at Pontypool Road just to top up its tender there.

No 4080 meanwhile was slogging away to good effect, but with 13 on for around 430 tons tare, this was the first of three heaviest expresses for the LMR to be allowed time at Abergavenny Monmouth Road to call up one of the Llanvihangel bankers. Two were on duty there 24hr a day and, carrying banking Target No 1, something really substantial like a '72xx' 2-8-2T might be involved. Not many passenger trains ever managed to obtain the services of one of these at any time.

Two trains in front of No 4080, the 9.5am Paignton–Manchester hauled by No 4980 *Wrottesley Hall* had lost at least 20min between Taunton and Maindee Jc North. There it was late enough for the two 'Britannia'-hauled midday South Wales–Manchester expresses to go on ahead. Fortunately, however, the 9.5 changed engines at Pontypool Road, and its prospects were greatly improved when No 1013 *County of Dorset* took over here working home to Shrewsbury. This enabled the whole raft of expresses in front of No 4080 to keep moving smoothly, even though the 9.5 was still running out of course and there would be some jockeying for position when five trains had to use the up platform at Hereford in quick succession.

This same compressed group of five runners would then cause problems after Ludlow for the signalman at Onibury, operating his level crossing gates across the busy A49 trunk road. Trains passing here were now well into the climb to Church Stretton. Making about

Above: Standing in for the usual Bath Road 'Castle', Shrewsbury shed's No 5968 *Cory Hall* picks up speed after clearing Patchway and starts its descent to the Severn Tunnel with the heavy 10.5am Penzance–Manchester on Saturday 10 September 1960. Most unusually on this train, No 5968 is working through from Plymouth, possibly due to rearrangements associated with the closure of Bath Road shed that weekend. *Richard Picton*

Right: The Longsight turn to Pontypool Road was a well-known feature of North & West operations until 1962, taking in the 9.30am Manchester–Swansea on its southbound leg. With unrebuilt 'Patriot' No 45549 appearing over the North & West hauling the 9.5am Liverpool–Plymouth on 9 July 1960 this picture of No 45519 *Lady Godiva* working the Longsight turn up from the Usk Bridge at Penpergwm towards Nantyderry on Friday 7 March 1958 is an illustration of continued close WR and LMR co-operation over this joint line. *R. O. Tuck*

50mph, each would be taking some 3min to come up from Bromfield. After one had passed the signalman had to try to clear the queue of road traffic before the next train was offered. He then needed to sight a break in road activity, close the gates again and be sure to clear his up distant signal in time to avoid any slackening of speed by the oncoming engine. With No 4999 *Gopsal Hall* on the 11.42am Manchester–Cardiff also needing to be cleared over the crossing in the other direction right at the busiest time, it would be touch and go whether damaging delays to up trains could be averted here.

No 4080 safely weathered the final stretch of collar work up over the shoulder of the Long Mynd, and then came down into Shrewsbury to arrive tight behind 2-6-0 No 7330 on the 3.10pm from Welshpool at about 4.5pm, 7min late. It had regained a useful amount of lost time from Newport. Shrewsbury then supplied Standard 5 No 73037 to take this heavy train forward and it started purposefully away up Crewe bank on to the LMR.

The old joint-line nature of the route from Shrewsbury to Pontypool Road was still clearly in evidence. Two through LM-worked express duties were as interesting as any, not to mention a full programme of Central Wales line expresses and reliefs sharing the same tracks as far as Craven Arms. The only 2-8-0 hauled passenger train arrived from the south not long

after No 4080. This was Llanelly-based '8F' No 48452 terminating on the 12.25pm slow from Swansea Victoria.

In the opposite direction 'Jubilee' No 45680 *Camperdown* penetrated through to Pontypool Road with the 9am Manchester-Swansea, but it was the following 9.5am Liverpool–Plymouth which enjoyed the greatest variety of engines. On Saturdays so far that summer 'Britannia' No 70047 was seen on 18 June, rebuilt 'Patriot' No 45529 *Stephenson* on 25 June and Caprotti 5 No 44687 on 2 July. On 23 July it was the turn of 'Royal Scot' No 46134 *The Cheshire Regiment* to appear with the 9.5am Liverpool.

On 9 July what should turn up but an ex-works unrebuilt 'Patriot' No 45549 being borrowed by Crewe North. The 9.5 arrived 12min late at Whitchurch where the 13-coach train had to be drawn up twice in the short platform, but No 45549 then obviously made good progress with this substantial train from there, calling only at Shrewsbury to Hereford. Later when the 9.5 Liverpool reached Exeter at 5.46pm with No 5059 *Earl St Aldwyn* on the front it was now 21min late, but by then No 45549 had long since completed its turn-round at Hereford. The 'Patriot' returned north on the 10.20am Kingswear–Manchester and was already back on LMR territory just beyond Shrewsbury.

Shrewsbury station had so many conflicting flows of traffic to be dealt with in a very cramped layout that it

was not surprising serious delays could arise here. Any evidence of these on 9 July is difficult to judge from records taken at the station, when most of the hold-ups would be out of sight while trains awaited access to a free platform. Changing engines, detaching restaurant cars and shunting stock in and out of bay platforms were all time-consuming operations over sharply curving trackwork, while access to carriage sidings on the up side of the Wellington line meant extensive occupation of the main running lines as well. To help speed things up, through train reversals in the station were eliminated on Saturdays, but even so, special arrangements were in force by means of electric plungers so that platform staff could advise nearby signalboxes when a passenger train was ready to depart, and which of six routes it would be taking. With the help of aids like this, allied to slick operating, trains were largely handled punctually, except for certain North & West expresses. Ultimately the timekeeping of these was well outside Shrewsbury's control, or anyone else's for that matter.

In 1960 rebuilding of Manchester London Road station was in full swing pending electrification. Manchester was starting point for over half of the extensive weekend services from the northwest to the West Country and many of these trains had to be diverted to start at Central, Exchange, Victoria or

even Mayfield instead of leaving from London Road. The LMR rescheduled departures to allow extra time over diversionary routes, but besides extending what must already have seemed like interminable journeys of between nine and 13hr, sometimes longer, there were inevitably greater chances of delay.

In fact the LMR did not do at all badly on 9 July. Coming south the main body of Liverpool and Manchester expresses appear to have been handed over to the WR something like 10min late, with the four noted at Whitchurch averaging 12min in arrears. Time lost on West of England trains V88, V89, V92 and V93 was a problem all the way, with all four reaching Taunton in very ragged order 12–48min late, and then averaging 37min behind time at Newton Abbot. These losses therefore seem to be largely debitable to the WR:

V88 8am Manchester–Penzance arrived at Newton Abbot 58min late with No 5029

V89 8.35am Liverpool–Penzance arrived at Newton Abbot 41min late with No 6811

V92 9am Manchester–Paignton arrived at Newton Abbot 24min late with No 5024

V93 9.5am Liverpool–Plymouth arrived at Newton Abbot 24min late with No 5059.

The previous week these same trains averaged 19min late reaching Newton Abbot even though V93 was actually early with *Australia* and *Abbotsbury Castle* in charge on the way down. By contrast, the following week, 16 July, V93 was worst of all, but the others didn't cope much better. They averaged 38min lost time, and this was before the start of the real holiday peak in late July. A year earlier on 18 July 1959 before any problems arose from diversions around the Manchester stations the same quartet clocked into Newton Abbot averaging 27min late. A year later, on 15 July 1961, although No 5055 *Earl of Eldon* steaming through from Salop on V92 was in a minute early, V88, now with diesel participation, was still 16min late, and V89, also with a 'Warship' from Bristol, arrived 11min late. It was a similar story most Saturdays for years.

Even more difficult was the position of the 11.15am Newquay–Wolverhampton and 11.10am Penzance–Wolverhampton through holiday expresses. In many respects they had the worst of all worlds. Heavy trains running at the tail of the day's main rush and suffering all the accumulated delays arising from other services around and in front of them; engines returning on 238-mile workings, for which they may not always have been in tip-top order when they started back; heavily dependent on at least three pilots each, and probably one banker too, over most difficult gradients on a slack infested route.

Eleven coaches were probably just about manageable. In fact the 11.10am Penzance was booked 13 and the 11.15am Newquay was due to load to 12 coaches. Seat regulation arrangements should have ensured that these limits could be observed. But the problem seems to have been that, having carried the holidaymakers down on non-regulated services, Western Region quite fairly felt it was also under an obligation to see them home again. This meant either running reliefs or augmenting the load. It was surprising that the 7.30am Penzance–Bristol was not extended to Wolverhampton for that purpose every Saturday, and not just at two peak weekends, because this would have helped solve the problem. But instead there were 12–14 coach loads each Saturday, and the timekeeping was diabolical. On 11 of the 13 1960 summer Saturdays when the two trains were observed at Tyseley, neither was on time once. The 11.15 Newquay was first up and did have what might be termed three acceptable trips 8-11min behind time. But it was 60–90min late on four other occasions.

The 11.10 Penzance was due to pass Tyseley at 7.39pm but it bettered an 8.30pm appearance only once. Seven other Saturdays saw it stealing through between 8.42-9.8pm, which perhaps showed some measure of consistency. The very worst trip on 6 August, which was the busiest weekend of the year for traffic into Birmingham, involved 140min of lost time. The following 2.55 and 3.10pm trains from Paignton also suffered in the backwash, but on that occasion both had thankfully got ahead of the Penzance when something seems to have seriously interrupted

the progress of both the Newquay and Penzance trains after they diverged on to the St Philip's Marsh line at Bristol.

An element of mystery followed these two services. They would leave Exeter about 15min late, disappear into the black hole of the Marsh avoiding line, and, for reasons often largely unknown, appear at Tyseley over an hour late. This was long after most lineside observers had gone home. In fact though, the trains were well worth waiting for, because power was amazingly variable.

The engine arrangements should have been quite straightforward: a Bath Road 'Castle' on the 11.15am Newquay and a Stafford Road 'Castle' on the Penzance, both through from Plymouth to Wolverhampton, remanned at Bristol. But at 1pm Laira would be scratching around for power after a busy morning, and it seemed that the normal engines were often either not ready or otherwise engaged. The Stafford Road 'Castle' made it back with one or other train on three of the first four weekends, but after 9 July it was seen only once again. On other occasions Laira would use one of its own locos, which may or may not have been freshly prepared to face such a long demanding job. For the remainder it was a matter of booking out any engine which was accessible. All 4-6-0 classes from 'Granges' to 'Castles' had a go. On 26 trains they originated at 12 different sheds as far apart as Penzance and Old Oak Common or Reading and Hereford. On this basis of random selection, events on 9 July 1960 unfolded more smoothly than most.

The 11.15am Newquay was loaded to 12 coaches. It had plenty of power over the earliest stage of the journey and curved round from St Blazey into Par behind No 1002 *County of Berks* assisted by Prairie tank No 5198. At Plymouth No 1002 was replaced by rebuilt 'Star' No 5092 *Tresco Abbey* piloted by No 6854 *Roundhill Grange*, and this pair took the 11.15 over Hemerdon to reach the first timing point at Newton Abbot 11min late. Detaching No 6854 took just over double the allotted 4min but in any case the 10.20am Penzance–Swansea was now only just ahead so departure had to await its clearance. The 10.20 then stopped to shuffle engines again at Exeter so No 5092 was able to nip ahead here, but by then it was 19min late.

To their great credit, the crew of No 5092 then really went for it up Whiteball with this heavy train. They would have made a stirring sight over the curve at Tiverton Jc as they crammed on speed ready to rush the last four miles to the top. By this means a time of 36min was achieved from Exeter to Taunton, an event unequalled since a diesel on the lighter up 'Mayflower' 5hr earlier. It only regained No 5092 2min, but this effort certainly goes to show that there could be merit in the performance of even the most unfancied train. It also didn't stop time being lost elsewhere, and largely invisibly at that.

Above: On Saturday 9 July 1960 Nos 5198 and 1002 *County of Berks* climb vigorously away from the coast near Quintrell Downs with the 11.15am Newquay–Wolverhampton. No 5198 will assist on this train as far as Par, leaving No 1002 to take the 12-coach load on to Plymouth from there. *Peter W. Gray*

It does seem unrealistic to expect that No 5092, routed over the vortex at St Philip's Marsh, would have managed to overtake the more punctual 11am Newquay–York in the Bristol area as it was supposed to. 'Grange' No 6804 on the York train had given way to No 45612 *Jamaica* at Temple Meads and the 'Jubilee' ran satisfactorily to reach Burton-on-Trent only 9min behind time at 8.20pm. So any delay to No 5092 between Yate and Standish Jc from this source would be minimal. Even so, once it was 25min late, No 5092 would be running almost in the path of the 11.10 Penzance service and there it stayed all the way to Birmingham.

But the fun wasn't over for the 11.15 yet, not by a long chalk. Word would already have been forwarded to Tyseley, probably from Bristol, to confirm that the Penzance needed assistance from Stratford-upon-Avon. But with only 12 bogies the Newquay was in a more marginal position whether or not No 5092 also required a pilot. However, No 5092 now had 200 miles behind it and was probably feeling the effects of many hours' exertion, so its crew decided they did need help at Stratford. 'Grange' No 6858 was already there, but was waiting to pilot the Penzance. It could

not be spared. The only other engines on hand were the two Stratford freight bankers. Of these 0-6-0 No 2267 was the most suitable for an express sortie. On went the Collett Goods coupled inside No 5092, and it remained there for 38 miles right through to Wolverhampton. They were still coupled on arrival at Stafford Road shed. Quite what the enginemen on the 0-6-0 thought as they came bucketing down behind the 'Castle' from Earlswood Lakes, very likely ankle-deep in coal tumbling on to the footplate from the tender, is not recorded. The duo joined the main line at Tyseley 33min late and picked up speed over the last lap into Snow Hill. Behind them the Penzance was doing pretty well by its usual standards. It was 51min late.

The 11.10am Penzance was among the last regular steam double-headers across Cornwall, and it had got away round Mount's Bay in good heart behind 4-6-0s No 6845 *Paviland Grange* and 6801 *Aylburton Grange* on a full rake of 14 coaches. No D6328 and 'Castle' No 5045 *Earl of Dudley* took over from Plymouth and these two found a free road in the rush at Newton Abbot 12min late. Away from here alone with its 480/510-ton train, No 5045 sallied out to face the music. This engine was in much better condition than No 5092 but it was still confronted by a hopeless task. Congestion at Newton meant that No 5045 was one path adrift leaving behind the 2.40pm Paignton–Paddington, so it was the 2.40 which managed to overtake No 4937 on the 10.45am Penzance–Sheffield at Exeter instead of No 5045. Even though the unusual

step was taken of stopping No 4937 at either Tiverton Jc or, more likely, Wellington so that the 'Castle' could go on ahead, No 5045 was still no less than 24min late through Taunton.

Assuming the 11.10 Penzance negotiated Bristol maintaining some 25min lateness, and was then given a most necessary shove up to Filton by 'Hall' No 6954 acting as Stapleton Road banker, No 5045 was now unfortunately placed to join the old Midland line at Yate just 10min behind the 5.15pm Bristol–Birmingham local. This was a really slow affair, which might be hauled by a '4F' 0-6-0 (No 44137 on 3 September) and had 3-5min stops at places like Berkeley Road and Stonehouse. Its progress, or lack of it, would impede the Penzance from passing Standish Jc until 6.54pm at the earliest, and by then the 11.10 Penzance would be at least 39min late.

After this the 11.10's schedule from Cheltenham to Birmingham was unrealistic to the extent of being no less than 9min quicker than the much lighter weekday 'Cornishman', so in this situation virtually all the 51min time lost by Tyseley can be accounted for. After attaching the pilot at Stratford-upon-Avon no amount of vigorous assistance for No 5045 from No 6858 *Woolston Grange* would make much impression on such a deficit. As the Penzance picked up speed on the relief line after its 15mph slowing over the junctions at Tyseley, the 6.10pm from Paddington with No 6017 *King Edward IV* was only 3min behind coming along the down main. No 6017 therefore received precedence where the four tracks were reduced to two through Snow Hill tunnel and the Penzance followed to arrive 57min late.

In 1961 diesel haulage of the Penzance–Wolverhampton as far as Bristol did not help one bit, and in any case Bristol had no spare 'Castles' to take the train forward at 5pm on a Saturday afternoon. At Tyseley it was less than an hour late on only one occasion out of eleven, and then by only 3min. That

this should have been the case probably surprised no one. Back in 1958 they were clocking up June arrivals on the Penzance 58min late, July arrivals 69–82min late and August arrivals 90–94min late. One wonders what the passengers had to say about it, as they went back to work building motor cars at Longbridge the Monday morning after.

So the Penzance took another step in notching up a record of late running rivalled on the Western only by the 9.25am Weymouth–Wolverhampton. There were about 12 trains on the Region which regularly ran well behind time, and they certainly did so on 9 July. These were made up of four down services from the northwest to the West Country, two trains from Weymouth to Birmingham or Wolverhampton, two more from Margate to Birmingham and three between Cornwall and Wolverhampton. Less is known about timekeeping of trains from the West Country to Manchester and Liverpool, but the evidence points to regular poor running before Shrewsbury by one or more up trains like the 8.30am Ilfracombe–Manchester or 7.50am Newquay–Manchester, both on 9 July 1960 and many other weekends in 1959 and 1960 too.

When staff all over the Western were straining every sinew to run a successful summer service, why was it that a dozen persistent really late runners were allowed to hold the reputation of the Region's 440 other expresses to ransom every summer Saturday? The offending trains were a constant headache. Their passengers were already underprivileged in terms of overcrowding, via slow roundabout routes, often using outdated stock, sometimes lacking restaurant car facilities too, about all of which not a lot could be done. The extra irritation of very late arrivals was a different matter. Unfortunately the attention that was so clearly required to schedules, pathing and locomotive preparation was not provided for far too long, and when it was, many of the trains had ceased to run anyway.

Above: 'Castle' No 5026 *Criccieth Castle* and '2251' No 2257 come through Acocks Green with the 10.30am Penzance–Wolverhampton 'Cornishman' routed via Hatton, on Friday 21 July 1961. No 5026 is working up from Bristol while the 0-6-0 will have been attached to assist at Stratford-upon-Avon. The train is running 13min late with a heavy summer Friday load of 13 coaches and making a final dash for Snow Hill. No 2257's fireman is very wisely keeping a firm grip on the side of the cab. *M. Mensing*

Below: Saturday 30 July 1960 and No 5032 *Usk Castle* is in the West Country, though it is hardly going in the direction its Old Oak Common shed foreman would have chosen. No 5032 will drop pilot No D6303 at Newton Abbot East up home signal and then set off solo for Wolverhampton with 14 coaches. Running true to form, No 5032 on the 11.10am Penzance–Wolverhampton will be 56min late at Yate and eventually, assisted by No 5927 from Stratford, pass Tyseley 85min overdue. The second class saloon marshalled at the front of the train will provide club-style accommodation for those families lucky enough to sample its well upholstered long bench seats. *Frank Tweddle*

Above: 0-6-0 No 2218 was stationed at Newport Ebbw Jc shed for many years, covering most, if not all, of the BR period up to the end of 1963. On Tuesday 9 May 1961 No 2218 leaves Newport High Street with the 6.55pm stopping train to Brecon while the first stages of the multiple aspect signalling scheme take shape in Newport station. *John Hodge*

Below: At Torpantau on a typically damp day at this inhospitable location, No 3661 with the 12.15pm Brecon–Newport tops the steep climb from Talybont into the station and crosses the 11.15am Newport–Brecon train on a Saturday in April 1961. *Mike Esau*

5. VALLEYS INTERLUDE AND SUBURBAN SUMMARY

Diesel multiple-units had been introduced to the Cardiff Valleys in January 1958 and with a full complement of Derby-built cars in operation by summer 1959 they quickly monopolised 90% of the extensive passenger network. In 1960 units were already operating all services to such unlikely spots as Senghenydd on the branch from Caerphilly, and even paid visits to Dowlais Central, which by then was only served by workmen's trains.

Although most Valleys routes still saw the odd loco-hauled passenger workings, mainly to convey parcels and rush hour traffic, as well as regular football and summer seaside excursions, just four lines within what was termed the Cardiff District still maintained exclusive steam services.

The old Brecon & Merthyr route from Newport to Brecon qualified by virtue of running through the Cardiff area between Pant and Pontsticill Jc. Infrequent and inconveniently timed stopping trains up the nearby Taff-Bargoed Joint line from Hengoed, Ystrad Mynach & Nelson to Dowlais Cae Harris still plied a dwindling trade, interspersed among coal trains in transit up and down the joint line to Taff Merthyr and Cwmbargoed Collieries. Further west nearer the Bristol Channel, Tondu remained a 100% steam shed. It supplied power for the one Valley passenger service north from Bridgend which now survived, running to the head of the Llynvi Valley through Maesteg, and also in the other direction south to the seaside at Porthcawl. Finally the old Barry Railway service, still competing for Pontypridd to Cardiff traffic via the spur on to the GW main line from Tyn-y-caeau Jc to St Fagans, was served daily by a couple of Rail Motors each way, though DMUs worked the sparse service from Pontypridd to Cadoxton or Barry via Wenvoe. (*Note:* In this context the term 'Rail Motor' is an interesting anomaly and needs to be clarified. The GWR said farewell to proper railmotors, formed of a coach with built-in steam power bogie, in 1935. It was strange then that after faithfully describing these trains as 'Auto' in the working timetable until 1954, the Western Region abandoned this term for the expression 'Rail Motor' from then on with the change of timetable format.)

All four of these steam routes were interesting, not least on account of the gradients involved. Only the old Barry line escaped relatively lightly with 1½ miles of 1 in 69. The others had stretches as steep as 1 in 35, 1 in 31 and 1 in 32 respectively (*Note:* Various

ruling gradients are printed for the up B&M and Taff-Bargoed lines in the 1960 Sectional Appendix and Working Timetables. The steepest shown are those given above, and, being steeper than those normally quoted, they go a long way to explain why engine loads had to be so severely restricted.) Each of them was sheer enough to reduce even a chunky '56xx' 0-6-2T down to a maximum load of between 130–145 tons when working regular passenger services. These limits also had to take account of sharp curvature, and where the B&M and Taff-Bargoed tracks emerged on to the high moors above Dowlais at an altitude of 1,250ft they were also subject to vicious winter weather conditions. Even though adverse weather was not usually a major consideration on summer Saturdays, train loads were as severely hampered by gradients here as anywhere on the Western since the Princetown branch had closed some years earlier in March 1956.

Newport–Brecon

Although the Brecon & Merthyr line formed part of the only direct railway route from densely populated southeast Wales, through the glorious countryside of Mid-Wales to resorts north of Aberystwyth, it was largely impractical for use as a through route. The same journey from Newport to Aberystwyth could in fact be made with a useful saving in time by travelling via Carmarthen. Whilst the fastest journey time of 6hr 42min from Newport to Aberystwyth changing at Talyllyn Jc and Moat Lane was available on a summer Saturday, this was only quicker than the weekly all stations service because there was a Saturday express connection over the Cambrian main line at Moat Lane Jc. Here passengers off the 1.20pm from Brecon could pick up the 3.15pm (SO) fast from Shrewsbury, hauled by 'Manor' No 7814. On the B&M itself no concessions were made to summer Saturday through passengers. Even the extra coach, added on Saturdays to the usual two-coach trains which sufficed for normal local traffic, was attached all the year round.

On 9 July 1960 all four trains between Newport and Brecon were augmented into three-coach sets as usual and worked by engines from Newport Ebbw Jc shed. Each locomotive made a return trip of 94 miles, with two of them, Pannier No 3798 and Collett Goods No 2236 being stabled overnight at Brecon. The two engines starting from Newport were both Panniers,

Nos 3772 and 9664. I had a lively run from Newport to Talyllyn Jc with No 3798 in April 1962 and few other regular tasks could show up these '57xx' tank engines in quite such a favourable light. They were the most powerful locomotives permitted over the full length of the B&M, being allowed 10 tons more than a Collett Goods, or the Ivatt Class 2 2-6-0s which were sometimes sent down from Brecon. While all these types were expected to manage four corridor coaches when allowed extra time, three bogies was usually quite enough to take both northbound up the 1 in 35 between Deri and Fochriw, or on the savage seven-mile climb at 1 in 38 from Talybont to Torpantau which took the line up to a height of 1,131ft.

The three panniers on this occasion obviously managed the job competently and on aggregate they clocked into Newport right time exactly. No 2236 arrived with the 2.5pm from Brecon 11min late, and probably owed its presence on the line more to its usefulness in working a pick-up freight like the previous day's 7.30am Bassaleg–Brecon goods than to any preference when compared with the performance of a pannier tank on the passenger services.

Ebbw Jc crews were dextrously adept at handling panniers on the steep gradients. They started vigorously in full gear. Once nicely on the move, steam was shut off for the briefest possible period while the driver adjusted the lever reverse. Then he smartly reopened the regulator and the engine accelerated off up the climb. There were 21 stops on the 47-mile route so the crews had plenty of practice. Whilst B&M trains were allowed to run at speeds up to the general Valley line's maximum of 50mph there were lots of lower restrictions on the way, so in practice deft handling of the vacuum brake was just as important for good timekeeping as their ability to make quick restarts.

Nelson-Dowlais

If traffic on the Newport-Brecon line suffered because the route it followed managed to miss all the towns of any significance except Bargoed on the way, passenger trains over the Nelson–Dowlais branch also lacked much in the way of attractions to help retain sufficient patronage. There were only three mining villages on the 9½ mile journey north along the Taff–Bargoed line, so passenger services were even more local in character than those on the B&M. They existed largely to fulfil colliers' needs. Trains started at 5.20am and finished late at night around 11.30pm in accordance with shift work at the pits. Additionally the five ordinary return trips each way were relieved at shift changeover times by three unadvertised workmen's trains which snaked along the steep-sided valley as far as Bedlinog, 3½ miles from Nelson. But in the middle of the day, when summer Saturday services everywhere else were in full swing, traffic between Nelson and Dowlais dwindled to virtually nothing. Only one arrival made its way up to

Dowlais Cae Harris between 10.10am and 3.50pm.

Regular interval services which had been established so successfully on the main Valley routes did not extend to the Taff–Bargoed timetable. Yet such were the varied requirements of travellers that the daily passenger service over this short line required three locos together with three sets of coaches, all of them non-corridor and second class only.

Trying to cater for ordinary passengers with such a sparse daytime service was an unenviable task, because there was no town on the branch round which to build up worthwhile business. Where links existed with other lines at the south end attempts were made to connect with Cardiff–Rhymney diesels and Pontypool Road to Neath steam stopping trains. Passengers off the branch could then fan out and visit local towns nearby, like Bargoed itself, Blackwood or Caerphilly. These connections took place at any of Hengoed High and Low Level stations, Ystrad Mynach or Nelson, so intending passengers needed to have their wits about them ready to get off at the right connecting stop. But unfortunately the resulting dilution of effort meant that gaps between connecting services were often longer than ever. Sunday excursions from Cae Harris to Barry Island were arranged in summer when every available coach would be pressed into service. Even though load limits for a single '56xx' were specially relaxed to 160 tons for return excursions, piloting back up to Dowlais would often still be required as trains going down in the morning could be made up to 220 tons.

The Taff-Bargoed was originally built jointly by the Rhymney Railway and the GWR and had been 0-6-2T territory since long before the Grouping. In 1960 it was exclusively operated by '56xx' class 0-6-2Ts, of which Cae Harris had an allocation of around half a dozen. Engines were rotated by the parent shed at Merthyr as required, but though the actual distance from Cae Harris to Merthyr was only three miles down the hill, so great was the difference in altitude that the shortest rail link via Quakers Yard measured 18 miles. In practice therefore Cae Harris ran its affairs largely independently.

On 9 July 1960 Cae Harris engine No 5635 was at the head of the 3.15 departure, starting for Dowlais from the upper level platform at Ystrad Mynach. Even though there was a 40min wait off the previous diesel from Cardiff this was a lot better than the situation on weekdays, when there was no connection at Ystrad Mynach at all. Instead the 3.15 started one stop up the line at Nelson, and then it could only connect with the 2.25pm Pontypool Road–Neath stopper. This was generally in the hands of another '56xx' tank, for example No 6685 two months later on 9 September. No 5635 had just two coaches to cope with on the Dowlais train, whereas most branch services earlier in the day were formed of a different three-coach set. The third locomotive and set of coaches arrived unadvertised on the 4.50am (SX) workmen's train

from Rhymney to Bedlinog. This involved yet another '56xx' hauling one of the last steam passenger duties remaining at Rhymney shed. It had to reverse on the Rhymney main line in the shadow of lofty Ystrad Mynach South signalbox before starting the climb up the branch to the collieries.

Even though No 5635 was hauling little more than its own weight, it would still have to dig in when the time came to restart on the sharp uphill curve out of Bedlinog. There the gradient sharpened from 1 to 40 to 1 in 36-31 for three miles, as the line resumed double track and climbed away from the valley floor up the south face of the mountainside towards Cwmbargoed. Here No 5635 breasted the summit and turned downhill round the mountain ledge high above Pentrebach to deposit its short train at Cae Harris around 4pm.

What the Taff–Bargoed lacked in passenger traffic, however, it more than made up for on the freight side. To handle heavy mineral trains exceptional measures were available when required to overcome the exceptional gradients.

One banker was usually sufficient to assist a train engine up most steep climbs on the Western, but over the Taff–Bargoed line operating instructions specifically permitted two engines to be coupled in front and two more behind if necessary. Main recipients of this treatment were the iron ore trains up to the Dowlais Works of Guest, Keen Iron & Steel, and they shook the ground they passed over when four 0-6-2Ts were on the job going flat out.

Whilst not suggesting that such a cavalcade as this was needed on 9 July 1960, there was coal to be worked up to Furnace Top at Dowlais even on Saturdays, and sometimes these mineral workings were booked to be assisted.

Carrying Cae Harris target K3, a '56xx' like Nos 5603 or 5610 would start its day by running down light with a brake van ready to bank the 4.15am Cardiff Stonefield Jc–Cwmbargoed empties from Ffeldcaiach Siding. It then made a loaded trip down to Aber Jc outside Caerphilly and returned through to

Furnace Top. K3 was then close at hand on weekdays to provide a second banker if required when K2 assisted K5 at 1pm. K6 was also available to provide still more assistance for K5 during its 8hr day, exclusively on banking work, during the week.

The '56xx' engine on K3 was then serviced and remanned at Cae Harris shed between 1.35 and 3.45pm, before going out again every day including Saturday. After remanning, the engine's target designation changed from K3 to K3R. It ran more trips to Furnace Top, took the 7pm loaded coal train from Cwmbargoed down to Nelson and then finished as it had begun, this time by assisting K1R on the final load of empties up to Cwmbargoed at 9.25pm. On Saturday 27 August 1960 when No 5650 came over the summit of the line on the 5.52pm Ystrad Mynach–Dowlais passenger, No 5605 was at Cwmbargoed forming up the 7pm departure. It was a gruelling but profitable day's work on K3 to which the Cae Harris '56xxs' were well suited.

Cae Harris's limited resources were frequently rather stretched, with two daily passenger turns and four to five freight workings for its six locomotives to cover. It was not uncommon for one Valleys shed to lend locos to another. Not surprisingly Radyr engines which arrived each day with the empties from Stonefield Jc were sometimes retained to help, and on 9 July one of these, No 6660, was also noted helping out along the branch.

The Llynvi Valley and Porthcawl Branches

Although Tondu shed was compactly situated in a triangle of branch lines, this depot enjoyed a much wider selection of work than Dowlais Cae Harris. So it was only to be expected that Tondu's all Great Western allocation of 40 or so engines would comprise much more in the way of variety than just 0-6-2Ts. Well over half the stud was made up of pannier tanks and in 1960 many of the other types represented there were already 30–40 years old. Nevertheless, Tondu was an efficiently run depot. Like Aberdare its engines

were maintained well up to the best main line standards, even though much of the route mileage involved at Tondu was only single track. All Saturday turns were economically covered using a bare minimum of engines, with a '57xx' pannier like No 3616 switching smartly between pilot, passenger and freight duties. Four Rail Motor turns for an allocation of three auto-fitted engines left no margin for casualties. All three were duly in service and ran like clockwork right through the day.

These three '55xx' Prairies were now the last WR 2-6-2T engines fitted up for Rail Motor operations in South Wales. Their replacement at Tondu by '64xx' panniers two months later was a sad acknowledgement that the days of four auto-trailers with the engine sandwiched between each pair of coaches were by now effectively over. The extra power of a '55xx' was no longer needed. Withdrawal of passenger services over the very steepest stretch at the top of the Llynvi valley between Cymmer Afan and Abergwnfi on 13 June 1960 would also make it easier for '64xx' pannier tanks to manage the passenger work on which they could handle three trailers.

In the meantime, however, the three '55xx' were still busy on 9 July. No 5592 started at 7.30am and handled the Porthcawl auto all day, connecting with the main line at Pyle 3¾ miles away. No 5529 returned to Tondu for a fleeting visit at 1.30pm, but then, with barely time to take water, it was off again starting the afternoon turn to Porthcawl at 1.45pm. Eventually No 5529 was relieved at 8pm by 0-6-2T No 6673. This engine had already covered two round trips to Blaengwynfi and a workmen's service to Tremains Platform on the Bridgend Trading Estate. No 6673 still had to make another journey to Blaengwynfi after finishing up the Porthcawl service at 9.15pm, and it was not due back into Tondu until the wrong side of midnight.

Unfortunately Pyle station was awkwardly situated in the middle of the eastbound climb to Stormy Siding, so none of the London expresses was booked to call there. Long distance passengers for the Porthcawl branch usually had to change at both Pyle and Cardiff. Oddly enough though, Porthcawl residents were encouraged to travel to other resorts by Saturday through connections at Pyle for Kingswear, Penzance and Bournemouth. The branch push-pull service was therefore greatly augmented on summer Saturdays and No 5529 would be on hand in the curved branch platform at Pyle when No 6936 *Breccles Hall* called on the up side with the 8.50am Swansea–Paignton relief. No 6936 then had to heave its train up the last mile of 1 in 93 to Stormy Summit. Here on a Saturday the loops would be empty as No 6936 turned downhill. But if things were going to plan No 6936 would then pass Mogul No 6336 blasting up the westbound climb from Bridgend on 6F04, the 7.20am freight from Severn Tunnel Jc as it cleared this congested section on to Margam as quickly as possible.

At Bridgend the Llynvi platform was sited on the up side of the station. From here No 5555 worked three Rail Motor trips to Blaengwynfi in the morning before handing over to No 6673's non push-pull set at 1.30pm. For the evening Rail Motor service No 5545 came off Tondu shed around 5.45pm ready for three more sorties up the valley from Bridgend. So at 6pm No 5545 was all ready and waiting to connect when 'Castle' No 7023 came sweeping smartly in round Bridgend East curve with the 1.55 down London, brakes hard on, and when the 13-coach train shuddered to a halt it was perfectly positioned alongside the cramped platform face at Bridgend Middle.

Sharing the other non-Rail Motor Llynvi passenger turns with Nos 6673 and 3616 were another Pannier

Right: '4575' class No 5534 has arrived at the head of the Llynvi Valley in Abergwynfi station with the 11.25am Rail Motor from Bridgend on Thursday 27 August 1959. In the background No 8710 is hauling a train of coal empties up the 1 in 32 gradient to Abergwynfi Colliery. *Steve Derek*

No 9606 and 0-6-2T No 5690. No 5690 was still carrying GWR lettering in plain block style, probably the last engine to be seen with this livery. Its black paint was still kept well groomed at Tondu and on Saturdays it sometimes worked to Cardiff with the 7.50am passenger from Porthcawl, though that train was hauled by No 4675 on this occasion. Instead No 5690, in the course of working Tondu Turn 1, made the only remaining trip to Abergwynfi on an unadvertised colliers' train from Maesteg. The set-up here was a bit confusing because Abergwynfi was still shown with a normal rail service in all the summer public and working timetables. Obviously withdrawal of traffic on 13 June 1960 must have come at very short notice, and instead trains now ran from Cymmer Afan up to the head of the valley at the neighbouring station of Blaengwynfi, terminating right outside the mouth of Blaenrhondda Tunnel. Part of both routes, which had once run separately up the valley, were still utilised. Because of a suspect viaduct on the old Rhondda and Swansea Bay Railway line all services were diverted onto the GWR Abergwynfi line to bypass it, returning to the R&SB route by a new connection southwest of Blaengwynfi.

Tondu shed also operated a couple of large Prairies. These were generally used for one of the Llynvi afternoon passenger turns, but on 9 July No 4144 was parked spare outside the shed, alongside a couple of panniers awaiting works or reallocation. The other Prairie, No 4121, made its way to Llantrisant ready to work the 9.45am special excursion to Porthcawl. This day out was organised by Pontyclun Social Club, and No 4121 returned from the coast at 6.45pm in plenty of time for members to enjoy a convivial evening at the club afterwards.

Meanwhile freight workings were bustling in and out of Tondu all morning. Swansea East Dock 2-8-0T No 4292 made two visits with empties from Margam,

returning on both occasions engine and brake van only. Two of Tondu's own 2-8-0Ts, Nos 4222 and 4218, also made three loaded trips to Margam. These were timed to take anything from 2–4hr for the return journey of 24 miles depending on the time of day and the route used, either via Pyle for down trains or the more northerly alternative past Waterhall Jc. All were banked from Tondu up to Cefn Jc by the Tondu No 3 pilot No 8710.

Two more 2-8-0Ts, Nos 4243 and 5208, were busy feeding Tondu yards from the north on trip workings DO3 and DO6. These originated at Blaengarw, Wern Tarw and, very locally, at Gelli Las.

Up the Ogmore Valley the 6.45am Tondu–Nantymoel empties was equipped only with Pannier No 3690. Even though its load would be progressively reduced before striking the steepest stretch of 1 in 32 gradient beyond Wyndham Colliery the train had to be assisted daily by the No 1 bank engine. Today Tondu South Yard pilot No 8453 fulfilled this role and the two engines filled the valley with their exchange of whistles and echoing exhausts. After parking the train at Nantymoel Nos 3690 and 8453 returned together coupled to a brake van. Sufficient traffic still remained for No 3690 to make a second trip part way as far as Ogmore Vale at 8.15am, this time without assistance.

After midday paths began to become available up the main line from Bridgend. No 4236 worked the 12.10pm Tondu–Cardiff coal train and No 3616, making its last appearance of a busy day, followed at 5.40pm. A number of other pannier tanks were busy on trip and pilot work, notably to Caerau and around Bridgend, but there was one other special goods which was a bit out of the ordinary when No 4269 set out with the 2.20pm from Tondu on to the Vale of Glamorgan line as far as Aberthaw power station. Generally its coal requirements were serviced from the Barry end. By the time No 4269 returned from

Aberthaw to Tondu Ogmore Jc yard with empties at 10.35pm the day's freight workings were complete, and only Nos 5545 and 6673 off the evening passenger turns remained to come in.

Abercynon Turn JB

On 9 July 1960 auto-fitted pannier No 6438 was the engine responsible for the two return Pontypridd–St Fagans–Cardiff Rail Motor services. However, these only served to get No 6438 and its two push-pull coaches into position for the main profit-making purpose of the day, which was to work five well-loaded shuttle trips between Cardiff General and Penarth.

No 6438 in lined green livery was due off Abercynon shed carrying target JB at 7.15am. After running light engine to Pontypridd it was coupled on to the Rail Motor stock, made up of a non-corridor third fitted with through auto-control gear, and trailer car No W196W dating from 1933. Spares kept for JB were Pannier No 6435, which was not as smart as No 6438 and apparently still in black livery; also postwar trailer No W241W. No 241 took over regularly from No 196 for the last month of Rail Motor working on JB at the beginning of August.

No 6438 then waited in the down bay position of the huge island platform at Pontypridd. Here it collected a number of passengers wishing to travel direct to the Western Docks area of Cardiff, who arrived on the 7am diesel service from Treherbert. At 7.46am the Pannier was due off, hauling its train over the steep 1 in 69 gradient up the hillside from Treforest to join the old Barry Railway main line at Tonteg. No 6438 then traversed some delightful scenery as it crossed from the Taff to the Ely Valley on a line which had hardly changed from the day it opened 71 years before. Somersault signals abounded, while at Efail Isaf the four-road through station with its spacious platform loops would have been handy in many locations on much busier routes than this, where expresses were so often delayed by stopping trains. Sadly, no overtaking manoeuvres were required at Efail Isaf any more; the Saturday freight service was now almost non-existent and the last down passenger train of the day called there before 2.30pm.

JB made three stops before joining the GW main line right under the rural shadow of St Fagans Castle. After another mile the Cardiff suburbs closed in beside the tracks and No 6438 completed its 14¾-mile run to Cardiff Clarence Road station, beside the Ely river mudflats, at 8.30am. JB was hardly in competition with the 7am Treherbert train along the more direct Taff Vale line from Pontypridd to Cardiff General. That had come and gone 15min before. However, No 6438 now had two Penarth round trips to fulfil, the first starting immediately at 8.35am, and, having escaped the usual South Wales gradients on its travels so far, it was now facing the right way round to propel its train up the 1 in 40 climb away from stops at Penarth Dock and Dingle Road Halt into Penarth Town station.

The 1958 economy cuts had unfortunately eliminated the useful mid-morning return trip from Penarth catering for city centre shoppers. This used to run at 10.40am to Cardiff Queen St, continuing from there up the Coryton branch. Instead No 6438 now sat idle at Cardiff General from 10.17 to 11.30am.

After its midday fill-in turn to Pontypridd and back JB would be wedged with trippers travelling to sample the triple Penarth attractions of seafront, pier and baths. Sometimes the '64xx' would be reluctant to start from Dingle Road at the first attempt and it was then allowed to roll back up to half a coach length for another try. Meanwhile the normally sociable atmosphere of the auto saloons would be rudely interrupted, as standing passengers were left holding on for dear life, when No 6438 finally got under way after smartly reversing direction up the climb. The

steepness of the gradient could be readily visualised from the train as it climbed up into the centre of Penarth and terminated there high above sea level.

Cardiff Clarence Road closed at 2pm on Saturdays, so three of JB's trips ended at the Riverside portion of Cardiff General station. Here No 6438 had the Riverside platforms virtually to itself during the afternoon, an oasis of relative calm while, nearby, mainline trains queued up to come in from Blackpool, Birkenhead, Newcastle, Portsmouth and Paignton a couple of platform widths away.

JB set off for its last journey from Cardiff General back to Pontypridd at 5.38pm, but in the week No 6438 then had to perform Turn JD, comprising passenger shunting duties around Pontypridd station, before it was finally released back to Abercynon shed at 8.52pm. When JB was taken over by a diesel multiple-unit on 13 September 1960 it marked a major change both to the atmosphere of Cardiff General and to the amount of steam working left on the Valleys passenger network. As a steam locomotive still had to be supplied to shunt Turn JD five days a week, any economies of operation resulting from the changeover were more limited than would otherwise have been the case.

Suburban Summary

Suburban Rail Motor services were retreating in the face of dieselisation at other locations too. Included among these was the area around Plymouth, where clear signs of the Tamar road bridge under construction were now rising out of the river waters. Completion of this road link would soon put pay to Plymouth suburban rail services across the Tamar altogether.

But in the summer of 1960 there were still two steam push-pull sets in daily use here, working intermittently between 5.45am and 7.45pm. By now off-peak suburban services were in the hands of DMUs, and only one of the Rail Motor rosters still involved journeys over the Royal Albert Bridge to Saltash and St Germans. The other operated exclusively along the attractive branch skirting Dartmoor as far as Tavistock South. Inevitably the number of '64xx' tank engines needed for the remaining auto trains had already been drastically thinned out. By the end of July 1960 only Nos 6400 and 6413 remained at Laira, reinforced as required by three motor fitted '55xx' tanks for the Tavistock duty.

The same pattern of rush hour remnants, left over from once busy steam suburban networks, was evident in the Birmingham and London areas. Here respectively, '51xx' and '61xx' large Prairies still held sway over the steam passenger turns which survived. On 9 July these mainly involved suburban trains during the Saturday morning and midday peaks.

Bristol, however, retained a significant proportion of steam suburban services working directly alongside diesel units all day, and a wide variety of tank engines was in use. Most of the WR's stock of BR Class 3 '820xx' 2-6-2Ts had gravitated from South Wales to Bristol Bath Road a couple of years before. These worked to Portishead, Yatton, Henbury and the Avonmouth line on 9 July. They also shared one or two Bath Green Park trains with the numerous Ivatt Class 2 2-6-2Ts. All but No 5561 of the once popular '45xx' small Prairies in the area had now been displaced, and that one was withdrawn from Bath Road for scrap during the course of the month. No 5508 did, however, maintain a small Prairie presence at Temple Meads when it arrived around 12.15pm with the 9.47am from Westbury to Bristol, routed over the Cheddar Valley line via Wells. Soon after a '57xx' pannier, thought to be No 8790, appeared to work the 12.35pm Temple Meads-Severn Beach, and during the afternoon No 8779 came rollicking in carrying express headcode on the 1.12pm Calne–Weston-super-Mare. A 48½ mile journey was involved, which was substantial for a small engine like this on what was usually an eight-coach train.

Though having no recognised suburban services as such, the Worcester area saw a lot of local steam working in all directions, and large GW Prairies were well represented here. Among these was No 4110 on a Worcester–Leamington–Worcester–Wolverhampton diagram. For a change those trains which weren't steam were often handled by one of the dwindling fleet of GW diesel railcars. No W22W was forming the 12.5pm Stratford–Worcester and No W26W made up the 2.5pm Kidderminster–Shrewsbury, returning at 4.20pm on a through service via Hartlebury to Worcester Foregate St.

Hereford–Paddington expresses had traditionally relied, more than any other WR main line service, on feeder traffic off secondary routes to help make the trains pay, but now the connecting lines which remained were struggling to stay open. Ledbury and Moreton-in-Marsh had already lost their junction status, while Cheltenham–Honeybourne stopping trains had been withdrawn just over a month earlier in June 1960. Only Evesham and Kingham were still busy and even these junctions were both surviving on borrowed time. 0-6-0PT No 9473 was waiting at Evesham to ply its trade on the 11.20am local to Stratford-upon-Avon, as No 7002 *Devizes Castle* hauling the 9.50am Hereford–Paddington made an Evesham stop to augment its modest load.

Secondary routes were sometimes able to rival main line expresses in the service they could offer. Across a beautiful Cotswold landscape for example, from Cheltenham to London the 2.25pm Cheltenham–Kingham and its onward connection at 3.42pm could manage a much quicker service than No 7035 *Ogmore Castle* hauling the 11.45am through train from Cheltenham via Gloucester; though as it turned out their journey times virtually tied on 9 July due to late arrivals at Paddington.

But the attractions of the rival route went no further than a 22min saving in schedule. The Kingham line

was no longer shown in the main line pages of the timetables as a through route and the 2.25pm service was innocent of any sort of refreshment facilities all the way to Paddington. Amazingly the 2.25pm by rail throughout to London received less prominence in the 1960 timetable than the 1.5pm road and rail service from Cheltenham via Oxford, though both resulted in the same 5.25pm arrival at Paddington. Cheap fares of 15s 10d (79p) by road and rail transport were clearly displayed, but the advertised through rail fare was inflated by an extra 6s 2d (31p) for the privilege of travelling an additional 12 miles via Gloucester. The most competitive price by rail was actually around 20s 6d for 109 miles via Kingham and received no mention at all. Small wonder then that this alternative line was languishing and little used.

As the sleek shape of double-chimney engine No 7006 *Lydford Castle* came flying over the Cotswolds into Kingham with the 1.50pm from Hereford the Cheltenham coaches were standing at one branch platform, while 2-6-2T No 4573 on the 4pm Chipping Norton train waited at the other.

Such busy scenes at branch junctions were still relatively commonplace but becoming fewer. It was surprising that the stump of the Chipping Norton branch, by now cut right back from King's Sutton and Banbury, lasted as long as it did on a meagre diet of two passenger and mixed trains each day. But at Kingham tracks on the bow-girder overbridge across the Oxford–Worcester main line, which had formerly carried the Swansea–Barry–Newcastle ports-to-ports expresses, were already rusty with disuse. Once one branch shut, the expense of running a substantial rural junction station like Kingham proved too heavy to be borne by what interchange traffic remained. Not even the busiest summer Saturday could make significant inroads into costs such as these, and ultimately even the main line service was able to survive better without them. So now it is time to retrace our steps on to the main line and see how 'Castle' No 7035 with its Cheltenham express was faring at Swindon.

Left: Standard Class 3 2-6-2T No 82006 arrives at Bristol Temple Meads with the 1.45pm from Portishead on Saturday 2 July 1960. Extensive use was still being made of '82xxx' tank engines on Bristol area suburban workings, but most local trains were now in the hands of diesel units, one of which is stabled on the middle line. *John Hodge*

6. PERSONAL VIEW — SWINDON JUNCTION

In 1960 many offices and schools required attendance as usual on Saturday mornings. In the middle of GCE exams that included me, and, whereas all exams were over by the following Saturday, so that I could then spend a full day at Swindon, on 9 July it was lunchtime before I was free to make for the lineside.

So I arrived outside Swindon station just before 1.30pm to find the up side platforms overflowing with trains. The 9.10am Kingswear–Birmingham was just leaving Platform 5, 12min late behind 'Grange' No 6813 *Eastbury Grange* of Exeter. Its train wound out on to the up main line as No 6813 started to regain 6min of lost time before Oxford. Meanwhile No 7035 was being held at the opposite side of the up platform on the 11.45am Cheltenham–Paddington. Well before the 'Castle' was signalled away at 1.33pm, 'Hall' No 7911 had arrived at Platform 5 with the 10.20am Weymouth–Wolverhampton, which was still running on time at this stage.

The six-coach set making up the main portion of this train was the last complete formation of ex-GW stock still carrying roofboards. At the start of the summer timetable the yard foreman at Wolverhampton Cannock Road carriage sidings had gathered together a set of Collett coaches with compartment doors. This stock suited the old style large carriage roofboards, brought out this year after their usual winter storage for the last time. So here they were, making their

weekly return trip proclaiming: 'Wolverhampton, Birmingham, Oxford, Swindon and Weymouth'.

On my way up to the platform I greeted Tom Hayworth, who was cheerily co-manning the ticket collectors' gate with his usual friendly good humour, in spite of the jostling holiday crowd surging through the subway. As I was swept past on a tide of humanity, he said 'Come to see the Trip specials then, have you?' Not being from Swindon I did not grasp the exact significance of Trip from this comment, and I had no time to ask. Though I frequently talked to Tom when we met on many other occasions, I never enquired about it and I did not discover the details for a long time afterwards.

On the up platform the station was heaving with activity, so it was a little while before I could draw breath and approach a couple of familiar faces at the platform end to find out what had passed through earlier in the day. In the meantime the main focus of attention was a 'Britannia' Pacific simmering gently at Swindon Station West up starter as it awaited a road

Below: No 6985 *Parwick Hall* arrives at Swindon on Sunday 26 April 1959 with the 8.50am Cheltenham–Paddington. This is the same train which was handled by No 6985 on 9 July 1960. On the right No 5066 *Sir Felix Pole* is just ex-works and will haul the train to Paddington, before taking up work from Old Oak Common primarily on the 'Torbay Express'. *R. C. Riley*

115

in. No 70029 *Shooting Star* on the heavy 8am from Neyland had maintained its usual weekday timing up from Newport, and this meant that on the Saturday schedule, involving an overall speed of less than 40mph, it had turned up outside Swindon 16min early at 1.32pm. So No 70029 was right behind No 7911 approaching from Wootton Bassett. Even after standing outside for 3min the 'Britannia' was still at rest in the platform 12min early. Though it then left right on time at 1.52pm, punctual running was much more difficult to maintain in the busy procession beyond Swindon. Three minutes lost before Twyford could not be regained and more delays afterwards made No 70029 7min behind time into Paddington, the same margin of lateness as No 7035.

On the down side there was a lull, and after No 5091 *Cleeve Abbey* had passed on the 11.55am Paddington–Pembroke Dock at 1.20pm — heard rather than seen, as I approached the station, with the sound of No 5091's distinctively noisy vacuum pump ticking away loudly at speed — the opportunity was taken to get some steam-worked local traffic away for Westbury and Kemble.

However, as 2pm came and went, with the 11.5am Wolverhampton–Weymouth nowhere in sight, a backlog began to build up. The 11.5 had left Oxford 16min late, with Weymouth Standard 5 No 73017 working home on the opposite leg of No 7911's Weymouth–Wolverhampton diagram. No 73017 probably had to tag along behind the 1.15pm Didcot–Swindon local as far as Shrivenham instead of overtaking it at Challow, and so it was 2.19pm before the Standard 5 eventually swung into the Swindon platform loop 23min late. The 11.5 now had to be dealt with promptly, otherwise it would delay the 1.15pm down fast from Paddington, which was due to pass at 2.33½pm. A couple of minutes were saved, enabling the Weymouth to set off for Chippenham at 2.24pm, with everyone hoping No 73017 would now get a good move on. A minute later No 6915 *Mursley Hall* slipped round the back into Platform 1 on the Didcot local and it began to look as if the 1.15 Paddington–Weston might get a clear run through after all.

Nonstop expresses were the main spectacle at Swindon. From the up platform — where the sun was unfortunately at totally the wrong angle for photography — you could see them coming for a mile in each direction on the long, gentle, southward curve. Brunel's broad gauge spacing of the middle roads allowed a grandstand view through the station, and every effort was made here to get the nonstops past without delay. No 73017 had made sufficient progress for all three double-pegged sets of down signals, homes, starters and distants, to come off virtually together for the 1.15. The loud whirr of the motor-operated distant arm for Rodbourne Lane box, dropping beneath Swindon West's home signal, meant

the down main was now clear. It was only 2.28pm. The 1.15 must be really going some, and all eyes at the platform ends turned Mecca-like to the east.

On Saturdays the 1.15pm Paddington–Weston-super-Mare was the fastest express of the day at Swindon. It was a train of the highest calibre and had a pedigree as long as your arm. The 2hr timing to Bristol stretched back over half a century, and, whilst it no longer ran nonstop any more, on weekdays in 1960 the 1.15's 66.8mph schedule to Bath was among a handful of the fastest steam-worked timings in the world. Now that the 39min booking from Darlington to York on the Eastern was usually diesel-worked, the 1.15 was not far behind Paris–Basle Rapide No 41 on the SNCF. This was run by ex-PLM four-cylinder compound Pacifics from Troyes Depot, like 231-G-87, at speeds of up to 67.5mph from start to stop. On summer Saturdays the schedule of the 1.15 to Bath was eased by 10min, but it was still the only mile-a-minute departure from Paddington for 12hr. This took some timing in the middle of a busy day with the usual load increased from seven to 11 coaches.

On weekdays since September 1958 the 1.15 was an Old Oak mileage turn, originally arranged for Gas Turbine No 18000 but now back in the hands of 'Castles' and sometimes 'Kings'. After a quick 60min turn-round at Bath Road the engine was back in London by 6.45pm. Engines used tended to alter quite frequently and performances varied to a similar extent from 'Bristolian' standards down to something less than mile-a-minute levels on occasion. On Saturdays the 1.15 reverted to Bath Road haulage, well established over many years, and despite the heavier Saturday load, progress to Swindon often equalled times achieved on weekdays.

Running a few minutes early and inside even time from Paddington the 1.15 appeared at speed passing Highworth Jc. Quickly the engine resolved itself into the unmistakable outline of a 'County'. It was trailing a dark dry haze of smoke and clearly going at full stretch. Sure enough this was No 1009 *County of Carmarthen* which came racing through the station with a healthy roar, having averaged 65.3mph from Twyford inclusive of any delays.

No 1009 had had an interesting day's work, with something of a rags to riches tale to show for it. In the morning the locomotive started out from Bristol on the 8.20am Weston for Paddington. This train was unusually loaded to 14 coaches, which would have been a handful for the regular 'Castle'. No 1009 fell behind No 5066 *Sir Felix Pole* hauling the preceding Bristol train, which was due through Swindon 12½min before-hand, and at Didcot the 'County' lost its path in front of No 7004 *Eastnor Castle*, which was coming off the avoiding line on the up 'Cathedrals Express'. No 7004 then preceded No 1009 all the way to Paddington.

By the time *County of Carmarthen* had arrived 25min late at 11.45am, and the empty stock was drawn out

Above: Standard 5 No 73017 is not performing very well as it approaches Oxford 16min late with the 11.5am Wolverhampton–Weymouth on 9 July 1960. More time was then lost on to Swindon. While No 73017 was waiting in the platform at Oxford, 2-6-0 No 6350 struggled past running 56min late in the opposite direction with the 9.25am Weymouth–Wolverhampton. *Mike Lake*

Right: On 9 July 1960, still carrying the reporting number off its up journey when it hauled the 8.20am Weston–Paddington, No 1009 *County of Carmarthen* has a lighter load on its way back with the 1.15pm down. No 1009 has a full head of steam and is already making good progress past West Ealing on its mile-a-minute run to Bath. The milk tanks in the background will soon be hauled out of this siding to form the 3.58pm milk empties to Neyland hauled by No 4957 *Postlip Hall.* The 2.40pm Wood Lane–Penzance milk empties with No 7024 *Powis Castle* will go round the west side of the West Ealing triangle instead, and proceed straight to Maidenhead for a pathing stop. *John Faulkner*

Right: On a date just given as July 1960, but which could easily be Friday 8 July, No 5049 *Earl of Plymouth* passes Langley Crossing box on the 8.20am Weston-super-Mare-Paddington with Driver Higby of Bath Road at the regulator. On 9 July 1960 No 5049 worked the 11.45am Bristol–Paddington nonstop via the Badminton route. *Kenneth Leech*

20min afterwards, there would be a rush to turn the engine at Ranelagh Bridge and trim the tender. There wasn't even time to replace the up 'A18' reporting numbers with correct 'B11' plates in the number frame, before it was time to back into No 1 Platform at the terminus, ready for a prompt departure just one minute late. On a weekday, going back with the slow heavy 1.40pm down, after a poor run up the Bath Road crew would have no chance of redemption. But on Saturday the 1.15 beckoned, and this was a challenge they were ready for, out past West Ealing in 9min and Twyford under 32½ with No 1009 nicely into its stride.

After passing Swindon within 75min, No 1009 was sure to have caught up with No 73017 before Chippenham at around 2.45pm. But the Saturday schedule made some allowances for a check like this, and just under 40min later No 1009 was seen curving round into Temple Meads punctually at 3.23pm, before working on through to Weston.

The main rush of down afternoon expresses started to appear at Swindon around 3.10pm. This sequence did not get off to a very good start, because the 1.38pm Paddington–Weston had to undergo an unscheduled engine change. 'Castle' No 5023 *Brecon Castle* had already come across from Swindon shed and was waiting in No 2 bay ready to take over when the 1.38 arrived. With no undue rush it replaced recently completed 'Warship' No D822 *Hercules* which then made its way back over to the Works. This had all the signs of a planned manoeuvre rather than a failure. The diesel was completing a test run which had started on the 7.5am ex-Cheltenham from Swindon to Paddington earlier and, it being a Saturday, the locomotive returned with the 1.38 instead of the customary Bristol portion of the weekday 2.55pm down.

Although No 5023 was eventually 9min late getting away for Bristol and Weston-super-Mare, the 'Warship' diesel had managed its timekeeping from Paddington more successfully than No 7926 following with the 1.45pm down Cheltenham express. Calling only at Didcot it was another 8min before this ran in at 3.30pm. *Willey Hall* was recently ex-Works in April, so the 1.45 with 11 coaches should have been a straight-forward enough proposition for Gloucester's best 'Hall'. However, there was an abnormally tight margin at Reading West Jc for No 6835 *Eastham Grange* on the 11.50am Bournemouth Central–Birmingham to cross the path of No 7926. If both trains were exactly on time, the crew of No 7926 passing Reading General at 2.28pm would actually be able to see No 6835 ahead of them coming off the Reading West Curve also at 2.28pm, as it crossed over the main lines to join the down relief. No 6835 was a minute late reaching Oxford; it would have precedence over No 7926 at Reading West Jc and No 6835 probably dealt No 7926 a nasty check there. This would diminish the chances of a race between the two engines, because otherwise

they were timed to run neck and neck along the four-track section to Didcot, with No 7926 gradually overtaking in the vicinity of Goring. A fair old curtain of spray would be hanging around there if both engines picked up water from Goring troughs at the same time.

Neither No 5099 nor No 7023 on the following 1.50 and 1.55pm down South Wales expresses fared any better in this queue. No 7023 was left kicking its heels at Swindon Station East signals, waiting to come into Platform 3 at 3.42pm, because Platform 1, which was vacant, was not long enough to hold a 13-coach train. Both locos made up almost all the 8–10min of lost time after Swindon however. *Compton Castle* ran to Newport in 63min and was a minute late at Cardiff. Its Canton compatriot *Penrice Castle* had to call additionally at Badminton and Severn Tunnel Jc. The 1.55 was the slowest South Wales train of the day and its schedule was no great challenge even with a 450-ton load. No 7023 was also on time at Cardiff.

Meanwhile, activity on local trains continued to reveal an absolute abundance of 'Castles' which had begun the day on Swindon shed, where they had no realistic prospect of carrying out any express work which would make use of their summer Saturday potential. These included Nos 4089 *Donnington Castle*, 5002 *Ludlow Castle*, 5068 *Beverston Castle*, 7016 *Chester Castle* and 7031 *Cromwell's Castle*, all of which were turned out to work trains which would not have taxed a 2-6-2T.

The situation was that Swindon shed had three turns for six engines each day which warranted Class 7 power. Even these were relatively undemanding by normal 'Castle' standards and two of them included a large proportion of milk and stopping passenger haulage. All could and often were handled quite comfortably by Class 6 'Counties' when required. One of the duties was a two-day cycle between Paddington and Swansea; another turn involved a Swindon–Paddington–Bristol–Swindon circuit and third was the working to Paddington covered by the 7.5am Cheltenham engine referred to above.

After borrowing No 5094 *Tretower Castle* from Bath Road for the Swansea job, substituting No 1027 *County of Stafford* also of Bath Road for another Swindon engine on the 10.5am Paddington–Bristol, and putting No D822 on the 7.5 working, there wasn't any more express work left. Add to the seven Swindon-based 'Castles' which were in traffic a couple of visitors (Nos 4089 and 7016), plus a supply of engines which had to be run-in (such as No 5044 *Earl of Dunraven*), then supplement these with four active 'Counties' (Nos 1010, 1015, 5007 and 7037 are all excluded, being away under Works control) and it can be seen that the Running Foreman would have had no difficulty at all in finding more than enough engines to cover his requirements.

Nos 5000 or 5009 and 5064 did find gainful employment on long distance parcels traffic, but the other 'Castles' were left hauling five and six-coach locals, with a succession of engines being steamed just to make one round trip from Swindon to Didcot and back. What wouldn't Weymouth shed have given to be able to borrow a couple of these spare 'Castles'?

Ordinarily this imbalance of engines at Swindon shed would not have been so glaringly obvious, firstly because more 'Castles' would normally be away on regular work, and secondly because Swindon engines were so often poached as a matter of course by other sheds. Old Oak usually had one or two 'Castles' lying over off Friday night's up milk train arrivals. Another would sometimes be on hand at Laira off the 3.30pm Hull–Plymouth fish. Here a good one like No 5000 *Launceston Castle*, or old Laira engines like Nos 5023 or 7031 of good reputation before being reallocated away to Swindon, would be welcomed with open arms for weekend express work. As we will soon see, however, No 7031 could rarely be plundered in this way. Instead on 9 July it was the 10 Swindon 'Halls' which were scattered to the four winds — just as well too, because there was no work for more than three of them at home. Two were borrowed by Old Oak Common, with one each at Bath Road, Canton, Tyseley and Laira. None of these 'Halls' actually ended up back at Swindon during the day, but they put in some sterling service filling gaps at other sheds by working to Newton Abbot, Paignton, Salisbury, Severn Tunnel Jc and Weymouth.

Although it never received a double-chimney, No 7031 *Cromwell's Castle* was absolutely resplendent and looked ready for any challenge when it came off Swindon shed as usual at 3.15pm in the afternoon. So many Swindon duties were conducted by night on milk and parcels traffic, with the engines away for

long periods, that it was inconvenient to keep them clean. There was such a plentiful supply of freshly painted ex-works machines on hand for any special requirements that a well turned out engine was always available at Swindon when necessary. So the shed cleaners just tended to concentrate on two of their own locos and in 1960 these were No 3440 and also ex-Laira favourite No 7031. Laira used to pack No 7031 off to Paddington on three single express trips to and fro every two days, but contrastingly through the first half of 1960 and now on 9 July No 7031 was used mainly on the 3.35pm Swindon–Banbury fish empties. This could load to 24 four-wheeled vans, but usually on Saturdays there was less than a handful to be consigned back towards the GC; sometimes just a guard's van. So this immaculate engine was coupled to three empty vehicles in the up carriage sidings and at 3.35pm sauntered off with its piffling train towards Oxford, when at any other shed, No 7031 would have been working hard to improve on its 56,370 annual mileage, instead of being held back for such an obviously uneconomic and nondescript duty.

By way of balancing the picture it should be noted that availability of Swindon engines was excellent, from 'Castles', through at least nine of the 10 'Halls', right down to the pannier tank which reached Weston-super-Mare during the afternoon. Swindon was

Below: On 9 July 1960 No 5981 *Frensham Hall* negotiates Hatton South Junction and heads for Snow Hill with the 10am Weymouth–Birmingham. It has been seriously delayed by the 9.25am from Weymouth in front and is now some 35min late. No 5981 is the locomotive which, no doubt still in the same old dirty Swindon shed condition, will make its mark working the down 'Mayflower' a week later. *D. K. Jones*

centrally positioned to be able to loan out locomotives with a minimum of light engine movements, and it was an advantage for Regional Operating Officers (called Traffic Officers by 1960) to know where they could find a couple of engines when they were sorely needed at short notice.

The previous weekend even No 5009 *Shrewsbury Castle*, an engine with worn inside cylinders which would lead to its withdrawal from service three months later, had been borrowed to work through from Plymouth on the 12.40pm Newquay–Cardiff.

The following Saturday, as seasonal traffic built up on 16 July, borrowing of Swindon engines was more widespread. Ex-works No 1010 *County of Caernarvon* was the loco at Plymouth this time, coming up to Bristol on the 7.30am from Penzance. At Old Oak Common No 1021 *County of Montgomery* was commandeered to work the 9.55am down to Swansea, possibly after arriving with one of the early morning empty stock trains from Didcot. However, when No 5981 *Frensham Hall* appeared from Swindon depot at 12.25pm that day no one could possibly have foretold where it would end up. No 5981 was probably booked for the same train as it worked on 9 July, taking over the 10am Weymouth– Wolverhampton from '9F' No 92222 at 12.40pm. Instead it had to replace ailing No 4988 *Bulwell Hall* on the 9.20am Ebbw Vale–Paddington. No 4988 was long overdue and came into Swindon with a Severn Tunnel pilot engine No 4130 coupled in front to provide emergency assistance. No 4988 must have been in really dire straits for No 4130 to end up coming all the way through to Swindon, so No 5981 was put on and worked to Paddington instead.

Meanwhile, an hour later 'Warship' No D823 failed while working the up Perranporth, and it was No 5981 which was roped in at 5.30pm to take over the diesel's return working from Paddington, none other than the down 'Mayflower'. On Saturdays this ran to a fast 'Special Load' schedule beyond Reading. No 5981 had 11 on as far as Exeter, so it was overloaded to the tune of three coaches but, even assuming a punctual departure and no delays, it was through Newton Abbot by 9.23pm, no more than 11min late. This was not bad going for an engine turned out to work to Wolverhampton which eventually finished up at Plymouth!

Returning to events on 9 July, No 7031 with its minuscule train of fish empties would need to skip along, because coming up the main line from Swindon 15min behind was No 7030. This was another engine from the strong running final batch of 'Castles', heading the 1.58pm from Locking Road excursion platforms at Weston. No 7030 *Cranbrook Castle* had had a busy time since being outshopped from Swindon with a new double-chimney in July 1959. It had since covered perhaps 53,000 miles, but was still running well and successfully holding its place amongst Old

Oak 'Castles' much more recently out of Works. The previous day, 8 July, No 7030 had been off to Wolverhampton on a 'King' turn; down with the 11.10am from Paddington and back on the 'Inter-City'. On Sunday 10 July it was down to Wolverhampton again on the 1.10pm.

This day No 7030 looked very spruce coming back with the augmented set of 'Bristolian' coaches in chocolate and cream livery. *Cranbook Castle* was quite at home with this set of stock. It had been the first 'Castle' to be booked for the postwar accelerated 'Bristolian' on 6 September 1954. No 7030 ran down successfully in 102min and pointed the way for 'Castles' to take over the 'Bristolian' service regularly once again, until dieselisation intruded in 1959. Meanwhile, No 7030 had further spells on the down 'Bristolian' in April/May 1956 and early in 1958.

On the 1.58pm up No 7030 had already regained all 10min of a late start from Bristol by the time it reached Swindon at 3.46pm. The 'Castle' continued to run well afterwards through a welter of delayed traffic on the up main. From Reading the 1.58 was allowed to leave ahead of three trains it should have followed and then passed Twyford just 1½min late. However, there were now two heavy Cornish expresses at 4min intervals in front, and so the punctual Paddington arrival which should have been within easy reach at 5.30pm was deferred for 10min.

No 5057 *Earl Waldegrave* on the following mid-afternoon express up from Bristol was a lot less fortunate even than No 7030. No 5057 had gone well with the down 'Merchant Venturer' earlier, coming off at Bristol 2min early. However, on Saturdays its return 2.58pm departure had originated from Minehead at 11.55am, and on 9 July the train left the branch terminus for Bristol in the tender care of No 6370, a decidedly run-down Ebbw Jc Mogul. This engine was in charge for 69½ miles off the branch. It reached Taunton 9min late and lost handfuls of time from there on to Bristol. During successive weekends in July, excluding 23 July, this stage of the journey attracted a real mixture of 2-6-0s, Nos 7327 from Didcot, 6309 of Swindon and 5376 from SPM, but No 6370 was certainly the roughest of this quartet. So No 5057 was 30min late leaving Temple Meads for London. At Wootton Bassett it had to follow both the 10.20am from Pembroke Dock and 11.5am Milford into Swindon where No 5057 arrived 38min late. Worse problems awaited here. The 4.20pm semi-fast from Swindon which connected for Challow and Didcot had already left long before with No 6957 *Norcliffe Hall*. Therefore No 5057 had to make these extra stops as well as its regular call at Reading.

Eventually No 5057 landed up at Paddington 61min late. Here it arrived behind No 5034 with the 2.15pm from Minehead which had started out 2¼hr after the 11.55. Bristol passengers had to endure a slow irregular service to London on Saturday afternoons, with no train at all to cover the fast weekday 4.15 or 4.30pm departures. Such a poor trip by the 2.58pm up from Temple Meads would have done nothing to improve their tempers. This was the worst runner of the day into Paddington and the only one to arrive there over an hour late.

As the afternoon wore on we had to wait some hours at Swindon for the first up nonstops to appear. But when they did come there were two in quick succession. First was the 10.20am Pembroke Dock–Paddington. This relief excited a lot of interest because if featured a Carmarthen 'Hall'. Quite a number of different engines appeared on successive Saturdays. However, when the summer peak approached, as was so often the situation when one shed, in this case Landore, had to rely on another, such as Carmarthen, to provide the power, the arrangement became rather ragged. Then 'Halls' from further afield like Gloucester and Worcester began to appear on the 10.20, though No 6810 *Blakemere Grange* from Llanelly did manage a rare run up on 27 August.

But on 9 July No 5937 *Stanford Hall* of Carmarthen was duly in charge. The tones of its warning whistle carried clearly on the wind and echoed back from the long walls of 'J' shop as it surged past the Works, before rattling through the station a couple of minutes early at 4.25pm with a lively chatter of fast exhaust. Prominent behind the tender was W4578W, one of the wide-bodied Centenary brake seconds built in 1935, at the front of a very mixed 11-coach train.

Also coming up from Swansea not far behind No 5937 was 'Star' rebuild No 5085 *Evesham Abbey*, fully loaded, filthy but in great shape on the 11.5am from Milford Haven. This splendid engine was right in the forefront of all the best 'Castle' action from the time it worked the last up steam 'Bristolian' until its withdrawal from service in February 1964. Though based at Bristol for much of this period, No 5085 took the 11.30am down on the day when it should have been the very last weekday Paddington–Plymouth express booked for steam haulage on Friday 8 September 1961. (Actually the 11.30 was still steam-hauled by No 7009 *Athelney Castle* to a new fast schedule on Monday 11 September.)

In the icy winter of 1963 No 5085 was frequently to be found replacing diesels on the North & West as well as helping out on Worcester line expresses. In April 1963 No 5085 was properly cleaned up for Newbury Race Special duty and finally it participated in working the Friday evening 5.50pm from Birmingham, which by 1963/64 was the last booked steam arrival at Paddington.

Though by no means going as fast as the thunderous 75mph tempo that the 'Bristolian' schedule demanded when No 5085 raced through Swindon in May and June 1959, *Evesham Abbey* was nevertheless whipping along at a good rate of knots on 9 July. By the time it passed Twyford No 5085 was 9min ahead of time and

5937 was 7½min early too. Only the tail end of the Cornish procession prevented this timekeeping being improved on into Paddington.

Over on Platform 1 at 4.55pm we were expecting No D804 *Avenger* back at Swindon with the down Plymouth parcels. When the long string of assorted vans came clattering in behind No 5018 *St Mawes Castle* there were suspicions of a diesel failure. Steam in the shape of No 6016 replacing a regular diesel on the Perranporth–Paddington earlier gave rise to suspicions of another. But perhaps we were wrong, because both situations were apparently linked up with the intricate arrangements needed to return diesel locos like D804 back into regular circulation at Plymouth after completing Swindon Works attention.

To accommodate No D804 even the best laid plans involved using four engines on the amended diagrams instead of the usual two. No D804 had set off from Swindon earlier on the 8.50am from Cheltenham to Paddington and was then forwarded to Plymouth on the 5.30pm down 'Mayflower'. This meant Laira still had to find an engine for the 5.30's up working, which explains how 'King' No 6016 came to be on the up Perranporth instead of a diesel. (An equally strong argument has been put to me that No 6016's appearance on the up Perranporth originated with the non-availability of the booked diesel at Laira, rather than a particular desire to return No D804 on the 5.30pm down. In this situation No 6016 would have been 'stepped up' from a later working at Laira. Both views are worthy of consideration.) Gloucester also had to provide power for the 8.50am from Cheltenham, even though this engine, No 6985 *Parwick Hall*, only worked to Swindon instead of through to Paddington and back as usual. Then of course another engine was needed at Old Oak for the return working off the 8.50am Cheltenham on the 2pm parcels to Plymouth as far as Swindon. Luckily this was less of a problem because, although heavy, the parcels was easily timed with a long pathing stop at Foxhall Jc. No 5018 had come into Paddington from Cardiff in mid-morning with the 3.30am ex-Fishguard Harbour. Ordinarily No 5018 would either require servicing or dispatch back to its home shed at Reading, but on this occasion it was considered fit enough for an easy run down with the parcels, leaving Swindon to solve the problem of how to return it home afterwards.

On the face of it, instead of using all these engines so that No D804 could be returned to Plymouth via London, it might have seemed less disruptive to send No D804 straight down on that morning's 7am Swindon–Penzance express in place of No 5084 *Reading Abbey*. The Old Oak 'Castle' could then have gone direct to London on the 8.50am Cheltenham instead. But this was probably out of the question because of difficulty in finding diesel-trained crews for the 7am. The crew situation would also help to explain why main line diesels had to be kept to their own regularly maintained diagrams at this stage of the transition from steam, rather than wandering off among a wide variety of different turns.

So No 5018 unexpectedly made a second visit to Swindon that day, distinctive because it was a green engine paired up with a black tender. There were very few of these 4,000gal tenders left around painted black, but Reading shed made something of a speciality of holding on to tenders in old liveries. The GWR lettered 3,500gal tender attached to 2-6-0 No 6324 was later handed on to 'Manor' No 7816 and lasted right to the end of Western steam. There was also an old tender, now used to store sludge, kept nearby in Reading Main Line West Sidings. This displayed its original MSWJR script in faded gold leaf which stood out clearly beneath peeling GWR black paint.

No 5018 gave way to No 5064 *Bishop's Castle* on the Plymouth parcels, but before it could leave at 5.27pm there was some outstanding business to be dealt with on the down main. This involved the second Fishguard and then the 'Capitals United Express'.

The first Fishguard had gone by an hour before with No 5048 *Earl of Devon* in charge on the first Saturday this train ran during its 1960 season. Now it was the turn of the 3.45pm down boat express, a daily train during the summer and one of very few daily restaurant car services still sporting a complete rake of GWR carriages. One would not call it a tidy set of stock. In fact, although it included four Hawksworth bow-ended corridors, these were spread out among a thoroughly motley collection of four other earlier Collett coach designs. Visually it was further fragmented by the corridor layout zig-zagging from side to side along the rake. The resulting variations in window design left hardly two coaches looking alike. In short it was like a typical WR train of the early 1950s, except for a mercifully uniform maroon livery. This

glimpse of successive Great Western coach designs all condensed into one train load was rounded off by the inclusion of an Edwardian Toplight restaurant car No W9538W. Although a couple of first class corridor Toplight coaches were out in service on succeeding weekends, No 9538 was the only Toplight to be seen at work on 9 July. This fully facelifted 70ft-long dining car actually predated some very similar vehicles built to inaugurate the transatlantic liner 'Ocean Express' services from Fishguard to Paddington back in 1909.

Old age was no guarantee of an easy life 50 years later, however. Along with 38-year-old No W9571W, one of the 1922 South Wales stock 70ft cars marshalled in the 6.55pm Fishguard, No 9538 had the longest 520-mile daily assignment of any WR restaurant car, new BR standard stock included. This was the last of many summers in service for the GW 70ft dining cars. So it was entirely appropriate that Nos 9538 and 9571 should share the honours, plying the longest run back and forth between London and Fishguard, fully provisioned with plenty of prime steaks and bottled Guinness, which was what the business on this route demanded.

Landore had used only single-chimney 'Castles' for its London turns so far. A couple of double-chimney engines were stationed there too, both modernised 'forties,' of which No 4093 was currently in pre-eminent condition. The 3.45 was the fifth homeward-bound Landore job of the day and so there were hopes at this point of sighting either No 4090 or No 4093 at speed. This was not to be, but when the 3.45 hove into view at 5.7pm, some 4min early, here was the next best thing. No 4094 *Dynevor Castle*, a single-chimney forty, was on the front approaching in some haste, silver-painted buffers clearly proclaiming its Landore parentage. With a swirling cloud of steam playing off the chimney No 4094 came storming

Left: A very woebegone Oxford 'Hall' is roped in to cover the non-availability of the booked Landore 'Castle' on the 3.45pm Paddington–Fishguard Harbour as No 6927 *Lilford Hall* picks up speed near Old Oak Common on Saturday 13 August 1960. The addition of a couple of strengthening coaches has produced a more harmonious set of stock since the mixture seen on 9 July, but more changes before the train ceased to run for the season meant it finished up with a very mixed bag of coaches once again by 9 September. *R. C. Riley*

Right: On 9 July 1960 'Britannia' No 70023 *Venus* passes West Ealing at the head of the down 'Capitals United Express'. Reaching Cardiff a minute early, No 70023 comes off there and No 7011 *Banbury Castle* will take the train on to Swansea. A through portion to Fishguard Harbour is on the front. *John Faulkner*

through, travelling rather faster than the 60mph ruling speed which was generally ample to time all Fishguard expresses except the 6.55 down.

Unfortunately, early running on the descent to the Severn Tunnel would mean No 4094 was almost certain to encounter delays from No 6921 *Borwick Hall* just ahead. No 6921 was working throughout from Newton on the 13-coach 10.20am Penzance-Swansea, and although it had regained a few minutes from Taunton, No 6921 was still about 6min late. With 13 coaches, including standard stock, this train would be very close to the 420-ton weight limit for a 'Hall' through the tunnel and No 6921 may even have had to stop at Pilning to take on assistance. No 4094 would then be held kicking its heels at Cattybrook Siding while the fireman tried to keep the safety valves quiet. However, after emerging from the Severn Tunnel No 4094 was then more fortunate. It managed to stay ahead of the 3.45pm Birmingham–Fishguard Harbour at Severn Tunnel Jc. This train behind fellow Landore engine No 5909 *Newton Hall* should have preceded the 3.45 Paddington all the way across Wales, but its 15min deficit was sufficient to allow No 4094 a clear road in front and a punctual arrival at 6.20pm across the Usk bridge into Newport. Even then the journey from Swindon had taken about 73min.

Fourteen minutes behind No 4094 at Swindon, Pacific No 70023 *Venus* was loping along comfortably with the 3.55pm down 'Capitals United Express'. So far it was not making quite such good speeds as the 'Castle' but its Canton crew knew exactly what they were up to. They stopped at Badminton, just kept clear of the 3.45pm Birmingham and still made Newport a minute early in a quicker time from Swindon than No 4094.

In the opposite direction odd freight workings were now beginning to find their way back out on to the main line, including one of the earliest surviving 2-8-0s, No 2807 on a Severn Tunnel Jc–Didcot 8A85 goods. 2-6-0 No 6327 had already edged past with the 2.15pm freight Stoke Gifford–Hanwell Bridge, which had so far averaged rather less than 13mph on its journey. This speed was about the right level for a very run-down No 6327 which had run its full mileage and was taken out of traffic to start a heavy general overhaul the following Wednesday. In contrast, the next up fast through express, the 12.5pm from Milford Haven, had started its journey with one of the most recently overhauled Moguls, No 5357, which came skipping into Carmarthen at around 1.20pm. Here the 12.5 reversed, attached its usual fish van and changed engines.

The 10-vehicle train required a 'Castle' on to Swansea if piloting was to be avoided from Gowerton up to Cockett. They were taking no chances at Carmarthen because all legs of this locomotive diagram involved full loads. So No 5067 *St Fagans Castle*, the most presentable Carmarthen 4-6-0 was at hand, already coupled to the 11.5am Milford Haven–Eastleigh fish van when it came backing gingerly into the platform to buffer up. No 5067 easily negotiated the onward run round the coast to Llanelly and then successfully scaled the climb to Cockett, over the neck of the Gower peninsula, before dropping sharply down with hot brake blocks into Swansea.

It was a pity that No 5067 was now facing the wrong way round when the 12.5 reached Swansea High Street terminus. This 'Castle' was in much better condition to work a heavy train to London than No 4075, the replacement engine standing in the up bay ready to add four more coaches, including a large 50-seater chocolate and cream restaurant car.

As No 4075 *Cardiff Castle* got away with 455 tons straight on to 1 in 90 gradients off the platform end,

and then thundered up round the curve past Landore loco, it would not have taken long for suspicions to harden that No 4075 might well be overdue for its second periodic valve and piston exam. The curtain of steam constantly leaking all round the front end was likely to mean an exhausting trip for the fireman, while the driver might have problems of his own sighting signals as the run progressed, when those leaks condensed and obscured his forward view in the cool evening air.

No 4075 was hard-pressed coping with constant stop-start demands along the South Wales main line. By way of minor respite the fish van — often an incongruous-looking dirty wood-planked four-wheeler — was now on the rear ready to be left at Cardiff. From there it would go forward to Eastleigh behind a brace of 'Halls' attached to the 4.25pm Portsmouth service. By this time No 4075 was outside Newport running 12min late. From there despite a comparatively easy schedule it took ages to pass Swindon. In fact the station clock showed 5.53 before No 4075 appeared past the Factory, plugging away gamely but slowly, 13min overdue, wreathed in steam and really struggling. After Swindon a bit of gravity helped No 4075 to keep moving at around 55mph but by Twyford a few more minutes had ticked away. No 4075 was ultimately 19min late arriving at Paddington, holding up 'King' No 6028 on the 12.30pm from Newquay in the process. So great was the demand for Old Oak 'Castles', however, that none of this prevented No 4075 being turned out for the 11.55am down South Wales express the following

Saturday, and little more successfully too. On this occasion it passed Swindon going rather better in terms of speed but in a terribly slow time of 100min from Paddington, against 96min for the easier up run. No 4075 then managed to regain 3min beyond Swindon and arrived at Cardiff 13min late.

No 4075 was in original mechanical condition, and it always sported fluted inside-cylinder covers, a two-row superheater boiler and single-chimney. Being in such poor condition, No 4075 did finally come to grief on 30 July when it was turned out for the 1.30pm down 'Royal Duchy' working to Plymouth. With 2-8-0 No 4703 on the 1.20 in front (itself a clear indication of an already tight loco situation at Old Oak Common) these two engines had a combined age of some 77 years between them as they set off from Paddington on long heavy load runs down the West of England main line. Already 12min late leaving Reading, No 4075 had to be replaced by No 5969 *Honington Hall* later in the journey and the 'Royal Duchy' was 35min late at Newton Abbot. It was a surprise when No 4075 survived a visit to Swindon Works in November 1960 and managed to remain in service for another 10 months.

Two more up West Wales expresses followed No 4075 through Swindon during the next 45min.

Below: Even after a Swindon Works overhaul in November 1960, No 4075 *Cardiff Castle* is still leaking steam heavily from its inside cylinders as it passes Lon Las with the 12.5pm Milford Haven–Paddington on Thursday 9 February 1961. This was the same train that No 4075 hauled with difficulty on 9 July 1960. *Huw Daniel*

Above: On Friday 8 July 1960 No 5049 *Earl of Plymouth* is at full stretch passing Didcot with the combined 1.40pm Paddington–Weston and Cheltenham. First vehicle is one of the 1926 Diagram K38 ocean mail vans, some of which were still marked 'Return to Plymouth Millbay' on the solebar in 1960. *Mike Lake*

They too had come into Carmarthen with Neyland-based 2-6-0s, and at Swansea the 12.5pm Pembroke Dock then changed from No 7012 *Barry Castle* to No 7914 *Lleweni Hall*. Conversely the up 'Pembroke Coast Express', 1.5pm from Pembroke Dock, managed the reverse, No 5953 *Dunley Hall* handing over to No 5042 *Winchester Castle* for the London leg. No 5042 had been a very welcome recruit at Old Oak Common when it arrived ex-factory from Swindon in April 1960. Now it simply played with the 'Pembroke Coast' job. Ten minutes early as it came purring smoothly through Swindon No 5042 had caught up with No 7914 by Reading, so it could gain no more than 14min on schedule at Twyford. The 'Pembroke Coast' called at Slough and Ealing Broadway on Saturday evenings, but only to set down passengers. So No 5042 did not have to wait time blocking the up main line at these two stops; it was able to restart straightaway and went on to reach Paddington 16min early. Four weeks later two Royal Trains were required for the Queen and her family to visit Cardiff. It came as no surprise then that No 5042 was rated such a good performer it worked both of them on successive days.

In order that the 'Pembroke Coast Express' could make its two London suburban stops on Saturday evenings, some really disruptive adjustments were inserted in the timetable. Firstly, no less than 40min was added to the weekday schedule of the 'Pembroke Coast Express' between Newport and Paddington. Secondly, the normal order followed by the 'Merchant Venturer' and 'Pembroke Coast Express' from Wootton Bassett was reversed on Saturdays, with the Bristol train now taking precedence.

To achieve this change of order, even though its load limit was increased from 420 to 455 tons, the 'Merchant Venturer' actually had to run a few minutes faster on summer Saturdays, almost a unique situation for a train making the same stops as on weekdays. The 'Merchant Venturer' was already quite quick intermediately. Lopping 3min off the uphill Chippenham–Swindon timing with a heavier load on Saturdays was therefore wildly optimistic.

The upshot of this on 9 July was that when the Wootton Bassett signalman was offered the 'Pembroke Coast Express' first he followed normal weekday practice and very sensibly accepted it. After that it was in everyone's interest to let No 5042 run and run, which of course it did. Meanwhile No 1024 *County of Pembroke* left Bristol 3min late on the 'Merchant Venturer' but predictably lost time to Swindon where it arrived 11min after the 'Pembroke Coast' had passed. Not unexpectedly, No 1024 never managed to get within spitting distance of No 5042 after that, and reached Paddington 13min late at 8.18pm.

Surprisingly, both trains were due to run in to Platform 11 at the terminus, though there was no chance of that on 9 July with only 9min separating them instead of the 20min interval scheduled. No 1024 probably ended up on Number 7 road instead, as there was plenty of time for that platform to be vacated by No 4088 *Dartmouth Castle* even though this had previously arrived 11min late at 7.41pm on the 3.50pm from Hereford.

Two down expresses due through Swindon around 6.20pm were usually successful in maintaining a close headway at speed. The 4.55pm 'Cheltenham Spa Express' and 5pm Paddington–Weston came down block and block every evening in 80–82min, hauled by two top-link 'Castles' returning to their country depots. On 9 July No 7035 braked smartly as it slowed to 10mph ready to diverge sharp right on to

the Gloucester line. The Swindon West bobby just had time to reset the road before No 5049 *Earl of Plymouth* on the 5pm was bearing down with seven league boots only 2min later, on course to make first stop Bath in 106min.

City of Truro was already out and waiting to go from Platform 4 with its Badminton line stopping train when No 5049 came past. At 6.30pm the magnificent 4-4-0 swung out on to the main line and strode off to Bristol, though with rather more vacant space in its five-coach load than was economically healthy. Even though No 3440's weekday train was well filled when I had a trip in it a few weeks later on 29 August, closure notices for local stations from Brinkworth to Winterbourne had already been posted. No 3440 lost its regular working on 3 April 1961 when stopping passenger services duly ceased.

City of Truro's appearance accurately reflected the changing nature of evening traffic at Swindon. The number of long distance expresses fell off, to be replaced in the normal way by more local trains, parcels and milk. All sorts of different steam types were represented on these incoming arrivals. They included No 5002 *Ludlow Castle* with the 5.38pm slow from Cheltenham, through No 6309, a dusty green 2-6-0, bringing up the 5.35pm from Westbury (which was made up of Eastern stock ready for the 7.33pm onwards to Sheffield Victoria) and small Prairie No 5536 capering in with the 7.11pm all stations from Kemble.

Add to normal services seven incoming Trip Specials with associated empty stock workings, and there were very few intervals when there wasn't at least one engine in sight until long after I left at 8.30pm. Engines at Swindon meant 4-6-0s. Out of 26 trains on the move between 6–8pm no less than 21 were hauled by 4-6-0s.

Even more remarkable was a concentration of five 'Counties' at Swindon within 1hr. In fact they were

nearly as plentiful as 'Castles' and that didn't happen very often. In addition to No 1024 on the 'Merchant Venturer', No 1014 *County of Glamorgan* followed on the next up Bristol express. This had originally started from Taunton with yet another, No 1028 *County of Warwick*, so there was a changeover between the two 'Counties' at Temple Meads on this train around 6.20pm.

The heavy 8.48am Fishguard–Paddington parcels would require almost a page of its own to recount the way its load constantly varied at a succession of stops along the way, and how it often used to end up with a Landore engine over the final stage up from Swindon, when all logic dictated it ought to have been the Swindon 'Castle' working up for next morning's Swansea express at 1am from Paddington. Suffice it to say that the engines used *en route* to shunt the parcels, haul it, bank it and pilot it almost run into double figures. A lot of coal had been burnt getting these parcels vans to Swindon. The appearance of No 1029 *County of Worcester* to take over the 8.48am from No 7036 was most unexpected, and not just because No 1029 was a Neyland engine. It meant that yet another diagram booked to be worked by Swindon shed had fallen by the wayside. It also helps to explain how, far away on its home patch, there was no 'County' ready for action at Neyland. That was why, just at this moment, 2-6-0 No 7306 was busy in its place blasting out like a good'un on the 6.50pm Paddington mail.

The other two 'Counties' were in the station together at 7.30pm. No 1027 *County of Stafford* had returned from Bristol on its booked return local off the morning's 10.5am express from Paddington. Alongside at Platform 5 on a very modest load of six coaches was plentiful power for the 7.33pm to Sheffield in the shape of Standard 5 No 73012 piloting No 1021 *County of Montgomery*. Both engines would probably work only as far as Banbury, while another

WR engine on the 10.25pm Swindon–York went through to Leicester. No 1021 would then return from Banbury in the early hours on the 6.40pm express from York, which this day conveyed Scarborough–Swindon through coaches starting off their 1960 season for the first time.

Only one of three 'Warships' managed to make it through Swindon on a nonstop express during the afternoon. This was No D813 *Diadem* which had worked up earlier on the 8.35am Falmouth–Paddington. No D813 was now making its way back to Plymouth with the 6.30pm down via Bristol. Against a 46min schedule from Twyford it had covered the 46.3 miles to Swindon in 51min.

Even more unusual here on 9 July was a 'King'. The last one in was No 6015 on the 4.55am from Fishguard Harbour at 10am, but now 10hr later No 6003 *King George III* appeared at 8.6pm on the 6.35pm Paddington–Cheltenham. This was journey's end because No 6003 was not permitted on the Gloucester line. It uncoupled and went off to turn before relieving No 5094 on the 3.50pm Whitland–Kensington milk. This duty formed a fairly regular fill-in turn for a 'King' in 1960.

The 6.55pm down Fishguard boat train was one of the most reliable runners on the South Wales service, even though it was not nearly as quick as its prewar equivalent. The 6.55pm was now a 12-coach formation, which did little for its pretensions to speed. Since 1956 the Fishguard had been progressively slowed from a Four Star limited load, then to a Three Star and finally a Two Star as the tonnage increased, and that meant trading 9min extra on the schedule to Cardiff for three additional coaches. Yet there was still some lively running to be had on the 6.55pm. A picked Old Oak 'Castle', especially one which had been round the right side of the coaling stage to fill up with choice Oakdale lumps in place of the ubiquitous ovoids, could certainly give

a good account of itself. Sure enough No 5037 *Monmouth Castle*, fleet of foot after a return trip to Bristol on the previous day's 1.15 down, had this job well covered. It came flitting through the evening shadows, whistle echoing across the town and surged past 2min early. From Swindon No 5037 just about tied with No 6925 *Hackness Hall*, which had experienced a miraculously clear run earlier hauling the 9.55am down, achieving the fastest time of the day on to Newport in 62min.

That virtually rounded off the evening as far as I was concerned, but not quite because the 2.30pm Neyland was now due. This was the day's last up Landore working and right on cue at 8.30pm in came double-chimney 'Castle' No 4093. The Landore cleaners had had all Saturday to work on this one and they had certainly done a good job.

The 2.30 set out originally from Neyland with local 'Hall' No 6909 *Frewin Hall* as far as Carmarthen. Here No 6909 was replaced by No 4935 *Ketley Hall* for the journey on to Swansea. After No 4935 had left, No 6909 backed out of the station. Rather than turn on the Carmarthen Jc triangle No 6909 utilised the nearby turntable at Carmarthen shed. It could then be stabled well out of the way ready to relieve No 4076 *Carmarthen Castle* on the 11.55am down for Milford Haven an hour and a half later.

Meanwhile, No 4093 *Dunster Castle* was running well with the 2.30 coming up from Swansea, on time at Cardiff, Newport and Swindon. As I set off for home along Station Road, No 4093 came past accelerating hard out of Swindon station. The fireman was busy with the flap down so the engine's exhaust was tinged bright orange twice over, once from the open firebox door and again from bright rays of evening sunshine. They were obviously in a hurry and No 4093 responded well. It picked up speed quickly with its modest load and was still audible storming away a good distance off.

Above: On 9 July 1960 No 7008 *Swansea Castle* comes sweeping round the curve towards Hatton station with the 9.30am Birkenhead–Bournemouth. After being held up north of Wolverhampton and leaving Snow Hill 9min late, No 7008 is regaining time nicely and will arrive at Oxford only 3min behind schedule. Later it will work the 11.30am Yarmouth–Swindon Trip special on from Oxford. *D. K. Jones*

Below: One generation of Swindon Works Trip Specials is depicted by 'Star' No 4056 *Princess Margaret* on a returning Works holiday train from Paignton crossing Aller Junction on Saturday 14 July 1956. The other two Specials from the West of England to Swindon seen that evening were train No 38 hauled by No 5038 and No 41 with No 4905. *Peter W. Gray*

7. Return Trip

Swindon Works customarily closed for summer holidays during the first two weeks in July every year. This holiday break was known to the workers and townspeople as Trip.

In Great Western days, when numbers employed at the Factory were considerably greater than the total in 1960, the Traffic Department very sensibly insisted that Trip took place midweek. Before World War 2, when only one week's holiday was involved, the Trip exodus occurred between 8.30pm Thursday and 7.5am Friday, well outside the weekend rush period.

By 1957 a very different situation applied. With the spread of a fortnight's paid summer leave for most workers, and pressure at resorts encouraging holidaymakers to book accommodation from Saturday evening to Saturday morning, Trip interference with ordinary peak weekend traffic could no longer be avoided.

A total of 10,000 Factory employees and their families were entitled to privilege ticket facilities in 1960 although their free travel usually had to be undertaken at inconvenient times and at no more than a leisurely pace. Most workers favoured seaside destinations, but Swindon was situated at least 60 miles away from even the closest holiday town at Weston-super-Mare. Other popular resorts at Weymouth and in the West Country were a lot more distant than that. A main line journey was therefore necessary for almost everyone going on Trip. Shops and schools closed while their customers and pupils were away, so many townspeople also joined the holiday exodus. The ordinary train service through Swindon could not possibly cope with a heavy influx of passengers like this.

An intensive programme of around 24 special trains was therefore required to convey employees away and almost an equivalent number of Specials was then needed to bring them back again.

In 1960 17 trains left Swindon between 9.55pm Friday 1 July and 10.45am Saturday 2 July, with another six on the following Monday and Tuesday too. Therefore, the problem was how to procure locomotives and two hundred coaches to form the initial 17 Specials on top of all the intense demands of that weekend's summer traffic. In addition more coaches were also required to strengthen regular trains conveying ordinary townspeople. The 7am Swindon to Penzance for example was made up to 15 vehicles on the first Saturday of Trip fortnight.

This was a very costly exercise. Even though the opportunity was taken to form a couple of trains with ex-works locomotives and coaches which were already on hand at Swindon, finding the rest of the accommodation required meant borrowing rolling stock from all corners of the Western, plus three sets from the LMR and three more from the Southern as well.

The expression 'Trip' was not referred to in the official Notice of Annual Holiday arrangements. This notice was fully self-contained and printed for widespread internal circulation. No Annual Holiday booklet has surfaced for 1960, but those produced in 1957 and 1961 have been available for consultation. These show that, although a number of trains were discontinued by 1961, the programme for those Specials which did run was remarkably consistent between 1957 and 1961. This information is more than adequate to paint the picture for 1960.

The scope of Trip was breathtaking. First empty coaches arrived from as far away as Newquay and Plymouth, in addition to what was lent by other regions. Sets had to be stabled, which meant working some of them in from Wootton Bassett, Marston Sidings and Marsh Pond. Early on Saturday morning 'B' Set Specials were arranged from Wootton Bassett, Purton and Highworth to connect with main line Trip workings at Swindon. The trains then ran loaded through to destination with every passenger meticulously accounted for. These destinations were everything from 60 to 250 miles away. They included complete Specials for Blackpool, Llandudno, West Wales, Cornwall, Torbay, Weymouth, all along the South Coast and Yarmouth, not to mention Weston and Paddington which were reasonably close at hand. Furthermore, there were additional connecting Specials to be organised. An 'M' set was laid on from Newquay to Perranporth at 6am carrying passengers who were already weary after spending $7\frac{1}{2}$hr aboard the 10.30pm Swindon–Newquay on Friday night. Five coaches were detached at Taunton from the heavy Exmouth Special for working on to Torrington. Most sets of main line coaches then had to be hauled back empty over the weekend, either for dispersal to their home depots, or back to Swindon to fulfil Monday and Tuesday's Trip programme. Some were stabled ready to start the return trek of eight trains the following Saturday, with about eight more programmed on the final Saturday.

The size of this enormous undertaking even rivalled that other great mass migration by rail, when Welsh Rugby supporters made their annual pilgrimage to either Twickenham or Murrayfield. Though the Edinburgh traffic required no less than 31 special trains in February 1953, demand had fallen off to around 20 by 1961. So in 1960 Trip was probably the biggest single long-distance passenger movement on the WR. The difference was of course that the demand for Rugby Specials came at a time of year when the resources required could easily be spared. Fares collected from rugby traffic covered costs, quite apart from catering revenue which, especially if Welshmen occasionally had to drown their sorrows after losing the match, was always substantial. The same could not be said of Trip which attracted very little revenue at all. As such it was a dinosaur.

In 1960 down Works Holiday Specials were worked away as usual on Friday evening 1 July and Saturday morning 2 July. This meant that 9 July was the middle Saturday of Trip fortnight, and the programme that day involved one last outward-bound Special leaving at 6.25am for Torquay and Paignton. Like the equivalent train the previous Saturday, new technology was on display and this Special was diesel-hauled.

Then later on, once the main summer Saturday rush had started to abate, the homeward procession back to Swindon began in earnest with a series of eight Specials arriving between 5.1 and 10.12pm. This was not all. First there were through coach connections to be added to the Penzance train from St Ives and Newquay. Then in all cases the stock had to be worked away from Swindon in many different directions for stabling between 7.10 and 10.30pm. This effectively doubled the number of Trip-related movements to be handled at Swindon.

First Special in was the 1.55pm from Weymouth with a very grubby No 6955 *Lydcott Hall*, another engine borrowed by Weymouth from Westbury Shed to help cover its commitments, arriving 10min late at 5.11pm.

No 6955 was due to work throughout on 9 July following close behind No 73020 on the 1.45pm Weymouth-Bristol. First No 6955 called at Weymouth Jc for a banker. It then picked up at Maiden Newton and Yeovil before stopping at Westbury for ticket inspection. Finally it paused at Wootton Bassett to set down. Both Nos 73020 and 6955 would have been delayed between Castle Cary and Westbury by the late-running 8.20am from Penzance in front. The schedule of the 1.55 was easy throughout. But even though an ample 29min was allowed between Castle Cary and Westbury, while No 73020 ahead made a couple of additional stops, No 6955 probably suffered its most time wasting delays somewhere along here. The following Saturday on 16 July Weymouth managed to find an engine of its own for this train and Standard 5 No 73041 reached Swindon 3min early at 4.58pm.

The 11.30am Yarmouth Vauxhall–Swindon Special was a surprisingly heavy train of 12 Eastern coaches including Gresley stock. The size of this load probably had something to do with its slow progress across East Anglia and the Home Counties. The Yarmouth had been running for 166 miles and well over 5hr before being handed over to the Western at Oxford. This shed then had the responsibility of providing power for the last 34 miles to Swindon and 'Castle' No 7008 was supplied. *Swansea Castle* had worked back from Chester to Oxford earlier with the 9.30am Birkenhead–Bournemouth West. Peter Ogden, who was travelling down from Manchester via Chester to spend the day at Shrewsbury, had had a run with it for the first 42½ miles during the morning. No 7008 was close behind Birkenhead 'Crab' No 42856 on the 9.20am Birkenhead–Bournemouth Central and so its style was a bit cramped all the way to Wolverhampton.

The Yarmouth train was due to reach Swindon at 5.42pm, but as it was running 25min late No 7008 found itself taking over the path normally reserved for the 10.8am Newcastle–Swansea instead. By contrast with arrangements for 1957 when the Yarmouth was due to change engines on the through road at Oxford, in 1961 it was booked to call at the up platform. However, on this occasion the Newcastle train also appears to have been running sufficiently late for it not to be delayed by the Yarmouth in either eventuality.

On arrival at Swindon No 7008 went off to turn. It would probably return to Oxford with the empty stock, which in 1961 was destined for the Eastern at 8.40pm as train No 3A79.

The next Special to Swindon didn't come into the junction station at all. This was the 3.1pm from Portsmouth Harbour collecting passengers from the Isle of Wight, which made its way up the Midland & South Western Junction route from Andover and terminated at Swindon Town. The 3.1 was formed of a Southern engine and stock throughout with arrival scheduled at 6.1pm. The locomotive could then turn on the 55ft turntable at Swindon Town and return with the empty coaches at 7.10pm, without needing any access to Swindon GWR shed at all.

Unfortunately this train must have been somewhat late because Bernard Cooke, who was watching out at Savernake, failed to see it pass before 5.20pm. The previous year the Portsmouth special was pulled by 'U' class 2-6-0 No 31804 as it threaded Savernake Low Level at 5.51pm. Whereas most trains passing Savernake could look forward to some easier gradients ahead of them, this was not true of up MSWJ traffic. The hardest bit was yet to come for No 31804, as it prepared to climb up at 1 in 65 round the fringes of Savernake Forest, whilst contending with a dead slow start and hauling the maximum permitted load. Its train of 11 coaches must have been carefully selected to come within the 320-ton weight limit over this section.

Of course SR power on this line was nothing unusual. The MSWJ's only remaining through service, the 1.52pm Cheltenham St James–Southampton Terminus, fulfilled only a local role by this time and its three coaches had gone down earlier on 9 July 1960 behind No 31803. Occasional shuttle services between Swindon and Savernake were left in the hands of Panniers Nos 8783 and 9795. I could have used one of these services myself instead of having to cycle to Swindon, except that the last MSWJ departure to the south worked by No 31795 left Swindon Town at 4.52pm and that was hardly practical for my purposes.

The previous weekend's southbound special to Portsmouth over the MSWJ had provided one of the last surefire '43xx' 2-6-0 workings on an annual Works' holiday train. These Moguls had been basic Trip power over all manner of routes in the past. However, as was the case on 9 July, 4-6-0s had gradually taken over the main line jobs. But on the MSWJ section, although 'Manors' and Standard 4s were permitted, '43xxs' were still the largest WR locos readily available. On the last occasion that Trip Specials ran this way while the line was open, our now overhauled friend No 6327 hauled train No 15 of LMR stock to the south, forming the 8.18am Swindon Town–Portsmouth Harbour on 1 July 1961. Train No 16, the 9.45am Swindon Town–Poole, followed later with 'U' No 31613.

Back at Swindon Jc on 9 July, the 1.45pm Special from Margate, numbered X42, was due at 7.7pm and it arrived 9min later with the same 'Hall' which would fail on the 9.20am Ebbw Vale–Paddington express a week later. This time, however, No 4988 Bulwell Hall had a much easier task to deal with. After the SR engine had brought its relatively light train into the relief line platform at Reading around 6pm, No 4988 had only to saunter gently down the main line following No 5929 Hanham Hall, which was hauling the 5.6pm Paddington–Weston. As the 5.6 called at Didcot and Challow on the way, No 4988's crew had to find ways of occupying some 55min before going round into the back platform at Swindon to detrain the passengers.

The Margate coaches were then worked across on to the up side where No 6955 off the Weymouth Special took them over. No 6955 then set off very promptly at 8.4pm, returning the empty stock as far as Reading en route back to the SR. In its turn No 4988 went forward on the stock of the Weymouth to Marsh Pond, so taking a second good stride back towards its home depot at Neath.

A 2hr break followed before the second set of Trip Specials was due to arrive at Swindon between 9.23 and 10.12pm. I had departed before that, so to cover the action on these four trains attention switches 140 miles west and north to Newton Abbot and Shrewsbury.

A recently overhauled SPM 'Grange' was ready at Newton Abbot for the Teignmouth Special, No Z83 —

a very appropriate choice this, in view of the amount of work these 'Granges' were getting through down in Devon during the day. No 6846 Ruckley Grange had arrived very early in the morning with Friday night's 9.10pm Manchester Victoria–Paignton, and its back working had then been arranged to accommodate an evening return on the Works Special. This might have been fixed up some weeks earlier by the diagramming office, or sorted out by the Newton Abbot Inspector in consultation with the Shed Foreman only hours beforehand, using the most convenient loco available. On the following Saturday when Works Specials again ran, it was the Torbay Special which was hauled by an SPM engine, but this one was working a completely different circuit as compared to No 6846. No 7907 Hart Hall on that occasion came down much later on the 8.50am Swansea–Paignton relief and was turned round in 2½hr at Goodrington before going back again. On the other hand, the Teignmouth train again had a loco off an overnight North Country express, and this time it was Didcot engine No 6969 Wraysbury Hall off the 8.27pm Friday Batley–Paignton extra. It really did take an experienced eye in the small Inspector's cabin on Newton Abbot down platform to decide how these foreign engines and their crews could be turned round to the best advantage, when the trains which had to be covered changed so much from week to week.

On 9 July No 6846 took over its stock in Newton Abbot yard and set off directly from there. It ran empty to Teignmouth ready for a 5.50pm departure along the seawall, and allowed holidaymakers a last look at the waves before their journey home started in earnest. Unlike the other two West of England Specials, this train travelled via Bristol, where crews were changed. It was then routed up Filton bank and at very modest speeds via Badminton to Wootton Bassett. On arrival at Swindon the stock had to be worked away, probably to Worcester or Kingham with the same locomotive. The following year on 15 July 1961 the coaches were destined for storage in Bentley Heath loop. Here they joined an accumulation of stock being gathered together, and filling every available carriage siding, ready to participate in the start of Birmingham Holiday fortnight on 22/23 July.

Meanwhile, the next Works train was from Torbay, making its way up with the same 'Warship' diesel and stock which had formed the 6.25am Swindon–Paignton Special that morning. No D823 Hermes started back from Paignton at 5.40pm and ran nonstop from Newton Abbot to Westbury on a schedule the 'Warship' diesel would have little difficulty observing. However, it was no good hurrying. The Special could not overtake the 7pm Taunton–Westbury Rail Motor before Frome, so the journey, though shorter in terms of distance than the Teignmouth train, was not a lot quicker. Reaching Swindon 23min after No 6846 by the book, another engine would then be required to work these empty coaches off to their immediate destination at Tyseley.

Then there was the 2.15pm Trip Special from Penzance, thought to be steam all the way with 'Halls' Nos 7929 and then 6904, as already recounted. The load was made up to 11 coaches across Cornwall by additions at St Erth from St Ives and Par from Newquay. No 6904 followed No D823 up the Westbury line and was due into Swindon at 10.10pm.

Arrival of the Penzance train should have closely coincided with the appearance of the final Works Special which had left Blackpool at 3pm. Unfortunately, however, the Blackpool was not doing at all well. When this train passed Tyseley at 9.26pm it was 98min late. A week later on 16 July the Blackpool was 61min late at the same point.

The Western obviously wanted to minimise costs payable to other regions for handling this train, so it was routed over as much WR mileage as possible via Chester instead of coming from Crewe to the rather more direct interchange point off the LMR at Shrewsbury.

In view of the late running, and uncertainty as to where so much time had been lost, it is not possible to say which loco hauled the Blackpool Special before Wolverhampton. If, on arrival there, the incoming engine went to Oxley, it is totally unknown. However, if the train arrived about 70min late, and the engine was then turned at Stafford Road, it was likely to have been 'Castle' No 5070 *Sir Daniel Gooch* which was booked on to 84A at 8.52pm. This would have been a nice touch in view of Sir Daniel's close association with Swindon Works. However, there was no corresponding engine movement the following Saturday and one has to conclude that No 5070's presence on the Blackpool Special was unlikely. No 5070 later returned to Shrewsbury on the 8.10pm from Paddington.

There was a 15min refreshment stop which the official notice stated 'must be maintained' at Wolverhampton. Afterwards the Blackpool was taken forward by No 4984 *Albrighton Hall* of Oxley. If the 1961 programme was maintained, this Special ran

loaded beyond Swindon to Wootton Bassett. From there, by now no doubt well after midnight, the nine-coach LMR set was due to be returned empty to what was once the old MR section at Bristol for immediate stabling.

This was a most comprehensive programme of special trains which has received very little attention over the years, no doubt due to the inconvenient time of day that many of the Trip Specials ran. The same was, however, true of many Charter Specials organised by BR even in those days; a lot of which were subject to early starts or very late finishes. By way of final illustration there was also a Dundee–Lavington troop train on 9 July. This must have left the banks of the Tay at around 9.30am, and passed Oxenholme somewhat short of its half-way point at 3.54pm. When the troop train came through Tyseley at 8.27pm it was running 13min early behind No 5959 *Mawley Hall*. However, there was still the prospect of at least 3½hr more travelling through Oxford, Swindon and Chippenham before this 500-mile marathon could be completed.

Troop trains from Scotland were organised regularly at this time of year and in 1962 the train carried a cafeteria car. I hope for the sake of everybody on board it had one in 1960 as well.

Right: A different generation of Works holiday train on 9 July 1960, as brand-new diesel-hydraulic No D823 *Hermes* prepares to leave Newton Abbot at 6.13pm on its return trip to Swindon with the 5.40pm staff holiday Special from Paignton.
Derek J. Frost

Below right: Holiday expresses were arranged from most centres on the Western Region for one or two weeks of the summer, running to a different resort each day. Paignton was a favoured destination and on Bank Holiday Monday 1 August 1960 No 6815 *Frilford Grange* brings the 'Somerset Holiday Express' from Bridgwater towards Creech on the down relief line. A smartly turned out set of coaches with descriptive carriage boards was unfortunately seldom matched by a clean engine. Definitely a wasted PR opportunity.
John Cornelius

Left: At Worcester No 7027 *Thornbury Castle* has completed a Worcester–Paddington–Hereford–Worcester round trip, and, still carrying its train number off the 12.45pm Paddington–Hereford, it waits to uncouple from the 5.50pm Hereford–Paddington. No 8109 is in the foreground on Thursday 28 July 1960 waiting to work the Kidderminster portion of the down 'Cathedrals Express'. *D. K. Jones*

Below: The 9.50am Hereford–Paddington runs into Oxford 2½min early on 9 July 1960 behind No 7002 *Devizes Castle.* This Worcester engine has a clean smokebox and tender emblem but not much else. *Mike Lake*

Left: There was a very cosmopolitan atmosphere at Oxford with the Eastern regularly represented. No 61137 of 15E (Leicester) worked in with the 8.35am Newcastle–Bournemouth on 9 July 1960 and here it is again arriving with the same train on 6 August 1960. *Mike Lake*

8. OXFORD — OPERATING SUCCESS ON A SHOESTRING

Oxford had two main distinguishing features as a busy railway centre. First was the great variety of locomotive classes to be seen there, working in all directions to a wide range of destinations. Second was the extremely restricted nature of the station layout for a city of such importance. The facilities comprised four running lines, but only one through platform face in each direction. These two platforms had to accommodate anything up to nine summer Saturday expresses in an hour, plus two or three local trains which also needed to make use of the through platform accommodation. During the same period from 1 to 2pm three of these long distance expresses were obliged to change engines in the station as well as making passenger stops. Fresh motive power therefore had to be ready and waiting to back down and couple up exactly when it was required, otherwise queues of trains awaiting a platform would soon build up.

Delays certainly did occur outside Oxford on 9 July but those hold-ups to trains like the 10.25am Poole–Bradford were comparatively minor. Punctual working was generally well organised in the shed and station areas throughout the busiest period of the day. Expresses were consistently changing engines at the down platform in 6–8 min. Up trains took slightly longer, due to difficulty in clearing incoming engines back through the station to the shed at the down end of the layout. Brisk station work constantly enabled scheduled stopping times to be cut by 2 or 3min. Few trains with locos working through stood for more than 5min, unless they had arrived early and were awaiting booked time before departure.

Timekeeping was certainly good in view of the volume of traffic being handled. Arrivals from as far afield as Birkenhead, Bournemouth, Hereford, Margate and Newcastle were in most cases recorded reaching Oxford within 5min of booked time. Excluding the 11.5am Wolverhampton–Weymouth, trains originating at Wolverhampton, Birmingham and Portsmouth were all early arriving, except 2-6-0 No 6365 on the 10.45am Birmingham–Brighton which was late — by all of ½in. Trains running behind schedule were helped on their way as stopping times were cut to an absolute minimum — 2½min only in cases of No 6929 *Whorlton Hall,* which was 7½min late with the 8.5am Bournemouth–Newcastle, and No 7332 44min in arrears during its trying journey on the 8.50am Margate–Birmingham. Other trains running well behind time, like the Weymouth–Wolverhampton

(inevitably) and Sheffield–Bournemouth, were absorbed into the traffic flow without undue delay to more punctual services.

One or two local trains had to be held up to accommodate expresses, notably 2-6-2T No 5167 on the 1.8pm Oxford–Banbury stopper. This could not leave until both the 8.50am Margate and 9.25am Weymouth trains had cleared at 1.30pm. Similarly the 1.20pm for Moreton-in-Marsh was not able to depart from the down end bay platform until 1.37pm. The engine was ex-works 'Modified Hall' No 6970 in spanking condition, hauling just two coaches, and its crew were in a good position to enjoy a lively run between stations over the Cotswolds, with plenty of power at their disposal to aid time recovery. Stopping times for local trains at Oxford were smart too. A break of only 3min was allowed for the 11.55am from Moreton-in-Marsh to change engines after its arrival with No 6349, attach Prairie No 4125 and then leave again as the 12.52pm for Princes Risborough. In the event this was too tight. No 6349 arrived 6¼min late, and it was 1.2pm before No 4125 got away round the cemetery curve towards Kennington Jc.

Only one express lost time heavily in the station, and that involved No 6366 on the 9.20am Margate–Birmingham. It was due past nonstop on the through road at 1.34pm, but after appearing 10min late, it then stopped for 7min, possibly to fill up the 2-6-0's small 3,500gal tender with water.

'Halls' and 2-6-0s handled the major share of WR passenger workings at Oxford between 10.30am and 3.30pm, with a smattering of 'Granges' and one 'County'. 'Castles' were in rather shorter supply then usual, with no representative from Landore on the Swansea–York, and only one 'Castle' each to be seen from Oxford and Reading Depots. While No 5082 *Swordfish* from Old Oak had worked through earlier with the 6.30am from Hereford, the London engine on the 10.45am down to Hereford was No 6973 *Bricklehampton Hall.* So it was Worcester shed which provided the main 'Castle' presence. Six engines originated from this source with expresses to Paddington during the day and at 2.12pm two of them were in Oxford station at the same time. No 7004 *Eastnor Castle* had gone up earlier on the 'Cathedrals Express' arriving in Paddington 5min late at 11.30am. There Worcester engines were booked for the quickest turn-round of any visiting express steam power, and after 75min No 7004 left again on a through journey to Hereford with the 12.45pm down. It was booked fast to the stop at Reading in 38min, then more slowly on to Oxford in 37min. So if a couple of minutes were dropped on the first stage they could generally be recovered easily enough over the second. However, approaching Oxford No 7004 was third in the queue behind No 6366 and it did not arrive until 2.8½pm, 4½min late. A minute before No 7004 was ready to leave again at 2.12½ No 7027 *Thornbury Castle* came gliding past into the up platform loop with the 11.50am from Hereford.

No 7027 left Oxford with nine coaches at 2.17pm, 2min late on a 70min schedule to Paddington. *Thornbury Castle* kept good time to Twyford, covering 32 miles in 37min, but by then it was right behind No 70029 on the 8am from Neyland. At West Ealing No 7027 was 6min late and it reached Paddington 5min in arrears, having passed its stablemate, No 7002 *Devizes Castle,* heading west with the 2.45pm Paddington–Hereford somewhere in the vicinity of Slough.

Worcester shed had a good reputation for the cleanliness of its 'Castles' and justifiably so, but in summer 1960 the depot had struck a bad patch and most of the engines looked very dingy. Only the oldest one was well kept, that being No 4088 *Dartmouth Castle*, amongst what was otherwise shortly to become an exclusive allocation of '70xx' series engines. This was a pity because a number of freshly painted 'Castles' had recently been transferred in, including Nos 7004, 7006 and 7027. Canton had reluctantly parted with No 7006 in flawless condition towards the end of June. It was therefore disappointing to see the shining finish being allowed to deteriorate so quickly at its new home. It took a year or so for standards to recover, but by summer 1962 Worcester had comprehensively turned the tables on Canton by maintaining an impressive fleet of well-polished 'Castles' for Worcester line expresses, while elsewhere standards of steam cleanliness were mostly in terminal decline.

The loads of trains through Oxford were not heavy, 11 coaches and a van being the length of the longest formation on 9 July. The 9.11am Portsmouth–Wolverhampton with No 5901 *Hazel Hall* was made up to no more than six bogies. However, it was still early in the season so far as this train was concerned. Four weeks later, on 6 August, the 9.11 was formed of 11 coaches, and holiday traffic was so busy that it had to be run in three separate portions. While most expresses were standing in the station their length was generally sufficient to foul the scissors crossovers situated half-way along each through platform face. As a result these crossovers were of very restricted value in enabling two trains to stand at a platform simultaneously. The lack of platform space therefore remained a handicap, but, despite this, the way so much traffic was efficiently handled at Oxford still compared very favourably with other more lavishly equipped stations elsewhere on the WR.

On 9 July Oxford nearly lived up to its reputation as the meeting point for engines from all four pre-Nationalisation companies. As far as ex-LMS visitors were concerned their contribution had been severely curtailed since BR DMUs were introduced on the Oxford–Bletchley line. Two representatives did work in from former LMS sheds during the day but both were standards — No 75038 from Bletchley, and ex-Crosti '9F' No 92028 with the 6.10am freight from Wellingborough. So no LMS locomotives were seen.

Off the Eastern 'K3/2' 2-6-0 No 61817 of Cambridge was on Oxford shed during the day. It had probably worked in with the 7.14pm Ipswich–Cardiff vacuum freight and was likely to be returning from Yarnton Sidings on 5E09, the balancing 12.10pm

Below: On 9 July 1960 'WC' Pacific No 34043 *Combe Martin* has been turned promptly at Oxford shed. Now with its earlier reporting number still prominently shown on the smokebox, No 34043 drifts quietly through Oxford station to await the arrival of its southbound train, the 12.10pm Birmingham–Bournemouth... *Mike Lake*

Above: ...and this arrives at Oxford 3½min early at 1.31½pm behind No 6866 *Morfa Grange* of Tyseley. This engine is fitted with one of the Collett intermediate tenders and its 10-coach train includes Eastern and London Midland as well as Western stock. *Mike Lake*

Llandilo Junction–Cambridge service. This freight was well loaded as it travelled up through South Wales behind Oxford-based 2-8-0 No 3823. From Severn Tunnel Jc it was routed to Yarnton via Gloucester, Ashchurch and Evesham.

At 3.37½pm 'B1' No 61137 arrived from Banbury and the GC line hauling the 8.35am Newcastle–Bournemouth running just 2½min late. No 5933 *Kingsway Hall* had set out from Banbury to Oxford earlier on the 10am Bradford–Poole and No 5933 now transferred to the Newcastle express in place of No 61137. No 5933 had been carrying the 042 reporting number of the Newcastle–Bournemouth ever since leaving Banbury, and it was due to work this train right through to Bournemouth West on a 3¾hr schedule from Oxford.

The Southern was well represented at Oxford with a series of tightly knit express rosters. Two daily duties from Bournemouth were expanded to four on Saturdays and Oxford was the point at which they all changed to Western motive power. First Southern visitor was Bulleid Pacific No 34043 *Combe Martin* with the 9.32am Bournemouth Central–Wolverhampton, looped into the down platform 5min late at 12.48pm. No 34043's replacement engine was a real contrast of size and style in the shape of 2-6-0 No 6364. This '43xx' did not run quite so successfully on the way back as it had when it arrived 3min before time with the 9.5am Birmingham–Portsmouth earlier. Hauling 10 coaches on the Bournemouth–Wolverhampton 6364 passed Tyseley 10min late at 2.30pm.

No 34043's arrival at Oxford was followed within 10min by the appearance of a rebuilt 'West Country' No 34046 *Braunton* which was heading the main 9.30am Bournemouth West–Birkenhead service. Oxford shed had nothing but grubby 'Hall' No 5966 *Ashford Hall* to take this train on, as all four home 'Castles' were away. No 5012 had handled Oxford's morning turn to Paddington at 7.10am, No 5025 was at Tyseley where it was thought to be under repair, No 5033 was making a return trip back from Plymouth and No 7008 brought the southbound Birkenhead–Bournemouth in for No 34046 to work home at 2.33pm. However, No 5966's dirty exterior belied its good mechanical condition and the 'Hall' passed Tyseley at 2.38pm before reaching Snow Hill right on time at 2.45pm. No 5966 worked through to Chester with this train hauling the WR set of coaches. These were balanced by an alternate SR set on the southbound train.

After its arrival No 34043 had less than an hour's turn-around before it was due to leave Oxford again for Bournemouth with the 12.10pm from Birmingham. While waiting for its train to come in, No 34043 would be stabled on one of the up loco sidings at the south end of the station. If No 34046 was able to turn quickly it could provide a spectacle of the two Bulleid Pacifics standing alongside one another as they awaited their return workings. However, there would not have been much time for this on 9 July because No 6866 *Morfa Grange on* Tyseley Turn 29 was at rest from Birmingham 3½min early and when No 34043 received the right away to depart it was still a minute early at 1.43pm.

As No 34043 was somewhere near Radley it passed 'Lord Nelson' No 30853 *Sir Richard Grenville* which was on the last lap of its northbound journey with the 10.25am Poole–Bradford. Both No 30853 and

No 5011 *Tintagel Castle,* which was heading the 8.55am Ramsgate–Wolverhampton in front, were running in close succession, but the 'Lord Nelson' was only $3\frac{1}{2}$ min late reaching Oxford. Here No 7905 *Fowey Hall* was waiting to work the Poole train to Banbury where Eastern motive power would take over, perhaps even a 'V2' making a rare visit on to Western territory.

Before No 30853 could return on the southbound Bradford–Poole at 3.26pm the fourth Southern locomotive had already made its appearance, 6min late at 2.38pm with the 11.16am Bournemouth–Newcastle. It was the third Bournemouth engine of the day's quartet but this time, instead of a Pacific, 'King Arthur' No 30781 *Sir Aglovale* was in charge, continuing the long association of 'N15' 4-6-0s on this Bournemouth duty to Oxford. No 30781 spent the rest of the afternoon at Oxford and was then due to start its return journey on the 6pm Worcester–Basingstoke perishables at 9.10pm.

No account of events at Oxford would be complete without a reference to the long-established 5.35pm 60min flyer to Paddington. However, equally, there is no room for dwelling on it too long because by summer 1960 the 5.35 was a very nondescript train indeed. Cut back from Wolverhampton to start at Worcester, and amalgamated with the old 3.7pm local from there, it was hardly a flyer now that it called at all 19 stations and halts except Yarnton to Oxford. There the 5.35 underwent a complete transformation into an express as it set out on the final nonstop sprint to Paddington.

In June 1960 the 5.35 had also been robbed of its buffet car, a long-standing feature dating back to prewar days which had once been one of the train's main attractions, where undergraduates travelling to London fortified themselves before they embarked on a lively night out in the Big City. On Fridays and Saturdays the 5.35 didn't even maintain its 60min schedule. With an unchanged six-coach load and 8min added on Saturdays it was a very easy job indeed,

having none of the 75–80mph cruising requirement needed by the weekday train to keep time.

Motive power had been too variable during the BR regime to provide the sort of consistent performance which was usually associated with some other Western Region 'Special Load' schedules. Although 'Modified Halls' had at times been noted for their extremely speedy running on the 5.35 during the mid-1950s, there was always a tendency to slip in a run-down 'Hall' which spoilt the picture. Though the 5.35 was generally 'Castle'-hauled by 1960 it still varied, and the occasional habit of substituting something substandard like a rough old Didcot 'County' persisted in 1961/62.

No 5071 *Spitfire* therefore had no occasion to live up to its name with the 5.35pm on 9 July. The Saturday schedule was quite unnecessarily easier all the way along the route, and not just at the conclusion of the journey where the extra minutes were needed to soak up terminal delays. So whereas No 7036 running to the 62min Friday schedule on 17 June was able to maintain the normal 60min timing as it passed Twyford, $32\frac{1}{2}$ miles from Oxford, in $29\frac{1}{2}$min (assuming a punctual start), No 5071 took $34\frac{1}{2}$min to cover the same distance. This meant that even on the Saturday schedule, No 5071 was $\frac{1}{2}$min late here, and right on the tail of the 11.55am from Minehead with No 5057. Ironically, if No 5071 had maintained the 60min schedule it could probably have overtaken the wayward Minehead train at Reading, in the same way that it passed the 4.15pm from Bristol there every other day of the week. But instead No 5071 had to trail along behind No 5057 and arrived at Paddington about 5min late around 6.48pm. On Saturday 27 August another Worcester engine, this time a good 'Hall', No 7928 *Wolf Hall*, performed very much better hauling the same load of six coaches, and it was into Paddington 6min early after successfully completing the journey at over a mile a minute from Oxford.

Left: On 9 July 1960 'Lord Nelson' 4-6-0 No 30853 *Sir Richard Grenville* has just arrived at Oxford with the 10.25am Poole–Bradford. After uncoupling it prepares to pull forward so that No 7905 *Fowey Hall* can take over for Banbury. *Mike Lake.*

Above: An animated scene at Banbury on Saturday 6 August 1960 where New England 'V2' No 60893 has just replaced No 6930 *Aldersey Hall* on the 10.25am Poole–Bradford. In the background is No 6829 *Burmington Grange* of Exeter waiting with the 9.10am Kingswear–Birmingham Moor St. This is the peak Saturday for return holiday traffic and many reliefs are running. At 3.37pm the Poole is 53min late and the Kingswear is already 47min late even before the starting signal clears. These deficits are due to weight of traffic and not poor locomotive performance. No 6829 at the end of its long run will lose very little if any more time on to Tyseley where it was 49min late. *M. Mensing*

Below: On Saturday 9 July 1960 the photographer receives a cheery wave from the driver of No 4941 *Llangedwyn Hall* as it approaches Fosse Road box pulling hard on the 10.42am Wolverhampton–Margate. No 4941 worked to Reading, reaching Oxford a minute early. *R. J. Blenkinsop*

Above: By 1960 the Sunday 10.40am Paddington–Penzance was usually diesel-hauled, but in 1959 when this picture was taken it was still steam-worked. Nos 7812 *Erlestoke Manor* and No 7006 *Lydford Castle* grapple with the climb from Totnes up to Tigley box on 9 August 1959. They are running 18min late, but No 7006, still in single-chimney form at this stage, has had to contend with the addition of what look like one or two Plymouth ocean stock saloons on the rear making up a formidable load from Paddington. *Peter W. Gray*

Left: No D821 *Greyhound* passes Exeter with the delayed down 'Torbay Express' on Saturday 9 July 1960. *John Hodge*

Below left: As on 9 July 1960, No 7033 *Hartlebury Castle* is again at the head of the 12.5pm from Paddington on Saturday 18 August 1962. However, this represents promotion because by 1962 the 12.5pm has become the down 'Torbay Express'. This 14-coach formation is well over the 450-ton limit for a 'Castle' up to Whiteball so No 7033, which has only five more months left to run, has stopped at Wellington for assistance, and 2-6-0 No 7305 is pushing vigorously at the rear up to Whiteball box. *Mike Fox*

9. THE BIG WEST OF ENGLAND RUSH

Holiday services between Paddington and the West of England were right at the heart of Western Region operations every summer Saturday. Judging by the amount of information which has come to hand, these expresses also created the greatest interest along the lineside during the day.

Of necessity additional westbound departures from Paddington to Cornwall were spread out over 13hr, while by contrast the bulk of up services were much more concentrated.

Down Traffic
In addition to the regular down night departures from Paddington at:

    10.20pm Postal, via Bristol for Penzance.
    10.30pm via Bristol for Penzance, the train including sleeping cars
    11.50pm via Bristol for Penzance, with sleeping cars as far as Plymouth
    12.30am Newspaper Train for Penzance, via the direct Berks & Hants line, and which also conveyed sleeping car passengers, although not advertised

there were additional departures on Friday nights/Saturday mornings at:

    10.05pm via the direct route for Penzance, with (normally) a three-coach portion for St Ives, detached at St Erth
    10.45pm via the direct route for Penzance, and which also conveyed sleeping cars for the use of passengers bound for the Scilly Isles
    11.15pm via the direct route for Newquay
    11.35pm via Bristol for Penzance
    12.35am via the direct route for Penzance, exclusively made up of sleeping cars, though there was also a brake composite at each end of the train for operating purposes.

Eight or more sleeping cars were marshalled in the formation of the 12.35 and its exact composition was advised by a weekly circular covering sleeping car arrangements. Some fairly basic second class sleeping cars with four berths per compartment were included, but the 9ft 7in width of these 1930 'Riviera'-style vehicles meant there was plenty of space for full length berths across the car. The arrival of overnight reliefs at Plymouth provided much needed express engines from the London end to help Laira cope with the return rush next day.

On Saturday morning crowds would start to throng on the circulating area behind the buffer stops at Paddington, known as the Lawn, from about 6.15am, ready for the first advertised departure to Penzance at 6.50am. This departed behind No 7923 *Speke Hall* which had been due to leave Southall shed light engine at 5.48am for Ranelagh Bridge. With the 6.50, No 7923 stopped at Reading and went on to pass Taunton 1min late at 9.28am.

Further departures left at 7am for Kingswear, 7.30 for Kingswear via Bristol, then 7.40am and 8.10am for Paignton. They were followed by departures at 8.25am for Penzance, with a portion for Perranporth which was detached at Truro, then at 8.45am and 9.22am for Paignton. The 7am and 8.10 departures were diesel-hauled, and one of the advantages of the new traction was evident when it was noted that their 'Warships' were able to return to Paddington from Kingswear and Paignton after a turn-round of less than 2hr, and without the need to go to shed for servicing.

An unusual one-off train joined the westbound procession by starting from Ealing Broadway at 7.25am. Engine and stock for this service had left direct from the Old Oak Common Goods Spur at 7am and then travelled on the down relief line calling at Ealing Broadway, Slough, Maidenhead, Twyford and Reading. This train provided a useful through service from these towns to Cornwall. However, return holidaymakers were not so well provided for, as only Reading was given the benefit of the through service from Cornwall. There was no direct down train from these outer London stations to the Torbay resorts, but Slough passengers had the advantage of a 4.15pm from Paignton which called at Torquay before running nonstop to Slough and Paddington.

With a substantial train of 12 coaches the 7.25am from Ealing needed a good loco to maintain the same running times as the daily Newbury twin diesel set between Slough and Reading. It certainly had one on 9 July with No 7018 *Drysllwyn Castle* at the head end. No 7018 was marking the second anniversary of a fine 'Bristolian' performance on Tuesday 9 July 1958 when Driver Newbury worked this engine up to 100mph at Little Somerford. The Bath Road team also went on to reach 93mph at Steventon during the course of a run to Paddington which was rounded off in 95min 55sec. This was one of a number of outstanding times achieved by No 7018 that summer, but the full 100mph maximum was not accomplished that often.

141

On the 7.25am Ealing–Penzance No 7018 was due to stop in the relief line platform at Reading from 8.19–8.23am. However, it could not cross over to take the Newbury route until No 5036 *Lyonshall Castle* with the 7.40am Paddington–Paignton had cleared Reading Station West Junction off the down main. The 7.40 had the fastest Saturday schedule of any advertised train through to Newton Abbot. Although No 5036 didn't quite keep time, it was still second fastest train of the day to this point. So No 5036 certainly showed No 7018 a clean pair of heels while the 7.25am Ealing made the only call by a down West of England express at Frome. No 7018 then ran 42½ miles from there to Taunton in not more than 50min start to stop. After Exeter No 7018's train reassumed its semi-fast role and was allowed until 1.20pm before it was due into Plymouth. No D6320 assisted No 7018 a minute late from Newton Abbot over the banks and at Plymouth No 6828 *Trellech Grange* took over about 10 coaches for Penzance, where the train was scheduled to terminate at 4.25pm. It was the slowest train of the day to Cornwall via the Westbury route, but it also made by far the most stops.

At Par the scheduled arrival of the 7.25am from Ealing was less than 1hr ahead of the 9.30am Paddington–Newquay, which by contrast had made only one passenger stop on its journey to this point. The running of the 9.30 on 9 July has already been described in Chapter 4.

Between 10.15 and 10.37am the main peak of four fast expresses running at 7/8min intervals developed around the regular 'Cornish Riviera' departure time from Paddington. None of them stopped before Newton Abbot. The first two for the Torbay line were steam, but on the way they had to negotiate a very slender margin between Blatchbridge Jc and Castle Cary. Here the 9.30am Reading–Weymouth came accelerating out of Frome only 6min before 'Castle' No 5060 *Earl of Berkeley* was bearing down with the 10.15. The 9.30 then had to travel uncommonly fast *and* make a 2min stop at Castle Cary before it could get out of the way of the 10.15. This was too close for comfort. It was trickier still when the preceding 9.40am Paddington–Minehead was probably a few minutes late leaving Westbury with No 6996 *Blackwell Hall*. That would inevitably make the Reading–Weymouth train, which was due out of Westbury just 5min afterwards, equally late. There might now be hardly any interval at all between the 9.30 from Reading and the 10.15 down at the point where their routes converged beyond Frome. However, the signalman at Blatchbridge Jc could hardly hold the Weymouth train there because, once stopped, it would have to wait at least 25min for all four sections of the 'Cornish Riviera' to pass. On the other hand, if he let it go on ahead any severe delay it caused to the 10.15 between here and Castle Cary would affect the three following trains too, and might explain why all four

were 7–11min late at Taunton on 9 July. No 5060 was going well and proved it was possible to make up all but 3min of the lost time before Newton Abbot. However, No 5977 *Beckford Hall* was not such a good choice following on the 10.22 from Paddington and it could not quite close up on No 5060. So the diesels with heavy loads on the 10.30 and 10.37 down Cornish expresses which were right behind No 5977 had no chance to show their paces.

Both the 10.30 and 10.37 were usually diesel-hauled throughout to Penzance. They were followed by the slower 11am and 11.40am down departures from Paddington with Nos 6021 and 7903 respectively. Not much is known about the workings of the 11.40 in Cornwall except to say that it seems to have been subject to some weekly variations between steam and diesel power. On 2 July two NB Type 2s relieved No 6902 and its pilot at Plymouth. Four weeks later No 5034 worked the 11.40 to Plymouth where in contrast Cornish stalwart No 4906 *Bradfield Hall* was then put on to complete the run to Penzance.

Whilst the 11.40 was the last daytime relief to penetrate into Cornwall, there was also a 12.5pm Paddington–Plymouth following the 'Torbay Express' which made eight stops on the way and performed a useful mopping-up function. With all these stops the overall timing of the 12.5 was not a quick one, and it took over 5½hr to reach Plymouth. However, the 12.5 had to run quite fast intermediately. It made a faster start to stop time from Reading to Newbury than the pass to pass booking of the Saturday 'Torbay Express' along here. After that the 12.5 was scheduled at the same speed as the 'Torbay Express' right through the Bristol District from Bedwyn to Castle Cary, covering 54½ miles in 48min.

This was certainly stretching it a bit when a '47xx' with its 60mph limit was booked out on the 12.5, as was occasionally the case. A 2-8-0 appeared fairly regularly on the last few summer weekends during 1952, and then less frequently in subsequent years until 1957. It was certainly a major surprise when No 4700 came out from Old Oak Common for the 12.5 on 6 August 1960. Unfortunately the failure near Newbury of No D604 on the 'Torbay Express', which was directly ahead of No 4700, completely ruined any chance of a reasonable performance by the 2-8-0. No 4700 was not able to overtake the casualty, and was therefore timed past Norton Fitzwarren 67min in arrears while the 'Torbay Express' was still in front running 80min late.

Generally during 1960 a 'Castle' or 'Hall' could be spared for the 12.5, and on 9 July the engine was No 7033 *Hartlebury Castle*. No 7033 had been fitted with a double-chimney in July 1959 and this confirmed it as a real flyer. It was a locomotive any shed would be pleased to have on its allocation. Not surprisingly all its short life was spent at Old Oak

Common, which had a knack of managing not to part with really choice engines like this one. Earlier in 1960, between 11 February and 18 March, No 7033 had been selected for four successive tours of duty on the Royal Train. It worked to Cheltenham twice, South Wales and Plymouth. These trains were easily timed, but when not engaged in Royal service No 7033 was first choice for the 1.50pm Bristol–Paddington. The 1.50 included, in an otherwise fairly unremarkable journey, a sprint from Swindon to Reading in 36min. At that time it was the fastest start to stop run on British Railways and the quickest steam schedule in the world. No 7033 had a much better chance of maintaining this booking than the 80mph speed restricted 'Warship' diesels which took over haulage of the 1.50 from 13 June 1960 onwards.

On 9 July No 7033 had 11 coaches in tow and left Paddington 1min late. It was due to call first at Reading and then Newbury. After that the 12.5 should have been up and over the top at Savernake by 1.37½pm. Bernard Cooke arrived to spend the afternoon at Savernake about 1.45pm. What he found was the 12.5 standing in the station. There the fireman was just in the process of throwing the bag off the tender as No 7033 finished taking water at the down end column. All West box boards would already have been off ready for it to restart and within a minute No 7033 was storming away down to Burbage Wharf, already looking out for those lost minutes on a fast run to Taunton.

Earlier No 7033 had obviously failed to scoop up an adequate supply of water from Aldermaston troughs, and unfortunately its passenger stop at Newbury cannot have enabled No 7033's crew to use one of the down side water columns there to top up the tender. One column was situated just beyond the station canopy roof on the platform, primarily for the use of engines arriving in the adjoining bay on trains from the south end of the Didcot, Newbury & Southampton line. The other used to be placed on the ramp right at the west end of the platform, but at some stage it had been moved to a position between the platform loop and the through line. This column cannot have been used very frequently and may have been faulty, or else No 7033's crew thought they could manage with the water they had left and then later changed their minds.

Savernake was certainly well placed if an unavoidable water stop had to be made. There was a downhill start followed by 26 miles of largely favourable gradients down to the next set of troughs beyond Westbury. Nevertheless, the price of having to stop would be a loss of 8min or so even at Savernake. The schedule was fast to Heywood Road Jc, so even if No 7033 passed here inside even time from the restart at about 2.10pm, no recovery would yet have commenced. But by running the next 48¾ miles, also with a downhill tendency, to Taunton in around 45min all the arrears of time were made up.

The 'Castle' ran into Taunton punctually at 2.55pm right alongside No 6907 *Davenham Hall* of Oxley which was passing through simultaneously on the relief line with the 10.18am Wolverhampton–Paignton.

No 7033 had covered the 72.6 miles from Savernake in 69min start to stop at 63mph. Kenneth Leech had 23 footplate trips on No 7033, his second highest total of any 'Castle', and he was not surprised to hear of its good performance. He told me the engine's speedometer read about 3mph fast at 90, so the crew might have thought they were going even more quickly then they really were.

Unfortunately there was no chance of No 7033 continuing its spirited progress beyond Taunton. Not even a 6min recovery margin up to Whiteball Tunnel and a further allowance of 3min for signal checks from there to Exeter could prevent a loss of 18min on schedule within 30 miles. It took No 7033 more than an hour to get from Taunton to Exeter. With only one down platform available for WR through traffic at St Davids, and four trains queuing up to use it solidly from 3.37 to 4.3pm, a single slow train was again able to hold up all the others behind. In this case the loss of time suffered by the 12.5 between Taunton and Exeter could be directly attributed to the poor running of No 5926 six trains in front on the 9.25am Wolverhampton–Paignton. No 5926's arrival at Taunton 34min late has already been related in Chapter 4. Even though a fresh crew took over at Taunton, that lateness had grown to 41min by Exeter, and at this stage No 5926 appears to have been responsible for cumulative delays of 108min to those six down trains which followed it. Within that traffic block No 6965 *Thirlestaine Hall* itself formed a mini-procession when it had to be held at Norton Fitzwarren to let No D821 *Greyhound* with the 13min late 'Torbay Express' overtake. No 6965 was working the 8am Sheffield–Kingswear which, from being early at Taunton, was 21min late into Exeter through no fault of its own. Behind No 6965 came No 5945 *Leckhampton Hall* with the 12.21pm Cardiff–Newquay. No 6907 was next on the 10.18am Wolverhampton–Paignton was not due to make a passenger stop at Taunton and so preceded No 7033 from there as scheduled. No 7033 bringing up the rear of this procession with the 12.5 could not avoid being held up all the way to Newton Abbot as a result.

At Exeter the 12.5 was alone in being booked to attach its assistant engine here. This pilot was No 4095 *Harlech Castle* which had already had an eventful day. At around 6.20am No 4095 first set out from Plymouth as train engine behind No 1002 *County of Berks* with 13 LMR coaches on the 9.15pm Friday night service from Manchester to Newquay. No 4095 worked through and then returned as far as Plymouth in front of No 6873 *Caradoc Grange* with the 11am Newquay–York. At North Road the 'Castle' pulled forward into one of the loco spurs to await the

10.20am Penzance–Swansea. No 4972 *St Bride's Hall* was the train engine for this and No 4095 assisted it to Newton Abbot. Here No 4972 was removed, No 4095 became train engine and No 6921 *Borwick Hall* was added as pilot. Finally, at Exeter, No 4095 had to be extricated so that No 6921 could take over as train engine. Off went the 10.20am Penzance on its way to Swansea 17min late at 3.20pm. Now, to complete this amazing catalogue of a whole day spent double-heading, No 4095 was in action again less than an hour later. At 4.10pm it set off back to Plymouth forming a twin 'Castle' combination coupled to No 7033. Two coaches were due to be left at Newton Abbot. Hopefully two 'Castles' on a load of nine coaches with only one 5min stop at Brent could then recover a good slice of what had by Newton become a 26min deficit, before the train was due into Plymouth at 5.38pm.

The next two departures from Paddington to the West of England unfortunately fared the worst of any down expresses. Involved were No 7034 *Ince Castle* on the 1.20pm Paddington–Kingswear and No 5069 *Isambard Kingdom Brunel* heading the 1.30pm 'Royal Duchy' for Penzance and Newquay. The 'Royal Duchy' should have been the crack 'Castle' turn of the day to Plymouth but unfortunately No 7034 failed and had to be removed from the 1.20 at Reading, so both trains were held up there. Although the delay to the 'Royal Duchy' was not severe in itself, it was sufficient to cost

Above: 'Castle' No 4095 *Harlech Castle* was no stranger to double-heading when it spent such a busy day assisting between Newquay and Exeter on 9 July 1960. Here, nearly a year earlier, No 4095, while shedded at Penzance, double-heads 2-6-0 No 6397 out of Lostwithiel with the 8.55am Wolverhampton–Penzance on 8 August 1959. No 5021 had brought the 14-coach train down from the Midlands and at Newton Abbot No 5021 arrived 65min late. Nos 4095 and 6397 are now 71min overdue, and hard at it on the steep climb to Treverrin Tunnel. *Peter W. Gray*

No 5069 its correct path at Taunton and No 5069 also suffered a further series of checks after that.

No 7034 was certainly one of the least successful double-chimney 'Castle' conversions to date and did not run particularly well during 1960. As a result, this engine was very slow building up its mileage. Although No 7034 should have been able to take 13 bogies from Paddington to Newton Abbot in its stride, it was more likely to be found hauling five coaches on the 5.55pm Bristol–Trowbridge local, which is what No 7034 had worked the previous Saturday, 2 July.

On 9 July *Ince Castle* left Paddington at 1.21pm and was in trouble at once. The first six miles to West Ealing took 17min. The next 25 miles as far as Twyford were covered slightly more quickly in 28½min, but by then No 7034 was running over 10min late. There was a long way to go and a decision had probably already been taken to call for another engine at Reading. It is likely that the crew of No 7034 sounded the standard whistle code of three crows to call up a fresh locomotive at their next stopping place when they struggled past Slough or Maidenhead.

This would give the men on the Reading down line pilot No 6923 a valuable 15min or so to clear the locomotive for action and start building up steam pressure. The standby engine had been on duty since 5.20am, so its fire would certainly need livening up by 2.15 in the afternoon.

Over a long period the Reading down line pilot had convincingly demonstrated its mettle on a number of occasions, none more successfully than the 'Saint' No 2937 *Clevedon Court*. In April 1936 it was recorded taking over the down 'Cornish Riviera' very capably, and soon after made an absolutely outstanding run on the 'Bristolian' when 'King' No 6015 had to be removed at Reading with a hot box. 'County' 4-4-0s like No 3820 *County of Worcester* had performed the pilot function before 'Saints', and now 'Halls' were generally in use. Shortly, when with the spread of dieselisation the Reading down line pilot was in almost constant demand, 'Castles' would be found hard at it well into 1964, stoutly trying their hand at accelerated diesel schedules with trains like the 'Red Dragon'.

On 9 July Reading pilot No 6923 *Croxteth Hall* was ready to replace No 7034 and they managed a very prompt changeover, so No 6923 was probably ready to go soon after 2.25pm. The 'Hall' was a high mileage example which nevertheless gave a good account of itself. Its crew were already firmly in the saddle as No 6923 came charging up the 1 in 106 through Savernake cutting with a blistering roar, and there they were running just 23min late.

This was certainly a much more successful salvage exercise than the one mounted a week later when No 6923 had to rescue No D808 on the down 'Cornish Riviera'. Despite such speedy action on 9 July, however, it was a pity that arrangements could not be made in time to transfer passengers for the 1.20 across to the relief line Platform 8 so that engines could be changed there. This platform was clear of local trains from 1.43 to 2.28pm and that would have enabled No 5069 following with the 1.30 to stop at Reading on the down main and go ahead without further delay. No 5069 was loaded to only 10 coaches and could be expected to stay well out of No 6923's way, even though the 'Royal Duchy' had a stop at Newbury. Unfortunately it had to be held at Reading Main Line East signals instead.

However, No 5069 did not have a perfect recent record either. On 2 July it had to be replaced at Westbury on the 12.18pm Newton Abbot–Paddington by No 4972 *Saint Bride's Hall*. The problem can have been nothing serious because only 20min later No 5069, running tender-first, banked No 6943 *Farnley Hall* out of Westbury on the 1pm Cardiff–Brighton. No 5069 returned from Warminster 1hr later coupled chimney to chimney with ex-works 'Hall' No 5940 *Whitbourne Hall*. No 5940 was probably forming the usual OC83 light engine movement back from Salisbury off the 9.20am Swansea–Brockenhurst, and No 5069 was coupled on at Warminster to save a path down Dilton Marsh bank. What this did show was that steam failures could take place almost unnoticed, whereas diesel breakdowns were usually only too obvious.

Meanwhile No 6923 on the 1.20 ran from Savernake to Taunton in 85min, which regained a creditable 3min. This 3min was crucial because it enabled No 6923 to cover up the evidence of No 7034's failure earlier, and to maintain the 1.20's

Below: On Tuesday 2 August 1960 No 7034 *Ince Castle* hauls a down train of LM empty coaches at 10.30am near Starcross. This is thought to be 3Z71: the 4.25am Paddington–Paignton ECS. No 7034 probably looked just as dirty as this when it failed with the 1.20pm Paddington–Kingswear on 9 July. *Peter W. Gray*

Above: Passenger engines were kept on standby at many locations, and some of them doubled as station pilots. Amongst these places were Banbury, Birmingham Snow Hill, Reading and here at Hereford. No 5952 *Cogan Hall* is the standby, while to the right No 6348 has arrived with the 12.48pm stopping train from Gloucester on Saturday 3 June 1961. *Gerald Adams*

booked path at Taunton just ahead of No 6842 *Nunhold Grange* on the 7.30am Newcastle–Paignton. No 5069 was not so fortunate. The 'Royal Duchy' had a booked stop to make at Westbury and this opened up a significant gap between Nos 6923 and 5069. The 'Castle' therefore had to follow No D818 *Glory* hauling the down 'Devonian' at Taunton, instead of preceding it. All trains were still losing time between Taunton and Newton Abbot, so when at 6.20pm No 5069 was eventually ready to attach No D6323 for assistance over the banks, its lateness had increased from 14min at Savernake to 31min on arrival at Newton Abbot.

By 7pm the day's westbound rush was effectively over. The last three direct Paddington–West of England expresses which arrived later in the evening were all diesel-hauled on fast schedules. With a much clearer road they kept good time. No D801 *Vanguard*, one of the original 2,070hp units, was a couple of minutes late at both Exeter and Newton Abbot with the 3.30pm down. But this was nothing that No D801 could not be expected to regain, on top of being able to take 11 coaches without assistance through to Plymouth. All other loads which were noted in both directions exceeding eight coaches were piloted over the South Devon banks.

Up Traffic

This was a satisfactory end to a day of mixed fortunes for down traffic. The morning had started promisingly, but recovery from later set-backs was agonisingly slow. It was much the same on the up road too.

For returning holidaymakers the eastbound rush to Paddington did not get under way across the Tamar until 10.29am on Saturday morning. Then, well within 2hr, five of the seven Saturday reliefs from Cornwall to London, plus the up 'Riviera' itself, had to be worked over the Royal Albert Bridge into Devon. These trains were the 8.15am from Perranporth, 8.35am from Falmouth, 8.20am from Penzance, 9.20am from St Ives, 10am from Newquay and the 10am from Penzance, the up 'Riviera'.

Within the same two-hour timetable, further east, three expresses from the Torbay line, together with what became at Brent one equally heavy departure starting from Plymouth at 11.15am, were interspersed among the six long trains snaking up from Cornwall. All of them contributed to the efficient movement of around 6,800 passengers in this peak cluster of 10 trains. The first two only loaded to 10 or 12 vehicles, and there was another, the 8.20am from Penzance, which fulfilled an intermediate role by stopping four times on the way up from Plymouth. But the others provided a spectacle of 13, 14 and 15-coach leviathans running nonstop in quick succession over long distances.

In few places was this parade more impressive than whilst covering the 100 miles from Cogload to Newbury. Firstly this was because such a rush of traffic was in total contrast to the usual low level of activity on a normal afternoon. Secondly, if there was any hard work to be done in the cause of time recovery after delays from congestion further west, it was between Taunton and Savernake that a real effort had to be made and sustained. This made the collective sights and sounds of these trains on the fast uphill stretches something quite out of the ordinary.

The importance attached to good performance by such a succession of heavy expresses was implicit in the standard of motive power provided. During earlier BR days before the first main line diesels appeared in 1958, the supply of steam locomotives on the peak 10 London trains divided up into something like four 'Kings', four 'Castles' and a couple of two-cylinder engines (often including a 'Britannia' Pacific until 1956). Now, even with such a limited number of diesels in service by 1960, Type 4 'Warships' had already achieved easy mastery of a majority of them.

Usually the general principle adopted for London trains was to provide diesel haulage from the Plymouth direction, and steam power for Torbay line traffic. There were normally about four exceptions where steam was used for trains from Plymouth and four more where diesels were generally supplied to work three Kingswear departures and one Paignton service to Paddington. This meant that seven Type 4 diesels were to be seen on the peak 10 up expresses at Savernake the previous Saturday, 2 July. Just one turn each remained for a 'King', a 'Castle' and a 'Hall'.

9 July was very different in this respect, however. For the last time steam outnumbered diesels on the main bloc of up London trains, as well as on the rest of the holiday service as usual. There was a distribution of four 'Warships', three 'Castles', two 'Kings' and a 'Hall', plus one other completely unexpected interloper which joined in right out of the blue. However, it cannot be said that the intervention of so many steam locomotives had entirely beneficial consequences for timekeeping. Only two of them ran at anything like their proper potential and these two were engines covering the lightest loads.

Some of the shortcomings might well be accounted for however if Laira had in fact found it necessary to step up the number of steam locomotive workings at short notice to cover a deficiency of diesels. The preparation of some engines may then have had to be rushed or even only partially completed.

Below: The down 'Royal Duchy' is very heavily loaded for a 'Modified Hall' on Saturday 16 July 1960. The train is approaching Hackney behind No 7917 *North Aston Hall* 39min late, and the practice of attaching empty Plymouth ocean stock saloons to heavy holiday expresses does not help. After an up 'Ocean Express' ran during the following week the stock had to be worked back to Plymouth all over again. On Friday 22 July two saloons went down from London on the 5.5am Bristol parcels, one on the 5.30am Paddington–Penzance and Nos W9111-3W were attached to the 12.5pm Paddington–Truro empty restaurant car train. *Derek J. Frost*

Bottom: 'Castles' had frequently been standing in for 'Kings' over many years well before the diesels arrived, and the sight they made at full stretch on the West of England main line is an abiding memory. Here is one such occasion when the 7.15am Plymouth–Paddington should have been a Laira 'King' on Monday 19 August 1957, and instead along comes No 4082 *Windsor Castle* setting a scorching pace past Patney & Chirton despite a full 'Castle' load for this schedule. No 4082 will be steaming hard on this train all the way after starting out of Westbury to mp 78 beyond Woodborough. *Rev A. C. Cawston Collection, National Railway Museum*

Above: No 7029 *Clun Castle* with the 11.30am Torquay–Paddington climbs to Brewham beneath the S&D route near Cole as '7F' 2-8-0 No 53805 crosses overhead with the 12.26pm Bournemouth–Nottingham on Saturday 13 August 1960. No 7029 also worked the 11.30am on 9 July, following this up by a run with the 'Torbay Express' on Monday 11 July. The DTSO's daily notice at Exeter gave specific instructions that on 11 July the up 'Torbay Express' MUST RUN TO TIME. ALL CONCERNED TO GIVE THE WORKING SPECIAL ATTENTION. Special attention may have involved arranging for No 7029 to be used instead of the usual 'Warship' diesel to ensure a punctual journey. The reason why this train had to run punctually was not disclosed. *Richardson Bros/Ian Allan Library*

Before the main rush began, up traffic to Paddington early in the morning had been handled both expeditiously and efficiently. All the first four trains from Plymouth and Kingswear to Paddington were diesel. As far as can be seen, they were relatively free from delays and were running early or on time when observed at West Ealing or Paddington. After arriving at Paddington by 1.40pm their 'Warship' diesels were ready to begin taking return workings to the west from 3.15pm onwards.

However, this meant that by 8.30am Laira was already in a position where about half the stock of 'Warships' which were likely to be available for London trains was already in use. To cover what had turned out to be a bigger deficiency of diesels than usual, those Old Oak steam locomotives off Friday's overnight reliefs were going to prove extremely valuable. So Laira was busy servicing two each of the visiting 'Castles' and 'Kings', as well as preparing a 'King' of its own, and all except one of them would be going off shed for London trains before midday.

At Newton Abbot shed locomotive preparation was also in full swing despite the effects of dieselisation. Here part of the shed was a building site for the new diesel locomotive service area, and a partial rundown of steam locomotive servicing facilities had already taken place. Various steam locos had been transferred away, others withdrawn, although of those which were left all the 'Castles' allocated were in service, except No 4037 *The South Wales Borderers* which was at Swindon Works. Some steam locomotive diagrams formerly handled by Newton Abbot depot were now covered either by Laira 'Warships' or steam power from Exeter and Bristol sheds. It was now Exeter's responsibility to provide or prepare engines for three Torbay–London services. The three trains being:

A47 9.45am Churston–Paddington
A88 1.30pm Paignton–Paddington
A92 1.55pm Torquay–Paddington

For these, locos from Exeter worked:
V79 10.22pm FRI Manchester–Paignton
9.30am Exeter–Kingswear
C60 8.10am Newport–Paignton

This left Newton Abbot to find power for London trains at 10.35am from Torquay, 11.30am from Torquay and 4.15pm from Paignton. Late deliveries of diesels meant that a likely intention to use 'Warships' on the 11.30 could not be fulfilled until later in the season, so for the 10.35 and 11.30 turns on 9 July Newton Abbot used two 'Castles' of their own which had probably been prepared earlier. No 5950 *Wardley Hall* was turned round off an early morning arrival for the third.

Some time during the morning Newton Abbot would also have been advised that 'Castle' No 5060 was heading their way on the 10.15am from Paddington. This was bad news for them, as the 10.15 should have been worked by a diesel which would then have returned to Paddington on the 4.35pm from Kingswear. It was not a good idea to try to send No 5060 back to London on the diesel diagram. It would probably run out of coal, lubricating oil and sand, but not of ash or clinker which might cause steaming problems. That meant NA had to find and prepare a suitable engine for the up train. No 5036 was used, after it had already covered a bit of extra mileage by working through to Paignton on the 7.40am from Paddington, instead of coming off at Newton Abbot on the down journey.

Contrary to what was shown in the public timetable, two expresses from Paignton and three more from Torquay actually made the longest nonstop runs on a summer Saturday over the Western Region system. The two from Paignton just exceeded 200 miles in length and on 9 July all five were steam-worked, two of them by engines supplied from Newton Abbot and two more by engines prepared at Exeter. The very long runs without public stops published in the timetable, such as the Paddington to Truro journey of the down 'Riviera' or from St Columb Road to London on the 10am Newquay–Paddington, were in fact interrupted by two operating stops for locomotive purposes on the way, as well as a crew change halt at Par Branch up home signal by the 10am.

First Paignton nonstop was the 9.45am from Churston to Paddington which was hauled by No 1007 *County of Brecknock*. It was followed by No 4083 *Abbotsbury Castle* on the 10.35am nonstop from Torquay. The 'County' overcame the delays it encountered rather more successfully than the 'Castle' and No 1007 made up 12min lost time between Taunton and West Ealing. There it was 10min late. Traffic built up all around No 4083's path as already recounted, and the 10.35 reached Paddington 19min late.

On its way from Kingswear to London the regular Mon–Fri 'Torbay Express' made four stops. However, it generated so much business on Saturdays that three separate trains were required to carry passengers originating around midday at stations between Kingswear and Exeter. On 9 July all three of these were steam-worked. The first of them was the 10-coach restaurant car express running nonstop from Torquay to Paddington at 11.30am. It was followed half an hour later by the 'Torbay Express' itself and then by the 12.18pm from Newton Abbot which ran nonstop up from Exeter.

On 9 July the 11.30 was in the capable hands of No 7029 *Clun Castle*. This engine had first emerged from Swindon Works with a double-chimney in October 1959 and by summer 1960 it was the only

one at Newton Abbot so fitted. No 7029 was due to leave shed and proceed light engine to Paignton at 9.55am. Here No 7029 collected the stock and at 11.15am returned with it empty to Torquay. On arrival No 7029 picked up a full complement of around 510 passengers with seat regulation tickets, and then moved off soon after 11.30am up the 1 in 55 climb towards Torre.

After converging with the line from Plymouth at Aller Jc, *Clun Castle* passed Newton 5min late. Further on at Exeter it overtook No 5090 *Neath Abbey* on the 10.58am Paignton–Nottingham. It also passed the 7.30am Penzance–Bristol hauled by No 7921 *Edstone Hall* at Taunton. But even then the prevailing procession of traffic from Newton Abbot had been moving so slowly that No 7029 was now 28min late. The first 45¼ miles had taken 106min. After Taunton where Bristol traffic diverged, the situation changed altogether. No 7029 found itself with a massive clear headway in front and, if anything was to be done to retrieve some lost time, now was the opportunity. The next 70 miles rising in aggregate about 450ft to Savernake were covered in 79min and *Clun Castle* passed there at 2.35pm. Seventy favourably graded miles and 73min now remained for a punctual Paddington arrival at 3.48pm, but in the event this was a target No 7029 was not quite able to meet. It arrived 8min late, possibly because of a check at Reading. There may also have been a couple of minutes delay during the final approaches, because the last five miles in from West Ealing occupied 8min. Nevertheless, time recovery of 20min since passing Taunton was a satisfactory outcome to this run.

Next day No 7029 was recruited amongst a series of diesels for Sunday morning departures to the West of England, and the 'Castle' returned to Plymouth on the 11am from Paddington. This was a stroke of luck, because when on Monday Laira found that there was no diesel available for the up 'Torbay Express' No 7029 was well positioned to take over what was now a Laira working. *Clun Castle* was very appropriately sent over to Kingswear and worked the 'Special Load' 'Torbay' schedule to Paddington. This and the appearance of No 5008 *Raglan Castle* on the down train the previous Thursday 7 July were by no means the only occasions that 'Castles' were to be seen on the 'Torbay Express' during July 1960. Curiously enough No 5008 was an equally appropriate choice for the down train, because this had been Old Oak Common's last regular 'Castle' on its alternate share of the 'Torbay Express' working in June and July 1959.

The next train after the 11.30am Torquay at Aller Jc was the 8.15am Perranporth–Paddington. This train had already travelled 98 very hilly miles with three different pairs of engines and at this stage it was making good progress. Initially the main section of stock for the Perranporth had started the day being hauled empty from Newquay along the branch towards Chacewater as far as its starting point. The load was made up of six coaches which formed the Newquay portion of Friday's 9.30am from Paddington. Included was restaurant car No W9574W, a 70ft-long 12-wheeler which had been used to victual the postwar 'Torbay Express' until 1956. No 9574 turned the scales at 49 tons, and this made it one of the heaviest coaches to be found anywhere on BR. So the weight of these six coaches was well in excess of the 170-ton limit for a single '45xx' 2-6-2T. Two engines were therefore needed, and these were dispatched light from Truro at 5.45am to collect the stock at Newquay.

After loading at Perranporth, the train faced a steep curving climb at 1 in 45-60 for five miles away from the coast up to St Agnes where it made just one stop on the way to Truro.

Only one of the pair of Prairies, No 4587, was noted when the Perranporth reached Truro. Nos 4593 and 5538 were also working the branch later in the day, but No 4587's assistant engine might in this case have been any one of Truro's allocation of 10 '45xx' engines. No 4587 was fast approaching its swansong and was withdrawn for scrap within the next five weeks.

At Truro the six-coach set from Newquay was reunited with Friday's Falmouth portion of the 9.30am from Paddington. However, these coaches had not originated at Falmouth on Saturday. They had been hauled up to Truro on Friday evening, demonstrating yet again the enormous non-productive cost of positioning all these trains for the Saturday rush.

Now with 12 corridors, mostly standard stock, this load was just heavy enough to require two smaller locomotives on the main line if no Class 6 or 7 was available. That was therefore the situation at Truro where No 7813 *Freshford Manor* from the local shed and No 6805 *Broughton Grange* of Laira were ready to couple on.

In order to leave sufficient accommodation for important stops at St Austell and Par, London passengers were not allowed to join the Perranporth at Truro. They had to await arrival of the 8.55am from Falmouth 12min later. After Par the Perranporth was deemed to be full of passengers for London and it made no more public stops.

Standards of locomotive performance over the Cornish main line were high, especially in view of the loads which had to be conveyed. The Perranporth was allowed 7min more than the weekday up 'Riviera' allowance of 55min from Par to Plymouth, but when one Class 7 engine was being used with three extra coaches, that was none too generous. Generally over the years Cornish expresses were handed over punctually at Plymouth, even during times of heaviest traffic.

After negotiating North Road station nonstop at 15mph, if they were lucky, Nos 7813 and 6805 drew up on the main line two miles further east alongside the shed at Laira Jc. Here 8min were allowed for the incoming engines to change places with Nos D6311 and 6016 *King Edward V* before the Perranporth was due away again at 10.51am. Arriving at Newton Abbot 5min late like No 7029 in front of it, the speed of No 6016's progress on to Paddington was largely dictated by No 7029 and in fact closely duplicated it. No 6016 passed Taunton 27min late, ran to Savernake taking 2min more than the 'Castle' and then also recovered a lot of time on to London. The Perranporth reached Paddington 7min late, still directly behind No 7029, after the sort of run up from Taunton in 153min that No 6016 had been successfully performing day in, day out for much of the 26 years it spent on the strength at Laira.

The 8.35am from Falmouth was right behind the Perranporth all the way up from Truro, the only difference being that it made alternative stops in Cornwall. Many of its 13 coaches would already be well-loaded by the time the train left Truro. However, there would still be a lot more passengers waiting to get on at Bodmin Road and Liskeard, where the Falmouth formed the main London service of the morning from these branch junctions. At Bodmin Road it connected with the 9.8am from Padstow which had reversed at Bodmin General on the way. Looe was served by a shuttle service of two-coach branch trains to Coombe Junction and Liskeard. These had been handled by 2-6-2Ts Nos 4552 and 4569 the day before on 8 July.

No seat regulation tickets were required on the 8.35am from Falmouth, nor could seats be reserved at the stops after Truro, so care would have to be taken to keep some vacant accommodation for passengers joining at Liskeard. Otherwise there would be a mad scramble to find unoccupied seats at this final pick-up point.

By summer 1960 haulage of the Falmouth was apparently an all-diesel affair. It was first taken over by 'Warships' east of Plymouth in 1959, and during 1960 seems to have been similarly equipped in Cornwall too. It is possible that the same diesel worked through from Falmouth to Paddington on this train. The big benefit here was that one Type 4 could manage 13 coaches unassisted as far as Plymouth. It would also have an advantage in restarting such a heavy train from Bodmin Road up the steep 5½-mile climb to Doublebois.

Once out of Cornwall on 9 July the Falmouth attached NB Type 2 No D6323 at Laira Jc in front of 'Warship' No D813 *Diadem*. They were then due to set off up Hemerdon 17min behind the Perranporth. At Newton Abbot the two diesels arrived 9min late and, after detaching No D6323, the deficit gradually increased to 26min past Taunton where an improvement in timekeeping could reasonably be expected. No D813 then totally failed to make any impression in reducing this substantial loss before Savernake. It took 90min from Taunton and was now 33min late. The usual large slice of recovery time before Reading then enabled the arrears to be substantially reduced to 19min at Twyford, and No D813, with what seemed to be a clear run in, eventually reached Paddington 13min late. As already reported, the return progress of this diesel on the 6.30pm down via Bristol later also seemed to be rather lacklustre, at least in the early stages as far as Swindon.

However, the standard of No D813's running was positively sparkling compared to what followed. With no diesel available for the up 'Torbay Express', those responsible for arranging a presentable substitute could feel justifiably satisfied when No 6966 *Witchingham Hall* was procured to work the train. This Old Oak Common engine was only five weeks out from works after a complete overhaul and repaint. If it had to be a 'Hall' this one should have been ideal. Unfortunately No 6966 never really got to grips with the challenge of a 450-ton load and was apparently unable to respond adequately when the opportunity for some time recovery arose. The 'Torbay' was made up to a full 13 coaches at Paignton and was on time passing Newton Abbot. Here the 12.18 departure was already loading at the up platform ready to leave for Paddington 6min later.

Inevitably No 6966 then lost as much time as the rest of the procession before Taunton and came through 24min late. After that the 'Hall' was not able to keep up with the three trains in front, and it took 94min from Taunton to pass Savernake. This now made the 'Torbay' 38min late. It is difficult to detect any extenuating circumstances, but, as the 'Warship' diesel on the Falmouth ahead also took 90min, both trains may have been held up somewhere along this stretch.

Down from Savernake No 6966 recovered some minutes before Reading, but only half as much as the preceding trains. It was still 28min late at Twyford. From there No 6966 managed to keep up an average of almost exactly 60mph on to West Ealing, but this was not enough to make any real impression on the arrears. The up 'Torbay' eventually drew into Paddington 26min late. It had taken 172min from Taunton.

Meanwhile the 12.18pm up had left Newton Abbot on time. This was a full 14-coach set-up headed by another London engine, No 7020 *Gloucester Castle*. No 7020 had followed the usual procedure for the locomotive on this diagram, being turned out by Laira to assist the 7.30am Penzance–Bristol from Plymouth. It headed No 7921 *Edstone Hall* to Newton Abbot and was then detached ready to work the 12.18pm to Paddington 45min later. This train called at Teignmouth and Dawlish before arriving at Exeter, where it should have been held up for the 11.15am

from Plymouth to overtake. However, the 11.15 had problems of its own, so No 7020 was allowed to go on in front still running right time.

Despite the potential hazard of No 1028 just ahead with the 12.45pm Exeter–Taunton local train stopping at intermediate stations, No 7020 was able to pass the 'County' at or before Tiverton Jc. The loss of time by the 12.18 as it passed Taunton was therefore limited to only 13min. In the prevailing situation that should have meant the prospect of a reasonably punctual trip was now within No 7020's grasp, or at least that no more time would be lost. Some hope! No 7020 made a disastrous run on to Savernake taking 104min. That represented an additional loss of 22min on schedule and was enough to throw all following services into disarray. There seems no obvious reason for such poor timekeeping, with no sign of any other train being squeezed into the ever increasing margin between Nos 6966 and 7020 to cause any hold-ups. The conclusion is that this loss of time was debitable against the engine, though of course anything from a missing tail lamp or open carriage door to animals reported on the line might have contributed to the delay.

No 7020 even lost time from Savernake to Twyford, taking 46½min for 39 favourable miles. A concluding time of around 37½min for 31 miles on to Paddington also seems to indicate a crew struggling with problems on the engine. By then there was a wasted gap of about 29min since any previous train had passed on the up main line into Paddington. No 7020 was straddling the paths of three following trains, which were struggling along behind as best they could.

A final arrival 40min late was a particularly disappointing performance for what was still a regular steam turn and on a train which, despite its heavy load, had managed well enough in the past when pulled by 'Halls' or 'Granges' when necessary. No 7020 itself was something of a contradiction. It was an engine with a reputation of running very high mileages between overhauls — in autumn 1958 it had amassed 116,000 since classified repairs and was still going strong on second link duties. Yet its total career mileage was low measured against contemporary 'Castles'. By July 1960, still in original condition with HB three-row superheater boiler and single-chimney, No 7020 would again be on a high periodic mileage and starting to get run-down. Even so, standards of servicing and quality of fuel might have had more to do with such a poor run than the condition of the loco. Perhaps the fireman may have spent much of his time recently working as second man on a route such as this which was now frequented by diesels. He might not be feeling as fit as he once was at the prospect of shifting over four tons of coal to power a jaded engine, struggling with a train of 455 tons for 4¼hr.

Earlier No 6024's journey on the 11.15am from Plymouth began encouragingly enough especially when

it was paired with No 4920 *Dumbleton Hall* at the start, in a scene which could still be duplicated by these two preserved engines today. They climbed Hemerdon with eight bogies and collected six more at Brent. These had been brought in by one of the Kingsbridge branch engines, No 5573 on 6 August, forming the 10.55am nonstop from Kingsbridge to Brent, and there they were attached to the rear of the express.

The two 4-6-0s then had the usual call of the 11.20am midweek local from Plymouth to make at Totnes, so instead of clattering through the station at 60mph on the middle road they had to climb Dainton with 14 coaches from a standing start. The 11.15 then stopped to set down local passengers at Newton Abbot, where it used the outer platform face, and arrived 3min late. Here, while No 4920 was being uncoupled, misfortune struck. One of the coaches was detected to have a hot box and had to be detached. This meant clearing all passengers and their luggage from the

offending vehicle, shunting it out of the way and then recoupling the two sections of the train. Problems could soon mount up in that sort of situation even if enough accommodation could be found for the displaced passengers. For example, when two coaches had to be recoupled it might now be found that they had non-compatible corridor connections. Unless one coach was fitted with adaptors, the gangway doors would have to be locked out of use, effectively splitting the train in two as far as passengers were concerned. But on 9 July no such hindrance was apparent. The whole operation was carried out very promptly in under 21min and by 12.50pm *King Edward I* was ready to go again 19min late.

While these shunting manoeuvres were going on at one up platform, No 6946 *Heatherden Hall* had left for Exeter from the other. It was on time with the 12.5pm Paignton–Cardiff and No 6024 had to follow it. No 6946 ran briskly to Exeter in 30min, but

No 6024 unfortunately took 41min, and so was not in a position to overtake before No 6946 restarted from St Davids at 1.13pm. No 6946 with its lighter load continued to run more quickly than No 6024, and was still a comfortable 9min in front at Taunton. Here the 'King' was 33min late.

By the standard of previous trains passing Taunton, even this amount of lost time was not completely irrecoverable, but now of course No 6024's crew had to contend with No 7020 which was in front of them losing pots of time. There was nothing they could do about that. At Savernake No 6024 was 52min late, just one block and 6min behind the laggard. By Twyford the arrears had grown to 57½min. But then, just to show what might have been achieved, the last 31 miles were reeled off inside even time from pass to stop enabling No 6024 to recover 6½min and arrive at Paddington 51min late. *King Edward I* was able to make a much more successful round trip to Wolverhampton a week later on 16 July. With 13 coaches (weighing 451/485 tons) No 6024 topped Saunderton at 53mph after starting from High Wycombe, and was not more than a minute late arriving at any stop. With a top speed of 77mph as it thundered past Tyseley, No 6024 clocked into Snow Hill 1½min early.

Returning to the West of England main line on 9 July, No D810 *Cockade* with the 9.20am from St Ives, No D814 *Dragon* hauling the 10am from Newquay and No D817 *Foxhound* on the 'Riviera' were all bogged down behind No 7020 as well. No 7020 passed Savernake at 3.41pm, No 6024 followed at 3.47 and the three diesels were in close succession at 3.55, 4.5 and 4.13pm respectively.

All these trains seem to have had steam participation at some stage of the up journey, though in the case of the St Ives train it may only have been over the St Ives branch itself. Along here two '45xx' 2-6-2T engines,

from the original square side tank series, were required to overcome the climb for a mile at 1 in 60 up to Carbis Bay. At St Erth, where the train reversed, two 'D63xx' Type 2 diesels were waiting to back on, and they also attached three more coaches bringing the total to 13. These two diesels took the train as far as Plymouth North Road station.

The 10am from Newquay was renowned as the heaviest regular express on the WR, being booked for a scratch set of 15 very variable coaches. On 2 July No 6816 *Frankton Grange* had piloted a 'D8xx' 'Warship' from Newquay to Plymouth, but on 9 July this theme was varied somewhat. No 4976 *Warfield Hall* was provided to assist two 'D63xx' Type 2 diesels working in multiple for the first 56¼ miles through Cornwall. There were some impressive sights and sounds, not to mention an unholy mixture of smells, as this enormous cavalcade came winding its way along the single-line Newquay branch, before continuing over the main line to Plymouth.

The up 'Cornish Riviera Express' was diesel-hauled right across Cornwall, serving the isolated branch from Helston at its Gwinear Road stop. Otherwise the 'Riviera' made public calls only at Truro and then at Plymouth. Here 'Warship' diesels were exchanged and No D817 took over, together with the usual pilot engine over the banks.

Identities of the assistant engines from Plymouth on these three Cornish expresses are not known. Their paths through Newton Abbot fell during a well-earned break taken by observers there, and in the absence of any Saturday records taken at Plymouth, only deductions can be made. The pilot of the 9.20am St Ives on 9 July may have been No D6313 if it followed the identical working covered by this engine on 23 July. On that occasion the same diesel came up on the 9.20, and then on both 9 and 23 July returned as pilot to Truro with the down 'Riviera'.

Left:
An idyllic branch line scene as the 10.55am Kingsbridge-Brent and Paddington train comes north between Gara Bridge and Avonwick at Bickham Bridge behind 2-6-2T No 5573 on Saturday 6 August, 1960. From Brent these Kingsbridge carriages will make up a 14-coach load for No 5029 on the 11.15am Plymouth-Paddington. No 5573 carries local headcode in 1960, whereas on 24 June 1961 No 5573 displayed express lamps on this train. *Hugh Ballantyne*

Left: During 1959 'Kings' were still in their element hauling the heaviest Saturday expresses from Cornwall. With 14 coaches forming the 9.20am St Ives–Paddington No 6004 *King George III* has just topped Savernake summit and is now coasting downhill over the speed-restricted curves as far as Grafton East Jc on Saturday 25 July 1959. Unlike 18 July 1959 when five 'Kings' in succession passed Savernake within 5min of scheduled time (including No 6021 which made a smartly executed stop for water in the station, also on the 9.20am St Ives) this week No 6004 is running late along with the whole up service. In due course it will pass Southall 30min adrift. No 6004 is the last 'King' still running with the early BR emblem on its tender. The old MSWJ route via Savernake High Level is visible on the right. *Kenneth Leech, Courtesy of Barry Haywood*

Left: Although they have a full Saturday load, Nos 7824 *Ilford Manor* and 6002 *King William IV* are in charge of a beautifully turned out uniform rake of stock forming the up 'Cornish Riviera' on 27 June 1959. They are already well settled in on the climb to Hemerdon, and No 6002 ran well all the way to Paddington. *Peter W. Gray*

Below: 2-6-2T No 4593 winds through the Cornish countryside near Mithian Halt west of Perranporth with the 4.25pm from Truro to Newquay on Saturday 9 July 1960. *Peter W. Gray*

By contrast 'Warship' diesels on the 10am Newquay and up 'Riviera' expresses may have been assisted by steam locos over the banks. On 23 July both were unexpectedly Canton engines; Nos 7925 *Westol Hall* piloted the 10am Newquay and 6859 *Yiewsley Grange* was coupled in front of No D819 *Goliath* heading the up 'Riviera'.

It is thought that No 6919 *Tylney Hall* may conceivably have helped work the 10am Newquay from Plymouth to Newton on 9 July, making its first move in a return journey to Bristol. No 6919 went on to Paignton and then back to Newton before finally making for home with the 6pm Plymouth to Bristol. No candidate for the up 'Riviera' assistant job has been identified. Its work done, this engine, whichever it was, apparently disappeared from sight on Newton Abbot shed to have its fire dropped, and usually didn't reappear for the rest of the weekend. It might be stabled on a long siding running the length of the shed and works, known as the 'Dead Line' to enthusiasts. Sometimes it might be Wednesday before the first engine into the siding the previous Saturday was taken out for use again.

Further east on 9 July there was still one train missing. The up procession should have reached its climax when the 10am 'Riviera' from Penzance came through Savernake at 4.13pm but even then there was no sign of the 8.20am from Penzance to Paddington. When the 8.20 was on time it ought to have materialised at 3.45pm and, even taking into account the current rash of late running, it should still have stayed ahead of the 'Riviera' all the way up.

Certainly the 8.20 appeared to be proceeding normally at least as far as Taunton. Two NB Type 2 diesels had started the train from Penzance and then made stops at 10 principal stations through Cornwall, one of the most important being at Lostwithiel. Here the 8.20 provided the main morning connection to London from Fowey, where 0-4-2T No 1419 was plying back and forth as usual with the Fowey branch Rail Motor. The 8.20's journey from Penzance to Plymouth occupied nearly 3hr and after reaching North Road it was then all change at the front end. Off came the two diesels, to be replaced by No 6826 *Nannerth Grange* and the London engine No 5065 *Newport Castle*. At Plymouth these fresh locos added three more coaches to make up 13, including No W9579W, a compact 60ft restaurant car. During the rest of the week this diner earned its keep between Plymouth and Swansea. Its use on the 8.20am from Penzance to Paddington meant that passengers travelling by the 10.20am Penzance–Swansea had to go hungry on Saturdays when no refreshment facilities were provided at all.

The 8.20 collected travellers at Brent and Totnes for intermediate stations to London and reached Newton Abbot 6min late. Here No 6826 was detached as No 6024 completed its unwelcome shunting at the adjoining platform. No 5065 departed after the 'King' 10min late. The 8.20 was due to stop at Exeter for 15min so that the 9.20am from St Ives could overtake, but as D810 on this train was already breathing right down the neck of the 'Castle' before Exeter, the 8.20's stop here could be cut to 6min. So No 5065 got away towards Cowley Bridge Jc only 6min late. Though time was inevitably lost to Taunton, No 5065 reached there only 10min after No D810 had passed through. This was quite acceptable bearing in mind the distinct likelihood of signal checks in awkward locations on the climb to Whiteball. At Taunton the 10am from Newquay was due to go past, which it did at 2.34pm and No 5065 would then be able to leave at once about 15min behind time. So far all was well.

At Savernake Bernard Cooke was having a good day on 9 July. It was proving much more interesting than the afternoon he and I had spent there the previous Saturday. Savernake station was an ideal vantage point, with engines working hard from each direction and an insignificant amount of road traffic anywhere nearby to disturb its rural tranquillity. At 4.20pm a large stain of black smoke appeared over Stibb Green Woods heralding the 8.20's approach. Then there was a hard rasp of exhaust and not one but two engines appeared on the bend near the entrance to the Kennet & Avon Canal tunnel. Both were throwing up large columns of dirty steam and, pulling hard, this unexpected pair rattled the windows of Savernake West box as they topped the summit. Then they came shouldering through the station, with 'Castle' No 5065 still on the front, and coupled up behind with flying rods and cut-away cabsides was 2-6-0 No 6360.

At some stage between Taunton and Westbury No 5065 must have developed a steaming ailment and a message was therefore passed on that this engine needed assistance. Despite his busy programme of cross-country trains the Westbury Running Foreman would not be surprised to receive that advice and he probably had an engine in mind for just this type of eventuality. So when No 5065 on the 8.20 Penzance was diverted into Westbury station, the very dingy run-down SPM Mogul must have been all ready to couple up inside the 'Castle' as the rulebook demanded, and promptly too. After clearing Taunton only 7min or so behind the 8.20, the up 'Riviera' just had time to go past on the avoiding line at Westbury before the 8.20's ill-assorted pair of steam locos were back out on to the main line at Heywood Road Jc and after it like long dogs. Even after stopping for assistance, No 5065 only took one minute more from Taunton to Savernake than No 7020. Here the 8.20 was 35min late at 4.20pm, after the up 'Riviera' had passed only 7min in front at 4.13pm, itself running 14min in arrears.

The final three Cornish expresses were now late enough to be outside the pathing slots set aside for West of England traffic at Reading and they had to

take their chance with other trains. The 8.20 Penzance was also held up by a final passenger stop at Reading, and No 7006 on the 1.50pm from Hereford had prior occupation here. But the main limitation was at Paddington. There coping with eight expresses which passed Twyford bunched up behind No 7020 in less than 45min was more than the terminus could manage. Whilst the 9.20am St Ives and 10am Newquay were able to squeeze in without further loss of time after Twyford, the up 'Riviera' and 8.20am Penzance lost 15 and 12min respectively. The 'Riviera' was 33min behind schedule arriving at Paddington and the 8.20 made it no less than 48min late.

No 6360 went all the way with No 5065, which provided the rare sight of a Mogul standing at Paddington on a Penzance express, but also indicated continuing difficulty with the 'Castle'. However, in view of poor performances by both Nos 7020 and 5065, together with No 6966 which is also thought to have originated at Laira, the problem may have been no more than skimped servicing or a poor batch of coal. 'Kings' Nos 6016 and 6024 did not suffer in the same way, and nor did No 6028 later, but 'Kings' would have more in reserve than the smaller engines to cope with adverse conditions.

There was nothing much wrong with No 5065. I had a mile-a-minute run with it double-heading No 5000 on the 2.55pm from Paddington less than a fortnight later. No 6360 on the other hand was nearly life-expired. It was condemned on 21 November 1960, worn out after running since October 1956 without a classified repair but it certainly gave good assistance to No 5065 on 9 July.

Three later expresses rounded off the day's Cornish arrivals at Paddington during the evening. First of these was the 12.30pm ex-Newquay on which the run up from Plymouth by 'King' No 6028 has already been described.

'Warship' No D815 *Druid* worked through from Penzance to Paddington with the 11.50am up 'Royal Duchy'. No D815 kept good time throughout what proved to be an exemplary trip. Six minutes lost before Exeter were comfortably recovered and No D815 passed Twyford on time. It came into Paddington a minute late at 7.51pm, 16min after No 6028 had arrived.

A week later on 16 July, quite by coincidence, power for these two trains was reversed, with 'County' No 1014 taking the 'Royal Duchy' and No D819 the 12.30pm Newquay. On 23 July the through Penzance–Paddington diesel working broke down again and 'King' No 6029 brought the 'Royal Duchy' up from Plymouth, with another diesel on the Newquay. Then for a couple of weeks both trains were diesel-hauled, until on 13 August No 6016 came out for the Newquay and so brought the wheel round full circle.

Last Cornish arrival was the 1.20pm from Penzance, due into London at 9.15pm, and against all the odds this was a regular steam working on Saturdays. With a load of 12–14 coaches it was also the hardest steam turn on the Western, bar none. The 1.20 was the first WR express to be accelerated as a result of 'Warships' being introduced and in 1960 it had acquired, along with a diamond diesel schedule, three extra stops at Westbury, Newbury and Reading without any additional time on the old Saturday schedule. Extra stops bred extra traffic and that meant a heavier load too.

In 1959 the 1.20pm Penzance was turned over to diesels after the first Saturday of the summer timetable. With the schedule alterations in 1960 it could surely be expected to remain diesel-hauled, but this was not so. In the absence of a 'Warship' on Saturdays 'King' power was certainly essential, but this was supplied only twice. The 6.50am from Paddington, although a dated train, could have provided an ideal outward working for a good Old Oak 'King' down to Plymouth. Even though a 4½hr margin would then be a bit on the tight side to turn the engine ready to come back at 4.10pm, it was still a better servicing interval than the actual arrangements sometimes adopted. For one reason or another the engines used instead left a lot to be desired on six occasions. They came from four different classes and were procured from a variety of sources.

Despite the earlier shortage of diesels and a heavy call on steam resources as a result, Laira had an ideal candidate for the 1.20 Penzance on 9 July in the absence of a 'King'. The only 'King' at Laira around 4pm was No 6002 off the 9.30am down and this could not be made ready to go out again until about 7.30pm at the earliest. So a 'Castle' had to step in, and this was No 5084 *Reading Abbey*. Outshopped from Swindon on 1 July and only released from running-in a day or two beforehand, No 5084 may still have been a bit tight. But all five engines like this one with the Davies & Metcalfe lubrication reservoirs were good runners and No 5084 was no exception. It had come down to Plymouth earlier on the 7am Swindon–Penzance and this back working after a 4hr turn-round was a good means of returning the 'Castle' home to Old Oak.

At North Road No 5084 relieved a pair of NB Type 2 diesels (Nos D6312/15 on 2 July) with a 12-coach train and received assistance from another, No D6323, as far as Newton Abbot, where they were 3min late. No 5084 was then three coaches overloaded on a diamond schedule of such severity that it included five stops in the course of a 237min timing from Newton to Paddington. The intermediate bookings included such choice snippets as a start to stop allowance of 43min for 42½ miles from Westbury, up through Savernake, to Newbury. Even the favourable half of this stretch included two permanent 60mph speed restrictions in the midst of constant curvature, and a 'Castle' could not be expected to observe such a tight schedule with 415 tons tare on the drawbar.

Engine and crew must have given it their best shot. Leaving Exeter 4min late, only 11 more minutes were lost from there and they did extremely well to achieve a Paddington arrival at 9.20pm. No 5084 was of course immaculate in its fresh paintwork and had given a good account of itself by covering 402 miles during the day.

However, this random diagramming policy for the 1.20 was not only unrealistic in terms of timekeeping on a week by week basis, but it was so flawed that there was a constant risk of the policy becoming unravelled altogether. On 16 July No 7922 can hardly have failed to lose a lot of extra time when the train was already 91min late at Newton Abbot due to a diesel failure in Cornwall, but on 27 August absolute disaster befell. The 14-coach load would have given any

'Warship' a searching examination, but instead a less than spruce No 5096 *Bridgwater Castle* from Bath Road was left to cope as best it could. Matters were well adrift before Exeter where the 1.20 was about 45min behind time. No 5096 gave up altogether in the Westbury area and was replaced by a single local 'Hall' No 4957 *Postlip Hall* which was in no better shape than No 5096. The arrival indicator at Paddington could register no more than 99min late and there it stuck as more time was steadily dropped. The train was announced as 160min behind time at Reading. One last person waiting near the Paddington buffer stops eventually saw two lights appear as No 4957 crept slowly in. It wasn't going to make it to the end of the platform and the driver had to open up again half-way along — not that he had much steam left, but No 4957 managed a few last gasps and dragged its way to the platform end in a very run-down condition. It was 12.18½am and the 1.20 was 193½min late.

Next week did draw a response and 'King', No 6003 was provided, but the damage had been done, and this was a situation which should have been nipped in the bud weeks before.

Laira had successfully turned No 5084 around on 9 July in just over 4hr, and Newton Abbot achieved the same with No 5036. We saw *Lyonshall Castle*, a Reading engine, making one of the fastest times from Paddington to Newton Abbot earlier while hauling the 7.40am down. It took this train through to Paignton and then came straight back ready to be serviced on Newton shed at 12.45pm. Later No 5036 reappeared to relieve 'King' No 6025 hauling the last Torbay departure for London, the 4.35pm from Kingswear, at 5.30pm. Though a considerably easier proposition than the 1.20pm Penzance 24min in front, both in terms of load and timing, the 4.35 was no push-over either. Its schedule of 155min from Taunton was still the fastest of any start to stop timing from there to Paddington that summer.

No 5036 fades from view 3min late at Exeter, hopefully ready to run as well on the return journey as it did earlier coming down. In the final analysis one can only applaud the way motive power resources were distributed around the key West of England services during the day. Difficulties with a couple of engines would not have been so obvious if they had not been aggravated by the hot box episode at 12.30pm which upset pathing. Once this happened the bunching up of so many trains made delays inevitable, and in assessing timekeeping it was line capacity as well as loco capability which were the most important factors.

There were 24 up expresses during the day from Newton Abbot or points further west to Paddington. Here the arrival time of 15 of them is known and a further three each were timed at West Ealing or Twyford. These 21 trains averaged 17½min late, which was not satisfactory for a comparatively early summer Saturday. It contrasts with a lateness figure of 10min for a similar but not identical selection of 21 up West of England expresses on peak Saturday 30 July 1960. It also contrasts poorly with a figure of 8min lateness for 23 down London trains at Exeter or Newton Abbot on 9 July and with comparatively excellent timekeeping on the Birmingham and South Wales routes the same day.

However, punctuality could still be worse than that covered by any of these figures. On 27 August 1960 a most comprehensive picture of all 24 up expresses shows an average lateness of 19.6min, even if the worst offending train is excluded. Adding it in raises the figure to 26.8min. There was no pattern to the trains which were latest on these three days under review.

Below: No 6025 *King Henry III* starts out on its return journey to Paddington with the 1.8pm from Kingswear on Sunday 10 July 1960. It has worked in from Newton Abbot earlier with the 9am Taunton–Kingswear local passenger train. *Hugh Davies*

Bottom: There are no apologies for including another picture of No 6016, because this one is thought to show the very last run by a Laira 'King'. The final pair of Laira 'Kings' were reallocated away at the end of the 1960 summer timetable, 11 September, and by then No 6002 had already gone. No 6016 was retained until Saturday 17 September 1960 when it was finally dispatched to London with 15 coaches on the 9.50am Newquay–Paddington relief. This picture shows No 6016, well cleaned up and running without a shedplate, at Newton Abbot, on this occasion with its enormous train stretching way back into the far distance. Pilot No 7907 *Hart Hall* has just been uncoupled and is now standing in Platform No 8 while No 6016 waits to start off alone. No one can say the Laira 'Kings' didn't go out in style. *Peter W. Gray*

10.
CARMARTHEN SNAPSHOT

Along the South Wales main line at Carmarthen, no time had been lost getting essential supplies of milk, fish and other perishables back on the move as the eastbound rush began to moderate soon after lunch. But of course the down peak had hardly commenced by then, and it was nearly 2pm before the main series of down line arrivals was due to begin with the 7.55am from Paddington. West Wales holiday resorts were mainly catered for during the next 6hr by eight other services originating at Paddington.

Birmingham also enjoyed through facilities to West Wales in the form of a 9.10am from Snow Hill to Pembroke Dock. This train had come to a stand at Cardiff 3min early behind No 4910 *Blaisdon Hall* of Tyseley. Here No 6818 *Hardwick Grange* relieved the

'Hall', left Cardiff at 12.35pm and then worked through to Carmarthen via the Swansea District line. This route avoided some of the worst main line gradients in South Wales and provided a useful 15/20min saving on the time required for reversal at Swansea High St. With eight coaches 2-6-0 No 6329 was then attached at 2.50pm while the train reversed in Carmarthen station. This engine should have been a 'Hall' working only to Whitland. There it would give

Below: On Saturday 12 September 1959 2-6-0 No 7318 and 2-6-2T No 5560 approach Manorbier with a substantial branch load forming the 12.5pm Pembroke Dock–Paddington. *F. K. Davies*

way to two smaller engines which were needed to negotiate the steep gradients of the Pembroke Dock branch. The 'Hall' should then have returned on the 5.15pm milk from Whitland as far as Canton. However, No 5013 *Abergavenny Castle* seems to have been sent out for the 5.15 milk, after arriving at Carmarthen on the 8.55am from Paddington. So perhaps, in view of its suitability for a Pembroke Dock train of eight coaches, No 6329 may have gone the whole way along the branch. A '43xx' 2-6-0 which would certainly have worked to Pembroke Dock an hour or so later with a similar load was No 7321, borrowed from Llanelly to haul the up and down 'Pembroke Coast Express' for 40¼ miles in each direction west of Carmarthen. Despite named status, the train called at all except two stations and halts on the way.

After diverging on to the branch, No 7321 had the tricky job of restarting from Narberth station on a 1 in 52 gradient and then climbing through the stifling single-line confines of Narberth tunnel. No 7321 would then have a struggle to maintain momentum as the line twisted and turned up wooded slopes, still climbing at 1 in 58 to Cold Blow Summit. Even though the Moguls were surefooted, it is likely that the load on this train would be so close to the 252-ton limit that a

Above: The 12.5pm Milford Haven–Paddington express, with its usual fish van coupled at the front, near Gowerton on Saturday 15 July 1961. The engine is Carmarthen 'Hall' No 4935 *Ketley Hall* which worked the 2.30pm Neyland–Paddington along this route on 9 July 1960. *Huw Daniel*

'45xx' pilot might be needed from Whitland. Other steep but shorter switchback gradients awaited No 7321 between Tenby and Pembroke Dock before the 'Pembroke Coast Express' terminated within sight of Neyland across the waters of the Cleddau estuary at 6.15pm.

Final holiday relief serving Carmarthen was the 1.50pm from Paddington. This train completed its journey there at about 7.37pm behind No 5961 *Toynbee Hall* from the local 87G shed. But no sooner had the 1.50 disappeared off the main line into Carmarthen Town station than it was time for the Irish boat traffic to commence, and 8min later the first Fishguard was duly expected past Carmarthen Jc at 7.45pm. This train was the 2.55pm from Paddington which made good progress from Cardiff using the Swansea District line. Scheduled over Morlais Jc near Pontardulais at 7.6pm, this was the point at which the 2.55 overtook the 1.55pm from

Paddington while the 1.55 was still standing at Swansea High St changing engines from No 7023 to No 5953 *Dunley Hall*. After rejoining the Swansea main line at Llandilo Jc the 2.55 made a brief call at Llanelly and then ran nonstop to Fishguard Harbour. Here it was the only train of the day to better a 6hr schedule for the 261¼-mile journey from London. Unfortunately the engine taking over the 2.55 at Cardiff from 'Castle' No 5048 was not recorded. Nor was the triangle at Carmarthen a vantage point where all traffic could be readily seen, so the 2.55, which ran via the direct line from Carmarthen Jc across Carmarthen Bridge avoiding the Town station, was not noted here either. However, it is possible that a Canton engine like No 70020 *Mercury* was turned round after a 7.50am arrival at Cardiff in the morning; or otherwise Neath 'Hall' No 5980 *Dingley Hall*, which had worked into Cardiff at 12.24pm with no other return working noted, may have been utilised for the 2.55.

An hour later the 3.45pm Paddington–Fishguard boat train was due, and the engine on this was observed, perhaps because it was a daily sight in summer whereas the 2.55 was dated to run to Fishguard on peak Saturdays only. The 3.45 was due to leave Swansea at 8.5pm for the climb to Cockett,

Above: 'Britannia' No 70027 *Rising Star* skims across Hendy viaduct above the Loughor river with what appears to be the 2.55pm Paddington–Fishguard Harbour on Saturday 5 August 1961. At this stage 'Britannias' had only five weeks remaining on the Western Region before they were transferred away to the LMR *en bloc. Huw Daniel*

where it stopped to put off the pannier tank pilot No 8789. Then the 3.45 with No 4099 *Kilgerran Castle* in charge was scheduled to run nonstop to Clarbeston Road, 54½ miles in 73min. Its Landore 'Castle' would be a fine spectacle taking water from Ferryside Troughs as No 4099 skimmed along the banks of the River Towy. For many years *Kilgerran Castle* had been a West Country favourite at Exeter, Newton Abbot, then finally Penzance, and now No 4099 was equally popular on the West Wales run. It slowed to 30mph over the curve and river bridge at Carmarthen before setting off with exhaust drumming up the climb past Sarnau. Hopefully all was now in good order ready for the 3.45 down to make its booked 10.10pm rendezvous at Fishguard Harbour with the *Innisfallen* steamer for Cork. This would leave the final 6.55pm Fishguard boat express from Paddington to bring in passengers for Rosslare when it arrived at 1.15am next morning.

Above: Only a few weeks before withdrawal from service No 5009 *Shrewsbury Castle* slows to stop at Patchway with the 6.5pm Bristol–Cardiff stopping train on Saturday 10 September 1960. The chalked reporting number and locomotive headcode depict 2F52. *Richard Picton*

Below: '57xx' pannier tank No 7780 eases the up 'Channel Islands Boat Express' away from Weymouth Quay while on the right the steamer *St Julian* prepares for its next sailing on Friday 4 September 1959. *Derek Phillips Collection*

11. EVENING ROUND-UP

The approach of evening brought only a gradual fall-off in volume of traffic over most routes, and many lines were still busy with passenger workings until 8pm or later.

Breaks in the incessant traffic flow through the bottleneck between Exeter and Taunton first began to appear from 5.20pm onwards. However, it was 7pm before the number of trains on this stretch subsided to a level approaching that of normal weekdays.

The South Wales main line was busy along its whole length for much of the evening, and this was certainly true westbound through the Severn Tunnel. In practical terms the down road here had been occupied at full capacity since midday, with 33 trains passing through in the next 6hr. The first significant break did not arise until 6.15pm after No 70023 went through running right time on the down 'Capitals'. But then at 6.40pm the down road had a renewed burst of activity, and there was a succession of 6–15min headways again which extended right through until 8pm. This spell should have begun as No 7907 *Hart Hall* left Pilning and entered the tunnel with the 6.5pm Bristol–Cardiff stopping passenger. However, No 7907 was running around 15min late and so the 5.55pm Bristol–Saltney express freight may well have preceded the Cardiff local to Severn Tunnel Jc. Six more trains then followed, finishing up with the 5.35pm from Salisbury to Cardiff, which on summer Saturdays started from Portsmouth Harbour at 3.57pm. This express was due through the tunnel at 8pm and was running virtually on time from Salisbury behind No 4084 *Aberystwyth Castle*.

In addition to the Fishguard boat express, trains connecting with ferry steamers from the Isle of Wight and Channel Islands also provided fruitful evening traffic with which to finish off the day's summer holiday services. At Portsmouth Harbour, beside the 3.57pm departure for Cardiff which was collecting passengers off the 2.50pm sailing from Ryde Pier Head, there was also a 3.40pm train for Wolverhampton loading nearby. In 1959 a WR 4-6-0 worked into Portsmouth at 1.18pm with the 10.45am from Oxford and the 3.40 then provided a balancing duty, with the engine returning right through from Portsmouth Harbour to Wolverhampton. On 1 August 1959 the locomotive concerned was No 7900 *St Peter's Hall*. There seems no reason why this diagram on to the SR should not have continued unchanged into 1960 and on 9 July No 7900 was again the engine. It took

over the down train at Oxford from 2-6-0 No 6364 and left at 10.45am. No 7900 looked like a fairly typical Oxford 'Hall' — travel-stained and rather ropy in appearance yet quite readily capable of many miles of good work. By the time it came through Tyseley running 5min late at 8.3pm on the return journey, No 7900 was well-placed to reel off 270 miles during the day.

This was by no means the final holiday express due into Snow Hill on 9 July. The late running Penzance was still outstanding, closely followed by No 5971 *Merevale Hall* with the 2.55pm from Paignton, which ran into Birmingham Moor Street station some 14min behind time at about 8.52pm. Next came the 3.5pm Paignton–Wolverhampton with No 6928, arriving at Snow Hill as scheduled around 9pm. However, another 50min were to elapse before what was undoubtedly the last holiday runner completed its journey across the Western Region.

This train was the fascinating 4.5pm Weymouth Quay and 4.18pm Weymouth Town–Cardiff and Birmingham Snow Hill. It connected with the steamer which had left Jersey at 8.15am that morning and initially the seven-coach Quay portion would be steam-worked round the Weymouth Harbour tramway. This engine would probably be saddle tank No 1361 or one of the three '1366' class outside-cylinder pannier tanks shedded at Weymouth. But if the 'Channel Islands Boat Express' for London (Waterloo) was running in two portions the 4.5 might be left for a '57xx' pannier instead. This arrangement persisted into 1963, and what was by then the 4.15 departure was often still steam-hauled by a '57xx' over the Tramway long after the '1366' type locos had been replaced by Drewry 204hp diesel shunters in 1961.

Meanwhile in Weymouth Town station No 6997 *Bryn-Ivor Hall* was coupled to five more coaches awaiting their 4.18pm departure. Then two minutes later at Weymouth Jc No 6997 stopped again while these carriages were amalgamated with the Quay portion to make up a truly formidable load of 12 coaches. Banking assistance would therefore be needed up to Bincombe box, and there were stops at Dorchester West, Maiden Newton, Yeovil and Castle Cary to be made while the full tonnage was in tow as far as Westbury. This train clearly called for Bath Road 'County' power but No 6997 must have been in good shape, and it obviously fared much better than one or two of the earlier Birmingham trains up this line. Any

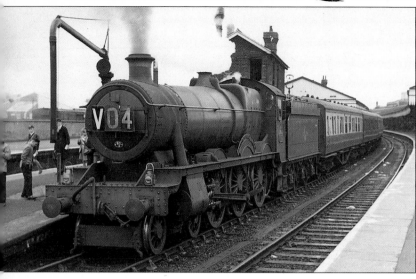

Left: The extensive inter-regional traffic through Salisbury attracted a wide variety of WR locomotives from 'Castles' to a 2-6-0 on 9 July 1960. Generally 'Halls' predominated and on Saturday 23 July 1960 No 6972 *Beningbrough Hall* has replaced an SR engine and waits to leave Salisbury on the 9am from Bournemouth to Cardiff. *Author's Collection*

time lost before Westbury was successfully recovered after No 6997 had detached the four-coach Birmingham portion there. After just two further calls at Bath and Stapleton Road No 6997 was at rest in Newport on time at 7.56pm with the Welsh section of eight vehicles. Final arrival at Cardiff was 2min early.

Back at Westbury No 6843 *Poulton Grange* was an unexpected choice to go on to Birmingham but, whether unexpected or not after if had already come through from Swansea to Salisbury previously, this engine was right on top of the job for the concluding 132½ miles. No 6843 added an extra three bogies to make up the Birmingham portion into a respectable load and the train then became the 6.19pm Westbury–Birmingham, leaving 7min after the Cardiff portion. No 6843 was probably handicapped by a few minutes' lateness to begin with, but at Swindon passengers had plenty of time to connect into the 7.33pm for Sheffield, which was drawn up in the neighbouring platform, before No 6843 left, next stop Oxford, 7min late at 7.25pm. The 'Grange' then successfully proceeded to gain 14min on schedule, so that the train was next seen passing Tyseley 7min early at 9.40pm. While 7min did little to make up for the welter of time lost previously by the other three Weymouth expresses during the day, No 6843 did at least demonstrate welcome signs of life on this neglected route. The 6.19pm Westbury went on to attain 'Castle' power in summer 1964 when with a six-coach train, and everyone anxious to get home, the running could be distinctly lively. However, No 6843 from Llanelly shed did very well at a time when Westbury would turn out anything available for this late turn, including Taunton 'Halls' which somehow managed to pop up on at least three Saturdays in 1960/61. No 6843 rounded things off by terminating at Snow Hill around 9.46pm and its passing was the sign that now was time for the

last lineside observer in the area to make for home.

No 6843 returned its stock to Tyseley Carriage Sidings and then headed for the shed itself. At many loco depots staff had been struggling during the evening to drop fires and dispose lines of engines where they would be available for the next turn of duty. This was straightforward enough at sheds like Tyseley where engines could be put away in spacious Churchward turntable unit buildings. But it might be awkward at the busier straightshed depots where accommodation was at a premium and every siding, however inconvenient, would be stacked full of engines until they could be sorted out by the shed pilot on Sunday.

Similarly sets of coaches had to be stabled and reformed ready for Sunday, restaurant cars revictualled and minor defects rectified. Although Saturday evening's freight service was kept down to a minimum there was still a regular programme of overnight sleeping car trains, newspapers and parcels to be dealt with, together with essential mail services which of course included the Penzance Postal.

Among sleeping car passengers travelling that night were David Wallis and his wife from Watford who had been married earlier in the day. They were going off to Cornwall for their honeymoon, and had booked sleeping accommodation on the 11.15pm from Paddington, which was really a Saturday night version of the Penzance newspaper train. It included two first-class sleeping cars tucked away in its consist among a string of newspaper vans. Berths were available only after prior reservation, so the train was not listed in the public timetable. This caused David Wallis considerable but fortunately only temporary alarm beforehand until he found the platform where his train was waiting. He observed that No D806 *Cambrian* was the motive power. This diesel had appeared in the afternoon arriving on the 2.40pm from Paignton, and it took the 11.15 back through to Penzance. Here David Wallis reckoned their arrival was about 5min behind schedule — not that he or his wife cared too much about that. They had both been up in time to see their train cross the Royal Albert Bridge into Cornwall, though Mrs Wallis was not as enthusiastic about the view as her husband at 5 o'clock in the morning!

Normally in summer 1960 'King' express operations ceased for the day at 11pm. On 9 July this would be when No 6001 *King Edward VII* pulled into Wolverhampton with the 8.10pm from Paddington. No 6003 was still on its way back from Swindon with the 3.50pm Whitland milk, and on some days there might be a 'King' returning from Westbury off the 6pm down with the 9.35pm parcels. But none was booked on express work. However, it is possible that one other 'King' may have been back in use before midnight and that was No 6002 which, as we have seen, had previously worked to Plymouth on the 9.30am from Paddington. It may have been used for the 8.15pm (FSO) Penzance–Paddington extra which departed from Plymouth at 11.45pm. Unfortunately there were no honeymooning couples that we know of on this train who can confirm or deny such a notion, although alternatively sight of a Sunday shed list for Old Oak Common would also reveal the truth. Any contributions from readers on these or any other matters concerning the Western Region around this time will be warmly welcomed.

As midnight approached, the 8.55pm Birkenhead–Paddington sleeper was drawing near to Wolverhampton behind No 6945 *Glasfryn Hall*. The engine had come on at Chester after arriving there previously with the 2.10pm from Paddington to Birkenhead, and it left Chester homeward-bound at 9.46pm. The sleeping car was augmented by ordinary stock totalling around 10 vehicles and No 6945 had this load to haul up Gresford bank into Wrexham. Further on there was another stiff climb to contend with

beyond Wellington, up through Oakengates to Hollinswood Summit. After disposing of the most difficult portion of the journey, No 6945 was due into Wolverhampton on the stroke of midnight. Engines were changed, and on 9 July No 5901 *Hazel Hall* was the last engine of the day off Stafford Road shed at 11.25pm on 9 July, ready to add more vans before hauling the Birkenhead sleeper on a typically leisurely overnight schedule to Oxford and Paddington.

Not all overnight services had easy schedules. Newspaper and mail trains did not hang around, and most important of all were the down and up West of England Travelling Post Office expresses to and from Penzance. The Penzance postal services were not heavily loaded but they had to run punctually. Special attention was always given to the working and they received priority over other trains when this was necessary to avoid delay. Once 'Warship' diesel-hydraulics became established they had to be seen to be trusted with such an important train as this. So by 1960 the Penzance Postal had been diesel-hauled in both directions for some time.

But on 9 July there were still a lot of Old Oak Common engines to be returned from Laira, and a continuing shortage of diesels meant steam had to fill in on the up 7am Penzance–Paddington Postal that night. Next Old Oak engine in line to head for home

Below: In spring 1961 the Western could offer no finer regular sight than this. Old Oak has some jealously guarded double chimney 'Castles' just out of works and among others Nos 5008, 5027, 5034, 5056 and 7033 are being turned out for the fast 1.15 Down. On Wednesday 18 May 1961 No 7033 *Hartlebury Castle* has come down Dauntsey bank 'Bristolian' style at about 90mph and is still travelling quickly near Langley Crossing. No 7033 has passed Swindon in 73min from Paddington and will soon be noted coming through Chippenham inside 86min. Kenneth Leech rode on 5027 *Farleigh Castle* with the 1.15 on 26 May 1961 when they also reached 90mph at Dauntsey. The 1.15 Down ceased running to Bristol after 50 years of 1.5 or 1.15 departures in September 1961. *Kenneth Leech*

was the 'Castle' off the 8.25am down Paddington to Penzance (with Perranporth portion).

So No 5093 *Upton Castle* found itself back on what had been a regular 'Castle' turn for many years, as it came on to the train of Siphons and brightly lit Post Office vans at Plymouth ready to leave at 9.30pm. Luckily there was still an observer at Newton Abbot who waited for No 5093 to complete a successful assault on the South Devon banks before it came into Newton 2min early. After another stop to exchange mail at Exeter the Postal was off to Taunton at 11pm on a brisk 36min schedule which left no margin for hanging around. It was then booked away from this Taunton call at 11.42pm. So, a few minutes later, No 5093 would be travelling at full speed across the Somerset levels if it was to pass Bridgwater on time at 11.56pm. Helped by a short downgrade it would be going even faster at midnight and here we leave No 5093 when it should be racing through Dunball, where its safe passage rounds off the events of 9 July on a high note. Anyone could be forgiven for believing that steam was certainly not finished yet, and that engines like No 5093 had plenty of useful life left ahead of them.

The sterling work of so many loco crews was a crucial feature contributing to the success of the day. Many top-link drivers and firemen, with the best engines from their depot, and experienced at working expresses over the same route almost daily, could do well with Nos 1009, 4080, 6002 and others. However, on a busy summer Saturday there would not be enough of these crews to go round. It was therefore likely that some men, who were more used to spending a day ambling from loop to loop at an average speed of about 25mph with a mixed freight, were called on to work expresses over demanding routes, often with the same indifferent motive power they were accustomed to having on the freights. Their role was every bit as

important as that of the top-link crews.

An account like this inevitably tends to highlight trains which gained or lost considerable amounts of time during the day. Out of all express trains noted on ex-GW lines, five were actually recorded running more than 1hr late on 9 July. These were:

> 7.42am Manchester–Penzance
> 8.50am Margate–Birmingham
> 9.25am Weymouth–Wolverhampton
> 11.55am Minehead–Paddington
> 3pm Blackpool–Swindon Special.

One suspects four more probably suffered a similar fate, these being:

> 7am Paignton–Colne
> 7.50am Newquay–Manchester
> 8.30am Ilfracombe–Manchester
> 11.10am Penzance–Wolverhampton.

Another 20 or so expresses were seriously delayed and ran more than 30min late at important points *en route*.

But on the other hand there were also a large number of instances where substantial time recovery took place, so that trains which were running over 10min late were able to regain all or most of the lost time. Similarly, Newport and Cardiff experienced only two significant late passenger arrivals all day. A train like the 9.20am Bradford–Paignton, which was reported passing Westerleigh 36min behind schedule, was able to cut back on waiting time at stations and unwanted recovery margins so successfully after it was turned over to No 6982 *Melmerby Hall* at Bristol, that it regained all 36min before Newton Abbot.

Overall, the verdict on 9 July was one where the overwhelming majority of passengers were likely to be well satisfied with the punctuality of their trains. It had been a Great day on the Western.

Left: The 'Midnight Intruder' from the Western. No 5922 *Caxton Hall* of Swindon leaves Rugby Central at approximately 12.40am on 4 August 1951 with the 9.35pm Swindon–York express. This locomotive working existed before Nationalisation and continued until after Hymek diesels took over the duty in 1962. *Rev A. W. C. Mace/Ian Allan Library*

APPENDIX

APPENDIX OF LOCOMOTIVE WORKINGS JULY 9th 1960

Notes to Appendix

Locomotives Covered
Express, Mixed traffic tender, Passenger Tank & 9F Classes
All "County" & "King" class engines were fitted with Double Chimneys by October 1959.
*Denotes "Castle" class engines fitted with Double Chimneys at 9.7.60.

Shed Codes
Shed Codes and Works Repair entries are generally extracted from W.R. Engine Record Cards held at the Public Records Office, Kew. These records are not altogether complete, and usually omit engines later transferred to the LMR on 1.1.63. In these cases information has been obtained from current periodicals.

Train Details: Abbreviations

(O)	Outward working
(R)	Return Working
( )	Trains shown in brackets assume that the engine followed its normal diagram. although it was not observed to do so.
?	Trains queried are no more than a guide to what are thought to be realistic guesses of balancing workings on this occasion. These assumptions should be treated with great caution, and are listed in the hope that some readers may be able to confirm or correct them.
A/E	Assistant engine specifically provided over the South Devon banks between Newton Abbot and Plymouth
D/H	Double-headed locomotive working.
ECS	Empty Coaching Stock traffic.
FRI	Allied Workings originating on Friday July 8th 1960.
LE	Light Engine
SUN	Allied workings originating on Sunday July 10th 1960.
TC	Through Coaches.
XT	Date a locomotive was taken out of traffic before dispatch to Works for Repair.

Train Numbers: These are shown for express services as they would appear in a number frame, chalk or pasted numerals on the locomotive.
Three digits appear for steam & early diesel locos: e.g. F54.
Four digits appear for diesel locomotives from D813 onwards: e.g. 1C30.
These numbers were generally, but not always carried on the engine for the major portion of the journey only.
Local reporting numbers have to be shown in four digit form to avoid confusion, e.g. 2A20; these numbers were not carried on steam locomotives, except a few main line trains originating in the Bristol area, and exceptionally elsewhere on the Western Region.

Notes on Loco Working
Include where available a punctuality report at a major point on the journey where notes of a passing time were taken. In a few cases where an approximate time is worth showing this is printed in brackets.
Place Name Abbreviations:

CF	Cardiff	P	Paddington	SL	Shrewsbury
EX	Exeter	S	Swindon	TM	Bristol Temple Meads
NA	Newton Abbot	SA	Salisbury	TN	Taunton
NP	Newport	SH	Birmingham Snow Hill	TW	Twyford
OX	Oxford	SKE	Savernake	TYS	Tyseley
				W	Westerleigh

Abbreviation for Early: E   Abbreviation for Late: L   e.g. EX 10L means Exeter 10 minutes late.
An indication of the page on which a loco is mentioned in the book is also given.

LOCO	SHED CODE	TRAIN	TRAIN NO	NOTES ON LOCO WORKING		PAGE REF
6MT						
4-6-0						
1000	82A	9.5 am Bristol-Swansea	2F42	To Cardiff	CF 7L	p 32
		9.50 am Carmarthen-Weston	B10	From Cardiff		
1001	87H					
1002	83E	9.30 pm FRI Manchester-Newquay	V75	From Plymouth D/H 4095		p 54
		11.15 am Newquay-Wolverhampton	H34	To Plymouth		p 103
1003	84G	2.35 pm Birkenhead-Paddington	V10	Chester to Wolverhampton		
		6.10 pm Paddington-Birkenhead	M21	Wolverhampton to ? Shrewsbury		
1004	82C	At Salisbury		At 82A Shed SUN		p 28
1005	82A	(5.25 am Bristol-Highbridge)	2B97	XT 22.7.60 for Works		p 32
		8.2 am Highbridge-Taunton Milk Empties	3C31			
		8.30 am Ilfracombe-Manchester	M14	Taunton to Bristol		
1006	83E	9.30 am FRI Paddington-Newquay	C28	From Plymouth		p 90
1007	83C	10.22 pm FRI Manchester-Paignton	V79	From Exeter		
		9.45 am Churston-Paddington	A47		TW 11L	p 48
1008	83G					
1009	82A	8.20 am Weston-Paddington	A18	From Bristol	P 23L	p 116
		1.15 pm Paddington-Weston	B11		TM 0L	
1010	82C	10.20 am Swindon-Didcot	2A76	Running-in	S 2L	p 32
		2.40 pm Reading-Swindon	2B76	Running-in		

LOCO	SHED CODE	TRAIN	TRAIN NO.	NOTES ON LOCO WORKING		PAGE REF
1011	82A	? 10.30 am Westbury-Salisbury	LE			
		1.0 pm Salisbury-Bristol	2B70			
1012	82C	(? 5.25 am Swindon-Salisbury)	2B91			
		(8.30 am Portsmouth-Bristol	V03	From Salisbury At 84E SUN		
1013	84G	5.10 pm FRI Cardiff-Crewe	2J91	To Shrewsbury		
		See Note D		Shrewsbury to Pontypool Road		
		9.5 am Paignton-Manchester	M89	From Pontypool Road	(SL 38L)	p 99
1014	82A	4.35 pm Taunton-Paddington	A38	From Bristol	S 6L	p 126
1015	82C	SWINDON WORKS Repairs		XT 22.6.60		p 32
1016	84G			At 84G Shed SUN		
		(O) Ex Shrewsbury See Note D		Shrewsbury to Exeter		
1017	84G	{ 8.10 am Newport-Paignton	C60	From Exeter	(NA 27L)	p 48
		1.55 pm Torquay-Paddington	A92		TW 9L	
1018	83D	11.4 am Bournemouth-Sheffield	E52	Basingstoke to Leicester	OX 8E	p 49
		See text		At 84G Shed SUN		
1019	82C			At 82A Shed SUN		
1020	87H	8.40 pm FRI Westbury-Neyland Parcels	3F18	From Cardiff		
1021	82C	7.33 pm Swindon-Sheffield	E50	To Banbury D/H 73012		p 126
		(6.40 pm York-Swindon)	V67	From Banbury		
1022	84G	10.55 am Reading-West London Parcels	3A11			
1023	83C	At Exeter Shed		? Stopped Repairs 83C		
				At 83C SAT & SUN		
1024	82A	4.41 pm Weston-Paddington	A20	From Bristol	S 12L	p 125
1025	84G	1.50 pm Chester-Wolverhampton	V08			
		4.10 pm Paddington-Birkenhead	M20	Wolverhampton to Chester		
				At 84G Shed SUN		
1026	84G	Stopped awaiting WORKS		XT 6.7.60 at 84G		
1027	82A	(8.30 pm FRI Whitland-Kensington Milk	3A44	From Swindon		
		10.5 am Paddington-Durston	C78	To Bristol	TM 3L	p 118
		5.45 pm Bristol-Swindon	2B77		S 5L	
1028	82A	6.55 am Bristol-Exeter	2C77			
		12.45 pm Exeter-Taunton	2C77			p 151
		4.35 pm Taunton-Bristol	2A70	TC to Paddington		p 126
1029	87H	8.48 am Fishguard-Paddington Parcels	3A24	From Swindon	S 2L	p 126
3MT **0-6-0**						
2214	89C	1.5 pm Shrewsbury-Welshpool	2J07			
		3.55 p m Welshpool-Salop	2J57			
2216	87G	10.25 am Newcastle Emlyn-Carmarthen Freight				
2217	89C	(9.10 am Aberystwyth-Carmarthen)	2F77			
		5.50 pm Carmarthen-Aberystwyth	2J77			
2232	89C	11.0 am Ruabon-Pwllheli	2J31	D/H 2294		
2236	86A	2.5 pm Brecon-Newport	2T66			p 108
		6.55 pm Newport-Brecon	2J95			
2267	84E	11.15 am Newquay-Wolverhampton	H34	D/H 5092 from Stratford		p 103
2268	82D	6.52 pm Westbury-Swindon	2B75			
2283	87H	9.30 am Pembroke Dock-Shrewsbury	J58	To Llandilo		
		12.25 pm Shrewsbury-Pembroke Dock	2F63	From Llandilo		
2287	89A	7.20 am Pwllheli-Paddington	A60	To Ruabon D/H 3200		p 88
2294	84J	11.0 am Ruabon-Pwllheli	2J31			
3200	89A	7.20 am Pwllheli-Paddington	A60	D/H 2287 At 89A Shed SUN		p 88
8F **2-8-0**						
2874	86C	3.50 pm Pylle Hill-Plymouth Parcels	3C04		NA 14L	
2879	82C	7.10 pm Victoria Basin-Basingstoke Freight	5O05	At 86C FRI		
28XX		Various other freights				
4P **4-4-0**						
3440	82C	6.32 pm Swindon-Bristol	2B78	Via Badminton		p 37
				On 82A Shed SUN		
7P **4-6-0**						
4037	83A	SWINDON WORKS Repairs		Until 12.8.60		p 148
4073		Stored withdrawn SWINDON				
4074*	81D	9.0 am Weymouth-Paddington	A37		P 2E	
		5.20 pm Paddington-Oxford	2A25	11.7.60 Ex Reading on Margate- Wolverhampton		
4075	81A	(O) See Note B		Paddington to Swansea		p 123
		(R) 12.5 pm Milford-Paddington	A11	From Swansea	P 19L	
4076	87E	11.55 am Paddington-Pembroke Dock	F32	Swansea to Carmarthen		p 28
		8.45 pm Carmarthen-Swansea	2F93			
4077	82A	At Weston Mid-day		? STANDBY Duty		p 43
4078	81A	SWINDON WORKS Repairs		Until 29.7.60		
4079	82A	10.40 am Weston-Paddington	A49	At Newton Abbot MON 11.7.60	TW 1E	
4080*	84G	(O) 10.29 am FRI Manchester-Plymouth	V92	Shrewsbury to Newton Abbot	E 0L	
		(R) 6.0 am Penzance-Liverpool	M91	Newton Abbot to Shrewsbury	(SL 7L)	p 99
4081	82A	9.35 am Bristol-Penzance	C21	To Plymouth	NA 5L	
4082	81A	3.10 pm Paddington-Wolverhampton	H24		SH 5L	p 45
		4.30 pm Birkenhead-Paddington	V12	From Wolverhampton		
4083	83A	10.35 am Torquay-Paddington	A54		P 19L	p 59
4084	86C	1.0 pm Cardiff-Brighton	O61	To Salisbury	SL 5L	p 71
		3.57 pm Portsmouth-Cardiff	V14	From Salisbury	CF 2L	p 163
4085	85A	SWINDON WORKS Repairs		Until 18.8.60		

LOCO	SHED CODE	TRAIN	TRAIN NO	NOTES ON LOCO WORKING		PAGE REF
4086	86C	8.30 am Pembroke Dock-Birmingham	H16	To Cardiff	CF 2L	
		12.15 am SUN Cardiff-Crewe	M65	To Hereford		
4087*	83D	7.45 am Paignton-Newcastle	N42	To Bristol	EX 0L	p 93
		Various locals Bristol-Kingswear				
		4.10 pm SUN Paignton-Paddington	A32	From Newton Abbot		
		Paddington-Bristol-Plymouth		11.7.60		
4088*	85A	3.50 pm Hereford-Paddington	A13	From Worcester	P 11L	p 136
		(9.45 pm Paddington-Worcester)	H77			
4089	85A	2.40 pm Swindon-Didcot	2A76			p 118
4090*	87E	4.55 am Fishguard-Paddington	A24	To Cardiff		p 11
		9.5 am Bristol-Swansea	2F42	From Cardiff		
4092	81D	At Bristol SPM in steam				
		? 1.5 am Paddington-Bristol West Depot Parcels	3B02			
4093*	87E	2.30 pm Neyland-Paddington	A44	From Swansea	S 1E	p 127
4094	87E	(6.50 pm FRI Neyland-Paddington)	A75	From Swansea		
		3.45 pm Paddington-Fishguard	F54	To Swansea	CF 1E	p 122
		⎧9.5 am FRI Liverpool-Plymouth	V93	From Bristol D/H 6910 to Exeter		p 143
4095	83D	⎨D/H workings all day		Between Newquay and Exeter		
		⎩See text pages 143/144				
4096	81A			Stopped REPAIRS Southall		
4098	83A	10.35 am Paignton-Wolverhampton	H22		TYS 8L	
		10.10 am SUN Wolverhampton-Penzance	C37	To Plymouth		p 161
4099	87E	3.45 pm Paddington-Fishguard	F54	From Swansea		

4MT 2-6-2T

LOCO	SHED CODE	TRAIN	TRAIN NO	NOTES ON LOCO WORKING		PAGE REF
4110	84F	7.10 am Stourbridge Jc-Wolverhampton	2H65			p 52
4112	84D	A/E 7.10 am Paddington-Wolverhampton	H45	From Leamington		p 111
4121	86F	Llantrisant-Porthcawl Excursion				p 135
4125	81F	12.52 pm Oxford-Princes Risborough	2A78			
		1.58 pm Princes Risborough-Oxford	2A78		OX 4L	
4143	88A	10.0 am Merthyr-Barry Island	2T61			
4145	83A	Local Trains		Between Newton Abbot & Kingswear		
4148	81F	9.45 am Princes Risborough-Oxford	2A78		OX 1L	
		2.50 pm Oxford-Princes Risborough	2A78			
4150	83A	6.38 pm Newton Abbot-Kingswear	2C91	TC off 9.5 am Liverpool		
4163	88A	7.30 am Treherbert-Barry Island	2T61		CF 2L	
4174	83A	5.0 pm Newton Abbot-Paignton	2C90	Unusually TC off both 8.35 am		
		(probably extended to Kingswear)		Liverpool and 7.42 am ex Manchester		
		7.20 pm Kingswear-Newton Abbot	2C76	D/H 4145		

4MT 2-6-2T

LOCO	SHED CODE	TRAIN	TRAIN NO	NOTES ON LOCO WORKING		PAGE REF
4552	83E	Looe Branch Passenger				p 150
4569	83E	Looe Branch Passenger FRI				p 150
4573	85B	Chipping Norton Branch Passenger				p 114
4587	83F	Chacewater-Newquay Passenger				p 150
4593	83F	Chacewater-Newquay Passenger				p 150

7MT 2-8-0

LOCO	SHED CODE	TRAIN	TRAIN NO	NOTES ON LOCO WORKING		PAGE REF
47XX		See text page 73				

5MT 4-6-0

LOCO	SHED CODE	TRAIN	TRAIN NO	NOTES ON LOCO WORKING		PAGE REF
4901	84B					
4902	81E					
4903	81D					
4904	83B	9.0 am Bournemouth-Cardiff	V04		CF 3L	
4905	83A	Ex 84A 10.35 am FRI		Working not known		
		At Banbury 10.30 am SAT		Ret 84A 5.35 am SUN		
4906	83E			Poor condition XT-Works 4.8.60		p 90
4907	85E					
4908	81D	? 5.30 am Paddington-Minehead	C58	To Bristol		p 89
		6.40 am Leicester-Paignton	V27	From Bristol	EX 1E	
4909	82D	2.15 pm Westbury-Swindon	2B75			
		5.57 pm Swindon-Westbury	2B73		S 1E	
4910	84E	9.10 am Birmingham-Pembroke Dock	F18	To Cardiff	CF 3E	p 159
		5.15 pm Cardiff-Crewe	2J91	To Shrewsbury		
4912	84B	7.15 pm Paddington-Bristol	B22			
4913	85C					
4914	82B			At 82B Shed SUN		
4915	81E					
4916	86G	(9.15 pm FRI Manchester-Newquay)	V75	Pontypool Road to Plymouth		p 54
		10.5 am Penzance-Liverpool	M96	Plymouth to Bristol	TN 14L	
4917	82D	7.43 am Nottingham-Plymouth	V31	From Bristol	NA 6L	p 56
4918	84A	SWINDON WORKS Repairs		Until 8.8.60		
4919	81A	9.45 am Paddington-Wrexham	J15	To Wolverhampton	(SL 0L)	p 68
4920	83A	A/E 11.15 am Plymouth-Paddington	A71	To Newton Abbot		p 152
		A/E 8.55 am Wolverhampton-Penzance	C33	Newton Abbot to Plymouth		
4921	81D	SWINDON WORKS Repairs		Until 17.10.60		
4922	82B					
4923	87G					
4924	83B	5.0 pm Tiverton Jc-West Ealing Milk	3A28	To Taunton		
		6.37 pm Taunton-Bristol	2B96			
4925	81C					

LOCO	SHED CODE	TRAIN	TRAIN NO	NOTES ON LOCO WORKING		PAGE REF
4926	86G					
4927	87A	LE at Chester 10.0 am				
4928	86C	7.35 am Cardiff-Blackpool	M66	To Shrewsbury	(SL 10L)	p 23
		9.15 am Blackpool-Cardiff	V55	From Shrewsbury	CF 33L	p 99
4929	85B					
4930	83C	10.15 am Teignmouth-Bradford	N47	To Bristol	(TN 13L)	
4931	86C					
4932	83B					
4933	82D					
4934	83A	7.40 am St Austell-Birmingham	H20	From Plymouth	TYS 11L	
4935	87G	2.30 pm Neyland-Paddington	A44	Carmarthen to Swansea		p 127
4936	83A	A/E 4.35 pm FRI Plymouth Millbay-Paddington Parcels	3A47	Plymouth to Newton Abbot		
		{ Up LE ex Paignton	—	Loco in poor condition		
		{ SUN p. way train to Hackney		XT For Works 17.7.60		
4937	86G	? 11.10 pm FRI Manchester-Penzance	V81	Pontypool Road to Plymouth		p 54
		10.45 am Penzance-Sheffield	E72	Plymouth to Bristol At 84G SUN	TN 18L	
4938	84A	STAFFORD ROAD WORKS Repairs				
4939	81E			At 81E Shed FRI		
4941	81D	8.47 am FRI Ramsgate-Wolverhampton	V82	From Reading		p 139
		10.42 am Wolverhampton-Margate	O48	To Reading	OX 1E	
4942	83C	{ 9.18 am Exmouth/	M90	Exeter Central }	(SL 4L)	p 25
		{ 10.4 am Exeter-Manchester		To Shrewsbury }		
4943	86G					
4944	83C	10.20 am Kingswear-Liverpool	M93	To Pontypool Road	TN 23L	
4945	82D	7.15 am Trowbridge-Paddington	2A70			
		2.35 pm Paddington-Weston	B14	Via Newbury	SKE 8L	
4946	84G			At 84G Shed SUN		
4947	82B					
4948	83C			At 82B Shed SUN		
4949	82B			At 82B Shed SUN		
4950	83D					
4951	84B	2.30 pm Plymouth-Exeter	2C76		NA 6L	
		2.21 pm SUN Exeter-Kingswear	2C91			
		5.20 pm SUN Kingswear-Bristol	2B96			
4952	86C	3.10 pm Trowbridge-Reading	2A87		SKE 17L	
4953	82C/82B					
4954	84A	9. 0 am Paddington-Pwllheli	J13	Wolverhampton to Ruabon		p 88
4955	83B	7.30 am Paddington-Kingswear	C68	From Bristol	EX 10L	p 89
		4.40 pm Paignton-Taunton	2C77			
		2.15 pm SUN Kingswear-Newton Abbot	2C90	TC to Cardiff		
4956	86C					
4957	71G/82D	? 8.15 am Frome-Paddington	A19	{ Officially loaned to Weymouth	SN 62E	p 56
		3.58 pm West Ealing-Neyland Milk Empties	3F 15	{ 27.5.60 to 16.8.60		
4958	86G					
4959	81E					
4960	82B	SWINDON WORKS Repairs		Until 27.7.60		
4961	82D	10.8 am Cardiff-Portsmouth	O56	To Salisbury	(SA 0L)	
4962	87G	8.55 am Paddington-Milford Haven	F15	From Carmarthen		p 87
4963	84B	10.50 am Wolverhampton-Minehead	C84	To Taunton	TN 2E	p 46
4964	84C	8.48 am Hastings-Wolverhampton	V77	From Kensington		
4965	81E			At Crewe Gresty Lane SUN		
4966	84B	OSWESTRY WORKS Repairs				
4967	83D					
4968	82B	? 10.40 pm FRI Wolverhampton-Paignton	C52	Off 84A 10.39 pm FRI		
				At Newton Abbot MON 11.7.60		
4969	81E			XT for Works 24.7.60		
4970	83B	? 11.40 pm FRI Taunton-Wolverhampton Parcels	3H05	At 84B Shed SUN		
4971	83B	12.30 pm Paignton-Manchester	M97	Bristol to Shrewsbury		
				XT for Works 4.8.60		
4972	82C	2.40 pm FRI Wood Lane-Penzance Milk Empties	3C05	To Plymouth		
		10.20 am Penzance-Swansea	F50	Plymouth to Newton Abbot	NA 4L	p 144
4973	86C	10.30 am Cardiff-Portsmouth	O58	To Salisbury	SA 3E	p 70
		2.43 pm Portsmouth-Bristol	V13	From Salisbury		
				At 82A Shed SUN		
4974	84F	STAFFORD ROAD WORKS Repairs				
4975	83A	6.35 am Paignton-Wigan	M85	To Shrewsbury		p 76
4976	83D	10.0 am Newquay-Paddington	A78	To Laira Jc D/H D63XX		p 153
4977	81D					
4978	83B	SWINDON WORKS Repairs				
4979	81F	At Banbury 10.15 am				
4980	82B	9.5 am Paignton-Manchester	M89	To Pontypool Road	(NP 22L)	p 99
		? 3.0 pm Manchester-Plymouth	V98	And/Or 5997 Pontypool Road to Bristol		
4981	87J					
4982	84E			At 84E Shed SUN		
4983	86G					
4984	84B	3.0 pm Blackpool-Swindon & Wootton Bassett Special		From Wolverhampton	TYS 98L	p132
4985	83B	11.0 am Ilfracombe-Wolverhampton	H28	At 84B Shed SUN	W 2E	p 97
4986	84A	8.43 am Wolverhampton-Portsmouth	O36	To Basingstoke		
		1.11 pm Portsmouth-Birmingham	V94	From Basingstoke	OX 6E	p 79
4987	81D	12.5 am Paddington-Birkenhead	M00	To Wolverhampton		
		1.10 pm Paddington-Birkenhead	M16	Wolverhampton to Chester	(SH 21L)	
4988	87A	1.45 pm Margate-Swindon	X42	From Reading		p 131
	SHED		TRAIN	NOTES ON		PAGE

LOCO	SHED CODE	TRAIN	TRAIN NO	NOTES ON LOCO WORKING		PAGE REF
		Down ECS from Swindon				
4989	85B		Z71	Excursion 6.7.60		
4990	85C					
4991	83B	11.5 am Paddington-Taunton	B09	From Bristol	TN 0L	
		4.50 pm Taunton-Exeter	2C77			
4992	83C	A/E 12.21 pm Cardiff-Newquay	C37	Newton Abbot to Plymouth		p 58
4993	85A	10.15 am Llandilo-Woodford Freight	7M36		NP 50L	
4994	81E	2.35 pm Shrewsbury-Paddington	A93	To Wolverhampton		
				At 82A Shed SUN		
				AT 86C Shed FRI		
4995	81C					
4996	85A					
4997	84B			At 84B Shed SUN		
4998	81D					
4999	86C	8.55 am Cardiff-Manchester	M68	To Shrewsbury	(SL 7L)	
		11.42 am Manchester-Cardiff	V57	From Shrewsbury	CF 7E	
7P 4-6-0						
5000	82C	? 5.5 am Paddington-Bristol Parcels	3B04	Or 5009 Identification unsure		p 118
5001	84G	5.10 pm FRI Shrewsbury-Birmingham	2H51	To Wolverhampton		
		6.10 pm FRI Paddington-Birkenhead	M21	From Wolverhampton		
		8.35 am Liverpool-Penzance	V89	Shrewsbury-Bristol		p 23
5002	82C	(7.58 am Swindon-Hereford)	2J90	To Gloucester		
		5.38 pm Cheltenham-Swindon	2B79	From Gloucester	S 2L	p 126
5003	83A	8.0 am Paignton-Colne	M87	To Coleham		p 94
		(9.0 pm Manchester-Penzance)	V76	Back at Newton Abbot MON 11.7.60		
5004	87E	SWINDON WORKS Repairs		25.4.60-13.7.60		
5006	87E	SWINDON WORKS Repairs		9.5.60-13.7.60		
5007	82C	SWINDON WORKS Repairs		28.4.60-5.8.60		
5008	81A	At Landore 8.15 am				p 149
		? 6.50 pm Neyland-Paddington	A75			p 118
5009	82C			See 5000 I/D unsure		p 138
5011	81D	8.47 am Ramsgate-Wolverhampton	V82	From Reading	TYS 40L	
				At 84A Shed SUN		
5012	81F	(7.10 am Oxford-Paddington)	2A70)		TW 3L	p 137
		2.3 pm Paddington-Didcot	2A25			
5013	87E	8.55 am Paddington-Pembroke Dock	F15	Swansea to Carmarthen		
		5.15 pm Whitland-Kensington Milk	3A33	To ? Canton		p 160
5014	81A					
5015	87E	11.45 am Swansea-Birmingham	H68	To Cardiff	CF 3L	
		4.50 pm Cardiff-Swansea	2F92			
5016	87E	(7.55 am Paddington-Carmarthen)	F11	From Swansea		p 80
		6.50 pm Neyland-Paddington	A75	Carmarthen to Swansea		
5017	85B	SWINDON WORKS Repairs		27.6.60-7.9.60		p 12
5018	81D	(R) 3.35 am Fishguard-Paddington	A06	From Cardiff		p 121
		2.0 pm Paddington-Plymouth Parcels	3C07	To Swindon	S 5L	
5019	84A	11.10 am Paddington-Birkenhead	M11	From Wolverhampton to Chester	(SL 7L)	p 62
		8.5 am SUN Birkenhead-Paddington	V05	From Chester to Shrewsbury		
				At 84G Shed SUN		
5020	83C	Presumed Exeter Standby	—	At 83C Shed SAT		p 82
				At 83C Shed SUN		
5021	86C	SWINDON WORKS Repairs		27.6.60-15.9.60		
5022*	84A	8.55 pm FRI Birkenhead-Paddington	V15	Chester to Wolverhampton		p 43
				Not out SAT		
				Down "Cornishman" 11.7.60		
5023	82C	1.38 pm Paddington-Weston	B12	From Swindon		
5024	83A	(R) 9.0 am Manchester-Paignton	V92	From Shrewsbury	NA 34L	
		7.15 pm Paignton-Newton Abbot	2C90	Up M87 MON/V92 TUES	NA 8L	
5025	81F			? Stopped REPAIRS Tyseley		p 137
				At 84E Shed SUN		
5026*	84A	(R) 6.8 pm FRI Paddington-Wolverhampton	H41			p 97
		D/H 8.55 am Wolverhampton-Penzance	C33	To Birmingham	SH 3L	
5027	81A					
5029	83D	(R) 7.42 am Manchester-Penzance	V88	Shrewsbury to Plymouth	NA 62L	p 23
5030	87G	6.35 am Taunton-Neyland	2F96	Swansea to Carmarthen		
LOAN	ex 87E	At Carmarthen pm		To Canton		
		? 6.45 pm Carmarthen-Wood Lane Milk	3A39	Out of use at 84A 7.7.60-11.7.60		
5031*	84A					
5032*	81A					
5033	81F	(O) See Note A	3A31	From Plymouth		p 137
		(R) 12.20 pm Penzance-Kensington Milk				
5034	81A	11.30 am Paddington-Minehead	C78	To Taunton	TN 4L	p 46
		2.15 pm Minehead-Paddington	A95	From Taunton	TW 4L	
5035	81A	SWINDON WORKS Repairs		11.5.60-28.7.60		
5036	81D	7.40 am Paddington-Paignton	C59		NA 8L	p 142
		4.35 pm Kingswear-Paddington	A36	From Newton Abbot	EX 3L	p 157
5037	81A	6.55 pm Paddington-Fishguard	F70	To Swansea	NP 2E	p 127
5038	84G			In use FRI V05-Wpn		
				At 84G Shed SUN		
5039	87E	8.35 am Paddington-Pembroke Dock	F13	To Swansea	NP 0L	p 87
5040	81A	9.5 am Paddington-Bristol	B06			p 88
		1.50 pm Bristol-Paddington	A74		P 7E	
5041	87E	7.30 am Pembroke Dock-Paddington	A55	From Swansea	P 9E	p 59
		(9.30 pm Paddington-Carmarthen)	F79	To Swansea		
5042	81A	(O) See Note B		Paddington to Swansea		p 125
		(R) 1.5 pm Pembroke Dock-Paddington	A23	From Swansea	P 16E	

LOCO	SHED CODE	TRAIN	TRAIN NO	NOTES ON LOCO WORKING		PAGE REF
5043*	81A	12.5 am SUN Paddington-Birkenhead	M00	To Wolverhampton		p 34
		4.55 pm SUN Shrewsbury-Paddington	A45	From Wolverhampton		
5044	81A	(4.7 am Swindon-Gloucester Newspapers)	2T32	RUNNING-IN		
		10.20 am Gloucester-Swindon Freight	8B68	RUNNING-IN	S 93E	
5045	84A	9.50 pm FRI Wolverhampton-Penzance	C10	To Plymouth		
		11.10 am Penzance-Wolverhampton	H37	From Plymouth	SH 57L	p 103
5046	84A			At 84A Shed SAT Not in use		
5047	84A	{ Wolverhampton				
		{ STANDBY 6.13 am-12.43 pm				
5048	82A	(7.5 pm FRI Paddington-Fishguard)	F71	To Cardiff		p 9
		9.20 am Ebbw Vale-Paddington	A40	From Bassaleg	Ealing 1E	
		2.55 pm Paddington-Fishguard	F47	To Cardiff	CF 9L	p 122
5049*	82A	11.45 am Bristol-Paddington	A43		P 10L	p 75
		5.0 pm Paddington-Weston	B17	To Bristol	S 3L	p 126
5050	84G	(? 6.58 pm FRI Glasgow-Plymouth)	V84	Shrewsbury to Bristol		
		8.30 am Ilfracombe-Manchester	M92	Bristol to Coleham		p 99
5051	87E	(R) 10.55 am Paddington-Pembroke Dock	F27	To Swansea	NP 1E	p 60
5052	81A	SWINDON WORKS Repairs		15.6.60-26.8.60		
5053	83D					
5054	81A	(O) See Note B		Paddington to Swansea		
		(R) 3.55 am Fishguard Hbr-Paddington	A09	From Llanelly	P 21L	p 12
5055	83A	7.40 am Newton Abbot-Swansea	F19	To Bristol		
		8.17 am Carmarthen-Penzance	C36	Bristol to Plymouth	NA 4L	p 58
		6.0 pm Plymouth-Bristol	B50	Plymouth to Newton Abbot	NA 3E	
5056	81A	(O) ?		? Late SAT to Plymouth		
		(R) 12.35 pm SUN Penzance-Kensington Milk	3A31	From Plymouth		p 47
5057*	81A	11.5 am Paddington-Taunton	B09	To Bristol	TM 2E	p 120
		11.55 am Minehead-Paddington	A86	From Bristol	P 61L	
5058	83D	7.55 am Penzance-Plymouth	2C74			
		8.55 am Wolverhampton-Penzance	C33	From Plymouth		p 97
5059	84G	(O) See Note D		To Pontypool Road		
		(O) 9.5 am Liverpool-Plymouth	V93	Pontypool Road to Newton Abbot	NA 24L	p 101
		(R) 5.10 pm SUN Paignton-Bristol	2B96	SUN at Bristol.11.7.60 at Paddington		
5060	81A	10.15 am Paddington-Kingswear	C71		NA 3L	p 142
		7.55 pm Kingswear-Newton Abbot	2C90			
5061*	86C	(12.45 pm Paddington-Carmarthen)	F02	Cardiff to Swansea		
		7.50am Fishguard-Paddington	A58	Swansea to Cardiff	CF 1E	
		7.20 pm Cardiff-Pontypool Road	2T06			p 54
		12 noon Penzance-Crewe	M99	Pontypool Road to Shrewsbury		
5062	82A	(O) 10.5 am FRI Penzance-Manchester	M96	Bristol to Shrewsbury		
		(R) (7.0 pm FRI Liverpool-Bristol)	V99	At 82A Shed SUN		
				No working traced SAT		
5063	84A	8.55 am Wolverhampton-Penzance	C33	To Plymouth	NA 37L	p 97
		10.30 am SUN Penzance-Wolverhampton	H32	From Plymouth		
5064*	82C	2.0 pm Paddington-Plymouth Parcels	3C07	From Swindon	S 5L	p 122
5065	81A	(O) See Note A		Paddington to Plymouth		
		(R) 8.20 am Penzance-Paddington	A79	From Plymouth	P 48L	p 155
5066*	81A	8.30 am Bristol-Paddington	A14		P 9L	p 116
5067	87G	12.5 pm Milford-Paddington	All	Carmarthen to Swansea		p 123
		11.35 am Paddington-Neyland	F29	Swansea to Carmarthen	arrive 11L	
5068*	82C	11.38 am Swindon-Didcot	2A76			p 118
		6.1 pm Didcot-Swindon	2B76		S 0L	
5069*	83D	1.30 pm Paddington-Penzance	C41	To Plymouth	NA 31L	p 144
5070	84G	7.15 am Chester-Shrewsbury	2V52			
		Shrewsbury to Wolverhampton		LE or train unknown		p 132
		8.10 pm Paddington-Shrewsbury	J28			
5071*	85A	3.13 pm Worcester-Paddington	A97		TW ½L	p 138
5072	84A	At Stafford Road. Stopped		XT for Works 24.6.60		
				To Swindon 14.7.60		
5073*	82A	{ (1.5 am Bristol-Neyland)	F01	To Cardiff		
		{ 6.5 am Cardiff-Bristol	2B78			
		{ 4. 0 pm North Filton-Weston	2B46			
5074	87E	7.30 am Swansea-Gloucester	2T51			
		2.14 pm Gloucester-Cardiff	2F52		CF 4L	
5075	83C	11.30 pm FRI Liverpool-Penzance	V83	Bristol to Plymouth		p 11
		12.38 pm Plymouth-Newton Abbot	2C75		NA 1L	p 82
		6.30 pm Kingswear-Exeter	2C76	From Newton Abbot		
5076	81D					
5077	87E	8.20 am Swansea-Paddington	A32		P 1E	p 91
		(9.25 pm Paddington-Neyland)	F78	To Swansea		
5078	82A	10.5 am Penzance-Crewe	M96	Bristol to Shrewsbury		p 8
		(7.0 pm Liverpool-Bristol)	V99	From Shrewsbury		
5080	87G					p 34
5081	85A					p 33
5082	81A	6.30 am Hereford-Paddington	A04	From Worcester	P 26L	p 135
5084*	81A	7.0 am Swindon-Penzance	C19	To Plymouth	NA 9L	
		1.20 pm Penzance-Paddington	A33	From Plymouth	P 15L	p 157
5085	82A	(O) ?				
		(R) 11.5 am Milford-Paddington	A90	From Swansea	P 6L	p 121
5087	81A	7.30 am Paddington-Kingswear	C68	To Bristol		p 93
		11.5 am Weston-Paddington	A51	From Bristol	P 4L	
5088*	84A	7.35 am Birkenhead-Paddington	V03	Chester to Wolverhampton		p 44
		9.45 am Pwllheli-Paddington	A89	From Wolverhampton	P 12L	
		7.30 pm Paddington-Wolverhampton	H49	via Oxford		
5089	84A	3.33 pm SUN Wolverhampton-Paddington	A91	No working traced SAT		
5090	82A	4.40 pm FRI Penzance-Manchester	M77	Plymouth to Bristol	NA 3L	

LOCO	SHED CODE	TRAIN	TRAIN NO	NOTES ON LOCO WORKING		PAGE REF
		(8.45 pm FRI Bradford-Paignton)	V14	From Bristol		p 93
		10.58 am Paignton-Nottingham	M23	To Bristol	TM 8L	p 149
5091	87E	11.55 am Paddington-Milford	F32	To Swansea	CF 2L	p 26
5092	82A	11.15 am Newquay-Wolverhampton	H34	From Plymouth	TYS 33L	p 102
5093	81A	8.25 am Paddington-Penzance/Perranporth	C25	To Plymouth	NA 4L	p 87
		7.0 pm Penzance-Paddington Postal	A69	From Plymouth	NA 2E	p 166
5094*	82A	(1.0 am Paddington-Swansea)	F05	To Swansea		p 34
		3.50 pm Whitland-Kensington Milk	3A27	Felin Fran to Swindon	CF 4E	
5095*	86C	SWINDON WORKS Repairs		14.6.60 - 8.9.60		
5096	82A	7.25 pm Bristol-Portsmouth	O67	To Salisbury		p 157
5097	82A			At 82A Shed SUN		
5098*	83D	10.15 am Launceston-Redruth	2C70	From Plymouth		
		3.0 pm Carn Brea Yard-Truro	ECS			
		(R) ?		{ Truro to Penzance or		
				Plymouth		
5099	86C	6.15 am Swansea-Paddington	A12	From Cardiff	P 10L	p 15
		1.50 pm Paddington-Carmarthen	F44	To Swansea	CF 1L	p 118
		(9.45 am SUN Swansea-Canton)	ECS			

4MT
2-6-2T

LOCO	SHED CODE	TRAIN	TRAIN NO	NOTES ON LOCO WORKING		PAGE REF
5153	83A	8.42 pm Newton Abbot-Kingswear	2C91	Portion of 11.55 am Manchester		
5167	84C	1.8 pm Oxford-Banbury	2H99			p 135
5191	86E	12.45 pm Newport-Barry Island	2F61		CF 3E	
		5.50 pm Barry Island-Newport	2T52		CF 1E	
5195	83A	A/E 3.50 pm Pylle Hill-Plymouth Parcels	3C04	From Newton Abbot to Brent or (unlikely) Plymouth		
5198	83E	9.22 am Par-Newquay	2C54			p 103
		D/H 11.15 am Newquay-Wolverhampton	—	To Par		
		1.38 pm Par-Newquay				

4MT
2-6-0

LOCO	SHED CODE	TRAIN	TRAIN NO	NOTES ON LOCO WORKING		PAGE REF
5326	82B	6. 25 am FRI Pengam-Moreton Cutting Freight	7A34	At 84B Shed SUN		
5339	82B	7.0 am Paignton-Colne	M86	Bristol to Shrewsbury		p 75
5351	87H	L.E. at Whitland				
5357	87H	12.5 pm Milford-Paddington	A11	To Carmarthen		p 123
5358	82D	? Hackney-Plymouth Freight		SUN pm also with 5318 at 83D		p 73
		3.55 pm MON Plymouth-Swindon Parcels	3B37			
5369	84E	10.20 am Birmingham-Margate	O45	To Redhill	OX 3E	
5376	82B	11.0 am Ilfracombe-Wolverhampton	H28	To Taunton	TN 5L	p 77
5385	82B			At 84J Shed SUN		
5399	84J			At 84J Shed SUN		

4MT
2-6-2T

LOCO	SHED CODE	TRAIN	TRAIN NO	NOTES ON LOCO WORKING		PAGE REF
5508	82D	9.47 am Westbury-Bristol	2B96	Via Wells		p 113
5529	86F	Porthcawl Railmotor				p 110
5536	82C	5.48 pm Swindon-Kemble & Others	2T79			p 126
5538	83F	Truro-Perranporth	2C52			
5545	86F	Llynvi Railmotor		Afternoon		p 110
5547	82C	7.5 am Swindon-Andover	2B81			p 110
		2.30 pm Andover-Swindon Freight	9C74			
5555	86F	Llynvi Railmotor		Morning		
5557	83F	4.35 pm Newquay-Truro	2C71			
5573	83C	9.30 am Exeter-Dulverton	2C87			

56XX & 57XX   Various local passenger and freight workings.

5MT
4-6-0

LOCO	SHED CODE	TRAIN	TRAIN NO	NOTES ON LOCO WORKING		PAGE REF
5900	84A	6.30 am Birkenhead-Paddington	V02	Chester to Wolverhampton		
		9.10 am Paddington-Birkenhead	M09	Wolverhampton to Chester		p 88
5901	81D	9.11 am Portsmouth-Wolverhampton	V87		SH 1E	p 136
		8.55 pm Birkenhead-Paddington	V15	From Wolverhampton		
5902	87G					
5903	86C	10.10 am Paignton-Cardiff	F30		CF 1E	
5904	82D	CAERPHILLY WORKS Repairs				
5905	87J			At 87J 6.7.60		
5906	81D	6.25 am Reading-Wolverhampton	2H52			
		4.40 pm Wolverhampton-Didcot	2A27			
5907	81D					
5908	87J	8.48 am Fishguard-Paddington Parcels	3A24	To Landore		
5909	87E	9.35 am Swansea-Birmingham	H12		TYS 8L	
		3.45 pm Birmingham-Fishguard	F52	To Swansea	CF 14L	p 123
5910	86C					
5911	86C	8.5 am Cardiff-Kingswear	C62	From Bristol	NA 35L	
		3.20 pm Kingswear-Cardiff	F60		CF 4E	
5912	84F					
5913	87E	6.15 am Swansea-Paddington	A12	To Cardiff		p 11
5914	85B	8.10 am Cardiff-Filey Holiday Camp	N37	To Gloucester		p 64
		6.33 pm Cheltenham-Swindon	2B79	From Gloucester	S 5L	
5916	84B	At Taunton 6.0 pm				
5917	85A					
5918	81E	SWINDON WORKS Repairs				
5919	84B			At 84B Shed SUN		

LOCO	SHED CODE	TRAIN	TRAIN NO	NOTES ON LOCO WORKING		PAGE REF
5920	83A	12.15 pm Kingswear-Wolverhampton	H31	At 84B Shed SUN	TYS 8L	
		Down MON Freight at Exeter		At 83A Shed 12.7.60		
5921	84E					
5922	82C					
5923	81A					p 55
5924	82B			At 82B Shed SUN		
5925	81C	SWINDON WORKS Repairs				
5926	84A	9.25 am Wolverhampton-Paignton	C76	Via Oxford	NA 35L	p 97
				Poor Condition–XT 20.7.60		p 143
5927	84E	7.0 am Birmingham-Paignton	C61		NA 12L	
		8.15 pm Paignton-Swansea	ECS	Loco to ?		
5928	87J					
5929	81A	5.6 pm Paddington-Weston	B18		S 5E	p 131
		(1.10 am SUN Bristol-Paddington Parcels)	3A09			
5930	84F					
5931	81A	10.29 am Oxford-Paddington	2A20			
5932	81A	11.35 am Paddington-Neyland	F29	To Swansea	CF 12L	
		8.5 pm Porthcawl-Carmarthen	2F91	From Swansea		
5933	84C	10.0 am Bradford-Poole	O41	Banbury to Oxford	OX 2L	
		8.35 am Newcastle-Bournemouth	O42	From Oxford	OX 2L	
5934	82A			At 82A Shed SUN		
5935	82D					
5936	81D	10.50 am Bristol-Portsmouth	O54	To Salisbury	SA 0L	p 93
		11.0 am Brighton-Cardiff	V11	From Salisbury	CF 8L	p 77
		8.25 pm Cardiff-Plymouth Parcels	3C10	At Newton Abbot MON 11.7.60		
5937	87G	10.20 am Pembroke Dock-Paddington	A87	From Swansea	(P 8L)	p 121
5938	87G	11.45 am Carmarthen-Swansea	2F93			
		3.40 pm Swansea-Carmarthen	2F94			
5939	81A			At 86C Shed on FRI		
5940	82A	9.9 am Portsmouth-Cardiff	V06	From Salisbury	CF 12L	p 145
		9.35 pm Cardiff-Chepstow	2T52	At 86E Shed SUN	NP 0L	
5941	82A			At 82A Shed SUN		
5942	84G	10.42 am Llandudno-Cardiff	V56	From Shrewsbury	CF 3E	
5943	81E					
5944	84B	SWINDON WORKS Repairs		9.5.60 XT for Works		
				30.5.60 until 21.7.60		
5945	82C	12.21 pm Cardiff-Newquay	C37	Bristol to Newton Abbot	NA 20L	p 58
5946	83C	8.15 am Exeter-Taunton	2C77			
		12.15 pm Taunton-Exeter	2C77		EX 7E	
		? 4.5 pm Exeter-Weston	2B97			
5947	84C	9.9 am Sheffield-Bournemouth	O40	Banbury to Basingstoke	OX 17L	
5948	86G					
5949	82A	A/E 11.0 am SUN Penzance-Paddington	A08	Plymouth to Newton Abbot		
5950	82B	? 9.5 pm FRI Newcastle-Paignton	V22	From Bristol		
		4.15 pm Paignton-Paddington	A30		EX 3L	p 148
5951	85B					
5952	85C	7.30 am Shrewsbury-Paddington	A16	To Wolverhampton		p 146
		10.15 am Wellington-Birkenhead	2M55	To Chester		
5953	87G	1.5 pm Pembroke Dock-Paddington	A23	Carmarthen to Swansea		
		1.55 pm Paddington-Neyland	F46	Swansea to Carmarthen		p 161
		8.30 pm Whitland-Kensington Milk	3A44	Carmarthen to Llanelly		
5954	82B			At 82B Shed SUN		
5955	87E	11.15 am Swansea-Manchester	M72	To Cardiff	CF 3L	
		9.0 am Manchester-Swansea	V54	From Cardiff		
5956	85A					
5957	81F			V. Rough on 8.10 am Newport-Paignton on 16.7.60		
5958	81A	12.21 pm Cardiff-Newquay	C37	To Bristol		
		5,0 pm Bristol-Cardiff	2F02		CF 6L	
5959	84E	11.40 am Birkenhead-Paddington	V07	Chester to Wolverhampton		
		Dundee-Lavington Special Troop Train		From ? Wolverhampton	TYS 13E	p 132
5960	81F	11.42 am Paddington-Reading	2A64			
5961	87G	1.50 pm Paddington-Carmarthen	F44	From Swansea		
5962	86C	CAERPHILLY WORKS Repairs		5.7.60 to 19.8.60		
5963	82D					
5964	82C	9.22 am Paddington-Paignton	C70		EX 2E	p 88
5965	84B	6.40 am Wolverhampton-Paignton	C63	To Exeter. At 83A Shed SUN	EX 23L	p 8
5966	81F	9.30 am Bournemouth-Birkenhead	M13	From Oxford to Chester	SH 0L	p 137
5967	82D	(9.27 am Westbury-Reading)	2A87			
		12.55 pm Reading-Westbury	2B73		SKE 3E	
5968	84G	9.0 am Manchester-Swansea	V54	Pontypool Road to Cardiff	CF 13L	
		(R) 4.40 pm Cardiff-Liverpool	M74	To Shrewsbury		
5969	87J			At Crewe Gresty Lane SUN		
5970	86G	7.20 am Pwllheli-Paddington	A60	Ruabon to Wolverhampton		p 53
5971	84G	(O) See Note D		Shrewsbury to Exeter		p 49
		6.40 am Wolverhampton-Paignton	C63	From Exeter D/H 6829		
		(R) 2.55 pm Paignton-Birmingham	H42		TYS 15L	
5972	87A	7.35 am Chepstow-Cardiff	2F52			
5973	81D	At Cardiff Canton				
5974	82D	8.30 am Bournemouth-Cardiff	V02	From Salisbury	CF 29L	
		4.25 pm Cardiff-Portsmouth	O65	Front loco with 6986		
				? 5974 to Westbury		
5975	82D					
5976	81A			At 83A Shed 12.7.60		
5977	81D	8.15 pm FRI Birmingham-Paddington	A53		NA 7L	
		10.22 am Paddingrton-Paignton	C74			p 142

LOCO	SHED CODE	TRAIN	TRAIN NO	NOTES ON LOCO WORKING		PAGE REF
5978	82C	12.50 pm Cardiff-Portsmouth	O60	To Salisbury	SA 1L	
5979	81D	? 7.20 am Hungerford-Paddington	2A70	Speculation only		
		12.55 pm West London-Didcot Parcels	3A03	Arrive 84A 1.25 am SUN	TW 11L	
5980	87A	9.50 am Carmarthen-Weston	B10	Swansea to Cardiff	CF 1E	p 161
5981	82C	10.0 am Weymouth-Birmingham	H15	From Swindon	TYS 42L	p 119
5982	81D	STAFFORD ROAD WORKS Repairs		Seen at 83C on 3.7.60		
5983	82C	4.4 pm Swindon-Bristol	2B70			
5984	87G	3.55 pm Swansea-Cheltenham	2T51	To Cardiff	CF 3L	
5985	84B	STAFFORD ROAD WORKS Repairs				
5986	82C	12.50 am Old Oak Common-Cardiff Freight	5F76		NP 107L	
		1.10 pm Pengam Sidings-Severn Tunnel Jc Freight	8T65		NP 7E	
5987	81E					
5988	84C	(O) ?				
		(R) 7.0 pm Paddington-Didcot	2A25		TW 0L	
5989	84C			At 84C Shed SUN		
5990	84C	9.20 am Chester-Paddington	V04	From Wolverhampton		p 68
		4.34 pm Paddington-Wolverhampton	2H01		TYS 0L	p 57
5991	84B	4.55 pm Wolverhampton-Stourbridge Jc	2H65			
5992	83B	7.20 am Taunton-Exeter	2C77			
		D/H 6.40 am Leicester-Paignton	V27	Exeter to Newton Abbot D/H 4908		
		8.0 am Sheffield-Kingswear	V33	From Newton Abbot		
		6.30 pm Kingswear-Exeter	2C76	To Newton Abbot	NA 11L	
		7.50 pm Newton Abbot-Taunton Parcels	3C46			
5993	81D	11.15 am Paddington-Cheltenham	T03	To Gloucester		
		4.0 pm Cheltenham-Paddington	A02	From Gloucester	P 16L	
5994	85A			At 84B Shed SUN		
5995	84B			At Crewe Gresty Lane SUN		
5996	85A					
5997	82A	8.20 am Cardiff-Llandudno	M67	To Shrewsbury		
		? 3.0 pm Manchester-Plymouth	V98	Shrewsbury to Bristol		
5998	85C					
5999	83B			XT 9.8.60		
8P						
4-6-0						
6000	81A	10.10 am Paddington-Aberystwyth	J17	To Wolverhampton (Shrewsbury FRI)	SH 0L	p 40
		2.35 pm Shrewsbury-Paddington	A83	From Wolverhampton	(P 4L)	p 2
6001	84A	7.25 am Wolverhampton-Paddington	A05		P 0L	p 88
		8.10 pm Paddington-Shrewsbury	J28	To Wolverhampton		
6002	83D	1.20 pm FRI Penzance-Paddington	A33	From Plymouth	EX 7L	p 40
		9.30 am Paddington-Newquay	C28	To Plymouth	EX 0L	p 88
6003	81A	6.35 pm Paddington-Cheltenham	T12	To Swindon	S 4E	p 127
		3.50 pm Whitland-Kensington Milk	3A27	From Swindon		
6004	81A	SWINDON WORKS Repairs		XT 16.5.60		
				7.6.60 to 29.7.60		p 40
6005	84A	SWINDON WORKS Repairs		XT 24.5.60		
				30.5.60 to 25.8.60		p 40
6006	84A	STAFFORD ROAD WORKS Repairs		Casual Repair		
				6.7.60 to 14.7.60		
6007	84A	4.35 pm Wolverhampton-Paddington	A05		P 3L	p 43
6008	84A	SWINDON WORKS Repairs				
6009	81A					p 40
6010	81A	11.10 am Paddington-Birkenhead	M11	To Wolverhampton	SH 11L	p 37
		2.35 pm Birkenhead-Paddington	V10	From Wolverhampton	P 0L	
6011	84A	7.30 am Shrewsbury-Paddington	A16	From Wolverhampton	P 6L	p 88
		1.10 pm Paddington-Birkenhead	M16	To Wolverhampton	SH 19L	
6012	81A	9.0 am Paddington-Pwllheli	J14	To Wolverhampton	SH 5E	p 88
		9.45 am Aberystwyth-Paddington	A70	From Wolverhampton	P 4E	
6013	81A	SWINDON WORKS Repairs		Until 8.8.60		
6014	84A	At Stafford Road Shed		Lt/Casual Repair STAFFORD ROAD Works 24.5.60-7.7.60		p 40
6015	81A	(12.45 am Paddington-Carmarthen)	F02	To Cardiff		
		4.55 am Fishguard-Paddington	A24	From Cardiff	P 8L	p 12
6016	83D	8.15 am Perranporth-Paddington	A65	From Laira Jc	P 7L	p 150
6017	84A	8.55 am Birkenhead-Paddington	V05	From Wolverhampton	P 1L	p 40
		6.10 pm Paddington-Birkenhead	M21	To Wolverhampton	TYS 4L	
6018	81A	7.10 pm FRI Paddington-Wolverhampton	H45	No work SATURDAY at 84A		
		6.30 pm SUN Shrewsbury-Paddington	A49	From Wolverhampton		p 40
6019	81A	SWINDON WORKS Repairs		21.6.60 to 19.9.60		
6020	84A	STAFFORD ROAD WORKS Repairs		Casual Repair until 15.7.60		
6021	81A	11.0 am Paddington-Penzance	C34	To Plymouth	NA 10L	p 95
		11.0 am SUN Penzance-Paddington	A08	From Plymouth	P 1L	
6022	84A	7.35 am Birkenhead-Paddington	V03	From Wolverhampton	P 1L	p 43
		4.10 pm Paddington-Birkenhead	M20	To Wolverhampton	SH 9L	
6023	81A	9.10 am Paddington-Birkenhead	M09	To Wolverhampton	SH 4L	p 88
		11.40 am Birkenhead-Paddington	V07	From Wolverhampton	P 3L	
6024	81A	(O) See Note A		Paddington to Plymouth		
		(R) 11.15 am Plymouth-Paddington	A71		P 51L	p 151
6025	81A	(2.25 am Paddington-Bristol Newspapers)	B00			
		6.35 am Walsall-Kingswear	V26	From Bristol	NA 19L	p 93
		4.35 pm Kingswear-Paddington	A36	To Newton Abbot		
		1.8 pm SUN Kingswear-Paddington	A92			p 157
6026	81A	SWINDON WORKS Repairs		XT 15.6.60		
				13.7.60 to 19.8.60		
6027	84A	6.30 am Birkenhead-Paddington	V02	From Wolverhampton	P 2L	
		2.10 pm Paddington-Birkenhead	M18	To Wolverhampton	SH 15L	p 86

LOCO	SHED CODE	TRAIN	TRAIN NO	NOTES ON LOCO WORKING		PAGE REF
6028	81A	(O) See Note A		Paddington to Plymouth		
		(R) 12.30 pm Newquay-Paddington	A12	From Plymouth	P 9L	p 38
6029	81A	8.30 am Paddington-Wolverhampton	H05		SH 1L	p 38
		7.20 am Pwllheli-Paddington	A60	From Wolverhampton		

Nos. 6000/1/7/11/12/17/18/22/23/27/28/29 were also working Paddington-Wolverhampton expresses on FRI.

4MT
2-6-2T

LOCO	SHED CODE	TRAIN	TRAIN NO	NOTES ON LOCO WORKING		PAGE REF
6109	81B	8.46 am Paddington-Hayes	2A51			
		11.37 am Hayes-Paddington	2A51	Also 2A73 later		
6117	81B	1.0 pm Slough-Paddington	2A57		W Ealing 5L	
		2.12 pm Paddington-Slough	2A57		W Ealing 3L	
6123	81F	7.5 pm Reading-Paddington Parcels	3A49			
6126	81B	1.42 pm Reading-Paddington			W Ealing 4L	
		5.3 pm Paddington-Reading			TW 1E	
6143	81B	1.0 pm Paddington-Aylesbury	2M60			
6150	81B	12.36 pm Paddington-Windsor	2A08			
6152	81B	1.2 pm Paddington-Slough	2A57			
6155	83B	(9.40 am Paddington-Minehead)	C71	From Taunton		
		2.15 pm Minehead-Paddington	A95	To Taunton		p 46
6158	81A	3.42 pm Paddington-Slough	2A64			
		Down LE Twyford 5.46 pm				
6159	81C	2.35 pm Worcester-Wolverhampton	2H65	? Running-in		

4MT
2-6-0

LOCO	SHED CODE	TRAIN	TRAIN NO	NOTES ON LOCO WORKING		PAGE REF
6309	82C	5.35 pm Westbury-Swindon	2B75		S 0L	p 126
6310	87H	12 .5 pm Pembroke Dock-Paddington	A18	To Carmarthen		
		11.35 am Paddington-Neyland	F29	From Carmarthen		
6312	82B	9.45 am Pwllheli-Paddington	A89	? Machynlleth to Wolverhampton	(SL 15L)	p 75
6313	81E	Exeter 9.0 am		At 82B Shed SUN		
6316	87G	10.40 am Carmarthen-Aberystwyth	2J77	At 84E Shed SUN		
				(possibly recorded in error)		
6324	81D	Oxford Station Pilot				p 74
6327	82C	2.15 pm Stoke Gifford-Hanwell Freight	8A77	XT 13.7.60	S 38L	p 123
6329	87G	? 10.35 am Neyland-Carmarthen	2F95			
		9.10 am Birmingham-Pembroke Dock	F18	From Carmarthen		p 159
6336	82C	7.20 am Severn Tunnel Jc-Landore Freight	6F04		CF 12L	p 110
6337	83B	(5.20 am Taunton-Ilfracombe)	2C34			
		9.22 am Ilfracombe-Cardiff	F36	To Taunton	TN 13L	
		(11.30 am Paddington-Ilfracombe)	2C34	From Taunton TCs dep 2. 26 pm		p 96
		(6.37 pm Ilfracombe-Taunton)	2C84			
6342	89A	10.55 am Aberystwyth-Manchester	M44	To Whitchurch	Whitchurch 4E	
6343	83B	? 8.30 am Ilfracombe-Manchester	M14	Barnstaple to Taunton		
		10.50 am Wolverhampton-Ilfracombe	2C34	From Taunton TCs dep 3.26 pm		
		(8.5 pm Ilfracombe-Taunton)	2C84			
6347	87G	3.55 pm Swansea-Cheltenham	2T51	From Cardiff	NP 0L	
6348	86A	7.30 am Blaina-Weston	B02	From Bassaleg Jc		p 91
6349	84F	8.14 am Wolverhampton-Moreton-in-Marsh	2H87			
		11.55 am Moreton-in-March–Oxford	2A90		SH 4L	p 79
		3.30 pm Oxford-Birmingham	2H03			
6350	82E	9.25 am Weymouth-Wolverhampton	H11	? To Banbury – failed. XT 19.7.60	OX 55L	p 74
6360	82B	8.20 am Penzance-Paddington	A79	Pilot 5065 from Westbury	P 48L	p 155
6364	84E	9.5 am Birmingham-Portsmouth	O34	To Oxford	OX 3L	p 79
		9.32 am Bournemouth-Wolverhampton	V90	From Oxford	TYS 10L	p 137
6365	85B	10.45 am Birmingham-Brighton	O46	To Redhill	OX 1/2L	p 79
6366	82C	9.2 am Margate-Birmingham	V83	From Redhill	TYS 56L	p 74
6367	84F	1.0 pm Wolverhampton-Stourbridge Jc	2H65	At Crewe Gresty Lane SUN		
6370	86A	11.55 am Minehead-Paddington	A86	To Bristol	TN 15L	
6374	82B	4.35 pm FRI Millbay-Paddington Parcels	3A47	To Bristol		p 76
		5.30 pm Paddington-Minehead	C58	From Bristol		
		12.20 pm Minehead-Taunton	2C33	TC to Wolverhampton		
6376	82E	4.30 pm Bristol West Depot. Trips				
6381	85B	6.43 am Cheltenham-Cardiff	2F52	From Gloucester	CF 7L	p 79
		10.35 am Pengam-Barnwood Freight	7T91		NP 36L	
6387	84C	3.35 am Park Royal-Bordesley Freight	6H27			

6300/01/20/30/39/61 were all XT or in Works for Repairs.

5MT
4-6-0

LOCO	SHED CODE	TRAIN	TRAIN NO	NOTES ON LOCO WORKING		PAGE REF
6800	83G					
6801	83G	11.10 am Penzance-Wolverhampton	H37	To Plymouth D/H 6845		p 103
6802	86G	8.15 am Bristol-Liverpool	M84	Pontypool Road to Shrewsbury	(SL 35L)	
		? 11.55 am Manchester-Plymouth	V95	Shrewsbury to Bristol		
				At 82A Shed SUN		
6803	84F			At 84E Shed SUN		
6804	82B	(O) See Note CF		To Plymouth		
		(R) 11.0 am Newquay-York	N53	To Bristol	(TM 0T)	p 58
6805	83D	8.15 am Perranporth-Paddington	A65	To Laira Jc D/H 7813		p 150
6806	84B	SWINDON WORKS Repairs		17.6.60 to 22.8.60		
6807	85A					
6808	83G					
6809	82B	A/E 10.5 am Penzance-Liverpool	M96	Plymouth to Newton Abbot	NA 2E	p 59
				ENGINE RECORD CARD		
				Marked "Ex Works 11.7.60" (sic)		
6810	87F	At Stafford Road Shed		At 84G Shed SUN		

LOCO	SHED CODE	TRAIN	TRAIN NO	NOTES ON LOCO WORKING		PAGE REF
6811	82B	8.35 am Liverpool-Penzance	V89	Bristol-Plymouth	NA 41L	p 10
6812	86G	7.15 am Cardiff-Birmingham	H62			p 53
6813	83C	{ 9.30 pm FRI Exeter-Newton Abbot	3C76	ECS		
		{ 9.10 am Kingswear-Birmingham	H17	Via Oxford	TYS 30L	p 115
6814	83B	6. 35 am Taunton-Neyland	2F96	To Cardiff	CF 12L	p 58
		8.17 am Carmarthen-Penzance	C36	Cardiff to Bristol	NP 1L	
6815	83B			At 83B Shed SUN		
6816	83D	8.42 am Shrewsbury-Paddington Parcels	3A29	From Wolverhampton		
6817	84B					
6818	87F	8.17 am Carmarthen-Penzance	C36	Swansea to Cardiff	CF 2E	p 58
		9.10 am Birmingham-Pembroke Dock	F18	Cardiff to Carmarthen		p 159
6819	86G	Running-in ex Stafford Road Works		At 84B Shed SUN		p 53
6820	85A					
6821	86G	At Exeter 11.30 am		At 83A Shed SUN		
		7.15 am Exeter-Paignton	2C90			
6822	86C	9..25 am Cardiff-Portsmouth	O55	To Salisbury	SA 0L	p 60
		5.45 pm Portsmouth Harbour-Cardiff	V16	From Salisbury	NP 4L	
		8.30 am SUN Cardiff-Goodrington	C62			
6823	83F			At 83F Shed 11.7.60		
6824	83G					
6825	83G	8.55 am Wolverhampton-Penzance	C33	From Plymouth D/H 5058		
6826	83G	A/E 8.20 am Penzance-Paddington	A79	Plymouth to Newton Abbot	NA 6L	p 57
		A/E 11.0 am Paddington-Penzance	C34	Newton Abbot to Plymouth		
		A/E 4.50 pm Penzance-Manchester	M78	Plymouth to Newton Abbot	NA 1E	
6827	82B	? 10.5 pm Hull-Paignton	V19	Newton Abbot to Paignton		
		9.30 am Paignton-Swansea	F24		CF 5L	p 60
		3.55 pm Paddington-Fishguard	F55	Swansea to Carmarthen		
6828	83F	7.25 am Ealing Broadway-Penzance	C22	From Plymouth		p 142
6829	83A	6.40 am Wolverhampton-Paignton	C63	From Exeter D/H 5971		
		3.10 pm Paignton-Wolverhampton	H44	? To Taunton or Bristol D/H 6928		p 53
6830	82B	? 10.5 pm FRI Hull-Paignton	V19	From Bristol to Newton Abbot		
		2.25 pm Paignton-Sheffield	E70	To Bristol	TN 19L	p 12
6831	82B			At 82B Shed SUN		
6832	87F	? 9.15 am Cardiff-Neyland Parcels	3F07			p 9
6833	82B	7.40 am Newton Abbot-Penzance	2C20			
6834	82B			At 82B Shed SUN		
6835	82B	(6.5 am Birmingham-Bournemouth)	O31	To Basingstoke		
		11.50 am Bournemouth-Birmingham	V91	From Basingstoke	TYS 1L	p 118
6836	83D	NEWTON ABBOT WORKS Repairs		Works Closed 16.7.60		
6837	83D	A/E 2.15 pm Penzance-Swindon Special	Z85	Plymouth to Newton Abbot	NA 1L	p 56
		A/E 10.30 am SUN Penzance-Wolverhampton	H32	Plymouth to Newton Abbot		
6838	86A	5.55 am Blaina-Paddington	A02	From Bassaleg Jc	P 7L	p 60
6839	84B	5.10 pm Shrewsbury-Birmingham	2H51	May work to Wolverhampton only		
6840	86G					
6841	82B	(10.5 pm FRI Nottingham-Paignton)	V07	From Bristol		
		8.40 am Paignton-Nottingham	M18	To Bristol	TN 8E	
6842	82B	(10.15 pm FRI Sheffield-Paignton)	V10	From Bristol		
		8.52 am Paignton-Leeds	N44	To Bristol	TN 4L	
		7.30 am Newcastle-Paignton	V38	From Bristol	NA 24L	
6843	87F	9.20 am Swansea-Brockenhurst	O59	To Salisbsury	SA 11L	p 60
		6.19 pm Westbury-Birmingham	H46		TYS 7E	p 164
6844	87F					
6845	83D	11.10 am Penzance-Wolverhampton	H37	To Plymouth D/H 6801		p 103
6846	82B	9.10 pm FRI Manchester-Paignton	V76	From ? Exeter		p 131
		5.50 pm Teignmouth-Swindon Special	Z83	ECS from Newton Abbot dep 5.35 pm		
6847	86C	10.0 am Cardiff-Swansea Freight	6F07			
6848	86G					
6849	83D	NEWTON ABBOT WORKS Repairs				
6850	83D/86A			In course of reallocation		
6851	85A					
6852	82B	1.0 pm Worcester-Severn Tunnel Jc Freight	8F73			
		LE Severn Tunnel Jc-Cardiff				
6853	84E					
6854	83D	A/E 11.15 am Newquay-Wolverhampton	H34	Plymouth to Newton Abbot	NA 11L	p 102
		12.21 pm Cardiff-Newquay	C37	Newton Abbot to ? Newquay		p 58
6855	84E	5.44 pm FRI Tyseley-Wolverhampton	2H52			
6856	85A	5.27 pm FRI Stourbridge Jc-Wolverhampton	2H65	Ex 84A 1.15 am SAT		
		9.20 am Leamington-Evesham	2H88			
6857	84B	9.20 am Birkenhead-Bournemouth	O38	Wolverhampton to Basingstoke	OX 6L	p 60
6858	84E	D/H 11.10 am Penzance-Wolverhampton	H37	From Stratford-upon-Avon	TYS 51L	p 104
6859	86C	7.48 am Bristol-Taunton	2C97			
		9.22 am Ilfracombe-Cardiff	F36	From Taunton	CF 8E	p 67
6860	83G					
6861	84E	11.10 am Pwllheli-Birmingham	H14	From Ruabon		p 88
6862	84B			At 84B Shed SUN		
6863	83D	A/E 12.0 noon Penzance-Crewe	M99	Plymouth to Newton Abbot	NA 7L	
		7.10 pm Hackney-Tavistock Jc Freight	8C30			
		10.30 am SUN Penzance-Wolverhampton	H32	D/H 5063, ? Exeter to Wolverhampton		p 97
6864	86C	5.40 am Wolverhampton-Leamington	2H56			
		7.45 am Leamington-Birkenhead	M04	To ? Chester		
6865	82B	11.45 am Swansea-Birmingham	H68	From Cardiff	NP 6L	
		Up ECS Birmingham -?		On Leamington line		
6866	84E	12.10 pm Birmingham-Bournemouth	O37	To Oxford	OX 3E	p 137
6867	86G	8.30 am Wolverhampton-Weston	B03		W 22L	p 53
		2.15 pm SUN Plymouth-Cardiff	F50			
6868	83B	9.35 am Taunton-Paignton Excursion	Z12	Carrying No IZ2	NA 8L	p 58

LOCO	SHED CODE	TRAIN	TRAIN NO	NOTES ON LOCO WORKING		PAGE REF
		6.20 pm Goodrington-Taunton Excursion	Z12		NA 4E	
6869	83G	9.5 am Liverpool-Plymouth	V93	From Newton Abbot		
6870	83F	7.0 am Swindon-Penzance	C19	From Plymouth		
6871	83B	10.40 am Minehead-Paddington	A52	From Taunton	P 16L	p 58
6872	86G	1.5 pm Saltney-Cardiff Freight	4F90		N P 4E	p 16
6873	83D	11. 0 am Newquay-York	N53	To Plymouth D/H 4095		p 58
		4.45 pm Plymouth-Exeter	2C76			
		4.15 pm SUN Exeter-Plymouth	2C75			
6874	83B	4.30 pm FRI Taunton-Exeter	2C77	Not seen SAT		p 58
6875	83E	12.42 pm Newquay-Cardiff	F58	To Plymouth		p 58
6876	86A	SWINDON WORKS Repairs				
6877	85A			At 84E Shed SUN		
6878	82B	2.5 pm Weston-Birmingham	H25		W 15L	
6879	84E	11.40 am Birmingham-Cardiff	F34	Back at 84E Shed SUN	CF 4L	
5MT 4-6-0						
6900	82B	SWINDON WORKS Repairs				
6901	86G			At Weston 12.7.60		
6902	82C	7.30 am Birmingham-Weymouth	B34			
6903	86G	6.30 am Bassaleg-Margam Freight	8F17		CF 37L	p 52
6904	84G	? Down ECS Wolverhampton-Plymouth		Ex 84A Shed FRI 10.37 pm		p 56
		2.15 pm Penzance-Swindon Special	Z85	From Plymouth		
		(Swindon-Cannock Road Sidings)	ECS			
6905	87A	8.55 pm FRI Birkenhead-Paddington	V15	From Wolverhampton		p 51
6906	84C			At 84C Shed SUN		
6907	84B	2.35 pm FRI Birkenhead-Paddington	V10	Chester to Wolverhampton		
		10.18 am Wolverhampton-Paignton	C82		NA 16L	p 7
		A/E 10.30 am SUN Paddington-Penzance	C30	Newton Abbot to Plymouth		
6908	82B					
6909	87H	2.30 pm Neyland-Paddington	A44	To Carmarthen		p 127
		11.55 am Paddington-Neyland	F32	From Carmarthen		
		⎧ 9.5 am FRI Liverpool-Plymouth	V93	Bristol to Exeter D/H 4095		p 16
6910	81E	⎨ 9.30 am Exeter-Kingswear	2C91	D/H 6914		
		⎩ 1.30 pm Paignton-Paddington	A88		TW 10L	p 46
6911	84C			At 84C Shed SUN		
6912	87E					
6913	83D	10.5 am Par-Newquay Passenger		D/H 7816		p 62
		12.30 pm Newquay-Paddington	A12	To Plymouth D/H 7816		p 150
		A/E Workings SUN		Newton Abbot to Plymouth & Return		
6914	83B	9.30 am Exeter-Kingswear	2C91	With 6910		
		12.30 pm Paignton-Manchester	M97	To Bristol	TN 6L	
		11.55 am Manchester-Plymouth	V95	Bristol to Newton Abbot	NA 18L	
6915	81E	1.15 pm Didcot-Swindon	2B76		S 11L	p 116
6916	84G	? 7.32 am Wolverhampton-Brighton	O93	To Kensington		
6917	85B					
6918	87E	10.55 am Paddington-Pembroke Dock	F27	Swansea to Carmarthen		p 60
6919	82A	3.10 pm Paignton-Wolverhampton	H44	To Newton Abbot D/H 6829	NA 0L	
		6.0 pm Plymouth-Bristol	B50	From Newton Abbot		p 155
6920	81A	6.5 pm Paddington-Oxford	2A27	At 81E Shed FRI	TW 8L	
6921	83D	10.20 am Penzance-Swansea	F50	From Newton Abbot	CF 7L	p 123
6922	84G	9.5 am Birkenhead-Cardiff	V53	From Shrewsbury	CF 14L	
6923	81D	4.40 pm FRI Wolverhampton-Didcot	2A27			p 145
		Reading DOWN Line Pilot				
		1.20 pm Paddington-Kingswear	C87	From Reading	NA 27L	
		8.45 pm Kingswear-Exeter	2C76		Teignm'th 8L	
6924	81D			At 84B Shed SUN		
6925	84B	9.55 am Paddington-Neyland	F21	To Swansea	NP 16E	p 127
6926	84A	SWINDON WORKS Repairs				
6927	81F			At 84B Shed SUN		
6928	86G	8.10 am Newport-Paignton	C60	To Exeter	EX 16L	p 53
		3.10 pm Paignton-Wolverhampton	H44	From Exeter	TYS 2L	
6929	84C	(9.40 pm FRI Newcastle-Bournemouth)	O29	Banbury to Basingstoke		
		8.5 am Bournemouth-Newcastle	N22	Basingstoke to Banbury	OX 9L	
6930	84A	At Stafford Road Shed		Did not work		
6931	83E	? 10.45 am Penzance-Sheffield	E72	To Plymouth D/H D63XX		
6932	86C	7.55 pm FRI Cardiff-Plymouth Parcels	3C10			p 15
		8.5 am Newquay-Newcastle	N50	Plymouth to Bristol	(TM 16L)	
		5.15 pm Bristol-Taunton	2C47			
6933	84A					
6934	84B			At 84A Shed SUN eve		
6935	86C	5.20 pm Milford-Paddington Fish	A57	Canton to Swindon		p 66
6936	86C	(1.5 am Bristol-Neyland)	F01	Cardiff to Swansea		
		8.50 am Swansea-Paignton	C73	To Bristol	CF 0L	p 110
6937	81E					
6938	83D			At 83F Shed 11.7.60		
6939	86C	SWINDON WORKS Repairs		XT 9.5.60 until 14.7.60		
6940	83A			7/10/11.7.60 at NA Shed		
6941	87E	8.10 am Swansea-York	N23	To Banbury	OX 2½L	p 90
		10.5 am Newcastle-Swansea	V66	From Banbury	CF 16L	
6942	81A					
6943	86C	8.30 am Pembroke Dock-Birmingham	H16	From Cardiff		
6944	84G	At Shrewsbury Stopped XT 6.7.60		Awaiting Works		
6945	84A	2.10 pm Paddington-Birkenhead	M18	Wolverhampton to Chester		
		8.55 pm Birkenhead-Paddington	V15	Chester to Wolverhampton		p 165
6946	86G	12.5 pm Paignton-Cardiff	F42	At 83A Shed 6.7.60	CF 8L	p 152

LOCO	SHED CODE	TRAIN	TRAIN NO	NOTES ON LOCO WORKING		PAGE REF
6947	85A	7.0 am Paignton-Colne	M86	To Bristol		p 76
6948	85A	9.45 am FRI Aberystwyth-Paddington	A70	Shrewsbury to Wolverhampton		
				No sighting on SAT		
				At 84B Shed SUN		
6949	84G					
6950	85A					
6951	82D	12.50 pm FRI West London-Didcot Parcels	3A03	At 84A Shed SUN		
6952	84C			At 84C Shed SUN		
6953	81D					
6954	82B	Stapleton Road Banker		XT 8.60		p 52
6955	82D	1.55 pm Weymouth-Swindon Special			S 10L	p 130
		ECS Swindon to SR	ECS	To Reading		
6956	84G	2.57 pm FRI Swindon-Didcot	2A70			
		3.5 pm Acton-Hackney Freight	5C51			p 18
6957	81E	4.20 pm Swindon-Paddington	2A20	At 82A Shed SUN	TW 0L	
6958	86G	8.10 am Birmingham-Birkenhead	M03	To Chester		p 53
				At 84G Shed SUN		
6959	81A	? 9.40 pm Basingstoke-Crewe Freight	4M43	To Wolverhampton arr 84A 2.45 am SUN		
6960	81D					
6961	81A	Ex Stafford Road Shed 12.3 am SAT		Workings unknown		
		At Newton Abbot Shed 2.50 pm SUN				
		4.30 pm SUN Newton Abbot to Paignton	2C90	TC from Wolverhampton		
6962	81A					
6963	86C	FRI Llantwit Major-Stratford-upon-Avon Excursion				
		3.35 pm Fishguard-Paddington Freight	4A15	From Cardiff	NP 17E	
				At 84G Shed SUN		
6964	84G			At 83C Shed FRI		p 19
6965	83C					
		? 6.50 am Paignton-Bradford	N40	To Bristol		
		8.0 am Sheffield-Kingswear	V33	Bristol to Newton Abbot	NA 16L	
6966	81A	? A/E 7.0 am Plymouth-Paddington	A27	Applies if 6966 started from Plymouth		
		8.0 am Exeter-Kingswear	2C91	From Newton Abbot		p 151
		11.20 am Kingswear-Paddington	A68		P 26L	
6967	81C					
6968	82D	10.34 am Portsmouth-Cardiff	V08	From Salisbury	CF 9L	
		8.31 pm Cardiff-Westbury Parcels	3B23	To Westbury		
6969	81E	11.38 am FRI Paddington-Didcot Parcels	3A18	No workings noted SAT		
6970	81F	1.20 pm Oxford-Morton-in-Marsh	2H86			p 135
		4.50 pm Moreton-in-Marsh-Worcester	2H89			
6971	84E	STAFFORD ROAD WORKS Repairs				
6972	82A	8.43 am New Milton-Swansea	V05	Salisbury to Cardiff	CF 16L	
6973	81A	10.45 am Cardiff-Hereford	J37		OX 1½E	p 135
		3.50 pm Hereford-Paddington	A13	To Worcester		
6974	81A	7.35 am FRI Severn Tunnel Jc-Hanwell Br Freight	8A63			p 52
		8.45 am Paddington-Paignton	C67	At Newton Abbot SUN	NA 13E	
6975	84B			At 84B Shed SUN		
6976	84C	11.16 am Bournemouth-Newcastle	N26	Oxford to Leicester		p 56
		? 3.5 pm Hull-Marston Sidings Fish	3V10	Leicester to Banbury		
6977	82B					
6978	81A	7.55 am Paddington-Carmarthen	F11	To Swansea	CF 3L	
6979	84C	Banbury Standby				
		? 9.25 am Weymouth-Wolverhampton	H11	Banbury to Wolverhampton	TYS 84L	p 53
		LE Wolverhampton-Banbury		84A Dep 6.41 pm		
6980	84B	? 5.5 pm FRI Marazion-Crewe Freight	5M44	? Exeter to Oxley		p 16
6981	82A	9.43 am Bristol-Weymouth	2B40			
6982	82A	9.20 am Bradford-Paignton	V42	From Bristol	NA 0L	p 166
		9.36 pm Paignton-Newton Abbot Parcels	3C49			
6983	81E			11.38 am Pdn-Didcot "C" 11.7.60		
6984	85A	11.25 am Wellington-Chester	2J51	At 84E Shed SUN		
6985	85B	8.50 am Cheltenham-Swindon	2B79	From Gloucester		p 121
6986	82B	9.10 am Bristol-Portsmouth	O51	To Salisbury		
		9.27 am Portsmouth-Cardiff	V07	From Salisbury	CF 14L	
		4.25 pm Cardiff-Portsmouth	O65	To Salisbury D/H 5974		
6987	84A					
6988	82A			At Newton Abbot FRI		
6989	85A					
6990	81A	5.50 pm FRI Birmingham-Paddington	A21			
		12.5 am Paddington-Birkenhead	M00	To Wolverhampton		
		5.55 pm SUN Worcester-Birmingham	2H59	Via Stratford		
6991	81C	6.18 pm Gloucester-Cardiff	2F52		NP 4E	
6992	85A					
6993	82C	6.50 pm Swindon-Cardiff Parcels	3F17			
6994	82D	SWINDON WORKS Repairs		Until 19.8.60		
6995	83B	(7.10 am Didcot-Paddington)	2A20			
6996	81E	9.40 am Paddington-Minehead	C71	To Taunton	TN 9L	p 96
		D/H 9.5 am Swansea-Kingswear	C75	Taunton to Exeter	EX 12L	
		(7.20 am Exeter-Paddington Freight)	5A20			
6997	82A	? 9.10 am Bristol-Weymouth	2B40			
		4.18 pm Weymouth-Cardiff	F59	Back at 82A Shed SUN	CF 2E	p 163
6998	84G	11.28 am Birkenhead-Birmingham Relief	V06	From Chester		
6999	86C	8.48 am Fishguard-Paddington Parcels	3A24	Landore to Cardiff	CF 10L	
		? 11.15 pm Cardiff-Bordesley Jc Freight	5H23	At 84E Shed SUN		

7P
4-6-0

| 7000 | 85B | | | | | |

LOCO	SHED CODE	TRAIN	TRAIN NO	NOTES ON LOCO WORKING		PAGE REF
7001	81A	Outside SWINDON WORKS for Repairs		XT 24.6.60		
7002	85A	9.50 am Hereford-Paddington	A42	From Worcester	P 19L	
		2.45 pm Paddington-Hereford	J43		TW 10L	
7003*	85B	Ex Stafford Road to Worcester		Off 84A 3.33 am		p 34
		4.35 pm Worcester-Gloucester	2H73			
7004*	85A	7.45 am Hereford-Paddington	A22	From Worcester	P 5L	p 116
		12.45 pm Paddington-Hereford	J39		OX 4½L	p 135
		5.50 pm Hereford-Paddington	A40	To Worcester		
7005	85A	SWINDON WORKS Repairs		16.5.60 to 10.8.60		
7006*	85A	1.50 pm Hereford-Paddington	A83	From Worcester	TW 14L	p 114
7007	85A					
7008*	81F	9.30 am Birkenhead-Bournemouth	O39	Chester to Oxford	OX 3L	p 130
		11.30 am Yarmouth-Swindon Special		Oxford to Swindon		
7009	87E					
7010	81A	6.0 pm Paddington-Weymouth	B41	To Westbury, D/H 73042 to Newbury		
		(9.35 pm Westbury-Paddington Parcels)	3A35			
7011	86C	3.55 pm Paddington-Fishguard	F55	Cardiff to Swansea		p 60
		(7.50 pm Neyland-Cardiff Parcels)		From Swansea		
7012	87G	12.5 pm Pembroke Dock-Paddington	A18	Carmarthen to Swansea		p 125
		2.25 pm Pontypool Road-Carmarthen	2F94	Swansea to Carmarthen		
		Up ECS of 1.50 pm Paddington-Carmarthen		From Carmarthen		
7013*	85A					
7014*	82A	8.20 am Weston-Paddington	A18	To Bristol		
7015*	84G	8.30 am Ilfracombe-Manchester	M92	Coleham to Chester		
7016	87G	(7.48 am Swindon-Didcot)	2A76	XT for Works that day		p 118
				9.7.60 until 29.9.60		
		10.25 am Didcot-Swindon	2B76			
7017	81A					
7018*	82A	7.25 Ealing Broadway-Penzance	C22	To Plymouth	NA 1L	p 141
				Back at 82A Shed SUN		
7019*	82A	SWINDON WORKS Repairs		10.6.60 to 19.8.60		
7020	81A	(O) See Note A		To Plymouth		
		A/E 7.30 am Penzance-Bristol	B46	Plymouth to Newton Abbot		
		(R) 12.18 pm Newton Abbot-Paddington	A72		TW 36½L	p 151
7021	87E	8.55 am Paddington-Neyland	F15	To Swansea	CF 1E	p 87
7022*	83D					
7023*	86C	6.30 am Swansea-Paddington	A13	From Cardiff	P 8L	p 15
		1.55 pm Paddington-Pembroke Dock	F46	To Swansea	CF 0L	p 118
		9.10 pm Swansea-Cardiff	2F03			
7024*	81A	2.30 pm Wood Lane-Plymouth Milk Empties	3C05		SKE 6E	p 47
7025	81A					
7026	84A	12.5 pm Paddington-Birkenhead	M00	Wolverhampton to Chester		
		8.55 am Birkenhead-Paddington	V05	Chester to Wolverhampton		p 40
7027	85A	11.50 am Hereford-Paddington	A62	From Worcester	P 6L	p 136
		4.45 pm Paddington-Hereford	J45	To ? Worcester	TW 2L	
7028	87E	7.30 am Carmarthen-Paddington	A35	Swansea to Cardiff	CF 0L	p 91
		7.40 am Newton Abbot-Swansea	F19	From Cardiff		
		(3.25 pm Carmarthen-Cardiff)	2F53	Swansea to Cardiff		
		(5.55 pm Paddington-Carmarthen)	F68	Cardiff to Swansea		
		11.30 am Torquay-Paddington	A63		P 8L	p 149
7029*	83A	11.0 am SUN Paddington-Plymouth	C34			
		11.25 am MON Kingswear-Paddington	A68	Up "Torbay Express"		
7030*	81A	8.50 am Paddington-Weston	B04			p 87
		1.58 pm Weston-Paddington	A85		P 10L	p 120
7031	82C	3.35 pm Swindon-Banbury Jc Fish Empties	3H13			p 119
		(3.5 pm Hull-Marston Sidings) Fish	3V10	From Banbury		
7032	81A	Awaiting SWINDON WORKS Repairs		XT 1.7.60		
7033*	81A	12.5 pm Paddington-Plymouth	C38		NA 27L	p 142/3
7034*	82A	1.20 pm Paddington-Kingswear	C87	To Reading – failed	TW 10½L	p 144
7035*	85B	11.45 am Cheltenham-Paddington	A56	From Gloucester	P 7L	p 114
		4.55 pm Paddington-Cheltenham	T09	To Gloucester	S 8L	p 125
7036*	81A	5.45 am Gloucester-Cardiff	2F52		CF 2E	p 47
		8.48 am Fishguard-Paddington Parcels	3A24	Cardiff to Swindon	S 10E	p 126
		6.35 pm Paddington-Cheltenham	T12	Swindon to Gloucester		
7037	82C	SWINDON WORKS Repairs		18.6.60-25.8.60		

4MT 2-6-0

LOCO	SHED CODE	TRAIN	TRAIN NO	NOTES ON LOCO WORKING		PAGE REF
7301	82B	9.0 am Cardiff-Portsmouth	O52	To Salisbury		p 77
		11.37 am Portsmouth-Cardiff	V10	From Salisbury	CF 8L	p 79
7302	82D	5.50 pm Bristol-Taunton	2C47	Booked DMU		p 8
7303	71G			Usually banking at Weymouth		
7306	87H	6.50 pm Neyland-Paddington	A75	To Carmarthen		p 80
		3.55 pm Paddington-Neyland	F55	From Carmarthen		
7308	86E	1.30 pm Barmouth-Birmingham	H19			
7316	83C			At Exeter Shed		
7319	83B	(8.30 am Taunton-Ilfracombe)	2C84			
		12.25 pm Ilfracombe-Paddington	A95	To Taunton		p 46
7320	87H	3.20 pm Milford-Carmarthen Fish	3F49			
		1.55 pm Paddington-Neyland	F46	From Carmarthen		
7321	87F	1.5 pm Pembroke Dock-Neyland	A23	To Carmarthen		
		10.55 am Paddington-Pembroke Dock	F27	From Carmarthen		p 160
7322	86E	LE Aberdare-Severn Tunnel Jc				
7330	84G	3.10 pm Welshpool-Shrewsbury	2J57			p 100
7331	81D	Reading Up Line Pilot				
7332	86C	8.50 am Margate-Birmingham	V80	From Redhill	(TYS 74L)	p 74

LOCO	SHED CODE	TRAIN	TRAIN NO	NOTES ON LOCO WORKING		PAGE REF
7335	83D	2.35 pm FRI Plymouth-Exeter Cen		Via Okehampton		
		3.0 pm FRI Waterloo-Plymouth		From Exeter Cen via Okehampton		
		7.58 am Plymouth-Penzance Parcels	3C12			p 73
7336	84G			At 84G Shed SUN		
7338	85B			At 86C Shed FRI		
MT						
4-6-0						
7800	89A					
7801	89A			AT 89A Shed SUN		
7802	89C	Ex Stafford Road 1.51 am (to Crewe?)				
		9.45 am Whitchurch-Welshpool	2J76			p 61
		10.15 am Aberystwyth-Shrewsbury	2J57	From Welshpool		
		4.22 pm Shrewsbury-Aberystwyth	2J76			
7803	89C	1.50 pm Oswestry-Whitchurch	2J72			
		4.10 pm Whitchurch-Welshpool	2J73			
7804	87G					
7805	86C	8.30 am Cardiff-Newcastle	N38	To Gloucester		p 62
		8.0 am Newcastle-Cardiff	V70	From Gloucester	CF 55L	
		7.35 pm Cardiff-Gloucester	2T52			
7806	83E	10.45 am Plymouth-Penzance	2C70			
7807	89A					
7808	83A	A/E 12.30 pm Newquay-Paddington	A12	Plymouth to Newton Abbot	NA 2L	p 62
		10.20 pm Hackney-Tavistock Jc Freight	8C33			
7809	89A					
7810	89A	10.45 am Manchester-Aberystwyth	V68	From Whitchurch		p 62
7811	84G	12 noon Aberystwyth-Shrewsbury	2J57	At 84G Shed SUN		
7812	83F					
7813	83F	8.15 am Perranporth-Paddington	A65	Truro to Laira Jc D/H 6805		p 150
7814	89C	7.35 am Aberystwyth-Shrewsbury	2J57			p 62
		3.15 pm Shrewsbury-Aberystwyth	2J26			
7815	89C	10.18 am Penychain-Carmarthen	F80	From Aberystwyth		p 64
7816	83E	10.5 am Par-Newquay	2C54	D/H 6913		p 62
		12.30 pm Newquay-Paddington	A12	To Plymouth D/H 6913		
7817	84J			At 84J Shed SUN		
7818	89C					p 62
7819	89A			At 89A Shed SUN		
7820	83E	LE Par-Newquay				p 62
		11.53 am Newquay-Par	2C54			
7821	83A	8.42 am Shrewsbury-Paddington Parcels	3A29	To Wolverhampton		
	84G	10.10 am Paddington - Aberystwyth	J17	Wolverhampton-Welshpool		p 61
		3.55 pm Welshpool-Shrewsbury	2J57			
7822	89A	11.32 am Swindon-Bristol	2B78	Running-in		
		4.50 pm Bath-Swindon	2B75	Running-in	S 2L	
7823	89C					
7824	84E					
7825	87G	2.40 pm Carmarthen-Aberystwyth	2J77			
7826	87G					
7827	89A	FRI Cardington-Bridgnorth RAF Troop Train		From Coleham.		
				At 84G Shed SUN		p 62
				No sightings SAT		
7828	84G	? 9.5 am Birkenhead-Cardiff	V53	To Shrewsbury		
7829	87G					
5MT						
4-6-0						
7900	81F	9.5 am Birmingham-Portsmouth	O34	From Oxford	TYS 5L	p 163
		3.40 pm Portsmouth-Wolverhampton	V98			
7901	82A					
7902	81A	(7.5 pm FRI Paddington-Fishguard)	F71	To Cardiff		
		8.15 am Abertillery-Paddington	A29	From Bassaleg Jc	P 15L	p 91
7903	81A	11.40 am Paddington-Penzance	C35	To Plymouth	NA 19L	p 52
7904	81A					
7905	84C	11.2 am Banbury-Oxford	2A99		OX 0L	
		10.25 am Poole-Bradford	N24	Oxford to Banbury		p 138
7906	81D	9.10 am Reading-Portsmouth	2A52			
		1.28 pm Portsmouth-Birmingham	V95			
7907	82B	6.5 pm Bristol-Cardiff	2F52		CF 14L	p 163
7908	84E	8.0 am Paddington-Wolverhampton	H04	Via Oxford		
		8.18 pm Birmingham-Paddington	A53	Via Oxford		
7909	82D					
7910	81C					
7911	81F	10.20 am Weymouth-Wolverhampton	H18		TYS 40L	p 115
7912	84E	6.58 pm FRI Glasgow-Plymouth	V84	From Bristol		p 11
		2.0 pm Penzance-Crewe Perishables	3M27	To ? Bristol	NA 1E	
7913	86C	6.30 am Severn Tunnel Jc-Landore Steel Works Freight	8F18	3½ hours late Newport XT for Works 9.8.60		
7914	81D	12.5 pm Pembroke Dock-Paddington	A18	From Swansea	TW ½E	p 125
7915	84B	8.10 am Oxley-Paddington Freight	5A12			
7916	83D	7.50 am Taunton-Paddington	A30	To Swindon		
		5.47 pm Swindon-Didcot	2A76			
7917	82D	(11.20 am Trowbridge-Reading)	2A87			
		4.36 pm Newbury-Westbury	2B73		SKE 1L	
7918	84E	10.10 am Birmingham-Margate	O95	To Kensington		
		7.10 pm Paddington-Wolverhampton	H45	At 84A Shed SUN	Solihull 4L	p 52
7919	81D					

LOCO	SHED CODE	TRAIN	TRAIN NO	NOTES ON LOCO WORKING		PAGE REF
7920	85A	? 7.55 am Worcester-Oxford	2A90			
		LE at Oxford 10.30 am				
7921	83D	7.30 am Penzance-Bristol	B46	From Plymouth	TN 32L	p 151
		1.30 pm SUN Paddington-Penzance	C41	{ D/H D802 from Taunton or Exeter to Plymouth		
7922	84G			At 84G Shed SUN		
7923	81C	6.50 am Paddington-Penzance	C18	To Plymouth	EX 8L	p 141
7924	83B	Awaiting SWINDON WORKS Repairs		XT 6.7.60 Into Works 24.7.60		
7925	86C	(12.5 am Cardiff-Liverpool)	M65	To Hereford		
		7.45 am Hereford-Cardiff	2F02		CF 1L	
7926	85B	8.0 am Cheltenham-Paddington	A08	From Gloucester	P 10L	p 34
		1.45 pm Paddington-Cheltenham	T06	To Gloucester	S 14L	p 118
7927	81A					
7928	85A					
7929	83E	? 2.15 pm Penzance-Swindon Special	Z85	To Plymouth		p 56
7MT						
4-6-2						
70016	86C	? 5.20 pm FRI Milford Haven-Paddington Fish	A57	At 86C Shed FRI, Cardiff to Swindon		p 65
70018	86C	12.28 pm Cardiff-Manchester	M12	To Chester		p 65
70019	86C	SWINDON WORKS Repairs				
70020	86C	6.30 am Swansea-Paddington	A13	To Cardiff	CF 2E	
70022	86C	SWINDON WORKS Repairs				
70023	86C	7.30 am Carmarthen-Paddington	A35	From Cardiff	P 1E	p 65
		3.55 pm Paddington-Neyland	F55	To Cardiff	CF 1E	p 123
70024	86C	5.20 pm Milford Haven-Paddington Fish	A57	To Cardiff		p 66
70025	86C	5.50 pm FRI Paddington-Swansea	F67	To Cardiff only		
		11.15 am Swansea-Manchester	M72	Cardiff & Shrewsbury		p 65
		2.55 pm Liverpool-Cardiff	V58	From Shrewsbury	CF 6L	
70026	86C	SWINDON WORKS Repairs		XT 9.5.60		
				At Works 16.6.60 to 11.10.60		
70027	86C			At 86C Shed FRI		
70028	86C	SWINDON WORKS Repairs		XT 6.5.60		
				At Works 19.5.60 to 25.10.60		
70029	86C	1.25 am Crewe-Cardiff	V51	From Shrewsbury		
		7.50 am Fishguard-Paddington	A58	From Cardiff	P 7L	p 65
		5.55 pm Paddington-Carmarthen	F68	To Cardiff	NP 5E	
5MT						
4-6-0						
73012	82C	7.33 am Swindon-Sheffield	E50	To Banbury D/H 1021		p 126
73017	71G	11.5 am Wolverhampton-Weymouth	B39		S 23L	p 116
73018	71G	12.45 pm Trowbridge-Weston	2B96	At 82A Shed SUN		
73020	71G	1.45 pm Weymouth-Bristol	2B20			
73021	87F	9.30 am Pembroke Dock-Shrewsbury	J58	From Llandilo		p 67
73023	87F	9.5 am Swansea-Kingswear	C75	To Cardiff	CF 1L	p 67
		8.48 am New Milton-Swansea	V05	From Cardiff		p 99
73025	84G	STAFFORD ROAD WORKS Repairs				
73026	84G	7.50 am Newquay-Manchester	M95	Plymouth to Pontypool Rd	TN 38L	p 67
73027	82C	8.50 am Swansea-Paignton	C73	From Bristol	NA 12L	p 67
				Still at Newton Abbot 11.7.60		
73035	84G	2.40 pm Shrewsbury-Swansea	F83			
73036	84G			At 84G Shed SUN		
73037	84G	6.0 am Penzance-Liverpool	M91	From Shrewsbury		p 100
73042	71G	11.12 am Weymouth-Paddington	A61		TW 6L	p 67
		6.0 pm Paddington-Weymouth	B41	To Newbury D/H 7010	TW 3L	
		7.18 pm Newbury-Trowbridge	2B94			
73092	84G	Also 73091/97		At 84G Shed SUN		
73093	84G	(11.1 pm FRI Crewe-Cardiff Parcels)	3V25	Newport 10.30 am		
		LE Cardiff-North & West Line				
73094	84G	9.55 pm Pontypool Road-Cardiff Parcels	3F16		NP 5E	
73096	84G	1.4 pm Stafford-Shrewsbury	2V66			
4MT						
4-6-0						
75000	84E	STAFFORD ROAD WORKS Repairs		Until 7.7.60		
75001	81F	Down LE at Oxford 10.45 am		At 82B Shed SUN		p 68
75006	84E			At 84E Shed SUN		
75024	84E			At 84E Shed SUN		
75025	85A	(7.15 am Worcester-Evesham)	2H89			
		8.0 am Evesham-Birmingham	2H59		TYS 6L	p 69
		5.45 pm Birmingham-Worcester	2H89			
75029	82C	(10.20 am Swindon-Bristol)	2B20			
		6.43 pm Weston-Swindon	2B25		S 1L	p 68
9F						
2-10-0						
92004	81C	1.20 pm Reading-Kensington Milk	3A13			
92005	86C	8.30 pm Whitland-Kensington Milk	3A44	From Cardiff to Swindon		
92213	84C	2.30 pm Kidderminster EMW-Cardiff Freight	7F70			
92216	86C	8.30 pm FRI Whitland-Kensington Milk	3A44	Cardiff to Swindon		
		2.30 pm Wootton Bassett-Old Oak Common Parcels	3A15	From Swindon	TW 8L	p 71
		8.30 pm Paddington-Neyland Parcels	3F20	To Cardiff		
92218	82B	? 7.30 pm Bristol-Oxley Freight	7H34/5H04	At 83A Shed 11.7.60		p 70
92219	86C			To Swansea		p 71
92220	86C	3.25 pm Carmarthen-Cardiff	2F53	At 86C Shed FRI		p 70

LOCO	SHED CODE	TRAIN	TRAIN NO	NOTES ON LOCO WORKING		PAGE REF
92222	83D	10.0 am Weymouth-Birmingham	H15	To Swindon		p 71
92227	84C	SWINDON WORKS Repairs				
92233	84C	11.5 am Banbury-Old Oak Common Freight	8A52			p 71
92236	86C			At 86C Shed FRI & SUN		
92237	86C	9.5 am Swansea-Kingswear	C75	From Cardiff	NA 10L	p 96
		5.30 pm Kingswear-Taunton	2C77	At 82B Shed SUN	NA 2L	
92238	81A	2.30 pm FRI Paddington-Penzance Freight	4C19	To Plymouth		p 18
		12.42 pm Newquay-Cardiff	F58	From Plymouth	CF 2E	
92239	81A			At 86C Shed FRI & SUN		
92247	81A	Also 92228		At 84B Shed SUN		
92249	83D	8.5 am Cardiff-Kingswear	C62	To Bristol		
		7.40 am Newton Abbot-Swansea	F19	Bristol to Cardiff	CF 0L	p 70
				Back at 83D Shed SUN		
Type 4 Diesel						
D600	ALL 83D	10.37 am Paddington-Penzance	C31	To ? Plymouth	NA 11L	p 83
D601		12.0 noon FRI Penzance-Crewe	M99	? Plymouth to Bristol		
		(6.55 pm FRI Weston-Paddington)	A50	From Bristol		
		(12.30 am Paddington-Penzance Newspapers)	C07	To ? Plymouth		p 83
		12.0 noon Penzance-Crewe	M99	? Plymouth to Bristol	NA 7L	
		6.55 pm Weston-Paddington	A50	From Bristol		
D6XX		11.10 pm FRI Manchester-Penzance	V81	Plymouth to Penzance		
Type 4 Diesel						
D800	ALL 83D	8.0 am Kingswear-Paddington	A33			
		4.15 pm Paddington-Plymouth	C47		NA 6L	
D801		8.30 am Plymouth-Paddington	A41		Ealing 2E	
		3.30 pm Paddington-Penzance	C43	To Plymouth	NA 2L	p 146
D802		9.45 am SUN Penzance-Paddington	A81	? From Plymouth		
		1.50 pm FRI Bristol-Paddington	A74			
D803		1.30 pm SUN Paddington-Penzance	C41	Not noted SAT		
D804		7.50 am Taunton-Paddington	A30	From Swindon	P 1E	p 121
		5.30 pm Paddington-Plymouth	C45		NA 4E	
D805		8.45 am SUN Plymouth-Liverpool	M87	Plymouth to Bristol		
D806		8.10 am Paddington-Paignton	C64		NA 4L	
		2.45 pm Paignton-Paddington	A03		TW 10E	p 82
		11.15 pm Paddington-Penzance	C07			
D807		? 8.45 pm FRI Penzance-Paddington	A90			
		10.30 am Paddington-Penzance	C30		NA 5L	p 81
		Up O/Night SAT ? 8.45 pm Penzance	A90			
		10.30 am SUN Paddington-Penzance	C30		NA 18L	
D808		4.50 pm Penzance-Manchester	M78	? Plymouth to Bristol		
D809		7.35 am Plymouth-Paddington	A39	Also up "Torbay Express" FRI	(P 2E)	
D810		9.20 am St Ives-Paddington	A76	From Plymouth	P 40L	p 153
D811						
D812		7.0 am Paddington-Kingswear	C57		NA 3L	
		1.40 pm Kingswear-Paddington	A08		P 5L	
D813		8.35 am Falmouth-Paddington	1A66		P 13L	p 150
		6.30 pm Paddington-Weston	1B20	To Bristol	S 5L	
		3.10 pm Manchester-Plymouth	1V98	From Bristol		
D814		(11.50 pm FRI Paddington-Penzance)	1C14	Bristol to Plymouth		
		10.0 am Newquay-Paddington	1A78	From Plymouth	P 33L	p 153
D815		11.50 am Penzance-Paddington	1A17		P 1L	p 156
		10.40 am SUN Paddington-Falmouth	1C31	To Plymouth	NA 16L	
D816		3.40 pm Penzance-Paddington Perishables	3A36	From ? Plymouth		
		12.0 noon SUN Paddington-Kingswear	1C80		NA 7L	
D817		4.50 pm FRI Penzance-Manchester	1M78	? Plymouth to Bristol		
		12.25 am Manchester-Plymouth	1V86	From Bristol	EX 0L	p 11
		10.0 am Penzance-Paddington	1A81	From Plymouth	P 33L	p 153
		1.10 pm SUN Penzance-Paddington	1A33	? From Plymouth		
D818	83D	8.45 am Kingswear-Bradford	1N45	To Bristol	TN 0L	p 146
		9.5 am Bradford-Kingswear	1V39	From Bristol	NA 12L	
D819				At St Blazey 11.7.60		p 82
D820		7.0 am Plymouth-Paddington	1A27		P 5E	
		3.15 pm Paddington-Kingswear	1C90		NA 3E	
		11.25 am SUN Kingswear-Paddington	1A68			
D821		7.0 am Weston-Paddington	A03	From Bristol	(P 4E)	p 82
		12.0 noon Paddington-Kingswear	1C80		NA 17L	
		6.30 pm Goodrington-Newton Abbot	2C90		NA 1E	
		11.55 am Manchester-Plymouth	1V95	From Newton Abbot		
D822		7.5 am Cheltenham-Paddington	1A10	From Swindon		
		1.38 pm Paddington-Weston	1B12	To Swindon	S 3L	p 118
D823		6.25 am Swindon-Paignton Special	1Z86			
		5.40 pm Paignton-Swindon Special	1Z84			p 131
Type 2 Diesel						
D6307				At Truro 11.7.60		
D6309				At Truro 11.7.60		
D6310		10.0 am Newquay-Paddington	A78	To Laira Jc D/H D6321, 4976		
D6311		A/E 8.15 am Perranporth-Paddington	A65		NA 5L	p 62

LOCO	SHED CODE	TRAIN	TRAIN NO	NOTES ON LOCO WORKING		PAGE REF
		A/E 10.37 am Paddington-Penzance	C31			
		A/E 6.0 pm Plymouth-Bristol	B50	At Newton Abbot SUN	NA 3E	
D6313		10.30 am Paddington-Penzance	C30	Newton Abbot to Truro D/H D807		p 153
D6314		9.0 am MON Wolverhampton-Penzance	C33	MON. 11.7.60 with D6329 at Truro		
D6316		A/E 9.35 am Bristol-Penzance	C21			
		A/E 10.45 am Penzance-Sheffield	E72		NA 20L	p 54
		A/E 8.17 am Carmarthen-Penzance	C36			
D6320		A/E 7.50 am Newquay-Manchester	M95		NA 0L	
		A/E 7.25 am Ealing Broadway-Penzance	C22			p 142
		A/E 11.10 am Penzance-Wolverhampton	H37		NA 12L	
		A/E 11.40 am Paddington-Penzance	C35			
D6322		A/E 8.5 am Newquay-Newcastle	N50		NA 3L	
		A/E 8.25 am Paddington-Penzance	C25			
		A/E 11.50 am Penzance-Paddington	A17	At Newton Abbot SUN	NA 3L	
D6323		A/E 8.35 am Falmouth-Paddington	A66		(NA 4L)	p 150
		A/E 9.30 am Paddington-Newquay	C28			
		A/E 1.20 pm Penzance-Paddington	A33		NA 0L	
		A/E 1.30 pm Paddington-Penzance	C41			p 146
D6326		At North British Locomotive Co. Works		Undelivered. Received at Swindon by 24.7.60		
D6328		A/E 7.0 am Swindon-Penzance	C19			
		A/E 11.0 am Newquay-York	N53			p 58
		A/E 7.43 am Nottingham-Plymouth	V31			

All A/E workings are between Plymouth & Newton Abbot.
A number of pairs of D63xx running in multiple between Plymouth and Penzance were not individually identified.

Working timetable details and times are used where known. These often differed by a few minutes from times shown in the public timetable.

Note A
Nos. 5065, 6024, 6028, 7020 and perhaps 6966 (all from 81A) plus 5033 81F were at Laira on Saturday morning.
These engines may have been utilised earlier for the following down expresses:

11.30 am FRI Paddington-Penzance	C35	if steam
12.5 pm FRI Paddington-Truro Empty RCs	C38	
9.50 pm FRI Paddington-Plymouth Parcels	3C12	
10.5 pm FRI Paddington-Penzance	C01	if steam
10.45 pm FRI Paddington-Penzance	C02	
11.15 pm FRI Paddington-Newquay	C03	
12.35 am Paddington-Penzance	C11	

Note B
Nos. 4075, 5042, 5054 (all 81A) and 7914 (81D) were at Landore on Saturday.
They may have worked in with the following trains booked for 81A engines:

5.55 pm FRI Paddington-Carmarthen	F68
6.55 pm FRI Paddington-Fishguard	F70
8.55 pm FRI Paddington-Neyland	F75

Note C
5092 (82A), 6804 (82B) and 6809 (82B) were at Plymouth on Saturday morning.
They may have been responsible for hauling the 7.15 pm FRI Sheffield-Newquay V49 or 11.35 pm FRI Paddington-Penzance C12 from Bristol to Plymouth.

Note D
84G Shrewsbury Locos on down workings overnight FRI/SAT

1013 Shrewsbury to Pontypool Rd	on ? 11.10 pm FRI Manchester-Paignton	V81
1017 Shrewsbury to Exeter	on ? 10.30 pm FRI Manchester-Paignton	V80
5059 Shrewsbury to Pontypool Rd	on ? 11.15 pm FRI Manchester-Paignton	V82
5971 Shrewsbury to Exeter	on { ? 10.15 pm FRI Manchester-Paignton / 10.22 pm in Public Timetable }	V79

Where locomotive diagrams have been referred to either in the text or the appendix it should be noted that these are generally based on a limited number of observations only, and may not apply to all dates through the season.